Interior Design
FUNDAMENTALS

Interior Design
FUNDAMENTALS

Steven B. Webber

Florida State University

FAIRCHILD BOOKS

NEW YORK · LONDON · OXFORD · NEW DELHI · SYDNEY

FAIRCHILD BOOKS

An imprint of Bloomsbury Publishing Inc

Bloomsbury Publishing Inc
1385 Broadway, New York, NY 10018, USA
50 Bedford Square, London, WC1B 3DP, UK
29 Earlsfort Terrace, Dublin 2, Ireland

BLOOMSBURY, FAIRCHILD BOOKS and the Fairchild Books logo are
trademarks of Bloomsbury Publishing Plc

First published in the United States of America 2020
Reprinted 2020, 2021 (twice), 2022

Cover design by Sam Clark / By The Sky Design | Cover photograph: *Bridge of Aspiration*, Royal
Ballet School, London, UK © Mark Sykes / AWL Images / Getty Images

Library of Congress Cataloging-in-Publication Data
Names: Webber, Steven B., author.
Title: Interior design fundamentals / Steven B. Webber, Florida State University.
Description: New York : Fairchild Books, Bloomsbury Publishing Inc, 2020. | Includes index.
Identifiers: LCCN 2019009868 | ISBN 9781501327087 (pbk.)
Subjects: LCSH: Interior decoration.
Classification: LCC NK2110 .W385 2019 | DDC 747—dc23 LC record available at
https://lccn.loc.gov/2019009868

ISBN: 978-1-5013-2708-7

Typeset by Lachina Creative, Inc.
Printed and bound in the United Kingdom

To find out more about our authors and books visit
www.fairchildbooks.com and sign up for our newsletter.

For Liz, Paige, and Claire. This wouldn't be worth it without you.

CONTENTS

EXTENDED TABLE OF CONTENTS

11 Lighting 247

12 Built Environment Support Systems 267

PREFACE

For educators and design students alike, the breadth of information needed to be introduced to interior design is daunting.

Interior design encompasses the analysis, planning, design, documentation, and management of interior non-structural/non-seismic construction and alteration projects in compliance with applicable building design and construction, fire, life-safety, and energy codes, standards, regulations, and guidelines for the purpose of obtaining a building permit, as allowed by law. Qualified by means of education, experience, and examination, interior designers have a moral and ethical responsibility to protect consumers and occupants through the design of code-compliant, accessible, and inclusive interior environments that address well-being, while considering the complex physical, mental, and emotional needs of people. (CIDQ, 2019)

Put another way, interior design is a practice-based discipline that possesses elements of both art and science. For this reason, interior design is one of a few disciplines that finds itself strategically placed between the worlds of fine art and the STEM (science, technology, engineering, and math) fields. This juxtaposition places a certain amount of additional expectations on the interior design profession to simultaneously be creative and achieve measurable results to real-world problems. Practicing interior designers experience this tension as they seek to create spaces that are aesthetically pleasing and functional. As a result, it may be best to think of interior design as an **applied art,** where artistic creative processes are used to address real-world problems. Due to this dichotomy of science and art, creativity and application, a text such as this will cover a breadth of topics ranging from design process to construction techniques and business practices.

Each chapter addresses a set of discrete topics while connecting the chapter content to design thinking and the design process. Beginning with the **Introduction,** the beginnings of interior design, the development of the discipline into a profession, and knowledge areas for interior designers are each discussed in turn. **Chapter 1** outlines the design thinking process and the design language of interior design, known as the elements and principles of design. **Chapter 2** provides a streamlined overview of architecture and design history providing a historical context for some of the later content. **Chapter 3** describes the design process from both the point of view of the client and the designer. These beginning chapters provide the context for much of the discussion that follows in the text.

The next grouping of content provides an introduction to fundamental critical knowledge that influences the design process and design outcomes. **Chapter 4** encapsulates several critical topics under the umbrella of spatial well-being, including universal design, the spatial sciences, human spatial behaviors, and sustainability. **Chapter 5** examines color theory in the built environment as it relates to both light and substantive color, or pigment. **Chapter 6** provides an orientation to the practice of interior design starting with ethics, the process of professional preparation, the legality of practice, and the financial aspects of practice. **Chapter 7** discusses the contextual factors present in any project that are outside of the designer's control but exert tremendous influence upon the design, including occupant demographics, location and existing construction factors, and design trends. As the designer combines knowledge from these diverse areas, design outcomes can be well-informed, purposeful, functional, and beautiful.

The last grouping of chapter content drives toward the application of design fundamentals in completed spaces. **Chapter 8** builds upon the prior chapters by walking the reader through the planning process, and describes each of the drawing types designers use during planning. **Chapter 9** begins the overview of design application elements by describing finishes as systems, specifically floor, wall, and ceiling systems. **Chapter 10** discusses the variety of furnishing types, including millwork, furniture, doors and windows, window coverings, textiles, accessories, and fixtures and equipment. **Chapter 11** introduces lighting, which includes both natural and electric lighting. **Chapter 12** concludes the text with an orientation to built environment support systems (mechanical; electrical; plumbing; fire monitoring, notification, and suppression; and acoustical) and the collaborative relationship between the interior designer and the engineering teams that specialize in these areas. The successful application of the content from these last chapters relies on a clear understanding of the breadth of design fundamentals and years of practice.

Interior design is a complex and rewarding profession where the practitioner has the opportunity to create beautiful places that enhance the lives of those who use the spaces. The key to a successful and long career in this profession relies on the enjoyment of the design process as much as the design outcomes. The path to becoming a great designer will be long, full of challenges and joys, and learning to love the design process is the best first step. Learning how to think like a designer, and developing a process to do so, will be any student's most valuable skill as he or she moves forward.

Sources

CIDQ. (2019). CIDQ 1 NCIDQ EXAMS 1 Definition of Interior Design. Retrieved February 22, 2019, from https://www.cidq.org/definition-of-interior-design.

Interior Design Fundamentals STUDIO

Interior Design Fundamentals STUDIO is an online multimedia resource specially developed to complement this book with rich media ancillaries that students can adapt to their visual learning styles to better master concepts and improve grades. Within the *STUDIO*, students will be able to

- Study smarter with self-quizzes featuring scored results and personalized study tips
- Review concepts with flashcards of essential vocabulary

STUDIO access cards are offered free with new book purchases and also sold separately through www.fairchildbooks.com.

Instructor Resources

- *Instructor's Guide* provides suggestions for planning the course and using the text in the classroom, supplemental assignments, and lecture notes.
- Test Bank includes sample test questions for each chapter.
- PowerPoint® presentations include images from the book and provide a framework for lecture and discussion

Instructor's Resources may be accessed through FairchildBooks.com (www.fairchildbooks.com).

Acknowledgments

An author of an introductory text, perhaps more so than other textbooks due to the breadth of coverage, relies on the knowledge of those who have come before, as they set precedent of expertise for the author to draw upon. Admittedly, this text cannot probe the depths of many knowledge areas, including design history, so the author applauds the educators who will provide students with the appropriate level of exposure from which students can analyze, interpret, and truly understand and apply these topics. In many ways, this text brings full circle the idea of what it means to be a practicing designer—one who collects, filters, analyzes, and synthesizes vast information that will then inform a design outcome. So, in light of this fact, the author commends the student for tackling this complex discipline that will one day become *your* practice.

I am forever grateful to the many mentors that have contributed to my development. My grandmother, Betty, was my first writing coach at around age fourteen, and Dr. Mark Eckel cultivated my inquisitive mind in high school as I set my mind toward that which will never pass away. He also demonstrated what it meant to be a caring and dedicated teacher, an example that I would return to more than once. My college professors at Lawrence Technological University, Dr. Virginia North, David Chasco, Bryan Koehn, and many others, fostered a love for the design process and architectural and interior design practice. Fellow practitioners in and around Detroit, Michigan, have inspired many of the content pieces in this volume and I am grateful to have called you

colleagues. My colleagues in the Department of Interior Architecture and Design at Florida State University have provided countless revisions of many writing pieces over the years, all of which, in some way, contributed to this effort. Thank you, Lisa, Jill, Jim, and others, for your patience and support. The team at Fairchild has been tremendous to work with on this project. Joseph Miranda has overseen the project and his wealth of knowledge and experience has been invaluable to this new author. Edie Weinberg has directed the extensive art for this book and she has patiently made this art program successful, not to mention she is a lot of fun to work with.

The publisher wishes to thank the following reviewers: Mary Ann Frank, Indiana University; Lee Kean, Louisiana State University; Kathleen Ryan, Washington State University; Mandy Berdami, Mississippi College; Stephen Anderson, University of Portsmouth; Wendy Hynes, Purdue University; Cotter Christian, Parsons New School; Elys John, University of South Wales; Rebecca Graaff, De Montfort University; Travis Hicks, University of North Carolina.

Bloomsbury Publishing wishes to gratefully acknowledge and thank the editorial team involved in the publication of this book:

Acquisitions Editor: Noah Schwartzberg
Development Manager: Joseph Miranda
Art Development Editor: Edie Weinberg
Editorial Assistant: Bridget MacAvoy
In-House Designer: Eleanor Rose
Production Editor: Ken Bruce
Project Manager: Rebecca Marshall, Lachina Creative

Introduction
What Is Interior Design?

Learning Objectives

As a result of reading this chapter, students will

1. **Possess an awareness of the evolution of interior design.**

2. **Possess an awareness of the priorities and goals of interior design.**

3. **Possess an awareness of the process to becoming an interior designer.**

4. **Possess an awareness of the knowledge areas within interior design.**

Historical Roots of Interior Design

The beginning of interior design was directly influenced by the development of human civilization and the cultural norms that grew from technological advancements. Necessity and the availability of materials motivated the invention of new building technologies such as stick and hide structures or clay brick. The cultural norms and lifestyle of a people group, such as Native Americans who relied on hunting roaming buffalo herds across the vast open plains of North America, led to the adoption of certain types of structures. In this case, the teepee, valued for its simplicity, speed of erection and mobility, in addition to providing shelter, allowed Native Americans to move the tribe to follow the herds across the plains and maintain access to a reliable food supply (Fig. I.1).

Some cultures were able to develop permanent, immovable structures as they moved away from nomadic ways of life based on hunting-gathering and herding toward an agriculturally based society. Occupying one location allowed people to utilize stronger building materials, including stone, brick, and milled lumber. A permanent location also allowed people to diversify their building types. Dwellings were the dominant building type throughout much of human history, but permanence allowed for the development of temples, palaces, and defense structures in addition to standard housing (Fig. I.2). As societies became more advanced across

Figure I.2 Following the settling-down period of human development, which was reliant on agricultural advances, permanent structures became the norm and, over time, grew in size and prominence.

Europe, the Middle East, and Asia, public forums, places for entertainment, education, and civic engagement, such as amphitheaters and marketplaces, came into being. In some cases, nomadic influences persisted, such as open-air marketplaces, as vendors sold their wares from mobile carts and beneath tent structures.

Overtime, various civilizations grew in their sophistication as technological advancements improved the quality of life for many individuals. The Industrial Revolution is one period of rapid technological advancement that transformed the built environment and European and American societies as a whole. The duration of periods of architecture and design following the Industrial Revolution were much shorter than style periods prior to the Industrial Revolution. One cause can be traced back to the growth in wealth and influence of the middle class enabled by the spread of democracy and representative forms of government. As a result, more people could afford to adopt new design styles for their

Figure I.1 Early human civilizations that relied on hunting, gathering, and herding followed a nomadic lifestyle, which benefited from dwellings that could be quickly and easily erected and dismantled.

Figure I.3 Current-day interiors are highly specialized and integrate a variety of disciplines, such that the interior designer must understand how to coordinate multiple disciplines in order to create a cohesive and well-designed interior.

homes and businesses (Fig. I.3). The built environment became both a place to provide shelter, security, and safety while also pursuing one's aesthetic ideals. As building types and interior spaces became more specialized in the twentieth century, the importance of the interior grew, and, therefore, so did the need for a specialized profession to design the interior.

Interior Design as a Profession

Interior design is a relatively new profession compared to its allied disciplines in architecture, engineering, and construction. The Council for Interior Design Qualification (2019) defines **interior design** this way:

> Interior design encompasses the analysis, planning, design, documentation, and management of interior non-structural/non-seismic construction and alteration projects in compliance with applicable building design and construction, fire, life-safety, and energy codes, standards, regulations, and guidelines for the purpose of obtaining a building permit, as allowed by law. Qualified by means of education, experience, and examination, interior designers have a moral and

ethical responsibility to protect consumers and occupants through the design of code-compliant, accessible, and inclusive interior environments that address well-being, while considering the complex physical, mental, and emotional needs of people.

The nature of this profession requires the practitioner to specialize in a few knowledge areas, but to be a generalist in many, able to coordinate the input of many other professionals, including architects, engineers, and other specialized design consultants, such as acousticians, fabricators, millworkers, and so on.

Mistaking an interior designer for an interior decorator is a common misunderstanding regarding the roles and capabilities of an interior designer. In the late nineteenth century, as the importance of the interior was just starting to grow in the eyes of the middle class, decorators were sought after for their knowledge in period styles of earlier eras and their associated revival styles to design new spaces or renovate existing ones. Decorators would use their knowledge of the flexible portions of the interior (floor, wall, and ceiling finishes and coordinated furnishings) to design spaces and then sell the goods necessary to achieve the vision as their means to earn income. This practice today is known as **interior decoration** and differs significantly from interior design.

While aesthetics is very important to designers and clients alike, an interior designer is also responsible for coordinating the technical aspects of the interior. Known as **space planning**, the designer is responsible for addressing the functional arrangement of built elements, such as partitions, interior windows, and doors, in addition to the movable components, or furniture, fixtures, and equipment, in a manner that complies with building codes while meeting the needs of the end user.

Nearly all interior design projects, whether residential or contract, require space planning to varying degrees. Interior designers who specialize in **residential design** will often blend the traditional role of a decorator with that of an interior designer as they may earn much of their income through the purchasing of furniture and fixtures on behalf of their clients. Interior designers who typically work on **contract design** projects earn their fees through providing design services, which includes space planning, as outlined in a contractual agreement with their clients. Contract project types include health

Figure I.4 Interior designers function as an integral part of a professional design team whose goal is to provide for the health, safety, and welfare of the public.

care, workplace, retail, and hospitality design among many others. The more complex contract projects will require a team of consultants, including mechanical, electrical, and plumbing engineers; structural engineers; lighting designers; and acousticians, among others (Fig. I.4). The interior designer does not need to be an expert in any of these areas addressed by the consultant, but the designer must know how to coordinate consultants' work into their own.

As interior designers address the aesthetic and functional needs of a project, the unifying priority of the practitioner is to provide for the health, safety, and welfare of those individuals who will occupy the space. In order to be able to design spaces with this priority in mind, interior designers should possess proper credentials that demonstrate they have been properly educated and trained to practice (NCIDQ, 2016). Ideally, this process begins with an education from an accredited interior design program, and may include a guided internship while still a student. Upon graduation, the new professional continues to work until they have met the requirements to take a professional examination, referred to as the NCIDQ (National Council of Interior Design Qualifications) examination in the United States. Possessing and maintaining professional interior design certification, such as the NCIDQ, demonstrates the base level competency and understanding needed to practice interior design, or interior architecture.

The legality of the interior design profession varies by country and even by state within a country, which is the case in the United States. This discipline is referred to as interior architecture in many countries, but is known as interior design in the United States due to the legal protections governing the use of the title architect. Depending on the jurisdiction, there may be no regulation of the practice of interior design, or the use of the title "interior designer," or very clear and strict regulations could exist. It is the responsibility of the professional to understand the laws and regulations governing interior design based up the project location, not simply the location of employment.

Knowledge Areas for Interior Designers

As mentioned, interior designers require a general knowledge of a diverse set of topics while also possessing expertise in a few specific to interiors. This text will address many interior design topics that the reader will encounter in much greater detail later in their education and practice. Chapters 1, 2, and 3 address subjects that are foundational to interior design. Chapter 1 discusses design thinking and the importance that it plays as an underlying current in the design process as the designer creates successful interiors. Along with design thinking, the chapter outlines the compositional building blocks of interior design, known as the elements and principles of design, so the reader can begin to understand the artistic aspects of the discipline. Chapter 2 provides a very brief introduction to the history of architecture and interior design so that the reader can gain awareness of the development of the built environment in relation to broad historical events and movements. Understanding the various periods of design and the stylistic qualities that accompany them helps the designer to place his or her own work in context with a broader movement of design. Chapter 3 focuses on the design process from the point of view of both the client and the designer. Approaching the design process from both of these vantage points will allow the student and practitioner to create relevant design solutions to meet their client's aesthetic and functional needs. The content of these first three chapters provides a foundation for the middle portion of the text, which looks at the psychological and practice-related knowledge areas.

Occupants' well-being in the built environment, discussed in Chapter 4, includes interpreting the effects of space through the five human senses, the psychological impacts of the interior on its users, and the ecologic and economic sustainability of the built environment. Spatial well-being is a holistic way for the designer to intentionally create an interior for the maximum benefit of the occupants and the environment. Color, arguably the single most impactful element of design, has been researched in great detail, and is summarized in Chapter 5. Color theory as it relates to both light and pigment can transform an interior into a highly impactful space, and the designer who wields color strategically can intentionally evoke certain sensations from the users. Lastly, in this section, Chapter 6 examines in broad terms aspects of interior design practice including business ethics, roles in a design firm, and relationships and agreements, among other topics. The topics addressed in these first two sections provide meaning, relevancy, and context for all of the decisions the designer makes in the design process.

The third, and final, section of the text addresses design outcomes and the methods designers use to communicate their design decisions at various steps in the design process. Chapter 7 begins this discussion by describing the importance of contextual factors, such as the project location, demographic influences on a design, construction type influences, and anticipating future design trends. Chapter 8 addresses the planning process and describes all of the drawing types a designer utilizes to communicate the design intent at particular phases in the design process. Chapter 9 broadly describes interior finishes by category—floors, walls, and ceilings—and the importance of the underlying construction in executing a successful installation of these finishes. Chapter 10,

Furnishings, introduces the critical aspects of furniture, fixtures, and equipment, referred to as FF&E, in addition to millwork and doors, windows and window coverings, and accessories. Chapter 11 provides an introduction to lighting, including design strategies, luminaire and lamp types, and control options. The final chapter, Chapter 12, discusses the integration of support systems for the built environment, including mechanical, electrical, and plumbing systems, known as MEP, as well as fire safety and acoustical systems. It is important to recall that student designers will likely engage in deeper study and application of each of these areas throughout their educational process. These topics will play a vital role in future courses and studio work as the student prepares to practice.

Summary

Interior design is a rewarding and complex profession where the practitioner has the privilege to greatly impact the lives of interior occupants for many years to come. The decisions designers make combine function and aesthetics to meet the needs of the client while creating beautiful places that can stand the test of time. The historical roots of interior design, its development from early cave dwellings to the modern-day complexity of specialized interiors, can be used to inspire and add to the body of knowledge of the profession. As future practitioners, student designers will be entering a growing profession in need of strong advocates for the legal recognition of interior design and the professionals that legally practice the discipline.

Key Terms

Contract design	Interior design	Space planning
Interior decoration	Residential design	

Resources

CIDQ. (2019). CIDQ l NCIDQ EXAMS l Definition of Interior Design. Retrieved February 22, 2019, from https://www.cidq.org/definition-of-interior-design.

Ireland, J. (2018). *History of interior design.* Bloomsbury Publishing USA.

NCIDQ Certified Interior Designers. (n.d.). Retrieved December 15, 2017, from https://www.cidq.org/find-ncidq-certified-int-designer.

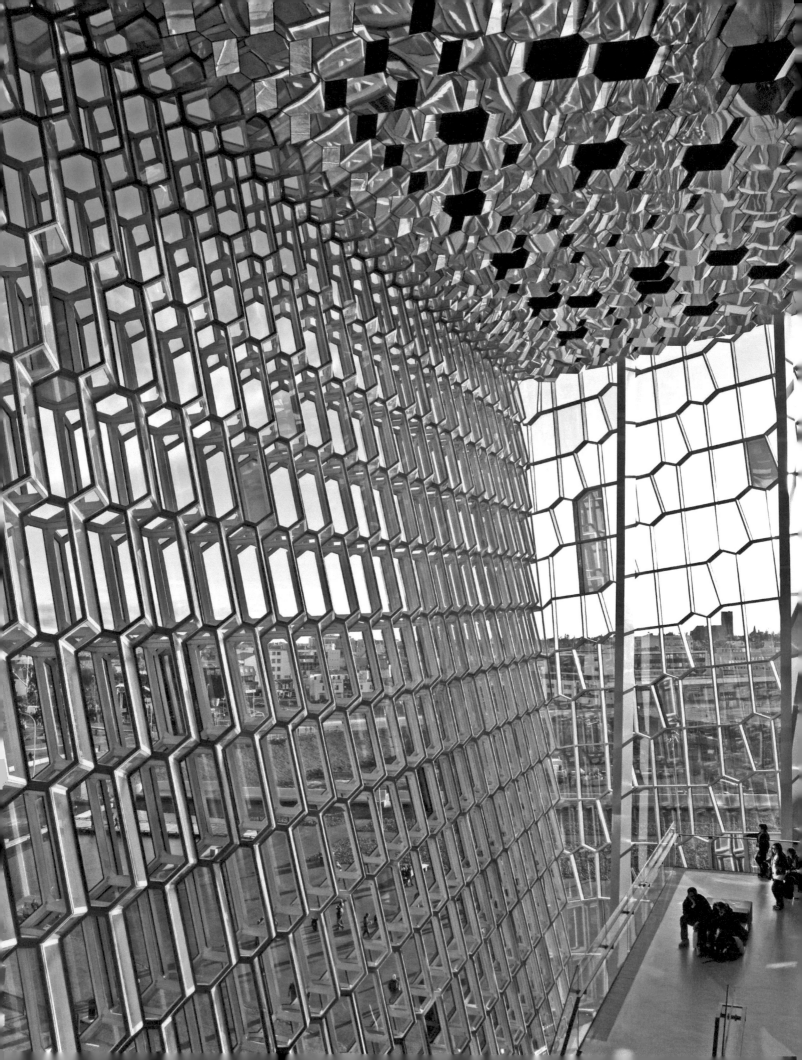

1

The Foundation of Design: Design Thinking and the Elements and Principles of Design

Learning Objectives

As a result of reading this chapter, students will

1. Possess an awareness of the purpose, history, and process of design thinking.

2. Possess an awareness of the elements of design: form, pattern, texture, scale color, and light.

3. Possess an awareness of the principles of design: proportion, balance, rhythm, and unity.

As a result of taking part in the learning exercises at the end of this chapter, students will

1. Demonstrate a deeper understanding of how to achieve empathy for a client/user of a space.

2. Demonstrate the ability to concisely define a design problem.

3. Demonstrate the ability to brainstorm ideas that may solve a design problem.

4. Demonstrate the ability to identify elements of design through imagery.

5. Demonstrate the ability to identify positive or negative examples of principles of design.

Design Thinking

Many companies and organizations that rely on innovation to create growth in their business have noticed a decline in the frequency of innovative ideas to solve problems and create new and impactful solutions. In architecture and design, professionals are consistently wrestling with the tendency to repeat a prior design solution or process for their current design problem. "This is the way we have always done it" is a common reason given for repeating a design or process without actually knowing the reasons why something is done.

Creative disciplines, including interior design, have always relied on creative people to solve very complicated problems. Sometimes, various things get in the way of "being creative." Design thinking is a methodology that seeks to address the need for innovation in a context that encourages stagnation. Broadly speaking, **design thinking** is "a formal method for practical, creative resolution of problems or issues, with the intent of an improved future result" (Faste, 1987). This definition is purposely broad as it can apply to many different professions and individuals across disciplines. Within the interior design profession, the tendency for stagnation can be high when under pressures of time, cost, and quality, which are present on every project. The goal of this text is to help the early design student see the role of design thinking in every context of design basics. This should help set the stage for the student to have a future career that seeks out the right process to encourage innovation with every design project.

History of Design Thinking

First, it is necessary to understand the roots of design thinking, its development, how it is being used today, and where it might be heading in the future. In 1969, Herbert Simon wrote "The Sciences of the Artificial," a research paper in which he outlined his research surrounding rational decision making. In the article, he identifies three stages of rational decision making: intelligence, design, and choice. Intelligence could be looked at as knowledge coupled with the ability to use the knowledge. Design speaks to the idea of identifying a problem and coming up with ways to solve it. And choice refers to selecting the best possible option, given the circumstances, to solve the problem. The process he outlined seems rather intuitive to us today, but it took someone unpacking the process of how one makes a decision to see it this way.

Expressing this process is sometimes challenging, depending on how an individual naturally processes information (verbally, visually, kinesthetically, etc.). For designers, visual processing through drawing is very common. That is why *Experiences in Visual Thinking*, written by Robert McKim in 1973, was very impactful. In this book, McKim describes perceptual thinking skills and the power they have on the ability of humans to change the world, or to solve problems.

Then, in 1987, Rolf Faste began to popularize the notion of "design thinking," providing the definition referenced earlier, and again here for convenience:

> Design thinking is a formal method for practical, creative resolution of problems or issues, with the intent of an improved future result.

Developing a formal method for the practical, creative resolution of problems that produces an improved result is actually a very difficult thing to do. Unpacking the mental and even physical processes of a designer who consistently innovates is tough. Sometimes, the designer isn't always aware of what they are doing in the moment of innovation unless they take the time to reflect on what it was that made the difference. For the early design student, it is important to understand that design thinking is not passive but a process of creative actions. It isn't something that "just happens," but it is something that one *makes happen*.

Process of Design Thinking

Recently, the d.school at Stanford University has been advancing the use of design thinking in many disciplines. Areas including business and organizational structures and product design and development have benefitted from the incorporation of design thinking concepts. The d.school has advanced the understanding of design thinking to include five active steps when solving complex problems:

1. Empathize
2. Define
3. Ideate
4. Prototype
5. Test

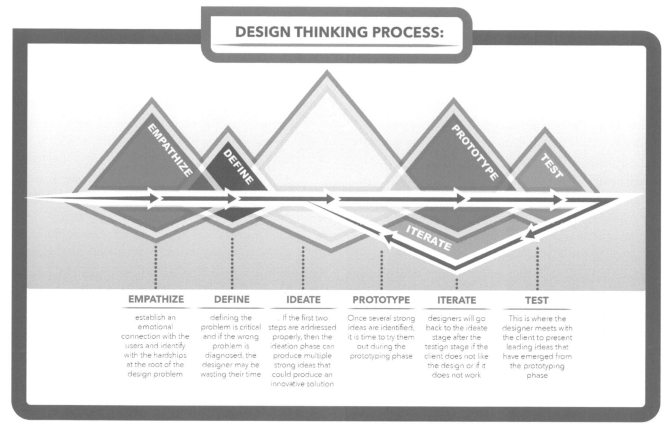

DESIGN THINKING PROCESS:

EMPATHIZE	DEFINE	IDEATE	PROTOTYPE	ITERATE	TEST
establish an emotional connection with the users and identify with the hardships at the root of the design problem	defining the problem is critical and if the wrong problem is diagnosed, the designer may be wasting their time	. If the first two steps are addressed properly, then the ideation phase can produce multiple strong ideas that could produce an innovative solution	Once several strong ideas are identified, it is time to try them out during the prototyping phase	designers will go back to the ideate stage after the testign stage if the client does not like the design or if it does not work	This is where the designer meets with the client to present leading ideas that have emerged from the prototyping phase

Figure 1.1 The design thinking process is a rhythm of gathering information in an outward focused manner (empathy, ideation, and prototyping) to focusing inwardly (problem definition and testing). The process also embraces iteration, as testing can often expose problems in a design prototype.

In the context of architecture and design, the process begins with the ability to **empathize** with the client, or users of the building or space (Fig. 1.1). For this to be successful, the designer needs to establish an emotional connection with the users of the design in an effort to provide the best possible solution to the design problem. Thomas Brown, CEO of IDEO and a proponent of design thinking, encourages users of this method to immerse themselves in the user's situation to fully understand the plight of the client (Brown, 2008).

Next, **problem definition** is critical. If the problem is misdiagnosed, the designer will be attempting to solve the wrong problem, or one that doesn't even exist.

The third step, **ideate**, is often where many designers jump to. However, if the designer cannot empathize with the client, or if the designer hasn't properly defined the problem, then the ideas that come out of the brainstorming sessions will be off base. If the first two steps are addressed properly, then the ideation phase can produce multiple strong ideas that could produce an innovative

solution. Brown suggests asking the "what if?" types of questions that drive toward what users want for a better future, rather than focusing too heavily on backward-looking data and past problems.

Once several strong ideas are identified, it is time to try them out during the **prototyping** phase. For designers and architects, this usually happens through sketching, preliminary material research and selections, and building models. It is important to allow this stage to take its course without jumping to a solution too soon. If the process is rushed, the probability of the design solution failing increases significantly. Brown has found that it is far better to develop prototypes based on evidence rather than gut feelings. The designer has to control the urge to design based on personal preferences and instead focus on the needs expressed by the users.

The fifth step in the design thinking process is the **testing** phase. This is where the designer meets with the client to present leading ideas that have emerged from the prototyping phase. Often, it is necessary to step back into the prototyping phase after testing a prototype with the client. The best designers are able to move back and forth between prototyping and testing quickly and efficiently. This process can take a while, but it is important to remember that developing multiple **iterations** is simply part of the design process. Working through multiple iterations is not failure. **Failure** is designing and building a space that does not meet the needs of the users, and it can be avoided if design thinking is followed closely. As a designer gains experience (closely related to the preceding discussion on intelligence), this process of prototyping and testing can be streamlined without losing quality.

It is also important to leverage the expertise and specialty skill sets of the design team members. Designing collaboratively is a necessary and critical aspect of design and is discussed further in later chapters. In Chapter 3, the conventional design process (pre-design, schematic design, design development, construction documentation, contract administration) often used on projects is discussed in further detail, placing it in context with design thinking. For now, though, it is necessary to develop a time-tested verbal vocabulary of design through the elements and principles of design.

Elements and Principles of Design

The psychology of how humans perceive space is at the heart of understanding the elements and principles of design. Gestalt theory, first proposed in 1890 by Christian von Ehrenfels, seeks to explain the ability of individuals to perceive consistencies, systems, or wholeness in a complex environment. The idea that "the whole is something else than the sum of its parts" (Koffka, 1935) summarizes the essence of the Gestalt laws (Metzger et al., 2006; Todorovic, 2008):

- Figure-ground articulation
  The notion that a form/object (figure) is separate from its surroundings (ground), similar to a barn in an open field.
- Proximity
  Clustered objects are perceived to be in groups with one another, similar to piles of sorted clothes in preparation to be laundered.
- Common fate
  Objects that move together are perceived as being of the same group, similar to vehicles moving in differing directions in traffic.

- Similarity
  Objects that possess visual similarities based on any number of characteristics, such as color, shape, or size, are perceived as being of the same group.
- Continuity
  Objects sharing an alignment with one another are perceived to be of the same group, such as an arcade of columns.
- Closure
  Objects are perceived as a whole if they are part of a discreet, or closed, whole, such as a series of chairs that completely ring a circular table.
- Good Gestalt
  Objects are perceived as a group if they are orderly and simple to discern, similar to ten children all wearing the same color shirt on a busy playground with forty other children wearing a variety of colored clothing.
- Past experience
  An individual's bias, or past experience, influences how objects are grouped and interpreted, which is the case when someone reads a language that is new to them—the individual is not familiar with the characters, or with how they should be grouped into words or ideas.

As Gestalt theory seeks to articulate how humans interpret the world around them in broad terms, the elements and principles of design describe the sensory qualities of a space more specifically. The **elements of design** are the sensory qualities of a design, concise and clearly defined in their own right. The **principles of design** are described as the composition of several individual elements of design within a space where each principle can use several elements in a variety of ways in order to be achieved. Understanding that the elements and principles of design fit together and complement one another is helpful when utilizing the elements and principles to achieve certain outcomes in a space.

Elements of Design

Both the elements and principles of design are defined slightly differently depending on the source and context of their use, whether it be within interior design, urban planning, industrial design, graphic design, or fine art. In essence, the elements of design include form, pattern, texture, color, light, and scale.

Figure 1.2 The intersecting lines of Paris streets create nodes, or points, of activity.

Form

Form is the shape, or geometry, of a space or object. At its most basic level, form is defined by point, line, plane, and volume. **Point** is technically a theoretical geometry, and is an infinitesimally small location in space represented through a dot on a two-dimensional plane or in a three-dimensional space. A point in the built environment can be expressed as a small object, or clustering of objects, such as a furniture arrangement in a vast and open interior space. Sometimes referred to as a **node**, a point can translate into designed space through an intersection of two paths, corridors, or lines on a surface. This idea of intersecting lines can be epic in scale, such as city streets (Fig. 1.2), or very detailed, such as the stitching pattern of an upholstered piece of furniture.

One of the most influential elements of design, the **line** is simply a point in motion, and that line can be

Figure 1.3 The Jewish Museum in Berlin utilizes many angular lines to guide the form of the exterior and interior design of the building.

straight or curvilinear. Straight lines can be described as vertical, horizontal, or angular (diagonal). Vertical lines serve to accentuate the height of a space, horizontal lines reinforce a sense of gravity within a space, and angular lines tend to create tension and evoke strong emotions within a space (Fig. 1.3). Curvilinear lines can be described as arcs or a set of arcs placed in sequence with one another and tend to softly guide the eye through a space and communicate a sense of relaxed freedom. Depending on context, curves can also place additional focus on a particular portion of the design. **Organizing lines** are incredibly helpful in planning a space as the designer seeks to bring certain boundaries or objects into alignment with one another. Organizing lines are also very useful in creating datum height lines on walls and other surfaces to create a certain sense of scale or proportion within a space. Organizing lines can also create clear paths of circulation, for example, providing a clear differentiation from the "usable area" within a furniture cluster or a room. In this case, the circulation is commonly thought of as **negative space**, and the room or furniture arrangement as **positive space**. Line is one of the most powerful elements of design, as it contributes to the overall form of the built environment.

Planes are created by a line moving in a single direction and can be easily described through Euclidian geometries, such as circle, triangle, and rectangle, among others. Planes can be interpreted as surfaces, such as floors, walls, ceilings, and roofs, as well as the ground plane (often pitched) upon which a building rests. Similar to lines, planes are very useful in organizing space and can be used in conjunction with a consistent material to link multiple spaces together.

Volume, also referred to as "space" or "mass," is created when a plane is extruded, such as a circle to create a cylinder, or extruded and tapered, such as a triangle or square to create a pyramid. Volume is often used to describe interior **space**, such as when an individual perceives the interior of the Pantheon in Rome. Or, **mass** can be recognized, for example, as one may hold an orange in the hand. These examples show that the same geometry, in this case a sphere, can be perceived as volume or as mass. Some volumes and masses are described as free form in nature. This description is reserved when the form in question does not strictly abide by the pure descriptions of a solid (sphere, cylinder, cube, pyramid, etc.) (Fig. 1.4).

Pattern

Pattern is utilizing a certain geometry, or combinations of geometries, repeatedly, even formulaically (Fig. 1.5). The visual effect can be dynamic when viewing the pattern at varying distances from the patterned surface. Many examples

Figure 1.4 The Oslo Opera House offers a free-form expression of volumetric space as contrasting forms create the edges of the multistory lobby space.

Figure 1.5 The grid pattern of the pendant light fixtures at Tomukun Korean Barbeque, designed by OX Studio, serves to reinforce the linear nature of the interior.

of pattern exist in textiles, where the visual pattern is linked to the technique used to weave the fabric. Historically, patterns also carry significant cultural meaning, such as in Celtic argyles and Islamic art and architecture.

Texture

Texture can be defined in both a visual and tactile sense. Visually, texture can be easily confused with pattern, because the two elements often contribute together to some of the same principles in design. The differentiator is that visual texture utilizes randomness, while pattern is very intentional and repeatable. Texture in the tactile sense is very important in the built environment, as well, because it describes how objects and surfaces feel to the touch. Descriptors such as rough and smooth can be used to describe the feel of surfaces. Texture also influences a space by adding visual interest, beauty, and character; reducing the reverberation of sound; altering the reflection of light from a surface; and often adding additional maintenance (Fig. 1.6).

Color

Color can be expressed in two ways, as substance and as light, and the two act very differently from one another. In terms of substance, color is technically expressed in terms of hue, value, and chroma. **Hue** describes the category of the color, such as red, blue, or yellow, and is what people often refer to in common language when using the term color. The primary hues are red, blue, and yellow. The secondary hues are created by mixing two of the primary hues in equal amounts: orange results from red and yellow, green from blue and yellow, and violet from red and blue (Fig. 1.7). **Value** is the term used to describe the tint or shade of a color. A tint is achieved by adding white to a hue, such as adding white to violet to create lavender. A shade is achieved when adding black to a hue, such as adding black to blue to create navy blue. **Chroma** refers to the saturation of a color. For example, a tonal color, one that is less saturated, is achieved when gray is added to a hue.

Color as light is described in terms of physics. In this context, color is expressed based on what we can see in the visible spectrum of light. Each color has a different wavelength, with red being the longest and violet the shortest. The colors of light can be seen together in a rainbow as sunlight passes through rain drops, or as sunlight passes through a glass prism and strikes a wall.

Figure 1.6 This close-up of the highly textured dimensional wood panels at the Oslo Opera House (previously referenced in relation to volume) demonstrates the impact that texture can have when viewed closely or from far away.

Figure 1.7 Powdered pigments are used to determine the color of paint and dyes.

Figure 1.8 The Festival of Lanterns utilizes colored lanterns to cast multicolored lighting effects.

These colors, in order from longest to shortest wavelength, are red, orange, yellow, green, blue, indigo (blue-violet), and violet (Fig. 1.8). The primary colors of light are red, green, and blue, as commonly expressed in old RGB computer monitors or in numbered RGB color values in photo-editing software, such as Adobe Photoshop. On the whole, color is one of the most easily recognized elements of design, and it has tremendous impact on the design of the built environment. More of the science and psychology of color is discussed in Chapter 5.

Light

Light affects all of the prior elements of design in some way. The most obvious is that without light, then form, pattern, texture, scale, and color would not be visible. The way occupants experience a space is directly impacted by light in most cases. Too little light can be unsafe, while too much can cause eye strain or even pain. Light can be overly uniform, creating a sense of boredom and weariness in a space. Lighting is categorized as either natural, coming directly or indirectly from the sun, or as electric, coming from light fixtures. Electric light is grouped into three categories: ambient (sometimes called general and is useful in illuminating spaces for circulation), accent (think of a washing of light across a painting, or pinpoint lighting focused on jewelry in a retail space), and task (typically takes the form of an adjustable lamp close to a surface as is commonly found on a bedside nightstand). Whether natural or electric, excellent lighting design can call attention to paths of circulation, provide for an efficient and comfortable work or living environment, accentuate texture and patterns, highlight certain forms, and provide for accurate rendition of colors and perception of scale (Fig. 1.9).

Figure 1.9 The integration of the mechanical apertures within the façade of the Modern Arab Institute by Jean Nouvel illustrates the impact of natural light on an interior space.

Scale

Scale refers to the size of a space or object in comparison to what someone would expect it to be based on an accepted standard, such as the human body. For example, if a residential doorway is typically expected to be 6 feet 8 inches tall, when one that is 10 feet tall is encountered, it would be characterized as large, or grand, because of the expectation of scale. Objects and components within the built environment, such as stairs, furniture, countertops, doors, storage components, and railings, are all designed and constructed in context with the scale of the human body. Scale is often described as intimate, where the space is designed to be snug around one, or a few occupants. Scale is also described as monumental, or grand, where the human form is dwarfed in comparison to the space (Fig. 1.10).

The key consideration of scale is the object, or space, in comparison to something else. The "something else" is often the human form, but can also be other objects in a space, such as a very large light fixture that is out of scale in comparison to the furniture in a space. Some designers, such as Philippe Starck, employ this technique to impose visual hierarchy, or emphasis, within their designs.

Figure 1.10 The grand scale of this atrium in a private residence, designed by OX Studio, contrasts with the intimate scale of the adjacent private spaces.

Scale can also be described in relation to a mechanical scale, such as an architectural drawing scale. In this case, the drawing becomes "scalable" in the sense that a drawing unit directly translates into a real unit, such as when one-quarter of an inch on a drawing equals one foot when the space becomes built, which is expressed as 1/4 inch = 1 foot. The definition of scale, the size of a space or object in comparison to an accepted standard, holds true in the case of drawings, as the accepted standard is the annotated scale (i.e., 1/4 inch = 1 foot). Without scalable drawings, designs would be very difficult to interpret and construct.

Principles of Design

The elements of design work as individual parts of an overall design. The elements, when orchestrated well by the designer, combine to create principles of design. Principles of design do not exist on their own. Rather, they rely on the elements of design working in combination with one another. The principles of design are proportion, balance, rhythm, hierarchy, and unity.

Proportion

Proportion references the size of an object, or space, in relation to itself rather than in relation to an outside standard. Proportion can have a tremendous impact on a person's perception of space and can elicit certain emotions. For example, spaces that have a small footprint and low ceiling can elicit feelings of confinement and increase stress levels due to their compressed proportions, while spaces that are larger in footprint and very tall, such as a cathedral, can inspire sensations of freedom and wonder due to their lofty proportions.

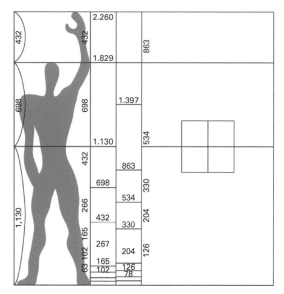

Figure 1.12 Le Corbusier (French architect from early to mid-twentieth century) developed a proportion based on the human body.

Figure 1.13 The Notre Dame Cathedral is known for its vertical proportion, a characteristic of Gothic architecture. The integration of natural and artificial light reinforces the pattern of the structural columns and rib vaults, drawing the eye upward while also illustrating symmetrical balance.

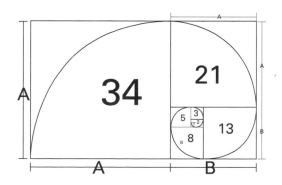

Figure 1.11 The golden section is a method of achieving the "ideal" proportion based on mathematics and geometry. Note the integration of the Fibonacci sequence in this diagram.

Design Thinking Methodologies Facilitated by the Stanford d.school

Project: Virtual Crash Course in Design Thinking
Organization: Stanford d.school
Creators/Facilitators: Thomas Both, Jeremy Utley, Scott Doorley, Dave Baggereor, and many others connected to the d.school
Web Location: https://dschool.stanford.edu/resources-collections/a-virtual-crash-course-in-design-thinking

The d.school at Stanford University offers the Virtual Crash Course in Design Thinking for those individuals interested in learning more about design thinking who cannot attend one of their many onsite person-to-person learning experiences. The tutorials introduce design thinking concepts and offer participants the opportunity to experiment with the five-step design thinking process. The website provides the following resources:

- Instruction and planning tools for organizing and executing a design thinking workshop experience including planning process lists and participant worksheets.
- A demonstration video that walks the viewer through The Gift Giving Project, a ninety-minute design thinking experience.
- Follow-up materials and strategies to help the facilitator continue the design thinking process after the workshop.
- The Design Thinking Bootcamp Bootleg.

The Bootcamp Bootleg document provides an overview of d.school Mindsets, the five steps, or modes, of design thinking, and a growing list of impactful design thinking methodologies. Currently numbered at thirty-nine, these methodologies are useful across the five steps of design thinking, which, with only a small amount of adaptation, a designer can use in designing the built environment. With an extensive, and still growing, list of design thinking methods, a designer would be best served to select the best methods for a specific project design scenario. Some of the methods, and how they could fit into the five-step design thinking process, are described below.

Empathy

Interview for Empathy

Purpose: Uncover the client's intentions, feelings, and desires for the project.

Techniques:

1. Ask questions that reveal the root cause of a problem.
   a. Ask why.
   b. Ask specific questions rather than general questions.
   c. Ask follow-up questions if something is confusing or unclear.
   d. Avoid questions that only have two answers such as yes/no.
2. Allow the interviewee to think.
   a. Silence is OK. It means the interviewee is contemplating their answer.
   b. Don't allow bias to creep into your questions.
   c. Stories are very telling and demonstrate that the topic is meaningful to the interviewee.
3. Observe.
   a. Read body language.
   b. Bring a partner to take notes or record the interview. It is impossible to fully engage with the person when trying to take notes yourself.

Definition

Design Principles

Purpose: Design principles provide an abstract way to create a set of action-based design guidelines that can also be communicated to other members of the design team.

Techniques:

1. Distill the problem.
   a. Building upon the outcomes of the empathy phase, create a set of guidelines that identify the most important aspects of the design problem that need to be solved.
2. Articulate.
   a. In this context, principles can be articulated based upon the designer's observations, interview results, or expressed needs by the client/user.
   b. A concise set of design principles are most effective when they discreetly articulate design goals, or define qualities of an anticipated successful solution.

Ideation

Facilitate a Brainstorm

Purpose: Complex design challenges often need a team of professionals to reach solutions collaboratively. Facilitating a brainstorming session is very important when generating ideas.

Techniques:

1. Pace
   a. By using the right questions to initiate a brainstorming session, the facilitator can set the pace of the session.
   b. The facilitator should monitor the energy level of the group and use follow-up questions to accelerate the pace of the session as needed.
2. Limitations
   a. Use hypothetical limitations in the brainstorming process through follow-up questions in order to solicit new ideas.

   b. Place a time constraint on a given set of ideation to come up with a certain number of ideas within a time frame.
3. Environment
   a. Create an environment that is scaled to the group size—not too small where people feel cramped and not too large where members of the group can disengage.
   b. Provide materials such as pens/pencils and sticky notes.

Prototyping

Prototype to Test

Purpose: The purpose of creating a prototype is to test it, so only create a prototype to the quality that is necessary in order to test. Save time by thinking of the prototype as an iteration. The idea is to learn something by making the prototype and to solicit feedback from a possible user during testing.

Techniques:

1. Begin by doing.
   a. Don't think about the prototype for too long—the making process can be very informative.
2. Informative not exhaustive.
   a. Don't spend too much time or energy on a single prototype. The idea is to solicit a reaction to an idea not represent the finished product with 100 percent accuracy.
3. User-centered.
   a. Create the prototype with the user in mind. Consider how they will perceive the prototype and what it is you plan to test.
4. Control the variables.
   a. Plan to answer a specific question with each variable in the various prototypes.
   b. Limit the number of variables for each prototype. Too many changes between prototypes can lead to confusing results in testing.

Testing

Testing with Users

Purpose: Testing a prototype design with the users of the proposed solution will lead to an improved solution. This is also more than an opportunity to present the design and gain feedback; this process helps the designer reconnect with the empathic roots of the design thinking process.

Techniques:

1. Orient the user to the design solution by reminding them of the problem definition and design context.

2. Show each design solution proposal, or prototype, rather than tell about it. Visuals allow the user to think and interpret for themselves.

3. Solicit feedback and ask questions regarding how the user feels about the design solution proposal.

4. Observe their reaction and interaction with your prototype. Which drawings do they spend the most time looking at, which finishes do they touch the most, what are their facial expressions while engaging with the different aspects of each prototype?

5. Dig into the reasons behind the user's reactions—both positive and negative. Ask follow-up questions that get at the reasons why.

Throughout history, much emphasis has been placed on finding and utilizing ideal proportions. In ancient Greek culture, the ideal proportion was clearly expressed through the golden mean, or golden section, and was commonly used by the Romans and later throughout Europe during the Renaissance period (Fig. 1.11). The Fibonacci sequence, developed in thirteenth-century Italy, is another way of expressing ideal proportions. The number series is infinite, beginning with zero and one, then progressing in an additive sequence: 0, 1, 1, 2, 3, 5, 8, 13, 21, 34, 55, etc. In other words, 0 + 1 = 1; 1 + 1 = 2; 1 + 2 = 3; 2 + 3 = 5; 3 + 5 = 8; and so on. One common place this proportion is used is in rugs and photography (Fig. 1.12). In the twentieth century, the French architect Le Corbusier developed another ideal proportion based on the human form. In each of these three cases—the golden mean, the Fibonacci sequence, and Le Corbusier's Modular scale—the proportions are extremely close to one another. On occasion, a designer will want to step away from the "ideal" for a very specific purpose, often to elicit a certain dramatic sensation or to communicate a specific intention (Fig. 1.13). In any case, the elements of design that most contribute to the design principle of proportion are form, scale, and light.

Balance

Balance is the quality that expresses a natural resting posture, or equilibrium, in a space. Various objects, surfaces, and effects in combination with one another create a general sense of balance in a space. Balance can be examined when space planning through the selection of appropriately sized furniture and through the placement of the furniture. Balance can also be examined vertically when designing walls by carefully taking into account the height and form of certain objects, such as furniture and light fixtures, in combination with the textures and patterns applied to surfaces. Lighting can also have a tremendous impact on balance within a spatial composition.

Three primary strategies are commonly used to achieve balance: symmetry, asymmetry, and radial arrangements. **Symmetry** utilizes an axial line to arrange

Figure 1.14 The interior of the Villa La Roche-Jeanerette by Le Corbusier, now known as the Fondation Le Corbusier, embraces the use of asymmetry in the design of the interior.

---

identical elements on each side of the line in a mirror-image arrangement. Symmetry is static, stable, and often characterized as traditional. **Asymmetry** relies on a more loosely defined visual axis and the visual weight of objects and surfaces on either side of the axis to achieve balance. Dense patterns, expressive forms, large scales, highly textured surfaces, and bright colors all increase visual weight. Creating asymmetrical balance is challenging compared to symmetrical balance, but it also communicates a different overall sense within the space with certain advantages. Asymmetry is typically viewed as more flexible when incorporating future design changes, is informal and more relaxed for the users, and is visually engaging (Fig. 1.14). **Radial** balance is achieved by arranging objects around a center point. This type of balance can be asymmetrical, relying on the visual weight of the objects and surfaces to create balance, or symmetrical, utilizing one axis or more running through a center point. A good example of radial symmetry can be found in the Greek cross plan of some church buildings.

With any of these strategies, form, scale, texture, color, and light are the elements commonly used to achieve balance.

Rhythm

Rhythm evokes a sense of movement as the eye traces various elements of a design through a space. This movement can be very regular, as if to a timed musical beat, or embrace variation with certain key markers, such as form or color, that make the rhythmic movement evident. Repetition, alternation, and gradation are common techniques used to achieve rhythm in a design. **Repetition** is most commonly witnessed in patterns and relies heavily on the same techniques used in musical compositions. **Alternation** is a type of patterning that uses two or more contrasting elements in sequence with one another. **Gradation** is achieved through slight variations in design components that create an overall progression, such as gradually changing a color from blue to red and then back to blue along a

Figure 1.15 The ceiling of the Welsh International Assembly in Cardiff illustrates rhythm through the gradation of the ceiling height changes, hierarchy through contrast and positioning, and a radial balance in the red cedar funnel that reaches to the floor of the upper mezzanine level.

wall (Fig. 1.15). The elements of design commonly used to address rhythm include pattern, form, color, and light.

Hierarchy

Hierarchy refers to a visual area of focus, or emphasis, within a space that draws the attention of the eye. In order for a visual hierarchy to exist, certain objects or surfaces need to take the focus over others. The designer can employ strategies to achieve hierarchy within a space, including degrees of contrast and dominance through positioning.

Contrast can be achieved through varying certain elements within a design. For example, contrast in form, scale, color, light, pattern, or texture can create contrast in relation to the space around that object or surface. Contrast can be bold or subtle and is best described through levels of contrast: dominant, subdominate, and subordinate. Utilizing more levels of contrast within a design begins to lessen the degree of contrast between each level, resulting in a design that lacks significant degrees of contrast. A **dominant** component of a design is what garners the greatest amount of attention at first glance. **Subdominant** components still exercise influence on the perception of the space but are perceived after the dominant component is noticed first. Finally, the

subordinate elements come into focus after detailed inspection of the space.

Hierarchy can also be achieved through dominance of **position**, which involves skillful placement of certain design components in a space. Within a space, certain positions call for more attention than others. For example, the design component at the center of a radial planning scheme demonstrates a high level of importance for the item in the hierarchical scheme of the design. In addition, design components that can be viewed from many angles and placed higher within a volume, such as a focal element in a ceiling, demonstrate hierarchical emphasis through positioning.

In order for a visual hierarchy to exist, certain objects or surfaces need to take the focus over others. One way to achieve this is through contrast. If the object of focus or surface is designed to contrast with its surroundings, then hierarchy is established. As a design becomes more complex, there can be multiple levels of hierarchy within a space, and the design can possess nuance and depth. Hierarchy can be incredibly rich, offering new and varied experiences as the user interacts with a space with increasing levels of detail. Hierarchy can be achieved through variation in scale, boldness of pattern, color, or texture, and through the skillful use of light (Fig. 1.16).

Figure 1.16 Hierarchy can be achieved through contrast, such as the daylight striking the stone wall in comparison to the relative darkness of the wood floor, or through positioning, such as the emphasis on the skylight at the top of the space. This interior also utilizes scale, pattern, color, texture, and light to achieve hierarchy, or emphasis.

Figure 1.17 This bedroom interior demonstrates unity by bringing together many design principles, particularly balance and hierarchy.

Figure 1.19 The Freelon RTP Office Upfit by the Freelon Group achieves unity through the use of proportion, hierarchy, and rhythm.

Figure 1.18 This worship space in the Vilki Church in Helsinki, Finland, utilizes proportion, hierarchy, and rhythm to achieve unity within the design.

Unity

Unity encompasses all of the design principles, and by extension the elements of design as well. This principle undergirds the entirety of a design and speaks to the base level structure of the design from which all other elements and principles are derived. One way to achieve unity is through a level of consistency in the design, possibly through a repeating form or color. While consistency is one unifying strategy, it is also important to integrate some variety into a design, so that the design doesn't become stale (Figs. 1.17, 18, and 19). The concept is one of the strongest ways to bring unity to a design. A concept provides a unifying direction for a project by addressing the functional and aesthetic priorities of an interior. Concept will be discussed further in Chapter 3.

Summary

By employing design thinking, designers can increase the likelihood of creating built environments that address real needs, both functional and aesthetic, of end users. The five-step process is founded upon the designer's empathy for their client, or user group, which progresses to accurate problem definition before engaging in an iterative process of ideation, prototyping, and testing. Strong design schemes that result from this process all employ the use of the elements and principles of design. Individual elements of design, including form (point, line, plane, volume), pattern, texture, color, light, and scale, combine to achieve principles of design, including proportion, balance (symmetry, asymmetry, radial), rhythm (repetition, alternation, gradation), hierarchy (contrast, position), and unity.

Key Terms

Alternation	Ideate	Proportion
Asymmetry	Iteration	Prototyping
Balance	Light	Radial
Chroma	Line	Repetition
Color	Mass	Rhythm
Contrast	Negative space	Scale
Design Thinking	Node	Space
Dominant	Organizing lines	Subdominant
Elements of design	Pattern	Subordinate
Empathize	Plane	Symmetry
Failure	Point	Testing
Form	Position	Texture
Gradation	Positive space	Unity
Hierarchy	Principles of design	Value
Hue	Problem definition	Volume

Resources

Brown, T. (2008, June 1). Design Thinking. Retrieved December 16, 2015, from https://hbr.org/2008/06/design-thinking.

Ching, F. D. (2014). *Architecture: Form, Space, and Order.* John Wiley & Sons.

Ching, F. D., & Binggeli, C. (2017). *Interior Design Illustrated.* John Wiley & Sons.

Cohen, R. (2014, March 31). Design Thinking: A Unified Framework for Innovation. Retrieved December 16, 2015, from http://www.forbes.com/sites/reuvencohen/2014/03/31/design-thinking-a-unified-framework-for-innovation/.

Crash Course. (2016). Retrieved April 14, 2016, from https://dschool.stanford.edu/resources/virtual-crash-course-video.

Faste, R. A. (1987). Perceiving Needs (No. 871534). SAE Technical Paper.

Koffka, K. (1935). Principles of Gestalt Psychology, International Library of Psychology, Philosophy and Scientific Method.

McKim, R. H. (1972). *Experiences in Visual Thinking*.

Metzger, W., Spillmann, L. T., Lehar, S. T., Stromeyer, M. T., & Wertheimer, M. T. (2006). *Laws of Seeing*. MIT Press.

Rengel, R. J. (2014). *Shaping Interior Space*. Bloomsbury Publishing.

Simon, H. A. (1996). *The Sciences of the Artificial*. MIT Press.

Todorovic, D. (2008). Gestalt Principles. *Scholarpedia*, *3*(12), 5345.

Review Questions

1. Define "design thinking."
2. Who popularized the three stages of rational decision making? What are these stages?
3. List the five steps in design thinking. For each step, describe why it is important and what can happen if the step is skipped or performed incorrectly.
4. What is failure in design?
5. List the six elements of design and define each.
6. List the five principles of design and define each. For each principle of design, list the elements of design that most commonly contribute to it.

Exercises

Using Design Thinking

Materials: camera, pens/pencils, drawing paper, notepad, tape measure

1. Preparation
   a. Each student should photograph a small space where they personally experience problems, such as a bedroom, design studio at school, or something else.
   b. Take basic measurements of the space so you know the location of walls, doors, windows, and furniture. Quickly and basically draw a plan view of the space.

2. Partner up (follow these steps for each partner)
    a. Show your partner the photos and plan sketch.
    b. Briefly describe your problem(s) within the space.
3. Divide
    a. Reflect on what your partner told you and showed you in the photos and sketch.
    b. Write questions that will help you to understand the problems they face within that space.
4. Come back together (follow these steps for each partner)
    a. Foster empathy. Ask your partner your questions about their struggles within the space. Be patient, ask follow-up questions as you think of them. Don't conclude until you fully understand the problem and have established an emotional connection with the person and/or the problem.
    b. Define the problem. Use diagrams to connect the ideas. Sketch cartoons that can add a sense of sincerity or levity to the problem, as appropriate. Write a statement that clearly identifies the problem so that others can understand it, too.
    c. Ideate. Brainstorm solutions with your partner to their spatial problem. Draw loose diagrams and use verbal descriptions that could lead to a possible solution. Come up with multiple iterations and ideas no matter how outlandish that could solve the problem.
5. Divide
    a. Prototype. Select the most interesting idea that you and your partner came up with to experience the prototyping process. Sketch ideas that could solve the problem(s). Root your prototype in the problem definition and the ideation process. Make sure you are motivated to solve your partner's problem (empathy). If you don't care, or simply go with what your gut tells you, your prototype will be lacking.
6. Come back together (follow these steps for each partner)
    a. Test. Present the prototype to your partner. Dialogue with your partner over the positives and negatives of the prototype.
    b. Write down the reactions of your partner on the sketches.

    c. This concludes the design thinking exercise. If the test resulted in a negative reaction by your partner, you would need to return to either the ideation or prototyping phase if this were a real-world project.

Identifying Elements and Principles of Design

Materials: magazines and/or internet search engine, printer (if using the internet)

1. Cut/paste images from magazines or print images from the internet that clearly express the elements of design. Each student should have one image that expresses each subcategory for each element of design, totaling twelve images.
    a. Form: point, line, plane, mass, and space
    b. Pattern
    c. Texture: visual and tactile
    d. Color: substance and light
    e. Light: natural and electric
2. Overlay tracing paper on each image and trace the portion of the image that expresses the element of design.
3. Cut/paste images from magazines or print images from the internet that clearly express the principles of design. Each student should have one image that expresses each subcategory for each principle of design, totaling ten images.
    a. Proportion
    b. Balance: symmetry, asymmetry, and radial
    c. Rhythm: repetition, alternation, and gradation
    d. Hierarchy: contrast and position
    e. Unity
4. Provide a written description for each image that describes why/how the principle is successfully, or not successfully, expressed.
5. The document could also be completed digitally using word processing and/or graphics software, if the student is comfortable doing so.

2

History of Architecture and Design

Learning Objectives

As a result of reading this chapter, students will

1. Possess a very broad awareness of the history of design periods.

2. Possess a very broad awareness of the transitions between design periods.

As a result of taking part in the learning exercises at the end of this chapter, students will

1. Demonstrate a base level understanding of post–industrial revolution design periods in Great Britain and America and how to identify their characteristics.

Introduction

Surviving buildings, interiors, furniture, and artwork positively influence our understanding of the history of architecture, interior design, and furniture. Likewise, war, natural disasters, the natural decay that comes with time, and selective demolition of buildings limit the body of knowledge. Based on this, it is important to realize that many design specimens have been lost to history, may only persist in literature, or are awaiting discovery through archaeology. In an increasingly global society, designers must understand the cultural and historical influences of the place and people for whom they will design. Due to the introductory nature of this text, the discussion on the history of design is cursory, and much has been omitted, or simply mentioned without an exhaustive discussion. The reader is advised to investigate the history of design as it relates to all cultures and places in later coursework.

Neolithic (10000–4000 BC)

Generally, **Neolithic** architecture includes shelters built between 10000 and 2000 BC. Construction techniques varied widely based on location and the materials available, such as mud brick in Mesopotamia or wattle and daub in Eastern Europe. Building types primarily included dwellings, ritualistic monuments, and tombs. Clustered settlements included Jericho in Palestine, Skara Brae in Scotland, and several locations in Turkey, including Catal Huyuk.

Catal Huyuk, located near present-day Konya, Turkey, was inhabited between 7500 and 5700 BC and realized its height of success around 7000 BC. The settlement included as many as 10000 inhabitants and consisted of mudbrick dwellings in direct proximity to one another such that there were no walkways, alleys, or streets dividing the buildings. Inhabitants traveled along the roofs of the dwellings and entered each building through holes or doors in the roofs. Ladders or stairs allowed access to the lower level of the dwellings. Interiors typically consisted of two primary rooms used for cooking and crafting and included a hearth, raised platforms for daily work and activities, and smooth plastered finishes. Wall murals depicting animals and humans have been found on interior and exterior walls.

Mesopotamian (4500–539 BC)

Mesopotamia was a large region centered around the Tigris–Euphrates river system and included the modern-day areas of southeastern Turkey, eastern Syria, Iraq, Kuwait, and portions of western Iran. The ancient civilizations that dominated this region from 3100 to 539 BC included the Sumerians, Akkadians, Assyrians, and Babylonians, with the Greeks, under Alexander the Great, conquering the land in 332 BC. The centralized location along primary trade routes that linked the Far East with Egypt to the southwest and Turkey to the northwest brought great influence and repeated war to the region. Some of the influential exports of Mesopotamia included technological advancements in architecture, including the first use of the true arch and the vault. In addition, columns and columns embedded within walls were first used; 500 years later they made their appearance in Egypt.

Due to the scarcity of wood and stone, sun-dried brick and fired brick were the dominant materials used in Mesopotamian building. Dominant building types included temples in the form of a ziggurat, or stepped tower, and domestic buildings, including palaces. One of the only surviving examples of Babylonian architecture, the Ishtar Gate, provided an entryway for the elevated outdoor paved pathway, or dromos, that acted as a formal processional to the palace and temples in Babylon (Fig. 2.1). The gate was constructed of glazed brick, included a circular archway, and was decorated with sculptural reliefs in the form of lions. These lions were used to demonstrate the prosperity of the civilization and to act as guardians for the city.

Very few examples of Mesopotamian furniture survive today, but further understanding can be gained through artwork depicting the use of furniture. Royalty and gods are often depicted in a seated position on stools and chairs and occasionally using footstools as well. Furniture legs were often turned on a lathe and were sculpted to resemble animal legs and feet, an aesthetic technique refined during the Middle Ages in many European designs.

Egyptian (3500–1100 BC)

Egyptian architecture from antiquity utilized sun-dried brick and stone due to the lack of wood in the region. Many non-ceremonial mud brick buildings built near the

Figure 2.1 A reconstruction of the Ishtar Gate is on display at the Pergamon Museum in Berlin, Germany. It is based on excavation findings in Babylon, or modern-day Hillah, Iraq.

Nile were lost to history because of the regular flooding of the river banks and the deterioration of brick structures. Areas that were not subject to flooding offer well-preserved brick structures due to the very dry climate of the region. As a result, the primary surviving structures are stone. Egyptian stone buildings predominantly used post and lintel construction techniques to carry loads across openings, and closely spaced columns to carry the heavy loads of flat stone roofs. Similar to other cultures that followed, the Egyptians incorporated round columns with ornately carved capitals into their architecture. Walls and columns were often covered in colorful decorative paintings and hieroglyphics that communicate much about the occupants' beliefs, status in society, and historical events.

One of the principle stone structures of ancient Egypt is the Pyramid of Khufu, which rests among the pyramid complex at Giza (Fig. 2.2). Built over the course of twenty years, and completed around 2500 BC, this pyramid is thought to be for the burial of the pharaoh Khufu, also known as Cheops. At 5.9 million tons and 480.6 feet in height, this pyramid was the tallest human-made structure in the world for 3,800 years, until the completion of the Lincoln Cathedral in AD 1300. Originally, the pyramid included an outer layer of white highly polished limestone blocks called casing stones, which would have created a much more striking visual contrast to the surrounding desert compared to what is visible today.

Figure 2.2 The Great Pyramid of Giza when it was first completed included an outer layer of white limestone that would have appeared very bright against the sandy desert.

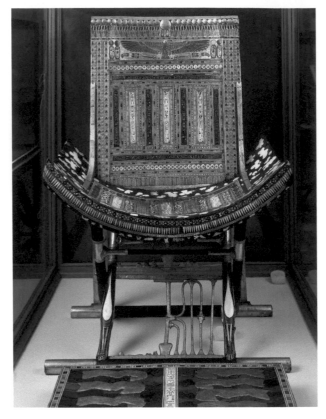

Figure 2.3 The ceremonial throne of King Tut included an innovative folding mechanism that allowed the chair to be transported and used by the pharaoh wherever he went.

in some areas of the cut limestone, the chisel marks of mason's tools are still visible.

As mentioned, wood was incredibly scarce in the region, so wooden Egyptian furniture was highly prized and carefully crafted to provide for an individual's comfort while also adding to the beauty of the interior. Egyptian furniture included chairs, stools, tables, and beds constructed of both domestic and exotic types of wood. Ebony wood was valued in Egyptian furniture and was combined with precious metal and stone decorative inlays. In the tomb of Tutankhamun, several chairs were discovered. One in particular, the ceremonial chair with an X-shaped base, demonstrates the high level of craft and design achieved by the Egyptians (Fig. 2.3).

Greek (776–146 BC)

Greek culture arose from the Minoan culture on the island of Crete and the Mycenaean culture on mainland Greece. Following the collapse of the Mycenaean culture in approximately 1300 BC, the Greeks lost the art of writing, which led to cultural stagnation, also referred to as a dark age, until about 1000 BC when Greek art and architecture began to flourish. Individual and independent city-states, known as the polis, initially developed organically, following the terrain of the countryside. Over time, polis plans became more sophisticated, imposing a grid upon the streets and building arrangements with an acropolis at the high point of the city where the religious temple was located. The agora, often located adjacent to the acropolis, was the center of culture, business, and entertainment.

The Greek orders of architecture were based on the design and proportion of the column, the central component of all Greek architecture. The three orders of Greek architecture—Doric, Ionic, and Corinthian—provided guidance to the design of the columns and the **entablature** (includes the architrave, frieze, and cornice), which runs around the entire perimeter of a building facade above the columns and below the pediment on the gabled ends and below the low edge of the roofline on the long sides. The **pediment,** or the triangular gabled form on the ends of a building, encapsulated the **tympanum,** or the triangular surface within the gable that contained rich sculpted ornamentation. The **Doric order,** developed in the eighth century BC, is characterized by columns with twenty flutes and lacking a base that were proportionally

The pyramid interior consists of an original entrance on the north side from which the descending passage leads to the lower chamber, which was never completed. Along the descending passage, shortly after leaving the original entrance, is an access point in the ceiling of the descending passage where the ascending passage begins. The ascending passage is blocked by large stone blocks, but it was originally designed to climb to the grand gallery. Due to the blockage, the only access to the ascending passage and grand gallery is through the robber's tunnel, which is used today for tours. The slope that begins with the ascending passage continues with the grand gallery, and it is near this transition in the grand gallery where a tunnel leads horizontally to the queen's chamber. At the top of the sloped grand gallery is the king's chamber, with five small chambers above, referred to as the relieving chambers, that served to relieve some of the weight placed upon the ceiling structure of the king's chamber. The king's chamber was dressed in polished granite, while the other compartments simply utilized cut limestone, and

Figure 2.4 The Greek Parthenon at the Acropolis in Athens was designed using the golden mean, a mathematical proportional relationship observed in nature.

massive in relation to the orders that followed. The Parthenon, designed and built by Ictinus from 447 to 432 BC in Athens, Greece, is considered an iconic example of the Doric order (Fig. 2.4). Comparatively, the **Ionic order**, originating in the sixth century BC, was graceful in its column proportions, with an articulated base, referred to as the **attic base**, a fluted shaft where the flutes were separated by narrow fillets, and a decorative capital in the form of a scroll. The **Corinthian order** first appeared in 420 BC and was very similar to the Ionic order in terms of the base and fluted shaft, but the Corinthian capital was far more decorative and resembled acanthus leaves. Each of the orders employed a technique called **entasis**, whereby each column was constructed with a slight bulge near its middle that served to correct the effects of perspective and cause the column to appear perfectly straight.

Greek interiors varied widely based upon the type of building—a public monument or domicile—and evolved based upon the prosperity of the Greek Empire. Floors were largely earthen in early Greek buildings, but evolved to include stone floors with intricate pebble mosaics in the later Hellenistic period. The interior walls were often painted white, or whitewashed, and a variety of functional items were hung from the walls, whereas the walls of the homes of the wealthy in the Hellenistic period were painted, paneled with stone, or faux finished to resemble marble. Most ceilings were likely painted, but coffers were also used, particularly in public buildings. Very little Greek furniture survives today because it was made from wood and has deteriorated

in the moist climate surrounding the Mediterranean, so most knowledge is gained through furniture depictions in pottery. Ebony and citron wood was prized above other species and was inlaid with ivory, tortoise shell, silver, or gold when constructed for the wealthy. The Greeks made significant advancements in a chair design known as a **klismos** by extending the angle of the chair backrest past the 90 degree mark, as they valued comfort in addition to appearance.

Roman (509 BC–AD 476)

The Etruscans controlled the central part of the Italian peninsula, known as Tuscany today, from approximately 700 to 300 BC. In 509 BC, when the inhabitants of Rome revolted against the Etruscans, a republic was established and the gradual expansion of the **Roman** civilization began until the entire Etruscan civilization was absorbed by 265 BC. The transition to an imperialistic empire marked by rapid expansion and conquest can be traced back to a civil war that greatly weakened Rome and led to the rise of Emperor Augustus in 27 BC. The empire quickly expanded to the west and east, enveloping the Greek Empire by 31 BC, and control became such a challenge that Diocletian created an east and west empire in AD 285 in an effort to maintain unity. In AD 330, Constantine moved the capital out of Rome and to Byzantium in the Eastern Roman Empire, which was later renamed Constantinople and is known today as Istanbul. As the Romans conquered new lands, the local people were assimilated into the Roman culture. Soldiers were granted citizenship, local seats of government were permitted to govern as long as peace was maintained, and the populace was encouraged to take part in commerce. The Romans brought certain improvements to the newly conquered territories, including sanitation, bridges, roads, bath houses, light houses, entertainment venues, and courts. Roman building technology, including the use of concrete and glass, and the development of the arch, spread with the empire.

Roman architectural orders were adaptations of the Greek orders and grew to include five orders—Tuscan, Doric, Ionic, Corinthian, and composite. The **Tuscan order** was a simplified version of the Greek Doric order; it incorporated a base, had a shaft lacking flutes, and its proportion was more slender than the Greek Doric. The

Figure 2.5 The Roman Pantheon, located in Rome, Italy, includes a dome constructed of stone with an oculus at its apex.

Roman Doric order continued the slender proportion and inclusion of a base established by the Tuscan order, and added fluting to the shaft. The **Roman Ionic order** included a base, fluted shaft, and scroll capital, but was more slender than the Greek predecessor, and also included a decorative application at the neck of the column, just below the capital. The **Roman Corinthian order** was used in interior and exterior applications, whereas the Greeks had reserved the Corinthian order for interior settings. The **composite order** joined the scroll forms of the Ionic with the acanthus leaf forms of the Corinthian and employed the most slender column shaft proportions of any of the orders. As the Roman architectural orders evolved, building proportions became more vertical in nature, voids between columns became slightly larger, and more daylight was able to penetrate the interior and covered exterior zones of buildings.

The Pantheon in Rome is one of many iconic examples of Roman architecture (Fig. 2.5). Commissioned by Agrippa during Augustus' reign (27 BC–AD 14), the building was completed in AD 126 and underwent several

modifications due to fire damage. The version of the building we see today is geometrically simple, consisting of a circular **rotunda** with dome and a rectangular **portico** attached to the south side of the rotunda and fronting an open plaza. The diameter of the rotunda and height of the **oculus** are identical, at 142 imperial feet (43.3 meters), or 150 Roman feet, the unit of measure in the ancient Roman Empire. The portico includes a front row of eight Corinthian columns with two rows of four columns each behind the front row and supporting the triangular portico roof form. The rotunda interior with the coffered dome and central oculus is the main attraction to this structure. The rotunda walls are decorated with elaborate stone carvings, **columns** and **pilasters**, and niches containing a variety of stone figures. These stone figures have been the subject of debate over the centuries, because the original sculptures of Roman gods were replaced with statues of Christian saints with the establishment of Christianity as the state religion. The colorful marble floor also includes a drainage system to divert rainwater that falls through the oculus.

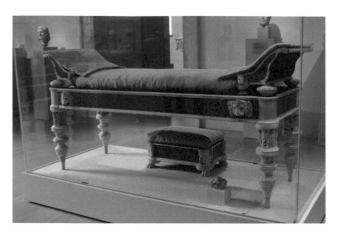

Figure 2.6 Roman furniture included couches and foot stools used for reclining while dining.

Roman furniture is scarce; the few surviving examples made of stone survive in ruins, such as the benches and thrones in amphitheaters. Most Roman furniture, however, was made of wood, and knowledge of these pieces is limited to what is depicted in relief sculpture, painting, or mosaics or that which has been found at archaeological sites in Herculaneum and Pompeii, sites of devastating volcanic eruptions. The elite of Roman society were known for reclining upon couches while dining. These couches were constructed of fine wood; were inlaid with bone, glass, or precious metals; and included cushions for comfort (Fig. 2.6). Examples of these furniture pieces survive as reconstructions based upon the fragments found at archaeological sites and depictions in Roman art.

Byzantine (AD 330–1453)

The Roman Empire allowed its citizens and conquered peoples to participate in their chosen religious practices so long as they acknowledged the deity status of the Roman emperor. Due to the tenets of Christianity denying any deity other than Jesus the Christ, Christians were persecuted within the Roman Empire until the god status of the emperor faded and Constantine legalized Christianity in AD 313. In 330, Constantine moved the capital out of Rome to Byzantium, which was later renamed Constantinople, and in 395, when Emperor Theodosius I died, the Roman Empire was officially divided into two halves—the Western Roman Empire, ruled from Rome, and the Eastern Roman Empire, ruled from Constantinople. Rome, and therefore the Western

Roman Empire, was conquered in 476, which began the Dark Ages in Western Europe and would last for almost 1,000 years. The Eastern Roman Empire, also known as the **Byzantine** Empire, on the other hand, would flourish with Constantinople (known as Istanbul, Turkey, today) as its center of cultural development. Constantinople would be the hinge in several wars pitting Western peoples, and largely Christian, against Eastern Islamic civilizations. Eventually, in 1453, Constantinople was conquered by the Turks and was renamed Istanbul. Functioning as the capital of the Ottoman Empire, it served as a closed gateway between the East and West, and, in the process, buildings that were once Christian became Islamic.

Byzantine architecture exhibits a set of traits that are characteristic of this period and that also paved the way for later architectural advancements, as can be witnessed in Russian architecture in the tenth century and following. This period is known for its widespread use of multiple domes, which create decorative **pendentives** on the interior where the round dome transitions to a square arrangement in plan, such as the case with the Greek cross plan arrangement so common in this period. Round arches and column **arcades** serve to divide the interior into bays, which are expressed in churches as the sanctuary and nave, a new development for this period. Clay brick was the dominant material for Byzantine exteriors, while the interiors favored more refined materials. Similar to Roman architecture, Byzantine architecture utilized marble as a flooring material. Marble was not domestically produced in the empire, however, and the material had to be imported or plundered from enemies. Walls and ceilings were heavily ornamented with mosaic tiles, frescoes, and panel carvings of alabaster, which were also used in windows to filter daylight. Byzantine furniture also reflects strong Roman influences, but with a higher degree of ornamentation, including more intricate inlays of ivory, gold, precious stones, and glass.

The Hagia Sophia is an iconic example of Byzantine architecture (Fig. 2.7). Built between 532 and 537 by Emperor Justinian, the structure originally functioned as a cathedral, the largest building of its kind for more than 1,000 years, until the completion of the Seville Cathedral in Spain. When the Turks defeated Constantinople in 1453, the cathedral was converted into a mosque; today the building serves as a museum. The primary central dome culminates at 182 feet 5 inches over the nave and is flanked by several other half domes. The iconic minarets

Figure 2.7 The Hagia Sophia in Istanbul, Turkey, has multiple domes and highly detailed mosaics throughout the interior.

are not original and were added after the Ottoman Empire conquered Constantinople. The building contains priceless artworks, including intricate Christian Orthodox mosaics that were covered over after the structure became a mosque and have since been restored.

Romanesque (800–1200)

While the Byzantine Empire was flourishing in Eastern Europe, Western Europe stagnated as a result of the fall of the Roman Empire. As the culture floundered, building technologies developed by the Romans were lost, including the engineering of domes and large vaults; development of the classical architecture orders halted. It wasn't until approximately AD 1000 that Western Europe began to advance once again and Romanesque architecture emerged as the dominant style from AD 1000 to 1200.

In general, **Romanesque** architecture is known for its round semi-circular arches, arcades of columns, groin vaults created by the intersection of perpendicular vaults, articulated structural bays, and a tripartite level arrangement in building facades (nave, triforium, and clerestory, from low to high, respectively). Churches were the dominant building type in the Romanesque period and typically were arranged with a Latin cross plan. The **nave**, or dominant central aisle, ran the length of the cross, with two side aisles, one on each side of the nave. The **transept** created the shorter legs of the cross plan resulting in the **crossing**, or the space where the transept and nave intersect, often resulting in a groin vaulted ceiling. The **apse** terminated the nave and the **ambulatory** allowed for circulation around the apse where a religious artifact would sometimes be located in certain churches. Churches that held artifacts would become destinations for Christian pilgrims. Some Romanesque churches, particularly in France, also included small chapels off of the ambulatory for small, private prayer gatherings or for individual meditation.

As Romanesque architecture spread across Western Europe, slight regional variations developed. In Germany, stair towers were emphasized, and churches included multiple octagonal towers and Lombard bands, open arcades located high on the building and just below the roofline. Italian Romanesque architecture included classical column orders with intricate plant-form carvings, domes at vault intersections, and multiple tiers of arcades, such as those on display at Pisa. Norman Romanesque architecture, located in England and northern France, included chapels that projected away from the main architectural form of the building, featuring repetitive rib vaults, groin vaults, slightly pointed arches and vaults (which would influence the development of Gothic architecture), dual towers near the primary entry, and Celtic decoration. French Romanesque architecture included repeating chapels around the apse, referred to as a **chevet**, a barrel vault over the nave flanked by a half vault over each side aisle, and intricate carved figures and masks on the building façade and interior. Spanish Romanesque architecture included cascading concentric stone masonry entry portals, four-part rib vaults, and large-scale stone block masonry.

The Basilica of Saint-Sernin in Toulouse, France, built between 1080 and 1120, is the largest preserved Romanesque cathedral in Europe, and is a UNESCO World Heritage Site (Fig. 2.8). The church held particular importance for pilgrims due to the many relics contained in the building, and it became a primary pilgrimage site along the route to Santiago de Compostela in Spain. Constructed of brick, the basilica includes a high barrel-vaulted nave, somewhat shorter side aisles made up of a series of rib vaults, and outer pilgrimage aisles that are shorter still also constructed of rib vaults. The outer pilgrimage aisles allowed Christian pilgrims to access the relics in the nine chapels off of the transept and apse without interrupting mass. The bell tower rises from the crossing of the nave and transept and creates a heavily ribbed dome at the underside of the tower.

Figure 2.8 The Basilica of Saint-Sernin in Toulouse, France, with a Latin cross plan, round arches, and more horizontal proportions, is a well-recognized specimen of the Romanesque period.

Gothic (1200–1500)

Between AD 1000 and 1200, Europe witnessed relative peace and the collapse of the feudal system, which had been the primary system of local governments across Western Europe. This led to monarchs providing increased freedom for towns, which extended to much of the populace and resulted in a strengthened middle class. Once peasants, people found themselves with the opportunity to pursue a trade and better their standing in a growing society. As the building trades grew, craftspeople and artisans formed guilds to advance their crafts and grow their businesses. These organized guilds enjoyed a period of great advancement in building technologies that came to define the Gothic style of architecture.

Building upon the Romanesque, **Gothic** architecture pioneered several technological advancements that resulted in much taller proportions, slender columns, large spans, and copious amounts of daylight penetrating the interior. This style of architecture sought to limit load-bearing walls and focus structural support to columns, resulting in **curtain walls**, or non-load-bearing exterior walls of stone, masonry, and glass between structural supports, which acted as the precursor to many modern structural advances. Slender Gothic columns departed from the classical orders to embrace circular, rectangular, and square forms, and supported **pointed arches** rather than the round arches of the Romanesque. The soaring heights of ribbed vaults placed significant horizontal loads on the slender columns, resulting in the birth of the **flying buttress** on the exterior of Gothic buildings to help carry this additional lateral force. Gothic planning included the traditional nave, side aisles, and apse, while including at least one transept, sometimes more. France led the way as the center of the Gothic period, and this movement matured such that a variety of building art forms became formalized into guilds and included stone masons, wood carpenters, stained glass artisans, furniture artisans, and many others. These guilds perfected their crafts to produce beautiful works, such as rose windows

Figures 2.9 and 2.10 Gothic architecture and design utilized several technological advancements, including the pointed arch, flying buttress, and curtain wall, each of which is on display at the Cathedral of Notre Dame in Paris, France.

and stone gargoyles. These defining characteristics are prevalent in many surviving Gothic churches across Europe; the Notre Dame Cathedral in Paris, France, standing out among them (Figs. 2.9 and 10).

Renaissance (1450–1649)

As the Gothic period was flourishing in France and Germany, Italy was engaged in the Renaissance, or a concentrated time of extraordinary artistic and intellectual advancement. The architecture to emerge from the Renaissance was certainly guided by classical design, but the artists and architects themselves pursued a liberated creative freedom that guilds could not provide. In many ways, the work to come out of the Gothic and Renaissance movements were at odds with one another at the time. History would demonstrate, however, that each would excel in their own way. The Gothic provided great technological advancements, as described previously, and the Renaissance would provide the creative mind of the artist, designer, and architect with liberated creativity, as evidenced by the world-renowned greats of the period:

Filippo Brunelleschi, Leon Battista Alberti, Leonardo da Vinci, Michelangelo Buonarroti, Raphael, Andrea Palladio, Donato Bramante, and many others. This focus on the individual was reflected in literature, art, architecture, and, generally, in a growing humanist philosophy. One product of this new mindset of the Enlightenment was the golden mean, or the ratio 1:1.618, which finds its origin in the human form where the navel acts as the center, the upper body is measured as 1 unit, and the lower body as 1.618 units. Closely related to the golden mean is the Fibonacci sequence, which follows the same proportion (see Chapter 1 for more explanation).

Renaissance architecture is characterized by many qualities that grew from this new focus on the individual. For example, Renaissance architecture has a much more horizontal proportion compared to the Gothic, utilizing semicircular arches and broad spans. In addition, Renaissance architecture utilized the classical orders; articulated facades with columns, pilasters, and pediments; arcades of columns to define open air space; and rusticated stone as a dominant material. St. Peter's Basilica in Vatican City is considered the most well-known example of Renaissance architecture (Figs. 2.11 and 12).

Figure 2.11 St. Peter's Basilica in Rome, Italy, is an architectural masterpiece. Its multiphase design and construction spanned several hundred years.

Figure 2.12 Bernini's baldachin and the Throne of St. Peter, two of the many great works of art and design within St. Peter's Basilica.

The current structure, initiated in 1506 and completed in 1626, rests on the location of Old St. Peter's Basilica, which was completed in the fourth century AD. The current design was realized through a multiphased process at the hands of a series of architects, including Bramante, Michelangelo, Moderno, and Bernini. The building is dominated by an enormous dome; standing at over 448 feet (136.57 meters) in height, it is the tallest dome in the world. The interior boasts grand proportions and exquisite details. Bernini's work, while classified as Baroque in style, in the cathedral's interior is extensive, with the baldachin, or canopy above the altar, and its twisted bronze columns and the intricacy of the Throne of St. Peter receiving the most attention.

Even though the Renaissance was centered in Italy, the style spread to various parts of Western Europe, including France, Spain, Germany, and England. Italian Renaissance characteristics would later influence revivals of the style in the nineteenth century, as well as other styles, including the Federal style in America, with Monticello, the home of Thomas Jefferson, a prime example.

Baroque (1600–1730) and Rococo (1715–1780)

Whereas the Italian Renaissance was largely secular in nature, communicating the glory of humanism, the Baroque style returned to more ecclesiastical ends. The Roman Catholic church was the dominant religious and political force in Europe, and it largely went unchallenged until the Protestant Reformation starting in 1517. In response, the Roman Catholic Church organized the Council of Trent in 1545–1563, which led to the Counter-Reformation. One strategy of the Counter-Reformation was to refocus art and architectural development back toward the populace and away from the aristocracy in order to draw people back to the Catholic Church. Baroque design was the result, and it was largely rejected in areas where Protestantism had taken a foothold due to its connection with Catholicism.

The **Baroque** style began in Italy, but then moved to France as the focus of artistic development. The style would spread into Spain, Portugal, the Netherlands, Russia, England, and, eventually, to America. Peter the Great of Russia would appreciate the style so much that he would recruit Giovanni Maria Fontana from Italy to design several buildings in St. Petersburg.

Baroque design is characterized by strong use of curvilinear, circular, and elliptical forms, undulating walls and details, prominent domes and pear- or onion-shaped domes in central and Eastern Europe, highly detailed staircases,

Figure 2.13 The Ottobeuren Abbey in Ottobeuren, Germany, is a showcase of the Rococo, with its ornate interior details and decorative arts.

extensive use of faux finishing, **trompe l'oeil** painting techniques creating the illusion of larger three-dimensional spaces or landscapes, and intricate details and gilding covering many of the interior surfaces. Baroque reached its height with the Rococo syle, particularly in the region of Bavaria in southern Germany. The **Rococo** falls in line with the Baroque, and is characterized by more expressive use of consecutive concave and convex forms, reserved use of asymmetry, and intricate detailing and gilding covering even more interior surfaces compared to the Baroque. The Ottobeuren Abbey in Ottobeuren, Germany, is respected as a masterpiece of the Rococo, with some of the best examples of the Rococo decorative arts (Fig. 2.13).

Neoclassical (1760–1830)

Neoclassical design resulted from a desire to return to the simplicity of classical Roman and Greek architectural forms and orders while also capturing a general dissatisfaction with the indulgent nature of the Rococo.

Fueling this renewed interest in classical Roman design were the discoveries made at Herculaneum in 1738 and Pompeii in 1748, two Roman cities covered and preserved by the eruption of Mt. Vesuvius in AD 79. Up to this point, Renaissance and Baroque architects and designers were guessing at the original design of Roman interiors, and, in their best guesses, were replicating the design of exterior forms on the interior. The new discoveries by archaeologists provided architects and designers with accurate examples to follow, further propelling the acceptance and spread of Neoclassicism. Similarly, Greek buildings were unearthed and the findings were published in 1758 and 1762, leading to a Greek revival style. Working parallel with the archaeological discoveries, people embraced the ideals of the Enlightenment, prioritized reason and natural orders over the supernatural, and, by extension, also desired to return to the democratic and republican forms of government established in Rome. The result in several places—the United States and France among them—was to throw off the oppression of the monarchy in favor of a representative form of government. The combination of these factors—archaeological discoveries related to ancient Greece and Rome, the dissatisfaction with Rococo excess, and the desire for self-rule—created the perfect storm for Neoclassical design to flourish across Europe, the United States, and in Central America.

Naturally, Neoclassical buildings followed the precedents set in Greek and Roman design styles. These characteristics included long colonnades, the proliferation of triumphal arches (particularly in France, e.g., Arc de Triomphe in Paris), domes elevated on drum forms, the use of temple facades on a variety of building types, symmetry, exterior entryways lined with glazed sidelights and transom windows, masonry belt coursings dividing facades based upon floor heights, and giant order pilasters used to rhythmically divide facades. As Neoclassicism spread, the style was customized to the location and often adopted new names, such as the **Empire style** in France, **Georgian style** in Great Britain, and **Federal style** in the United States. The U.S. Capitol building in Washington, D.C., presents the characteristics of Neoclassical design, particularly the Federal style, in the United States (Fig. 2.14). The building is divided into three primary masses, divided from one another by smaller rectangular forms called hyphens. The central portion of the building is dominated by a grand dome. The **Greek revival style** became popular in the United

Figure 2.14 The U.S. Capitol Building in Washington, D.C., demonstrates the height of Neoclassical architecture and design in the United States.

States as well and embraced brick masonry. When wood **balloon framing**, where the wall studs span vertically multiple stories uninterrupted, was developed, it became possible to adapt the Greek revival style to all building types, including middle-class dwellings.

Victorian (1840–1920)

The Industrial Revolution occurred between 1760 and 1840 as the world witnessed the rapid development of mechanized methods for processing raw goods such as cotton into textiles, the harnessing of steam power, and the refinement of iron ore into structural materials. These rapid technological advancements occurred at a time when England sought to revive the architectural styles of old. This dichotomy would eventually create a division in design styles between those that would look longingly to the past while others would seek to harness the technological developments of the Industrial Revolution to create new design styles.

The **Victorian era** was named for Victoria, Queen of England from 1837 to 1901, the longest reigning monarch in the history of England. Her reign would witness a rapid series of style changes, several of which were revivals of prior styles. Interestingly, the technological advancements of the Industrial Revolution, including the development of power tools, would enable the execution of many of the ornate architectural details and furniture decorations that would come to characterize the styles of this period. Many of the styles would be shared between England and America, often with America following England by a decade or more. The **Gothic revival** (1820–1870 in England, and 1840–1860 in America) would initiate this progression with Britain's Houses of Parliament providing a primary example. The **Italian villa** (1830–1880) and **Italianate** styles (1845–1880) overlapped with the Gothic revival and were characterized by asymmetrical arrangements, stucco over brick facades, semicircle arches, and ornate details. Several **exotic revivals** (1835–1890), including Egyptian, Moorish, and Byzantine, referenced buildings from earlier times and would often blend characteristics from one of these earlier styles with new materials, forms, or details. The **stick style** (1855–1875) possibly draws influence from medieval timber-frame houses by decoratively articulating panels of wood shingles or siding in wood frames painted or stained a contrasting color and integrating intricate wood trim details at railings, windows, and overhangs. The **Romanesque revival** (1860s–1870s) in America was led by Henry Hobson Richardson. Many of his buildings, including the Trinity Church in Boston, are described as "Richardsonian Romanesque" and utilize many signature forms, such as semicircle arches in stone. **Queen Anne** style (1880–1910) utilized many of the same forms as Romanesque revival style, added additional characteristics, such as wrapping porches in steep-pitch roofs, to the style, as many of the works were domestic in scale, and generally favored the use of wood and brick rather than stone. **Colonial revival** (1880–1955) houses were a conglomeration of various styles, including Georgian and Cape Cod houses that were common during the colonial period of American history but were modified to include non-characteristic forms and details. This "style," as undefined as it is, endured in part for the nostalgia but also for the affordability due to its simplified construction and architectural detailing.

The affordable quality of design would become a hallmark of the Industrial Revolution, as the middle class expanded its wealth, and technological advancements allowed more people to purchase goods. One example is the work of Michael Thonet, with his bentwood chair and bentwood rocker, both of which continue to be produced today. Utilizing a minimum of wood components, simple fastened joinery, and little or no decorative details, these chairs became icons for their simple elegance and durable construction. Thonet's work would be recognized in the 1850s with multiple awards at the London and Paris Expositions.

One of these expositions, the Great Exhibition of 1851 in London, was housed in the Crystal Palace, designed by Joseph Paxton (see the image on the opening page of this chapter). Constructed of cast iron and glass, the Crystal Palace is widely recognized as marking the transition from historic architecture and design styles to modern design. The technology that produced this structure would eventually lead to the development of wrought iron, known for improved strength and corrosion resistance over cast iron. The Eiffel Tower in Paris was constructed of wrought iron in 1887/89 and served as the entrance to the 1889 World's Fair.

Figure 2.15 The Gamble House by Greene and Greene is an iconic example of the Craftsman style in America.

Arts and Crafts (1880–1915), Craftsman (1897–1930s)

The negative effects of the Industrial Revolution, poor working conditions, and a perceived decrease in the appreciation of highly designed and crafted items created opponents to the mechanized nature of the new society in England. Led by William Morris, John Ruskin, and A.W.N. Pugin, a renewed desire for high design and high craft became known as the **Arts and Crafts Movement** (1880–1920). Although architecture did result from the movement, interiors and furnishings were the primary areas of focus. Characterized by authenticity and honesty of materials, exposed joinery, unique textile and wall covering patterns, the style was known for highly crafted furniture, millwork, and exquisite details. The enhanced tools of the Industrial Revolution allowed artisans to produce goods and crafts with precision, but the goods were also expensive, and, as a result, the middle class was not able to enjoy the fruits of the Arts and Crafts Movement. The Red House, designed for William Morris by Phillip Webb, embodied the ideals of the Arts and Crafts Movement and stands as the prime example of this period, which would go on to influence much of early modern design.

Arts and Crafts style emigrated to America through the American Arts and Crafts Exhibition in Boston in 1897 and became known as the **Craftsman style** due to *The Craftsman*, a popular magazine of that time by Gustave Stickley. Through the magazine, design guidelines were established that sought to simplify the design of the middle-class American home while valuing highly crafted interiors and

architecture. A new type of house structure emerged, known as the bungalow, that utilized one or one and a half stories, high first-floor ceilings, clerestory windows for ventilation, shallow pitch roofs, deep overhangs to provide shade for windows and therefore the interior, exposed construction details in wood, and also incorporated clean-line Asian influences. The influence of Japanese architecture and design in particular was felt in Craftsman style circles and would especially influence the work of Frank Lloyd Wright. The Gamble House, constructed in 1908/09 in Pasadena, California, and designed by the firm Greene and Greene, is considered one of the most sophisticated examples of Craftsman style (Fig. 2.15). Similar to Arts and Crafts, the Craftsman style succeeded in promoting highly crafted and well-designed interiors, architecture, and furniture, but it was not always affordable to the masses.

Art Nouveau (1892–1910)

Art Nouveau was the first truly new style since the Gothic and drew influence from the English Arts and Crafts, French Gothic, and advancements in wrought iron. Equally, Art Nouveau was a reaction against the Ecole de Beaux Arts, a school of art and design in France that sought to preserve and revive the use of the classical orders. This reaction against the classical influences resulted in a rejection of right angles in favor of compound curvilinear lines, asymmetrical balance rather than strict symmetry, parabolic arches rather than pointed or semicircular, glass expanses, and exposed ironwork. Influential Art Nouveau works of architecture

Figure 2.16 Art Nouveau is known for curvilinear lines as demonstrated in the Tassel House by Victor Horta in Brussels, Belgium. (Image by Henry Townsend—qwn work (own photo), public domain, https://commons.wikimedia.org/w/index.php?curid=3846745)

include the Tassel House in Belgium, designed by Victor Horta (Fig. 2.16); the Paris subway entrances by Hector Guimard; and La Sagrada Familia by Antonio Gaudi, in Barcelona, Spain. The high-craft influences of the Arts and Crafts influenced the design of furniture and interiors of the Art Nouveau, particularly in the design of interior iron railings, iron columns, and decorative motifs.

Modernism (1910–1940)

Modernism embraced technological advancements of the early twentieth century, including electricity, steel, concrete, and large-pane glass windows, at a time when the developed world could communicate faster due to the telephone, travel greater distances in airplanes, and work fewer hours per week due to manufacturing automation. Culturally, the movement rejected traditional

autocracy and historical influences, valued rationality, and embraced the empowerment of the masses. Together, these factors led to buildings that prioritized the health of the occupants, embraced views to the exterior, and simplified architectural forms to right angles and straight lines. Influential modernist architects include Le Corbusier, who designed Villa Savoye in Poissy, France, which embodied his Five Points of a New Architecture:

1. **Pilotis**: structural loads are carried on columns rather than on load-bearing walls.
2. **Free plan**: with the structure carried on columns, interior walls can be arranged with greater freedom.
3. **Free façade**: the exterior walls are free from structural constraints and can be more expressive.
4. **Ribbon window**: an application of the free façade, windows should wrap the building horizontally to provide daylight to the interior equitably.

Figure 2.17 The Villa La Roche-Jeaneret, now known as the Fondation Le Corbusier, demonstrates the clean lines and lack of decoration so prevalent in Modernism.

5. **Roof garden:** the portion of the building that meets the sky, the flat roof plane, is designed to be usable, extending the occupied space.

Modernism would eventually become refined into the International style, but would share many characteristics (Fig. 2.17).

De Stijl (1917–1931)

The **De Stijl** movement developed in the Netherlands while the Bauhaus was active in Germany. The movement, led in part by Otto Wagner, advocated the role of the artist and designer to influence the desires of the public rather than simply continuing in the stylistic tastes of the day. Subscribers to the De Stijl movement advocated abstract forms, non-intersecting planes, and the use of

gray scale and primary color schemes. In relation to form, it is possible that Frank Lloyd Wright's development of the Prairie style impacted the ideals of De Stijl. Gerrit Rietveld designed the Schröder House in Utrecht, Netherlands, one of the few buildings to fully embrace De Stijl principles. In addition, Rietveld designed the Red and Blue Chair (Fig. 2.18) and the Zigzag Chair, two iconic furniture pieces from this style.

Art Deco (1920–1939)

Art Deco was the first nontraditional style to gain wide acceptance in America. It capitalized on a cultural desire for opulence following lean economic times during World War I. The term Art Deco was first used by Bevis Hillier to refer to the variety of work to come out of and to be inspired

Figure 2.18 Rietveld's Red and Blue Chair was a milestone in the short-lived De Stijl movement, which would go on to influence many other designers and architects of the twentieth century.

Figure 2.19 The Chrysler Building exhibits many Art Deco characteristics, including stepped forms, sunbursts, and streamlined edges.

by the Society of Decorative Artists, an organization established in France after the 1900 Universal Exposition in Paris. Art Deco style encompasses architecture, interior design, furniture, jewelry, clothing, glass art, graphic art, and film. Whereas other styles that departed from historical underpinnings did so based on philosophical reasons, Art Deco focused entirely on aesthetics and decoration. The style was characterized by stepped forms that were inspired by the stepped pyramids of ancient civilizations, including Egypt; chevrons and zigzag lines; sunburst reliefs; sharp angles with rounded corners; high sheen materials, including stainless steel and aluminum; and the free use of a variety of colors. Architecture, interiors, and furniture utilized all of these characteristics to achieve a unified overall design, as evidenced in the iconic Chrysler Building in New York City (Fig. 2.19).

Bauhaus (1919–1933) and International Style (1930–Present)

The **Bauhaus**, located in Dessau, Germany, was a school of Modernist design and craft that brought each student under the direction of an artist and craftsperson. The education was geared toward unifying art and technology and was conspicuously light on the traditional subjects of mathematics and art history. The Bauhaus building, with its expansive use of glass and unadorned exterior, serves as a strong example of the architecture that came out the school.

Ludwig Mies van der Rohe, one of the most influential architects to come out of the Bauhaus, would move to the United States, first to New York and finally to Chicago, along with several other architects, following the closing of the school by the Nazis in 1933. With the dispersal of architects trained at the Bauhaus around the world, the International style was born. The term, however, was established by Philip Johnson and Henry-Russell Hitchcock in connection with an architectural exhibition at the Museum of Modern Art in New York in 1932. The ideals of the International style include

1. The emphasis of volume over mass when defining form.
2. The idea of balance beyond the symmetry.
3. The elimination of ornamentation.

The **International style** shares many characteristics with Modernism, through the embrace of advanced construction technologies, the use of concrete and steel structure as a means to provide a free design of the interior plan and building façade, and large expanses of glass often with minimal framing members in the continual effort to eliminate ornamentation. The aesthetic nature of the style lends itself to building types other than single-family residential, but a few limited examples of International style houses exist, including the Farnsworth

Figure 2.20 The Farnsworth House by Mies van der Rohe embodies the strict clean-line designs of the International style that builds upon Modernism.

Figure 2.21 The Jewish Museum in Berlin, Germany, embodies much of the Deconstruction philosophy with its angular forms and slicing fenestration.

House in Plano, Illinois, built in 1951 and designed by Mies van der Rohe (Fig. 2.20). Also designed by Mies van der Rohe, the Seagram Building in New York City is representative of the more common application of the style in nonresidential buildings.

Postmodern (1960s–Present) and Deconstruction (1980s–Present)

The **Postmodern** style emerged as a countermovement to the International style. Rather than the strict rectilinear forms, this new style embraced sculptural form expressions in concrete combined with steel reinforcing and liberal use of glass allowing daylight to penetrate into the interior. Proponents also recognized historical influences of architecture in this style, often expressed in simplified historical forms through the use of advanced building materials. Robert Venturi expressed the motivations of Postmodernism in his book, *Complexity and Contradiction*, as a desire to recognize the influence of history

and ornamentation as connection to a building's place rather than the lack of context and austerity expressed in Modernism and the International style. This notion of complexity and contradiction could result in awkward design solutions, which was often brought to light by critics of the style. One of the primary architects to practice the style was Michael Graves, with the Denver Public Library, built in 1995, serving as an example of the style.

Keeping in line with the established pattern, Deconstruction, also referred to as **Deconstructivism**, would evolve as a reaction against Postmodern architecture. The new architectural expression would enter the design vocabulary with the Parc de la Villette design competition in Paris, France, with particular notice being given to the architectural installation by Bernard Tschumi. The style is known for its disjointed and free expression of architectural form divorced from the building interior, often requiring acrobatic structural engineering to make the building a reality. A primary example of Deconstruction comes from Daniel Libeskind's Jewish Museum in Berlin, Germany (Fig. 2.21).

Parametricism (1993–Present)

Parametricism, or parametric design, has developed as a response to the prescriptive nature of Modern and Postmodern design, and each of the subsets of styles and movements that accompany them. Parametricism utilizes digital programs, computers, and algorithms as tools for the designer to address and balance complex functional and formal needs of the built environment. Each of the

Chapter 2 Case Study

Adaptive Reuse: A New Tech Industry Incubator Unifies Three Historic Building Interiors

Project:	Cahoots Tech Hub
Location:	Ann Arbor, Michigan
Client:	Nutshell
Architect/Designer:	O|X Studio
Project Type:	Technology hub and workplace set in an adaptively reused historic structure
Site Characteristics:	Three early 1900s structures unified into one structure in an urban setting
Year Complete:	First phase complete in 2017
Cost Estimate:	$4 million
Facility Size:	25,000 square feet of interior space with a 5,000-square-foot rooftop deck

Project Context

With office space in downtown Ann Arbor, Michigan, being scarce and demanding a premium cost, local tech entrepreneurs and founders of Nutshell decided to purchase three landmark historic buildings on one of the city's busiest thoroughfares. In addition to moving their own growing business into the space, the company is developing the complex into a tech hub incubator in an effort to attract companies and investors to the area. Named Cahoots, the collaborative work environment provides different tech startup companies with all the amenities of a large and well-established workplace in a dynamic and creative open work environment. These shared amenities will allow the different companies to work alongside each other and create a dialogue that will enhance creativity and growth for all those involved. By purchasing the three historic structures for this project, the client made a firm commitment to honoring the historical roots of this section of the city while simultaneously breathing new life into an underutilized structure. This decision is historically, economically, and ecologically sustainable for the community affected by Cahoots.

Design Challenges

Due to the historic nature of the existing buildings, dating back to the early 1900s, the design team encountered several challenges as they sought to adaptively reuse the three buildings and combine them into one cohesive tech hub work environment:

1. As a result of long use and lack of maintenance, the buildings possessed a decaying structure.
2. The aging infrastructure, including utilities and availability of modern technology systems, was seriously outdated.
3. Due to the three buildings being separate from one another, each had varying floor levels from one another, making it an interesting challenge to unite the buildings.
4. Like many historic structures, the basement ceilings are very low, making these subgrade spaces difficult to use.
5. The "unknown": with any very old building it is challenging to know exactly what is inside or behind a wall, below a floor material, or above a ceiling finish.

Impact of an Adaptive Reuse Project Scenario on the Design Process

The design team addressed each of the design challenges through a wholesale revamping of the primary interior spaces. Interventions included the removal of walls, framing and vertical circulation, the creation of new openings in the floor structure, and the design and integration of new systems and infrastructure as part of the interior build-out. With all of the interior changes, the historical integrity of the exterior façade needed to be maintained.

The ultimate challenge in such a scenario is the issue of the "unknown", that is, what is behind the existing walls and other interior elements. As components of the building were to be retained, O|X Studio needed to make assumptions during the documentation phase regarding existing conditions that were not evident prior to the start of demolition. These assumptions were rooted in the depth of the team's knowledge and experience working with old and historically significant structures. This experience allowed them to make an invaluable assessment of the existing conditions based on visual evaluation to effectively minimize any potential impact during construction.

The challenges of this process were communicated up-front to both the owner and the contractor. Stating the concerns and addressing them in a timely fashion was critical to maintaining costs and schedule. Further, O|X Studio addressed this issue head-on during the construction phase when the "bones" of the building were ultimately exposed. Knowing the potential pitfalls in advance, they budgeted time to assess and resolve the issues in the field. Once again, this intent was clearly communicated to both the owner and the contractor.

The process of assessing the unknown existing conditions and facilitating communication with the owner and contractor was enhanced by the team's proximity to the project site. Regular and frequent site visits were conducted to assess issues as they arose and provide immediate direction to the contractor through sketches and other documentation. These sketches where then formally incorporated into the construction documents. The overall decisions, in particular those that impacted costs and schedule, were then communicated to the owner on a weekly basis during the standing weekly construction meetings. The obvious take away is that experience, commitment, responsibility to the project, and, ultimately, broad and direct communication were the keys to resolving these design challenges unique to an adaptive reuse project in a timely fashion.

Innovative Solutions for this Adaptive Reuse Project

The adaptive reuse of the three historic structures addressed each of the design challenges in the following ways:

1. Altering the building interiors to comply with modern building codes and accessibility laws.
    *   Adding an elevator
    *   Updating stairs
    *   Installation of fire suppression systems
    *   Added structural reinforcement
    *   Added a 5,000-square-foot roof deck accessible from the new elevator
2. Modernizing the building utility connections, infrastructure, and environmental controls.

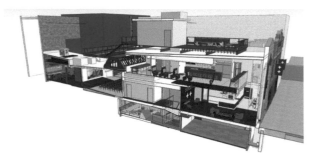

The design team analyzed the whole of the three buildings as they brought them together into a cohesive design by normalizing the floor levels and making all aspects of the building usable, including adding a rooftop amenity to the project.

As a tech incubator, flexible work environments will be a critical component to the client's success.

- Updated plumbing systems to be more efficient
- Installation of modern HVAC systems
- Installation of updated lighting, electrical, and data systems appropriate to a tech hub
3. Normalization of floor levels across the three buildings through the creative use of ramps, stairs, and a new elevator.
4. Underpinning the foundations in the basement level so that the slab could be lowered, allowing the subgrade spaces to be used as a spa and exercise facility.

These four innovations set the stage for an innovative interior to be designed for Nutshell and the future tenants of Cahoots. The resulting work environment encourages collaboration among multiple companies through the use of shared amenities and shared work areas. Movable partitions and work stations allow the organizations that work at Cahoots to expand and contract with fluid market conditions.

Long-Range Impact or Benefits Realized

One of the key goals that will be realized with this project is the ability of the ownership group to attract, assemble, and assist a variety of startup tech companies under one roof. It's a unique twist on the co-working and tech incubator models that have come to prominence of late, one that is focused on consolidating a broad swath of tech companies in order to promote collaboration and provide direct resources to promote the success and growth of the firms. To facilitate this and express their commitment to this collaboration, the primary owners are headquartering their own companies within the building. This puts them and their teams front and center. The spaces are developed to facilitate the ultimate goal of the project— to create a collaborative, interconnected tech community.

Further, the overall project is designed to provide amenities beyond the stereotypical coffee and foosball tables that evoke a cartoon of a tech space. The model being adapted is a fluid, hospitality-type space. This starts with a central large-volume entry lobby akin to a hotel lobby with a café that will be open to the public, accommodating a unique public interaction with the occupants. Further, there will be a variety of support spaces for the occupants, including private getaway spaces, such as a "library"; a fitness center with a sauna, steam room, and showers; a full-size bocce ball court; performance and event spaces; and a 5,000-square-foot rooftop terrace for outdoor work along with public performances and networking. The goal is to provide a high level of amenities for the users that will likewise be adaptable for use by the public, including local symphonic and musical groups.

The character of the urban fabric is maintained through this adaptive reuse project, and activity in the vicinity is enhanced with the new tenants that will occupy this new venture.

Interior amenities such as an exercise facility and this café/kitchen with prime views overlooking the downtown enhance the desirability of this workplace.

O|X Studio

O|X Studio is a full service architecture and design firm located in Ann Arbor, Michigan, with a broad base of experience in many project types. For more information on the Vectorform Headquarters Office or O|X Studio visit http://oxstudioinc.com/.

The rooftop amenities provide a high-end social functionality to augment the program of the interior.

variables in the parametric equation are controlled, with specific values and emphasis, by the designer in such a way that if one variable changes it will impact all of the others, leading to a different iteration and potential design solution (Fig. 2.22). The values of Parametricism include

1. Whole buildings that can serve multiple typologies.
2. Individual spaces that can adapt to multiple functions.
3. Malleable forms.
4. Variety of forms.
5. Unity of order.
6. Mass customization rather than mass production.

Mid-Twentieth to Early Twenty-First-Century Furniture

As architecture and interiors witnessed rapid change following the Industrial Revolution due to the technological advancements that followed, furniture design underwent a similar rapid change in the mid-twentieth century. Following World War II in the United States, the growth of consumerism combined with the tendency of individuals and families to change residences often created a demand for light-weight and mobile furniture. Heavy furniture pieces constructed of solid wood gave way to furniture

Figure 2.22 Parametricism is a contemporary period of design and architecture currently in development. It is valued for its tendency to catch the eye of onlookers, as is the case with the Dalian International Conference Center by Coop Himmelb(l)au.

Figure 2.23 The Eames Lounge Chair is recognized as an iconic mid-twentieth-century furniture piece. Charles and Ray Eames, among many other mid-twentieth-century designers, revolutionized the design of furniture.

constructed of tubular steel, plywood, fiberglass, plastic, aluminum, and tensile fabrics. Furniture forms became more amorphous, curvilinear, soft, and more responsive to a relaxed human posture. Advancements related to bent plywood and fiberglass molds allowed for mass production of high-quality furniture pieces. The Eames Lounge Chair and Ottoman, designed by Charles and Ray Eames and manufactured by Herman Miller, became one of the many iconic furniture pieces from the middle of the twentieth century (Fig. 2.23). In addition, the Barcelona Chair by Mies van der Rohe, the Womb Chair by Eero Saarinen, the Wassily Chair by Marcel Breuer, the LC4 Chaise Lounge Chair by Le Corbusier, and the Noguchi Coffee Table by Isamu Noguchi have all been recognized as prized furniture pieces from the mid-twentieth century. Arguably, the Aeron Chair, designed by Donald Chadwick and William Stumpf and manufactured by Herman Miller, is the most well-known piece of furniture from the latter portion of the twentieth century. The Aeron Chair set the standard by which all subsequent task chairs would be measured for its ergonomic adjustability and health benefits that users experienced as a result of using it on a daily basis. Other furniture from the late twentieth and first two decades of the twenty-first centuries include the Cross Check Chair by Frank Gehry, Carbon Chair by Bertjan Pot, and Victoria and Louis Ghost Chairs by Philippe Starck.

Summary

The constant in design history is change. The catalysts for transitions in style and period include political upheaval, cultural revolutions, new knowledge as empires spread or as society becomes more connected globally, advancements in technology and materials, or in reaction against what came before. One could argue that proponents of each new style had employed the design thinking process as they empathized with their clients/users; defined new problems that design should solve; developed new ideas, prototyped them, and tested them. The prototyping and testing phases of design thinking are particularly interesting in terms of the development of styles when successive examples of a given style are analyzed. For example, differences or improvements can be witnessed when evaluating multiple examples of the Gothic, or when comparing the application of the Baroque in various regions of Europe. As mentioned at the beginning of this chapter, design history is selective, whether that be by war, natural disaster, or demolition. It is likely that in the process of prototyping a new style that several experiments in building technology or material did not work as planned. After all, the flying buttress wasn't invented overnight. Regrettably, this chapter only scratches the surface of design history, and the intention is to allow this discussion to provoke further inquiry by the reader.

Key Terms

Ambulatory	Entasis	Pilasters
Apse	Exotic revivals	Pilotis
Arcades	Federal style	Pointed arches
Art Deco	Flying buttress	Portico
Art Nouveau	Free façade	Postmodern
Arts and Crafts movement	Free plan	Queen Anne
Attic base	Georgian style	Renaissance
Balloon framing	Gothic	Ribbon window
Baroque	Gothic revival	Rococo
Bauhaus	Greek	Roman
Byzantine	Greek revival style	Roman Corinthian order
Chevet	International style	Roman Doric order
Colonial revival	Ionic order	Roman Ionic order
Columns	Italian villa	Romanesque
Composite order	Italianate	Romanesque revival
Corinthian order	Klismos	Roof garden
Craftsman style	Mesopotamia	Rotunda
Crossing	Modernism	Stick style
Curtain walls	Nave	Transept
De Stijl	Neoclassical	Trompe l'oeil
Deconstructivism	Neolithic	Tuscan order
Doric order	Oculus	Tympanum
Egyptian	Parametricism	Victorian era
Empire style	Pediment	
Entablature	Pendentives	

Resources

Frampton, K. (2014). *Modern Architecture: A Critical History*. London: Thames & Hudson.

Hinchman, M. (2016). *History of Furniture: A Global View*. New York: Fairchild Books.

Ireland, J. (2018). *History of Interior Design*. Bloomsbury Publishing USA.

Lucie-Smith, E. (1979). *Furniture: A Concise History*. London: Thames and Hudson.

Winchip, S. M. (2010). *Visual Culture in the Built Environment: A Global Perspective*. New York: Fairchild Books.

Review Questions

1. List the periods and associated time frames.
2. On graph paper, draw a proportional time line that articulates each period and include the associated time frames.
3. Consider each of the periods from Egyptian through Romanesque with particular attention placed on the transitions that occurred between adjacent, or slightly overlapping, periods. Select one transition and describe the causes.
4. Consider each of the periods from Romanesque through Victorian with particular attention placed on the transitions that occurred between adjacent, or slightly overlapping, periods. Select one transition and describe the causes.
5. Consider each of the periods from Victorian through Postmodern and Deconstruction with particular attention placed on the transitions that occurred between adjacent, or slightly overlapping, periods. Select one transition and describe the causes.

Exercises

Identifying Design Examples of the Modern Era

Materials: magazines and/or internet search engine, printer (if using the internet)

1. Cut/paste images of building exteriors or interiors from magazines, or print images from the internet that clearly fall into one of the design periods from the modern era. Each student should have one image that expresses each period, totaling nine images.
   a. Arts and Crafts (1880–1915)
   b. Craftsman (1897–1930s)
   c. Art Nouveau (1892–1910)
   d. Modernism (1910–1940)
   e. De Stijl (1917–1931)
   f. Art Deco (1920–1939)
   g. Postmodern (1960s–Present)
   h. Deconstruction (1980s–Present)
   i. Parametricism (1993–Present)
2. Provide a written description for each image that describes the characteristics of the building exterior or interior that specifically relate to the characteristics of the period or style.
3. The document could also be completed digitally using word processing and/or graphics software, if the students are comfortable doing so.

Make this exercise more experiential by touring your campus, or city, in search of examples of each style/period and photograph the examples yourself.

3

The Design Process

Learning Objectives

As a result of reading this chapter, students will

1. **Possess an awareness of the importance of point of view in relation to the design process.**

2. **Possess an awareness of the typical phases of the designer's process and how each phase builds upon the prior phases.**

As a result of taking part in the learning exercises at the end of this chapter, students will

1. **Demonstrate an understanding of the phases of the design process from both the client's and the designer's point of view.**

2. **Demonstrate an understanding of how the design thinking process overlays the phases of the design process.**

Introduction

The prior chapters discussed design thinking, elements and principles of design, and, briefly, architecture and design history. It is important to see that while these topics are addressed separately, they influence one another in significant ways. Design thinking addresses the methodology of a designer's thought process that seeks to produce the best results on a consistent basis. The elements and principles of design are used to express the categorical qualities of those results that work well. When considering the great architectural and design works of history, those great works are honored because they possess the elements and principles of design with a sense of harmony that other works may not. In addition, one cannot deny the role of nature, war, and the quality of construction on the body of architectural and interior design work available to us from ages past. Earthquakes, floods, erosion, conquests, world wars, looting, crime, and construction knowledge and techniques have taken their toll on design history. Great works from the past may have been lost, with only archaeology, art, and literature to bear witness to their prior existence. As architecture and design have evolved over time, so has the design process that produces these great works. This chapter details the design process as it is typically used in professional practice today.

Design Process Point of View

The **design process** is greatly affected by one's point of view. A professional designer views the process very differently compared to the client, for example. The designer has a very in-depth view of the process, while a client may have never been through the process before. It is important for the designer to educate the client on the design process prior to beginning and throughout the process. Fostering an open dialogue with the client on the design process will help the designer build trust with the client and prevent major misunderstandings during a project.

POV: The Client

As mentioned in Chapter 1, developing empathy for the client is an important part of design thinking as the designer seeks to create an innovative solution. This idea of empathy starts with the process of design itself, particularly with the designer realizing that the client sees the design process differently than the designer sees the process. The American Institute of Architects offers a very client-friendly five-phase description of the **client's POV** of the design process, which applies to both residential and nonresidential project types (Fig. 3.1):

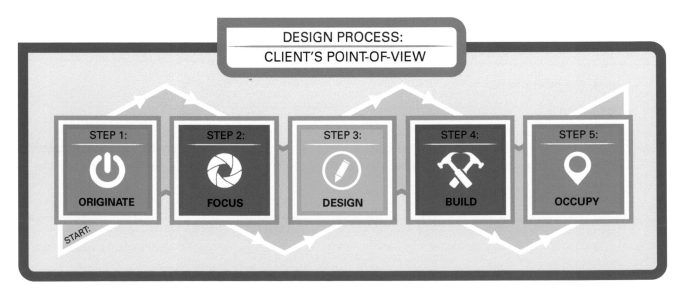

Figure 3.1 The design process from the client's point of view begins prior to hiring the designer. The client doesn't typically see the intricacies of the design process like the designer does.

1. Originate
2. Focus
3. Design
4. Build
5. Occupy

Phase one, **originate**, begins as the client considers the need for a new, or additional, space. The designer is not always involved in this phase, as the client may choose to handle this first step alone. This stage concludes when the client decides that a new, or more, space is needed to address their current and planned needs. This phase often concludes with the decision to hire a professional designer. Note that the designer enters the process after the client perceives a need.

Phase two, **focus**, relies on the client having hired a professional designer to guide them through the next several steps. A written contract is necessary during this stage that clearly identifies the specific services that the designer will provide to the client. Once the formalities of the contract are established, the designers and client develop the intent of the design and brainstorm goals and qualities that the design must have to be successful. This step parallels the first two parts of design thinking: empathize and define the problem. The focus phase involves extensive information gathering, where the client and users of the space should have a tremendous amount of input.

Phase three, **design**, is where the client's involvement tapers off slightly. The prior two stages focus largely on the client's role, whereas the design phase shifts focus toward the designer. Here, the designer begins the process of creating potential design solutions. This phase allows the client to see what the design could look like before it ever gets built. As the designer and client work back and forth to narrow the options and eventually arrive at a design direction, the process by which decisions are made becomes critically important. The design thinking steps of ideate, prototype, and test parallel this phase of the design process. In the section that follows on the design process from the designer's point of view, it is clear that this phase is broken into several additional steps. As the process progresses, a design will be agreed upon by the client before construction commences. This phase concludes when a set of detailed plans is drawn by the designer, and a general contractor, or construction manager, prepares to begin construction.

Phase four, **build**, provides for another shift in focus further away from both the client and designer

toward the contractor, or builder. The designer remains intimately involved with the project, however. The pace of construction is often fast, so close communication and time lines are critical during this phase. Changes during construction are common, and the designer is responsible for keeping the owner appraised of these changes. The owner will have input and be a part of the decision-making process should any changes come up that affect the vision, or intention, of the design. Elements of design thinking do crop up in this phase, mostly in the form of ideate, prototype, and test, and must be addressed in rapid fashion due to the pace of construction. This phase concludes when construction is complete and the client is prepared to occupy the space.

Phase five, **occupy**, concludes the design process for the client. This phase begins once construction is complete and the terms of the contract between the owner and contractor are fulfilled. Occasionally, the contractor may offer move-in services, but this should be spelled out in the contract between the owner and building contractor. The designer can also offer suggestions to the client on move-in contractor services. In theory, this phase never ends. The client, tenant, or users are always in some process of occupying the space. The bulk of the initial process of occupying a new space happens shortly after construction is complete, however. As the occupation of a new space continues on, it is a good idea for the client to maintain a strong line of communication with the designer, in the event that the client would like to renovate or make other significant changes to the space.

POV: The Designer

The designer sees the design process in much greater detail than the client. The designer acts as the maestro of the design process, controlling the pace and approach to each phase. Even though the design process is viewed a bit differently between the client and designer, the steps share many similarities (Fig. 3.2). The design process from the **designer's POV** include these steps:

1. Pre-design
2. Schematic design
3. Design development
4. Construction documentation
5. Contract administration

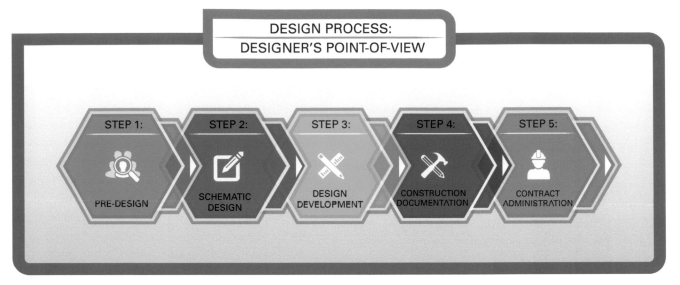

Figure 3.2 The design process from the designer's point of view begins before a contract is signed, and continues after construction is complete.

Pre-Design

At the beginning of **pre-design**, the client has not yet hired the designer—no contracts have been signed. When a designer becomes aware of a potential project, the client has already been thinking about it for some time. At this stage, the designer lacks knowledge regarding the specifics of the potential project, and will need to ramp up quickly if he or she wants to be awarded the contract by the client. A large amount of time and effort goes into pursuing a potential project. This is often referred to as business development, and is addressed in more detail in Chapter 6. Overall, the pre-design phase consists of client and location research, the use of evidence-based design, programming, and concept development. Depending on the type and complexity of the project, each of the parts of pre-design will change in relation to importance and the type of work that is needed to complete the work. Assuming that the contract is awarded, the designer moves on to gathering information on the client and project location.

The client and location research portion of pre-design often begins before a contract is signed (Fig. 3.3). The designer often wants to know as much as possible about the client, their business (especially if the project is commercial), and the project location in an effort to win the contract. Once the contract is signed, however, client and location research will continue in earnest. In design-thinking speak, client research is referred to as

developing empathy for the client. As stated in Chapter 1, empathy is crucial to eventually developing the best design solution for the client. If the designer cannot identify with the client and their needs, then developing a great design solution will be nearly impossible. Client research will vary based on the project type, but will often consist of studying the client's history and future goals, interviewing the specific users of the space (i.e., employees, patrons, or family members), executing a questionnaire or survey, conducting on-site observations, and other types of information-gathering techniques. Nonresidential projects, such as commercial office, hospital, or higher education projects, can take on a very formalized approach to gathering this information with high-level meetings in a formal conference room, whereas with residential clients, the information gathering processes may be less formal, occurring over a cup of coffee in their existing living room.

Understanding the location context of the design is also very important. The designer needs to understand the immediate location, neighborhood, and surrounding conditions of the space that will be designed (Fig. 3.4). Location context begins at the edge of the space to be designed and extends outward from there. The extent of that location context is difficult to define, as it can be different from project to project. In the case of a corporate office interior in an urban center, the location context starts at the elevator lobby; includes the neighbors around, above, and below within the building; and extends out

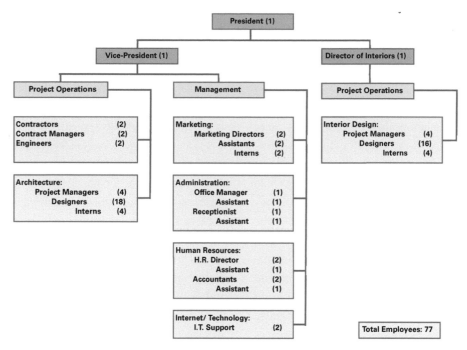

Figure 3.3 Client research in the pre-design phase gathers the important information regarding the client that will influence the upcoming design, for example understanding a corporate client's organizational structure.

location analysis

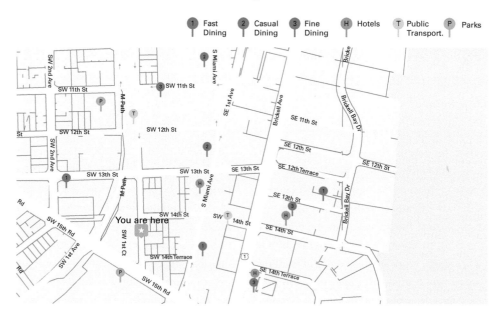

Figure 3.4 A location analysis catalogues and visualizes information regarding the project location that will influence the design of a space.

into the city to include the views of landmarks and nature, exposure to natural elements such as direct sunlight, as well as the functional and entertainment amenities within the neighboring buildings. More discussion is provided on the importance and impact of design context in Chapter 7. As the designer gains a strong understanding of the client and the project location, the designer moves on to an often-neglected phase of pre-design called evidence-based design (EBD).

Evidence-based design is "the use of research to inform the design process" (Hinchman, 2014). To say that EBD has a tightly defined time period within the design process isn't entirely accurate. EBD is something that can, and often should, be present throughout the design process. EBD is important because the success of a design can, and often should, be measured. If a designer is relying on whim or personal preference (a.k.a. "Because I like it" syndrome), the likelihood of failure increases drastically. Does this sound familiar? As described in Chapter 1, design thinking principles reinforce the use of EBD. The two philosophies can work together to improve the likelihood that a design will be successful. As the design profession builds a more extensive knowledge base regarding various design typologies and trends, EBD will grow in popularity and usefulness. One example comes in the design of health care spaces. In the last several decades, the contribution of healing environments to the health care profession has been increasingly documented. Topics such as environmental psychology, color theory, and advancements in material sciences have become crucial to designing the most effective spaces for healing. Without the disciplines inherent within EBD, these advancements may not have been realized, or at least may have been further delayed in application.

The **programming** stage is where the designer and client work together to determine what functions will occur in the new or renovated space. Based on specific user needs, lessons learned through professional experience, and EBD, the designer determines the types of spaces needed, the size of the spaces, and the contents of each space (Fig. 3.5). In the case of a corporate office environment, or workplace, types of spaces could include private offices, open work areas, lounge and kitchen spaces, conference rooms, informal collaborative work and meeting areas, and spaces for storage. Area is expressed in square feet, or square meters, and the quantity of space is dictated by functional requirements, such as the number of people that will occupy the space or the amount of storage needed in the space. Quantity of space can also be dictated by hierarchy within an organization, as the CEO will often have a larger office than a mid-level manager, 350 square feet as compared to 120 square feet, for example. The contents of the space, such as furniture or equipment, would typically be determined by the function of the space. A conference room used for private meetings, for example, would contain at least one table and several chairs for the occupants along with display surfaces, such as a projection screen or dry erase boards used to facilitate meetings and discussions. A similar approach is used in residential projects, but the types of spaces are domestic in nature, and include a kitchen and dining space, social and gathering zones, and sleeping and bathing quarters, along with appropriate facilities for storage. All of these pieces of information, the list of spaces, their required floor area, and their specialized furniture and equipment needs, should be efficiently presented in the form of a table. The goal of programming is to identify the spatial needs of the client and users and to summarize these needs in the form of a programming table that the designer can use as a guide during space planning in the schematic design phase.

As pre-design draws to a close, an overall guiding principle, or set of principles, should emerge that will guide the project through schematic design. Based on prior research and programming, a **concept** should be developed for the project and will serve as the link between pre-design and schematic design. Whether or not it is clearly stated, every well-executed and highly designed space has a vision to guide the design process and outcomes. This vision can be expressed in a creatively written statement, a list of functional goals and aesthetic characteristics, or a series of sketches and images. Some designers choose to use these various techniques in combination with one another to express the big idea of the project to the client and even a wider audience if needed. In design education, the concept statement is commonly taught as a way to express the big idea and form intentions of a design project. Many techniques are available, and one that works well is the two-step concept development process proposed by Patricia Eakins in her book *Writing for Interior Design*. This process starts with identifying the idea generator of the project and follows with a description of the forms that idea inspires. Combined with descriptive language surrounding the elements and

Programming Table

Organization	QTY	Type	Furniture	Sq.Ft	Total
Vice President	1	Executive office	Desk, Task chair, Credenza, Storage, Computer	120	120
Admin					
	2	Executive Office	Desk, Task chair, Credenza, Storage, Computer	120	240
	8	6' x 6' Work Stations	Desk, Task chair, Computer	36	288
Engineering					
	1	Executive Office	Desk, Task chair, Credenza, Storage, Computer	120	120
	2	6' x 12' Project Manager Work Station	Desk, Task chair, Computer, Storage	72	144
	14	6' x 6' Work Stations	Desk, Task chair, Computer	36	504
Architecture + Interior Design					
	4	Executive Office	Desk, Task chair, Credenza, Storage, Computer	120	480
	6	6' x 12' Project Manager Work Station	Desk, Task chair, Computer, Storage	72	432
	26	6' x 6' Work Stations	Desk, Task chair, Computer	36	936
Distributed Office Space					
	2	Private Phone Rooms/ Enclaves/ Wellness	Seating for 1-2 People	60	120
	2	4-Seat Conference Room	Conference Table, 4 Task chairs	115	230
	1	6-Seat Conference Room	Conference Table, 6 Task chairs	147	147
	2	8-Seat Conference	Conference Table, 8 Task chairs	150	300
	1	Design Library	Storage, Seating, Work Tables, Lounge Seating	400	400
	1	Reception and Waiting Area	Lounge Seating, Coffee Tables	400	400
	4	Coffee Bars	Coffee Table	21	84
	1	20-25 Seat Workcafe	Bar Height Seating, Tables, Chairs	400	400
	4	Open Area Soft Seating	Lounge Seating, Coffee Tables	200	800
	1	I.T Equipment Room	Seating, Work Tables	150	150
	4	Multi- Functional Network Printers	Tables	6	24
	3	Supply Closets	Storage	60	180
	1	Stairwell	N/A	180	180
Sub-Total					6,967
Circulation					1,393
Total Sq. Ft					8,360

Figure 3.5 A programming table lists all of the individual spaces; associated area in square feet (or square meters); and particular needs within the space that relate to furniture, fixtures, and equipment, along with any other particular concerns such as privacy or acoustic needs.

principles of design, the concept statement can provide a rich mental picture of how the design could develop. Concept statements are broad in their scope, as they can address both functional and aesthetic ideas about the project. The concept statement can serve to help the client envision the design before it comes to fruition and help the designer make design decisions as the project develops. That said, it is not impossible for a concept to change as the project develops. As the design process unfolds, new priorities can be revealed, and the designer should feel free to adjust the concept as necessary. Even after the space is built, the concept can help to describe the design process in marketing and promotional materials.

Overall, the pre-design phase of the design process is firmly joined with the philosophies of design thinking. Designers and architects have been intuitively abiding in design thinking principles for a very long time, but the

rigor of this process is now being elevated to a discipline within design. This phase of design can require a team of individuals to complete highly complex and long-term projects. If the client is a large organization, the pre-design team may divide the work by category in order to leverage the expertise of the individuals on the team. In the case of smaller projects, such as single-family residential and small nonresidential projects, the designer may complete the pre-design phase alone. For continuity and quality purposes, it is advisable to keep the pre-design team intact as the project moves into schematic design. This makes it much simpler if an issue is uncovered during schematic design that the pre-design phase did not directly address. A hand off from a pre-design team to a schematic design team can lead to additional errors or problems later in the project. Keep in mind that as the next design process phases are described, the pre-design phase is the bedrock on which the others stand. If the designer, or design team, takes shortcuts in pre-design, the quality of the end result will suffer, or the process will have to backtrack to address items that were left out.

Schematic Design

With the bulk of the research, programming, and concept work addressed, the designer begins the **schematic design** phase, where the designer studies spatial adjacency and form. These two critically important items can often progress simultaneously, as one drives at the functionality of the space through adjacency and the other addresses the aesthetic needs of the design. The function and the form should inform one another.

The designer conducts adjacency studies using the adjacency matrix and bubble diagram. These two tools work from an idealized vantage point, seeking out the "best" arrangement of spaces based upon inherent adjacency requirements. The diagrams place emphasis on certain adjacency connections, as some spaces have a primary connection to one another, while others have a secondary connection, and still others are purposely separated from one another. This hierarchy lends itself to establishing a priority of adjacency and will help the designer make compromises in the space-planning process later.

The adjacency matrix and bubble diagram both address adjacency, but in different languages. The **adjacency matrix** takes the form of a table, listing all of the programmatic spaces along the left-hand side and utilizing a turned, 45-degree grid to create intersections between each space where the designer can articulate the priority of adjacency (Fig. 3.6). It is important to use discreet descriptors, such as "primary," "secondary," and "separate," in the legend, or key, of the table so that the hierarchy of adjacency is 100 percent clear. In cases where certain cells are empty, the meaning is also clear: the adjacency of these two spaces is unimportant, or inconsequential. Allowing blank spaces to exist in the matrix is important, as visual emphasis is placed on the primary, secondary, and purposely separated spaces. The 45-degree nature of the matrix takes some practice to read, but it is far more efficient than utilizing a 90-degree matrix where the list of spaces is repeated along the top and side. Color can also be integrated into the list of spaces along the side of the matrix to communicate different ideas, such as the privacy needs for each space.

The **bubble diagram** is typically characterized as a more visual method of communicating adjacency. It utilizes circles, or other geometric shapes, to represent individual spaces that are connected by lines to indicate level of adjacency (Fig. 3.7). Line types, such as thick lines, thin lines, or dashed lines can be used to indicate primary and secondary adjacencies and primary paths of travel through the various spaces. Other priorities, such as connection to nature and privacy level, can be communicated through symbols and color. Dedicated circulation zones, such as corridors, stairs, and elevators, can also be shown in the bubble diagram if needed. Space labels and other notations also become critical aspects of the well-executed bubble diagram in order to communicate the intricacies of the designer's thought process.

While starting with an ideal is helpful to establish adjacency priorities, the realities presented by an existing building footprint and structure must be addressed quickly by prototyping the ideas through the blocking diagram. The **blocking diagram** is a plan-view drawing completed at an architectural scale, 1/8 inch = 1 foot

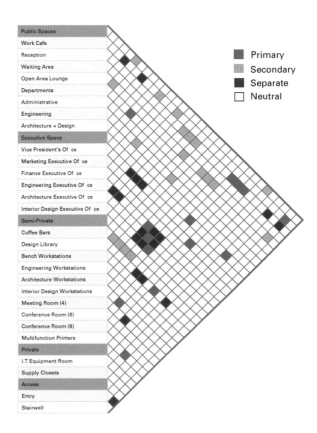

Figure 3.6 An adjacency matrix lists the spaces to one side and uses a 45-degree turned grid to show how spaces relate to one another by showing levels of required adjacency or separation.

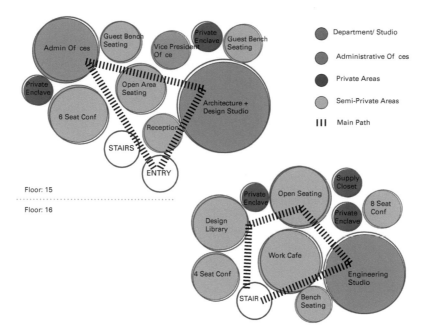

Figure 3.7 A bubble diagram utilizes graphic language to communicate priorities regarding adjacency.

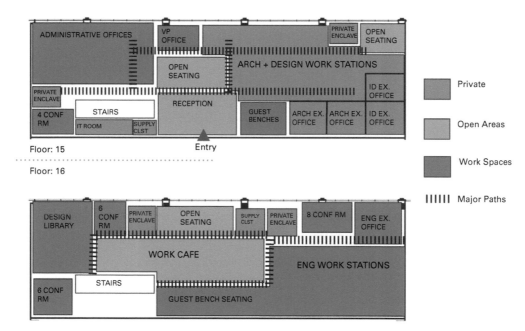

Figure 3.8 The blocking diagram utilizes the bubble diagram or adjacency matrix alongside the quantified areas in the programming table to conceptualize adjacency and proportion/quantity of space simultaneously in a to-scale diagram. A base floor plan showing the extents of the available space is necessary to complete this diagram.

for example, on top of an existing floor plan at the same scale (Fig. 3.8). The existing floor plan shows any and all exterior walls; building structure, including columns; and other building elements that cannot be moved. Looking at the programming table, which shows the types of spaces and their area quantities, the designer can begin placing accurate rectangles as representations of specific spaces

upon the existing floor plan. Notice that the blocking diagram is largely functional at this stage. Variety in forms stemming from the concept have not been integrated yet.

It is not unusual for the designer to create several blocking diagrams, each with their advantages and disadvantages as they relate to the needs of the adjacency matrix and bubble diagram. Corresponding to each blocking diagram, the designer may also generate several iterations of stacking diagrams. A **stacking diagram** analyzes vertical adjacencies across multiple levels with a specific eye toward multistory spaces, views between levels, ceiling heights, interconnecting stairs and lifts, and any acoustical design concerns between levels. The stacking diagram begins the process of designing a space in the third dimension, which will continue throughout the schematic, design development, and construction documentation phases of the design process.

With a visual representation of a rudimentary plan, the designer will begin to address issues of form that relate back to the concept. Several iterations, often completed by hand sketching on tracing paper overlays, will result in this step of schematic design (Fig. 3.9). The designer will create a form layout that corresponds to each blocking diagram option and will then begin to design more detailed space plans that incorporate furniture, fixtures, and equipment. Completed space plans will showcase placement of walls, windows, doors, millwork, furniture, and divisions of flooring materials as it contributes to the definition of functional space. Along with the potential for several plan iterations, the designer will offer several options for millwork, furniture, finishes, and lighting selections (discussed in greater detail in later chapters).

At the end of schematic design, the designer and client should have agreed upon a space plan and the primary furniture, finish, and lighting fixture selections. In addition, it is beneficial for the designer to articulate the planning concept through a very simple diagram, known as a parti. The **parti** is a diagram that captures the essence of the design, either in plan, section, elevation, or in a three-dimensional view, such as an axonometric (Fig. 3.10). The parti will work in conjunction with the concept statement to communicate the guiding ideas behind the design.

Design Development

Design development begins with adding additional layers of detail to the design. Whereas schematic design focused on planning of space and primary selections of furniture, finishes, and lighting, design development

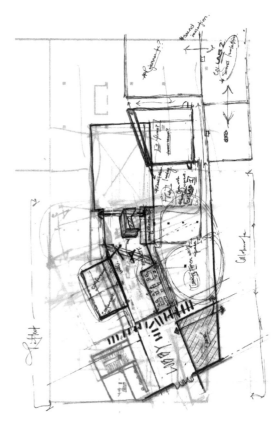

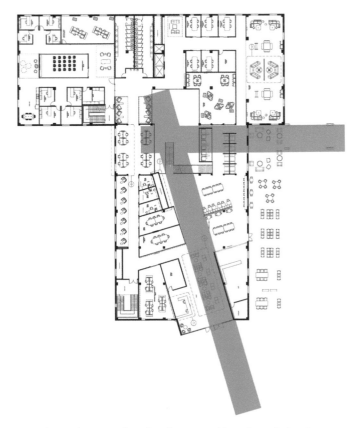

Figure 3.9 The designer takes into account many factors when studying the form of a space plan, therefore several iterations of planning studies are needed to arrive at a clear and well-executed plan arrangement. In this case, the designer created several sketch overlays, shown on the left, prior to arriving at the final space plan on the right. The blue bars indicate two primary planning influences—the exterior path approaching the building on a slight angle and views to the east of the building.

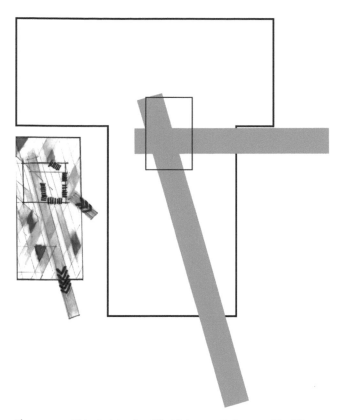

Figure 3.10 This sketch, simplified into a parti diagram, identifies a framework for space planning. The diagonal pathway addresses circulation from the exterior of the building to the interior, emphasizing pedestrian access from a campus center. The horizontal path calls attention to a major pathway connecting this building to an adjacent building on an upper level while also providing views between them.

addresses the question, "How do all these elements come together?" The first task is for the designer and the client to come to an understanding regarding the secondary furniture, finish, and lighting fixtures. Second, the designer will complete more specific drawings, including elevation and perspective views that serve to pave the way toward the design of specialty millwork, cabinetry, interior architectural details, and other detailed elements that will result in a rich design. It is also common for the designer to consider appropriate ways for materials to transition from one to another during this phase (Fig. 3.11). A good example is addressing a flooring transition from ceramic tile to carpet. These sorts of everyday transitions require the designer's planning and attention in order for them to be built properly. Design development seeks to identify these important transitions, and construction documentation creates the construction detail drawings that will describe how the transitions should be executed.

The design development phase concludes with a set of design development plans that will begin to look similar

to a set of construction documents. Although these documents are not yet ready to be used for construction, they will serve as the bones from which the designer creates the set of construction documents. To complete this phase, it is often helpful for the designer to be well versed in using computer-aided drafting software or building information modeling software. Along with the design development drawings, a preliminary specifications document should also be produced. The specification is a written document detailing the selection of materials, installation or construction techniques, and the care and maintenance processes needed to maintain the quality of the materials long after construction is complete. If it is part of the designer's scope of work, this is also the phase where selection of art and accessories in the space begins. Final decisions may not be made until sometime during construction documentation.

Figure 3.11 Transitions between flooring materials need to be anticipated by the designer and thought through in detail. During design development, the designer begins developing options for some of the more detailed design elements in a space.

Construction Documentation

The goal of the **construction documentation** phase is to create a set of large drawings and detailed specifications from which the design can later be built. This phase can take much longer than any of the prior phases due to the level of detail invested in this phase. Most of the drawings produced in this phase can be in the construction details, which typically consist of section drawings detailing out the layers of substrates and finishes necessary for construction. This process is needed to achieve the design intent that was shown to the client way back in the schematic design phase.

Without a doubt, this phase is highly technical in nature. As the designer becomes more experienced in this phase of project development, the early phases of the project will go more smoothly. The designer will learn in which areas to innovate or push the envelope, and in which areas to use best practices and tried-and-true methods.

In relation to design thinking, design development and construction documentation will touch upon ideation, prototyping, and testing as the designer seeks innovative ways to address the technical aspects of the design.

Figure 3.13 During contract administration, the designer spends time on the construction site observing the progress and quality of construction.

Depending on the organization of the design team, the construction manager and engineers may have significant input during both of these phases.

The construction documentation phase of the project will result in a set of drawings and specifications that can be used to hire a general contractor who will then build the design, bringing the vision of the designer and client to reality (Fig. 3.12). Sometimes, the general contractor will already be hired by this point and may even serve as an important consultant during the prior phases of design in an effort to keep the cost and schedule of construction in check sooner rather than later. The stronger the relationship between the designer and contractor, the better the contract administration phase will go.

Contract Administration

The **contract administration** phase is where the designer works to ensure that the design intent becomes reality on the construction site (Fig. 3.13). To do this, the designer acts as an advocate for the client. Because clients are typically not well versed in the construction process, they need an experienced designer to act on their behalf, to speak for their best interests.

Some may say, "Well, if the client and the designer worked so hard to come up with a great design, and thought through all the details, shouldn't it be a straightforward matter to just follow the drawings and specifications to construct the new design?" Ideally, yes, that is the case, but construction is very complicated and unexpected things come up during the construction process. Those unexpected situations require decisions to be made,

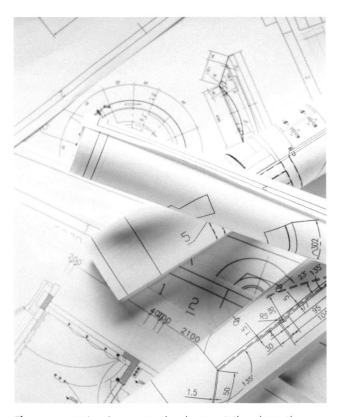

Figure 3.12 During the construction documentation phase, the designer prepares a set of very detailed drawings that the contractor will use to build the project.

A User-Centric Design Process Heightens Design Outcomes

Project: University of Minnesota–Duluth, Kirby Student Center

Location: Duluth, Minnesota

Client: University of Minnesota

Architect/Designer: Workshop Architects

Project Type: University Student Union

Site Characteristics: Unique natural setting on a university campus with multiple adjacent building connections

Year Complete: 2015

Cost Estimate: $3,158,078

Facility Size: 19,615 square feet

Project Overview

Kirby Student Center is the geographic and historic center of the UMD campus, and is the keystone of UMD's campus master plan to create a grand entrance for campus visitors. The renovation of the first-floor space was intended to provide a significant increase in lounge space for students; to use design principles that encourage students to connect with one another and with UMD faculty and staff; and to open up what was a cramped, dark, and dated space. A previous renovation in 1979/84 sectioned off the spaces and was designed to accommodate a student population that was 40 percent smaller than enrollment at the time design was initiated. The design for the renovation supports UMD's strategic goals of integrated curricular and co-curricular learning, sustainability, equity and diversity, and connection to the Duluth community. The renovated space contributes to the part of UMD's mission that strives to integrate education and engagement to prepare students for lifelong learning.

This project is remarkable because of how it achieved the stated needs within a confined space and how it addressed the particular needs of the campus' traffic patterns. A unique feature of the UMD campus

The primary circulation flanks the student service areas and areas for student collaboration and socialization.

is its thirty-two interconnected buildings on a hillside overlooking Lake Superior. Students, faculty/staff, and campus visitors navigate from building to building via concourses, skyways, and the occasional tunnel. Kirby Student Center is connected on all four sides to other buildings, so there was no opportunity to expand the building footprint to gain more space for students. Rather, the design team was required to rethink the use of existing space and use it more efficiently.

The new design eliminated wasted space in odd corners and strange partitions of the previous renovation and provided space that could be fully utilized. It increased lounge space by more than 4,000 square feet within the existing 22,000-square-foot renovation area without eliminating any existing student organization or staff office spaces. It also provided one-of-a-kind elements, such as an interior porch, meeting space that can expand into a performance space, and a design that connects student casual areas across a busy hallway that supports over 10,000 trips a day. The integration of a natural aesthetic, connection with the surrounding landscape, and the use of school colors and branding links the space to campus heritage and identity.

Innovative Design Process

One of the most unique aspects about the project was the above-and-beyond collaborative process between the design team and the campus community. During pre-design, while the team was focusing on research and programming, the designers went straight to the source in an event called Kirby's Big Week. They set up shop in the existing student center, embedding themselves into the space they were designing, and developed concepts with students, displaying and presenting drawings each day, and inviting other students and faculty to sketch, write, and express their ideas and feedback. The process allowed for real-time responses to student input and reinforced the power of student voices in the conceptualization of their new student center. The results were then compiled into a comprehensive program study that became the framework for the final design.

Construction was divided into two phases in order to avoid a complete shutdown of an already active zone. Phase I included the student lounge space and phase II included student organizations and support services. The inclusive process created a sense of ownership and pride in a space that will continue to enhance the connection between learning and the community.

Prioritizing Inclusion Produces Higher Satisfaction

Vast insight gathered throughout the master plan in 2012, and multiple phases of the Kirby Student Center renovation, lent itself to creating a vibrant, welcoming, and engaging space that resonated with the community. Workshop's intensely collaborative efforts with UMD administration, Kirby staff, and hundreds of students stood at the forefront of creating a remarkably inclusive environment prior to the team having the exact language to describe it. Since opening after the first renovation in 2014, and the second phase in 2015, Workshop's design has greatly enhanced the physical and information environment of Kirby Student Center while creating an exceptional backdrop for UMD's attitudinal, policy, and program environment. Overall, the result of the improvements made to Kirby Student Center has rebooted UMD's institutional culture and furthered their commitment to inclusivity.

Design Priorities Resulting from Kirby's Big Week

Campus Identity

What once functioned as a dark and dated corridor and merely a pass-through for students is now a vibrant and open hub of activity that attracts students and encourages them to linger. Subtle infusion of branding and thoughtful use of color speaks to campus culture and creates a space that is wholly unique to University of Minnesota–Duluth.

Mixed-Use Innovation

The garage functions as a flexible conference room by day and a stage for student programming or presentations by night. The student life porch is a subtly raised collaboration zone and social platform. It pulls the social spaces out of the student organization offices and aligns them along a highly visible platform that increases interactions between different groups.

Open Space and Circulation

The high traffic central corridor is flanked on both sides with programs for innovative learning and interaction

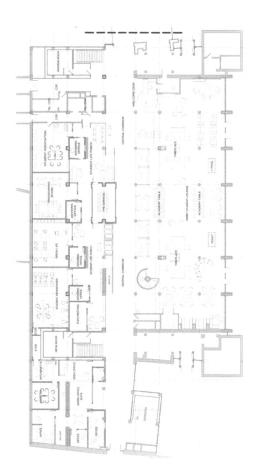

This complex interior renovation included all 22,000 square feet of the existing facility and made very efficient use of the space to create a new hub for the university community.

between students, faculty, and the rest of the campus community. Glazing on the east wall allows for abundant natural daylighting as well as stunning views of the campus, the city of Duluth, and Lake Superior below.

Space Utilization

The west side of the corridor houses the more structured services, including student organizations and administrative support. The east side opens to a student lounge, offering a variety of seating, nodes of activity, expansive views, and natural daylighting. The two spaces—private and public—are buffered with the student life porch, the highly visible social platform that provides a thickening of the threshold between both zones.

Student Life and Support

The open layout emphasizes visibility and ease of access for students and faculty. Student organizations, once hidden, were turned inside out to create a strong presence on a heavily trafficked path. The overall layout serves all aspects of student life and support in one versatile space.

Workshop Architects is a full-service architecture and design firm located in Milwaukee, Wisconsin, specializing in the design of higher education spaces, particularly student unions, with a refreshing focus on an inclusive design process. For more information on the University of Minnesota–Duluth, Kirby Student Center, winner of an ACUI Facility Design Award, and Workshop Architects, visit http://www.workshoparchitects.com/.

The main socialization area embraces natural light and warmth to encourage students to remain in the space for as long as they desire.

often involving the contractor, designer, and client to communicate clearly with one another. If the designer is removed from the situation, the client may not receive the best options to choose from, or they may not be able to make the best choice. This is where client advocacy by the designer is so critical. More on this in Chapter 6, the professional practices chapter.

To advocate for the client, the designer will often put on work boots and a hard hat to visit the construction site and observe the progress. On occasion, additional drawings will need to be produced to answer questions from the contractor. This phase is often very rewarding for the designer, as ideas on paper become built space. The quality of decisions made early on now become clear.

The punch list is often the last opportunity the designer has to advocate for the client prior to the general contractor walking away from the construction site. This step involves the designer visiting the nearly completed space and taking note of any problems in quality of construction, such as scuffs on walls, misaligned light fixtures, and other very small errors. Solutions to these problems should only involve touching up paint, some additional cleaning, or slight adjustments. The designer should have been visiting the site frequently during the construction process, or contract administration, so that there are no surprises at this point.

When the construction is complete, the designer and contractor can give the client notice that the space is ready for occupation and normal use. The client then takes occupancy, beginning the normal operations of their business in their new space, or living in their new residence. This process is often accompanied by a celebratory event, assuming that the design and construction process was viewed favorably by the client (Fig. 3.14). The client inviting the designer to a "grand opening" of sorts is a good sign that the designer built a strong relationship with the client.

Figure 3.14 When construction is complete, the client takes occupation of the space, often with great anticipation and celebration.

In order to make sure that the next project goes well, the designer would be well-advised to conduct a **post-occupancy evaluation** (POE). A POE often consists of an on-site observation by the designer coupled with a survey or interview of the client and users after they have been using the new space for a while. The observation and survey should drive at how the design intent matches up with how the client and users interact with the space. Did the design intent match closely with reality? If not, how might the design process change in the future to arrive at a better solution? The findings from a POE will serve to inform the pre-design process on the next project. So, the cycle begins anew.

Summary

The design process, whether from the client's perspective or the designer's, is critical to the success of a built space. The client initiates the process and the designer designs the space to become everything it can be. Without the designer ushering the client through the process, the space would not become the solution to the client's spatial problems. As discussed earlier, the design process utilizes elements of design thinking throughout. For a big-picture view of how design thinking relates to the design process from both the client's and designer's point of view, see the Gantt chart in Figure 3.15. Much of the process involves a rhythmic back and forth interaction between the client and the designer, but portions of the design process, especially design development and construction documentation, is more inwardly focused within the design team. All of the parties, including the client, designer, engineering consultants, and general contractor/construction manager must come together to make the design a successful built environment. Chapter 6 addresses some of the nuances of professional practice and how design teams composed of multiple professional disciplines can come together to create successful spaces for the client.

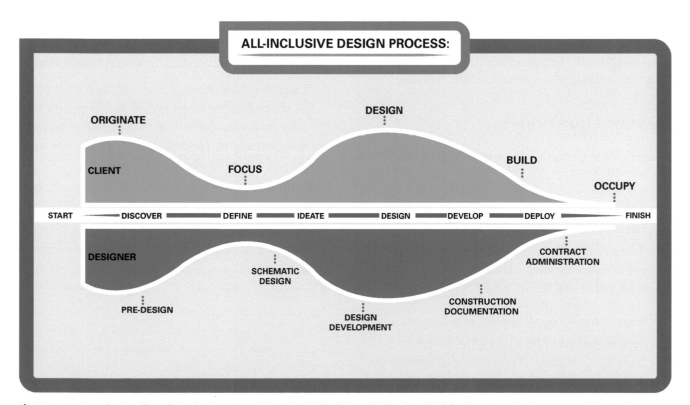

Figure 3.15 An understanding of the design process integrated with design thinking is critical for the young designer to envision. A clear understanding of the divergent and convergent processes that accompany each stage of design thinking as it overlays with the designer's and client's point of view is helpful in developing a personal approach to the design process.

Resources

AIA. (n.d.) (http://www.aia.org). Retrieved January 15, 2016, from http://howdesignworks.aia.org/fivephases.asp.

Aspelund, K. (2014). *The Design Process*. Bloomsbury Publishing.

Eakins, P. (2005). *Writing for Interior Design*. Fairchild.

Hinchman, M. (2014). *The Fairchild Books Dictionary of Interior Design*. A&C Black.

Piotrowski, C. M. (2001). *Professional Practice for Interior Designers*. John Wiley & Sons.

Rengel, R. J. (2014). *Shaping Interior Space*. Bloomsbury Publishing.

Winchip, S. M. (2012). *Professional Practice for Interior Design in the Global Marketplace*. New York: Fairchild.

Review Questions

1. List the steps in the design process from the client's point of view.
2. List the steps in the design process from the designer's point of view.
3. What are the components of pre-design?
4. What information is included in a programming table?
5. What pre-design components and diagrams combine to create a blocking diagram?
6. What is the end result of schematic design?
7. What is the end result of design development?
8. What is the end result of construction documentation?
9. What is the end result of contract administration?
10. What does POE stand for? What is it, and how is it used?

Exercises

Understanding the Design Process

1. List the design process phases from the client's POV across from the corresponding phase from the designer's POV. Some client phases will bridge multiple phases as viewed by the designer, so some answers can be used more than once.

Client POV	Designer POV
_____	Pre-design
_____	Schematic design
_____	Design development
_____	Construction documentation
_____	Contract administration

2. List the design thinking steps as they would most likely correspond to phases of the design process from the designer's POV. Some design thinking steps will be used in multiple design phases, so some answers can be used more than once.

Design Thinking	Designer POV
_____	Pre-design
_____	Schematic design
_____	Design development
_____	Construction documentation
_____	Contract administration

4

Spatial Well-Being

Learning Objectives

As a result of reading this chapter, students will

1. Possess an awareness of the physiological and psychological impacts of the built environment on building occupants.

2. Possess an awareness of the importance of universal design and the role the designer plays in advocating universal design principles.

3. Possess an awareness of spatial sciences, including anthropometry and ergonomics.

4. Possess an awareness of human spatial behaviors, including the expanded eight-tier Maslow's hierarchy of needs, prospect-refuge theory, territoriality, personalization, and proxemics, and how these behaviors relate to the built environment and the role of the interior designer.

5. Possess an awareness of sustainability in the context of interior design and the role of sustainability guidelines.

As a result of taking part in the learning exercises at the end of this chapter, students will

1. Demonstrate the ability to analyze interior spatial experiences through the physiological senses.

2. Demonstrate the ability to analyze a service or volunteer experience in context with the eight-tier Maslow's hierarchy of needs theory of human behavior.

Introduction

Spatial well-being is a broad topic that prioritizes the fundamental betterment of the users in a built environment. Foundational to spatial well-being are the physiological methods humans use to interpret space through the five senses. A designer must have a thorough understanding of universal design because sensory and physical impairments among building occupants is common. Several branches of human physiological study have produced the spatial sciences known as anthropometry and ergonomics. In addition to understanding human physiological needs within space, designers must also understand human psychological needs in space. This chapter offers an overview of human spatial behaviors, beginning with Maslow's hierarchy of needs and progressing to prospect-refuge theory, territoriality, privacy, personalization, and finally proxemics. The chapter closes with an overview of sustainability and sustainability guidelines that offers an awareness of attempts at measuring sustainability and spatial well-being.

Incorporating every topic related to spatial well-being into every space may not always be possible, but striving for this ideal is worth the effort and presents a complex problem worthy of the design thinking process. At times, aspects of well-being may be in conflict with one another, or with other tangible aspects of a project, such as budget and quantity of space. The responsibility of balancing these potentially conflicting project needs rests at the feet of the designer, because it is quite possible that no one else on the project team has the knowledge, ability, foresight, or motivation to be able to address these complex topics. Adequate attention to the empathy stage in design thinking is the only way to identify which of these topics are most important in the problem definition stage. Only then can complex problems related to universal design, proxemics, and sustainability, for example, be addressed in ideation, prototyping, and testing.

Sensory Interpretation of Space

The built environment is perceived and interpreted through the five physiological senses—sight, hearing, smell, taste, and touch. A disability, in whole or in part, in any one sense will alter an occupant's experience within a space. **Sight** impacts an individual's ability to navigate a space, to know where to go in the event of an emergency, and it enables the aesthetic enjoyment of an interior. Circulation through a complex environment, such as a transportation terminal or hospital, is far more challenging for a blind individual, who must rely on a cane, the aid of an animal, and Braille signage. In general, users can be disoriented when visiting a place for the first time, and this feeling can be heightened for those who have impaired vision. This condition is heightened further in the event of an emergency that requires evacuation of a building when someone cannot see the source of the problem, such as a fire or security breach. In cases of colorblindness, signs that are low in color contrast can be difficult, or impossible, to read. Enjoyment of spatial aesthetics is limited for those who are visually impaired, as the material and color palette does not have the same level of impact as it does for those who possess full use of their eyes. Bland views can also negatively impact a user's experience, such as in a workplace that lacks views to the exterior, particularly of nature (Fig. 4.1). Conditions such as these have a tendency to decrease productivity (HOK, n.d.; Jaffe, 2013).

Hearing affects one's ability to navigate, discern conversation, heal, perform a task, and concentrate. In relation to navigating space, hearing can aid in understanding one's immediate surroundings outside of the peripheral vision. A person who has slight to moderate hearing loss will often struggle to engage in conversation in spaces with high levels of ambient noise, which is often the case in active restaurants. The overlay of sounds from health-monitoring equipment can affect the pace of

Figure 4.1 The influence of sight within interiors tends to be the focus of much of the design process, but it is also important to embrace views to the exterior.

healing in hospitals, and can negatively affect the concentration of health care staff while administering care. Excessive noise can distract workers in open office environments, particularly those who are more introverted (which is approximately 50 percent of the population). Students in noisy classrooms, or classrooms with poor acoustics, will often find it very difficult to focus and to understand what the teacher is saying, which affects learning outcomes (Treasure, 2012) (Fig. 4.2).

The olfactory senses of **smell** and **taste** work in tandem to interpret aromas, odors, and tastes within space that extend beyond the dining experience (Fig. 4.3). Retailers employ scent strategies in some stores, particularly in the fashion industry, to influence the customer's tendency to make purchases (Klara, 2012). Smells can help with wayfinding in hospitality environments when a visitor is seeking the location of a banquet hall in a large convention center. Smells and tastes also serve to strengthen the bond between pleasant memories and places, which results in individuals wanting to spend more time in places that cater to their sense of taste and smell. As with each of the

Figure 4.2 Noise impacts one's ability to concentrate, communicate, and can even lead to increased stress levels and headaches in the event of prolonged exposure.

senses, smell and taste can deteriorate with age, leading to an elderly person not being able to locate the source of an odor, such as spoiled food or a soiled carpet.

The sense of **touch** is one sense, in addition to sight, that can be used to interpret textures and gives us sensations of comfort and warmth. Tactile textures add

Figure 4.3 The role of the olfactory senses, smell and taste, is largely indirect in relation to interior design, but does provide occupants with heightened memory associations, both positive and negative, in relation to certain types of spaces.

aesthetic variety to interiors and influence performance qualities of a space rooted in anthropometrics and ergonomics. Skillfully wielding natural textures within work environments can positively influence productivity, memory, and creativity (Bromberg, 2016) (Fig. 4.4). Touch is also how occupants interpret temperature changes and generally experience a space as "warm" or "cold." Individuals differ on this particular characterization of space so widely that it is impossible to please everyone in shared spaces, such as workplaces, through centralized heating and cooling controls. For this reason, many architects, designers, and engineers recommend allowing the users more control over their environment (HOK, n.d.). For the blind, the ability to sense touch becomes imperative for wayfinding, just as a seer's cane and Braille writing become very important in navigation and communication.

Figure 4.4 Tactility can provide nuance to a complex experience within the built environment.

Universal Design

Universal design is an approach to designing spaces, and components within spaces, that allows inhabitants to fully utilize the built environment despite any physical challenge, mental challenge, or age (Fig. 4.5). Physical challenges include partial or full sensory disability, mobility challenges, strength and endurance challenges, or body size considerations. **Sensory disabilities**, including blindness and deafness, result in design guidelines that account for the use of white canes, the inclusion of audible and visual fire alarms, the provision of listening enhancement devices at performance and entertainment venues, and Braille-equipped signage and indicators in public buildings. **Mobility challenges** that require the use of a support cane, walker, or wheelchair impact the design of stairs so that each step is not too high for a cane user to climb, encourage the use of ramps and lifts to aid users of walkers and wheelchairs to traverse vertical changes in floor height, and require certain minimum clearances to be maintained at doorways, next to door handles, in restrooms around fixtures, and at corridor junctions. A user's strength and endurance challenges lead a designer to design handrails and specify door handles and faucet controls that can be gripped easily, and strategically disperse resting places throughout long circulation spaces such as malls, transportation terminals, and hospital corridors. Body size considerations, such as individuals that are very tall or short, impact the specification of taller doors and longer beds, and the design and detailing of storage items such as cabinetry

Figure 4.5 Universal design prioritizes the needs of all users by seeking to eliminate physical and psychological barriers that would otherwise prevent someone from utilizing and enjoying a space.

and the specification of appliances and equipment that accommodate a user's reduced range of reach, which is also the case for wheelchair users. Anyone can encounter temporary challenges due to an injury, surgery, illness, or pregnancy, which means that anyone can also benefit from the principles and application of universal design.

The Seven Principles of Universal Design were developed from the work of a collaborative group of architects, engineers, product designers, and researchers at the North Carolina State University in 1997, with funding support from the U.S. Department of Education National Institute on Disability and Rehabilitation Research. The Seven Principles of Universal Design (Connell, B., Jones, M., Mace, R., Mueller, J., Mullick, A., Ostroff, E., Sanford, J., Steinfeld, E., Story, M., Vanderheiden, G., 1997) are:

- Principle One: Equitable Use
  The design is useful and marketable to people with diverse abilities.

- Principle Two: Flexibility in Use
  The design accommodates a wide range of individual preferences and abilities.

- Principle Three: Simple and Intuitive Use
  Use of the design is easy to understand, regardless of the user's experience, knowledge, language skills, or current concentration level.

- Principle Four: Perceptible Information
  The design communicates necessary information effectively to the user, regardless of ambient conditions or the user's sensory abilities.

- Principle Five: Tolerance for Error
  The design minimizes hazards and the adverse consequences of accidental or unintended actions.

- Principle Six: Low Physical Effort
  The design can be used efficiently and comfortably and with a minimum of fatigue.

- Principle Seven: Size and Space for Approach and Use
  Appropriate size and space is provided for approach, reach, manipulation, and use regardless of user's body size, posture, or mobility.

Some countries have enacted laws that require all new construction of public spaces, both indoor and outdoor, to accommodate certain physical challenges. In the United States, the Americans with Disabilities Act (ADA) was signed into law in 1990 by President George H. W. Bush. It resulted in gradual implementation at the local level over the course of the years and decades that followed. Amendments to the law have sought to clarify and improve it, especially in regard to implementation of barrier-free design guideline requirements. In the context of interior design and architecture practice, a space that is in compliance with all aspects of the ADA are said to be **barrier-free**, or **accessible**. It is important to note that laws such as the ADA include many universal design principles, but these laws do not currently mandate all universal design principles. It is up to the designer and owner to prioritize the creation of inclusive spaces.

Individuals with mental challenges also benefit from universal design solutions. Neurological and cognitive mental impairments present from birth, resulting from an injury, or caused by aging impact how an individual perceives space and reacts to various stimuli within the built environment. In the case of individuals on the Autism spectrum, the designer can design spaces, such as classrooms, that account for the social, communication, and behavioral aspects of the disorder. In cases of Alzheimer's disease and dementia, which have become more common as people are living longer, designers can craft spaces that accommodate the memory and cognitive effects of the disease. Specifying finishes in assisted living facilities that do not utilize bold, high contrast patterns help users navigate the various spaces and remember where they are. Emotional depression resulting from seasonal affective disorder (SAD) is caused by a prolonged lack of exposure to daylight that often occurs in rhythm with the change of seasons in fall and winter. Several types of treatment and therapy are available, including **phototherapy**, or the use of full-spectrum lighting or light boxes to mimic the type of light produced by the sun.

Age, whether advanced in years or very young, presents interesting design challenges and opportunities for the designer to address. In the case of an aging population that is living longer than prior generations, the intent for the designer is to help the user utilize a space as fully and independently as possible for as long as possible. This concept is referred to as **aging in place**, and requires significant planning and foresight on the part of the designer and client to implement with as little economic cost and inconvenience as possible (Fig. 4.6). The impact has become, and will continue to be, significant in residential design as the vast majority of

Figure 4.6 Many types of design strategies and products can provide disabled or elderly users with the freedom to stay within their homes, and many complicated design changes can be anticipated to minimize expensive alterations later.

Spatial Sciences

Successful implementation of universal design principles relies on understanding the physical capabilities and needs of the human body articulated through anthropometry and ergonomics. Anthropometry is the measurement of the human body. The resulting data, or **anthropometrics**, are used to categorize large populations in an effort to design products and spaces for public consumption. Products, such as automobiles, chairs, and mobile phones, and spaces, whether residential, corporate, health care, or any other typology, are designed to accommodate the greatest number of individuals (Fig. 4.7). Specifically, products and spaces are designed to fit the needs of the middle 90 percent of the public, or those between the 5th and 95th percentiles, but what about the outliers, or those at the edge of the anthropometric scales? This is where universal design steps in to attempt to provide products and spaces for as close to 100 percent of the public as possible. Basic standards, including countertop heights in kitchens at 36 inches and in restrooms at 30 inches, desk and table heights at 28 inches, and chair and bench seat heights at 18 inches all stem from the middle 90 percent on the anthropometric data tables, but these designs may need to be adjusted based on universal design principles, or on the specific needs of a client or user group.

It is also important for designers to note that populations go through changes in body measurements, as evidenced through the growing rate of obesity in Western society. As anthropometrics change, so must the design of certain products, such as chairs. Waiting areas for hospitals, clinics, and dental offices are impacted by this trend where bariatric seating options are included in the seating arrangements. The designer also needs to understand that anthropometrics differ between some global populations and it is their responsibility to apply appropriate data for a given population group based on the location of the project and the dominant user group.

As defined by the International Ergonomics Association, **ergonomics** is "the scientific discipline concerned with the understanding of interactions among humans and other elements of a system, and the profession that applies theory, principles, data and methods to design in order to optimize human well-being and overall system performance." The systems referred to in the definition include work systems found in a factory or an office space, food preparation systems found in kitchens, and driving and navigation systems found in vehicles, among many other

the aging population desires to stay in their homes rather than move to specialized facilities.

At the opposite end of the aging spectrum, children present a set of design needs that require particular attention by the designer. Children are in a developmental stage of life where the built environment can provide safe opportunities to grow, experiment, and learn. For young children, mental concepts of logic, safety, and security have not yet developed, so physical injuries are common. The frequency of severe injuries can be reduced by eliminating sharp protrusions from furniture and millwork and along paths of circulation and controlling access to storage cabinets while offering safe and controlled environments where children can climb, play, explore, and hide. Naturally, children have smaller bodies and need furniture designed based upon their anthropometrics and ergonomics in order to effectively accommodate them.

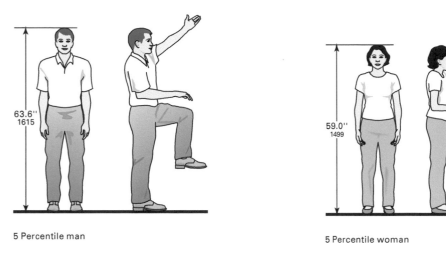

5 Percentile man

50 Percentile man

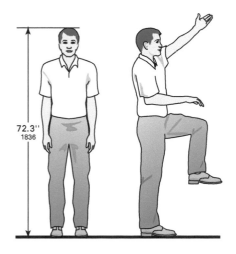

95 Percentile man

5 Percentile woman

50 Percentile woman

95 Percentile woman

Figure 4.7 Anthropometric measurements are helpful in understanding the vast majority of a user groups' body measurements, but the extremes, the bottom 2.5 to 5 percent and the top 2.5 to 5 percent, are often not represented, which can conflict with universal design ideals.

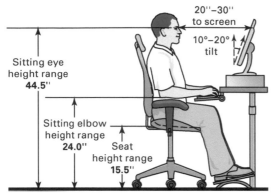

Men—1% ergonomic office desk, chair and keyboard height calculator

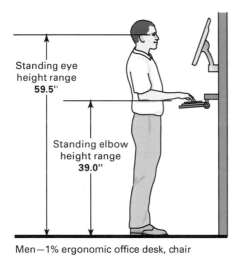

Men—1% ergonomic office desk, chair and keyboard height calculator

Figure 4.8 Designing with ergonomics in mind results in a work environment, such as an office, that encourages the occupants to use healthy postures, which helps the user avoid injury or health problems caused by the built environment.

systems (Fig. 4.8). The well-being of the individual is the primary goal of ergonomics, as products and systems that are ergonomically designed can help to prevent injury and even improve a person's well-being. Likewise, ignoring ergonomics, or applying the science improperly, can result in injury, pain, unnecessary fatigue, or even a chronic medical condition. For individuals, proper ergonomics result in an improved lifestyle, better physical health, and improved mental and emotional state. For businesses, the benefit comes in a happier, healthier, and more dedicated employee base that misses fewer days of work due to illness or mental fatigue, and increased productivity leading to higher profitability.

The most valuable resource of any company is its employees, not the equipment or products produced by the employees, making ergonomics an important part of a successful company. As a result, ergonomic office furniture has been developed for workers who use computers for prolonged periods of time. These improved products seek to minimize many ailments associated with computer use, including eye strain, mental fatigue, lower-back and neck pain, poor blood circulation—especially in the legs—joint stress, and carpal tunnel syndrome. Furniture innovations include ergonomically adjustable task chairs that can accommodate a wide range of body sizes and proportions and adjustable-height work surfaces that can allow an individual to stand while working at the computer. More recent innovations also include the incorporation of treadmills into standing-height desks that can be set at low speeds while working to improve dietary balance and blood flow resulting in a less sedentary lifestyle. These products have been pioneered and embraced by many furniture companies, including Steelcase, Herman Miller, Haworth, and Humanscale.

Human Spatial Behaviors

The study of human spatial behaviors is strongly rooted in environmental psychology. Environmental psychology is the study of individuals in their environment, which includes the natural, social, learning, informational, and built environments. The correlation with interior design is mostly found in the built environment portion of the discipline, and tends to focus on broad populations. Observations within the built environment are influenced by a number of factors, including culture, upbringing, and location of the space. It is up to the designer to know how to apply broad observations in a differing culture or location. This discussion will address Maslow's hierarchy of needs; prospect and refuge; territoriality, privacy, and personalization; and proxemics.

Maslow's Hierarchy of Needs

Maslow's hierarchy of needs is a motivational theory that places the root cause of human behaviors in perspective in such a way that can be very useful for designers in understanding the role of design in context with the life of the "typical" client or user. **Maslow's hierarchy of**

SELF-TRANSCENDENCE
Helping Others, Spiritual Experiences

SELF-ACTUALIZATION
Achieving Individual Potential

AESTHETIC NEEDS
Pursuit of Beauty and Creativity

COGNITIVE NEEDS
Pursuit of Knowledge and Understanding

GROWTH NEEDS

DEFICIENCY NEEDS

ESTEEM NEEDS
Self-con dence, Respect from Others

SOCIAL/BELONGING NEEDS
Family, Friendship, Intimacy

SAFETY NEEDS
Security, Finances, Freedom from Fear

PHYSIOLOGICAL NEEDS
Air, Food, Water, Shelter, Sex

Figure 4.9 Maslow's hierarchy of needs can be categorized by deficiency needs (physiological, safety, social/belonging, and self-esteem needs) and growth needs (cognitive, aesthetics, self-actualization, and self-transcendence needs). This diagram was created by the author based on work from Zhang and Dong, 2009.

needs includes eight categories, beginning with the most basic and progressing to the higher order needs (Fig. 4.9):

1. Physiological needs
2. Safety needs
3. Social/belonging needs
4. Esteem needs
5. Cognitive needs
6. Aesthetic needs
7. Self-actualization
8. Self-transcendence

The first four needs are considered the deficiency needs—if any one of them are deficient, then the individual will quickly seek them out prior to the higher-level needs. For example, if the **physiological** need of thirst, hunger, rest, or shelter from the natural elements is not met, then someone will need to drink, eat, sleep, or acquire shelter before they can focus in the classroom in order to meet their need for knowledge and understanding. The same is true if someone lacks **safety** or is afraid of danger, lacks the **love and acceptance** of friends and family, or possesses low **self-esteem**. Architecture and interior design affect each of these deficiency needs by

1. Providing a place to store and preserve food and water, providing a place to eat, drink, and sleep, and providing shelter from natural elements (physiological needs).
2. Preventing intrusion by those who intend to do harm (safety needs).

3. Providing a place for family and friends to gather and experience love and belonging (love and acceptance needs).
4. Providing a place to practice a skill or a sport, and display achievements (self-esteem and respect from other's needs).

The four deficiency needs can be considered as fundamental to survival, or coping with life. By contrast, the growth needs of acquiring **knowledge and understanding** and pursuing **aesthetics and beauty** are characterized by growth, and only become a priority after the four deficiency needs are met. Architecture and interior design impact the growth needs by

5. Providing environments that are conducive to learning, experimenting, observing, contemplating, and meditating (knowledge and understanding needs).
6. Expressing beauty and aesthetic excellence through the built environment, and providing spaces where beauty can be on display, such as a gallery or performance hall (aesthetics and beauty needs).

Design has a tremendous potential to positively affect a person's growth in both of these areas (Fig. 4.10). In particular, interior design is geared towards meeting the aesthetics and beauty needs of the client and the user. Designers also understand that their own need for beauty and aesthetics is fulfilled through the practice of interior design. In this context, the needs of both the client and professional are being met.

Figure 4.10 Many interior environments provide for multiple needs simultaneously, such as this gathering among friends as they celebrate a special event with food and drink in a safe place.

The **self-actualization** need embodies the desire for one to reach his or her full potential once the basic and growth needs are met. Designing spaces where an individual, or group of individuals, can reach their full potential is not prescriptive by its very nature because each person and his or her full potential is unique. Spaces that are tailor-made to the client and users require a dedicated designer who will listen to the client by building empathy for them and their needs, accurately define problems that a well-designed space can help to solve, develop ideas that could address those problems, prototype the ideas, and finally test them. The designer addresses this need in him/herself by pursuing excellence in the interior design profession, constantly practicing the craft of design, refining the design process, and reaching his or her full potential.

The final need, as described by Maslow, is **transcendence**, or helping others meet their needs (physiological through self-actualization). As described in detail already, a variety of spatial types can meet the many needs outlined in Maslow's hierarchy. This means, that at some level, designers have the opportunity to engage with their own need for transcendence by practicing interior design and helping others meet their needs. It is important to understand that this system of analyzing human needs is broad and does not address an individual's nuance and particular circumstances, so it is in the designer's hands to know how best to apply this system of understanding clients and user groups.

Designing for the Greater Good

Designing and conducting built environment research for the betterment of humanity is one way that professional

Figure 4.11 Exercising their own need for transcendence, Dr. Jill Pable and Kenan Fishburne, designed the interiors of the Kearney Comprehensive Emergency Services Center. This housing environment offers residents a safe place to reside that provides for their basic psychological needs so they can focus on their growth needs, enabling the residents to one day independently provide for themselves.

interior designers seek to fulfill the highest orders described in Maslow's hierarchy of needs. Certain project types, such as hospitals and clinics, shelters for the homeless, low-income housing, and others, by their nature address certain basic needs of the clients and users and offer the designer the opportunity to exercise their own need for transcendence. Designers are paid for the services they provide to their clients, but, occasionally, a client comes forward with a project that they cannot pay for. In situations such as these, the designer has the opportunity to offer their services for free, on a pro bono basis, to a nonprofit organization that works to further a cause that the designer wants to support (Fig. 4.11).

In addition to working on projects for the greater good, designers and educators study the impact of the built

Figure 4.12 The Design Resources for Homelessness website offers a variety of useful resources for those interested in improving and applying design techniques in homeless shelters and transitional housing.

environment on users' physical and psychological health and well-being. Often a designer or educator will focus research efforts on a particular project type or a known problem affecting interior design. Other times, the research will center on an issue the designer or educator is passionate about, such as design for underprivileged or underrepresented populations. An excellent example is the online knowledge base Design Resources for Homelessness (http://designresourcesforhomelessness.org/), organized by Dr. Jill Pable of Florida State University (Fig. 4.12). The website offers a growing body of knowledge focusing on the positive impacts that interior design can have for

individuals in crisis through a collection of case studies of completed projects and access to broad research topics that can be used to improve homelessness recovery.

Prospect-Refuge

Jay Appleton, an English geographer, first proposed the **prospect-refuge theory** of human aesthetics in *The Experience of Landscape* written in 1975. The theory proposes that people have an innate desire for opportunity and safety, or prospect and refuge (Fig. 4.13). This theory has been mostly applied in context

Figure 4.13 The refuge of this living room, with its low ceilings, offers the occupants the opportunity to survey, or prospect, the land and seascape.

with urban and landscape planning, but has also made inroads with architecture and interior design. In relation to interiors, one can see the prospect-refuge theory at work through the coveted table or booth in the corner of the pub, coffee shop, or restaurant that offers a clear view of the entrance. Prospect-refuge theory also posits that views to the exterior are desirable in order to gain a vista of the landscape where opportunities can be surveyed and approaching danger can be prepared for from a safe haven. This principle can be witnessed when one considers the desirability of a corner apartment near the top of a residential high-rise in an urban setting or the mountain lodge with a wall of windows overlooking the valley below. Undoubtedly, other forces are at work in these cases, such as the desire to witness a beautiful view, the prestige of owning such a desirable apartment or property, and the positive effects on the human psyche and body associated with views of nature and daylight. The possible discrepancies uncovered in the way users respond to the application and observation of the prospect-refuge theory warrants further investigation as designers use this theory, and others, to justify design decisions (Dosen & Ostwald, 2016).

Territoriality, Privacy, and Personalization

Territoriality in the built environment is the tendency to claim entire or partial ownership, whether permanent or temporary, of a space. In context with public or shared spaces, people will often mark their territory by placing a bag or book down on a table in a coffee shop while they place their order, purchase a ticket for a specific seat at a music performance or sporting event, or display personal effects on their desk in an open office setting. In the private realm, homeowners will build fences and walls at the edge of their property; siblings will display "keep out" signs on their bedroom doors; and roommates will claim certain cabinets, shelves in the refrigerator, or a specific chair in the living room. These displays of territoriality will vary in importance from the critical, such as someone's private bedroom in an owned residence, to the moderate, such as a seat that has been purchased for a sporting event, and finally the more casual territorial claims such as those found in a coffee shop. The level of importance for these territorial displays may differ by the individual based on the level of personal identity, personalization, and privacy that is embodied in the particular space or object.

People also have a tendency to defend their territory in proportion to the level of importance that the space has for them. In the case of a home, great defensive measures may be employed, including locks, electronic security systems, and even physical violence if the occupant is threatened by an intruder. In the example of a sporting event, someone occupying a seat they have not purchased a ticket for is expected to move when the ticket holder arrives. In the more casual coffee shop example, a regular patron may arrive to find that "their" booth or table is occupied by another customer and the regular has no grounds to demand the other customer to move.

Privacy in many ways is rooted in the fundamental need for security and can be a motivator for many of the territorial tendencies just described. Privacy can be visual or acoustical and can be described in degrees of each. Visual privacy can range from total opacity, such as a solid gypsum board wall, to completely open vision, as is the case with a clear glass wall, or something in between, such as a frosted glass wall. Complete acoustical privacy prevents any sound from transferring from one adjacent space to another, functional acoustical privacy prevents distracting sounds and intelligible conversation from transferring from one space to another, and spaces that are open acoustically do little to nothing to mitigate the transference of sound from one space to another. The need for complete privacy will vary by project type. In the case of multifamily residential buildings, such as apartment or condominium high-rises, both types of privacy are very desirable between dwelling units. Office interiors, on the other hand, must balance the need for visual and acoustic privacy with other important needs, such as collaboration and ease of communication. When people need privacy but cannot obtain it, then they will likely make modifications to their environment or alter their behavior, and may experience heightened anxiety or fear.

Personalization is the tendency of users to adapt a space to reflect their individual desires, traits, and characteristics; stake claims to certain portions of a space (territoriality); and to increase their comfort levels in a space. Personalization tendencies are often very noticeable in the workplace where people may display photos of family members, awards and diplomas, or artwork and baubles that possess intrinsic meaning to the owner. The freedom to personalize a space increases a person's comfort level, allows them to pursue beauty and aesthetics, can lead to higher morale and lower turnover in the workplace, and can even improve healing rates in health care environments.

Proxemics

Proxemics is the study of the way people behave, communicate, and socialize in space as population density changes. Edward T. Hall, a cultural anthropologist, first proposed the term proxemics in his book *The Hidden Dimension*, in 1910. Through studying the ways that people use space, several key proxemics categories of space can be observed (Fig. 4.14):

1. Intimate: Ranging from zero to 1.5 feet, intimate space is reserved for touching, affection, and close/private talking and whispering. This space is shared between individuals who have a very close relationship with one another and occurs often in residential spaces. When intimate space is violated, a person typically feels threatened, unsafe, and fearful.

2. Personal: Starting at 1.5 feet and extending to 4 feet from the individual, this space is reserved for friends and family and can include dining settings or travelling in a vehicle. Personal space is "owned" by the person psychologically, and intrusion into this space by strangers, such as in an elevator, can be tolerated for only a limited amount of time or under certain circumstances, such as a plane flight.

3. Social: From 4 feet to 12 feet, the social circle of space tends to include interaction with acquaintances or friends in large groups and can include the workplace and classroom settings. When social conventions are maintained, entering an individual's social circle of space can have positive results.

4. Public: Outside of 12 feet and extending to 25 feet, the public circle includes individuals with little or no personal knowledge of one another. Individuals enter into one another's public zone at public speaking events, a house of worship, or a sporting event. In these contexts, violations of personal and intimate zones are particularly concerning for some people and can result in an avoidance of public venues.

The distances described for each of the four zones are approximations, which can differ by circumstance or cultural norm. Certain settings, such as a crowded subway car, necessitate the intrusion upon an individual's intimate and personal spaces, which can trigger a variety of coping mechanisms, including avoiding eye contact or focusing attention on a mobile phone or newspaper (Fig. 4.15). Cultural differences also influence proxemics, particularly in context with how interaction with strangers is perceived within the intimate and personal zones. Designing with culturally and situationally relevant proxemics in mind will help to guide space planning for a variety of spatial types based on the anticipated level of interaction between the users of the space.

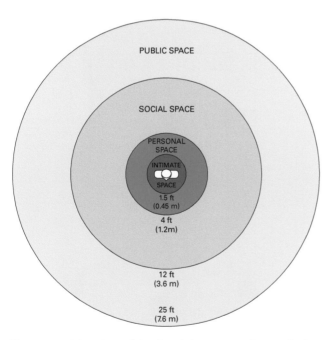

Figure 4.14 Edward T. Hall developed the concept of proxemics by studying the ways people use space and was able to articulate the four zones of individual space: intimate, personal, social, and public.

Figure 4.15 When needs to express territoriality, privacy, and personalization cannot be met, individuals often employ coping mechanisms, including avoiding eye contact, until the environment becomes less crowded.

Sustainability

Sustainability in the built environment is a broad concept encompassing ecological, economic, and health ideals. The definition provided by the World Commission on Environment and Development in 1987 drives at this dual role of sustainability, and still rings true today:

> **Sustainable development** seeks to meet the needs and aspirations of the present without compromising the ability to meet those of the future. Far from requiring the cessation of economic growth, it recognizes that the problems of poverty and underdevelopment cannot be solved unless we have a new era of growth in which developing countries play a large role and reap large benefits.

Interior designers should understand the impact that the design and construction of their spaces have on the world's ecology in relation to the materials and furniture specified, the construction and fabrication processes required to make the design become reality, and the energy required to operate and maintain a space. The materials utilized in construction of interior spaces extends beyond the visible finishes to include the underlying structural materials and substrates. Most manufacturers of interior finish products have a firm grasp on reducing waste, reusing scrap and discarded materials, and recycling byproducts from the manufacturing process. Certain manufacturers, such as Interface Flooring, Inc., with their GlasBac carpet tile backing material, will even accept old materials left over from a demolished construction site and use them in the manufacturing process for new finishes.

The **life cycle** of a furniture piece, taking into consideration what happens to its various components once it is no longer usable, is also very important in managing the sustainability of the manufacturing waste stream. In the case of the Think Chair by Steelcase, up to 95 percent of the chair is recyclable, allowing the chair to be processed into materials usable to make another product once the chair is no longer useful (Fig. 4.16). Planning for obsolescence by utilizing materials that can be reused or recycled one day, reducing the amount of waste in manufacturing, reusing materials whenever possible, and recycling materials for new uses are each a part of a sustainable **closed-loop** manufacturing strategy. Cradle to cradle (McDonough, 2002) is a unifying manufacturing strategy that draws inspiration from nature, also known as **biomimetic**. In essence, cradle to cradle strategies utilize waste from the manufacturing and consumer process as part of the manufacturing stream of future products.

Each project has nuance based on a variety of factors, including location, the condition of the existing building

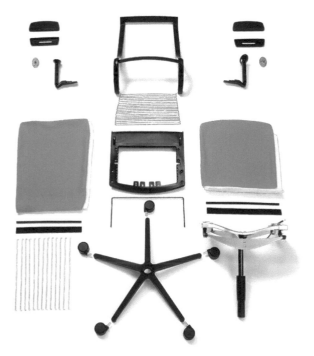

Figure 4.16 The Steelcase Think Chair is strategically designed to be disassembled for maintenance purposes or to be recycled when it has reached the end of its usefulness.

Figure 4.17 One of the most effective sustainability strategies is found in the reuse of materials, which requires that these materials be carefully preserved during the demolition phase of construction.

Figure 4.18 Effective sustainability strategies embrace a balance between ecology and economy, and seeks ways to maximize both.

(if it is a renovation or addition), and the available methods of construction and fabrication. Part of the design process that prioritizes sustainability will take an inventory of all of the existing project conditions to determine the most sustainable approach for construction. Reducing waste, reusing as many materials as possible, and recycling any materials resulting from the demolition of an existing space or building is the first priority related to sustainable construction techniques (Fig. 4.17). Second, the project location brings certain opportunities and challenges related to the availability of materials and products. Due to energy consumption related to transportation, it is wise for the designer to specify as many materials and products as possible that can be obtained close to the project site. The typical standard of "close" is within 500 miles, the standard dictated by the United States Green Building Council (USGBC) **Leadership in Energy and Environmental Design (LEED)** guidelines, but this can vary depending upon the sustainable design and construction standards used to guide the project.

The energy required to operate and maintain a space, while easy to overlook, is critically important for a designer to consider while planning and specifying products for a new project. The orientation of the building in relation to sun exposure and the resulting heat that is gained within the space from direct sunlight should determine how spaces are planned and what window treatments are specified in order to leverage the positives of daylight while minimizing the negatives. Efficient HVAC planning in collaboration with a mechanical engineer will reduce

the consumption of electricity in heating and cooling a space. Automatic lighting controls that can sense daylight and the movement of occupants and then can dim or turn off light fixtures will save energy (Fig. 4.18). Specifying efficient lamp types (bulbs) in light fixtures may have a higher initial cost, but will save energy in the long run.

Each of the sustainable strategies just described in relation to energy can also reduce the economic costs of operation and maintenance. Specifying efficient lamps in light fixtures, automatic lighting controls to dim or turn off fixtures, window treatments that reduce heat gain, and planning with efficient HVAC performance as priorities will decrease the utility costs associated with owning or leasing a space. Efficient lamps also reduce maintenance costs, as they will not burn out as quickly or need to be changed as often.

Economic and health benefits go hand in hand due to the increased health benefits for occupants that result from sustainable design and construction practices (Fig. 4.19). Healthier occupants do not require costly health care as often, nor are they absent from work as often, which can reduce the operating efficiency of a company. Healthy people also tend to be happier, with higher morale, which can increase the profitability of a company. While an interior environment is clearly not the only influence on a person's health, it will have an impact. Certain spatial qualities, such as access to daylight and views of nature will improve a person's mood.

Negative health can result if sustainable design practices are ignored. Some interior finishes, such as paint, carpet, and wood products, have been found to release toxic gasses into the air, which can cause illness to those who are exposed for prolonged periods. Proper maintenance of HVAC systems,

Figure 4.19 Views to nature from the interior will improve an individual's overall mood, increase morale, and improve productivity in the workplace.

careful lighting design, and thoughtful acoustical design are all critical in the health of building occupants. If these items are neglected, a variety of conditions, generally termed **sick building syndrome**, can result where occupants experience an increase in illness frequency, such as headaches and fatigue often related to poor lighting, excessive noise, or thermal discomfort. In certain extreme cases, **building-related illness**, where occupants can become infected by bacteria, viruses, or certain forms of fungi, can result. One example is the breakout of Legionnaire's Disease that periodically causes problems in buildings where the cooling towers, a critical component of a HVAC system, harbor bacteria which then is distributed to all of the interior spaces via ductwork. The disease is deadly, as was the case for 21 individuals out of 127 who were infected in a Canadian nursing home in September 2005.

Sustainability Guidelines

Various government-related bodies seek to oversee the application of designated levels of sustainability

practice as it relates to the manufacture of products and the design and construction of buildings. In the United States, the Environmental Protection Agency (EPA) created and oversees the Energy Star program, which publishes a set of performance requirements that must be met and maintained by manufacturers of products, such as residential appliances, in order to receive Energy Star product labels. It is up to the manufacturers to understand and meet or exceed the requirements of the guidelines, and test their products to ensure compliance. Historically, this program has been met with controversy, as some manufacturers have exploited loop holes in the testing requirements resulting in some inefficient products receiving Energy Star approvals.

The USGBC oversees LEED, the primary certification program for sustainable buildings and interiors. With a variety of specific programs related to building design and construction (BD+C), interior design and construction (ID+C), building operations and maintenance (O+M), residential design (Homes), and neighborhood development (ND), the LEED system offers design, construction,

Design for the Greater Good

Project: Bakhita Gardens

Location:	Seattle, Washington (USA)
Client:	Catholic Housing Services
Architect/Designer:	Environmental Works Community Design Center, Bill Singer
Occupants/Users:	Single, adult homeless women
Site Characteristics:	Urban; main street frontage with alley flanking the side
Year Complete:	2010
Cost Estimate:	$14 million
Facility Size:	38,000 square feet; six levels

Bakhita Gardens stands as an excellent example of the role that great design can play in contributing to the well-being of the users of a built environment. The facility uses specific design strategies to balance sometimes competing needs for the betterment of the single, adult women who call Bakhita Gardens home. The design balances such competing needs as security with visibility and ease of access, individual privacy with community connectivity, and personal control with the resident policies agreed to by residences and supported by the Catholic Housing Services staff.

While it may seem like a small feature of Bakhita Gardens, the entrance fronting the main street rather than the alley is an intentional way for the architect, Bill Singer of Environmental Works Community Design Center, to invite residents into the interior with dignity. Staff offices are distributed across the resident levels of the facility to offer a sense of security for the residents, but the offices are arranged in such a way to embrace sightlines strategically so that residents do not feel as though they are under surveillance. Each resident has her own personal cubicle with 54-inch high partitions that includes a bed, lockable storage, shelving for display, a personal refrigerator, and lighting with a localized control. These cubicles provide residents with a sense of visual privacy without being cut off from their community audibly, security for their belongings, and the opportunity to personalize their space while also exercising control over their space.

Community spaces, such as the dining room, provide residents with options to engage in conversation, or to retreat to a window seat with a view of the bustling city below while still being able to engage with a group if they so choose. Amenities such as the media room, library, and basement storage offer residents with

The contemporary architecture stands with pride in context with the other buildings of immediate vicinity.

opportunities to socialize and engage with one another, better themselves through study and professional preparation, and securely store additional belongings where they can be accessed conveniently. The open-air raised deck offers fresh air, views of the city and surrounding neighborhood from an elevated vantage point, and a small garden for those who wish try their hand at horticulture. The interior of Bakhita Gardens embraces tall proportions with its high ceilings as a way to welcome maximum daylight to the interior in a climate known for its cloudy weather. The color palette is calm and subdued, offering a safe haven from the occasionally hostile outside world, and the art features inspirational female subject matter as a consistent reminder to the residents that they are strong, capable, and valued.

Environmental Works Community Design Center "empowers Washington's most vulnerable people and communities to create the spaces they need to succeed." For more information on Bakhita Gardens, and other

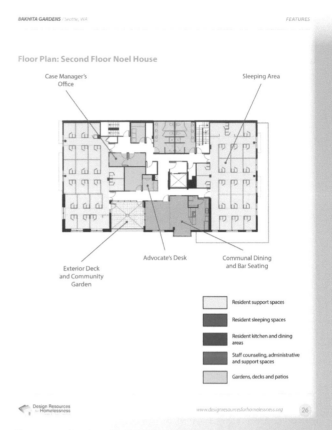

Floor Plan: Second Floor Noel House

Case Manager's Office

Sleeping Area

Exterior Deck and Community Garden

Advocate's Desk

Communal Dining and Bar Seating

Resident support spaces

Resident sleeping spaces

Resident kitchen and dining areas

Staff counseling, administrative and support spaces

Gardens, decks and patios

Design Resources for Homelessness   www.designresourcesforhomelessness.org   26

The space planning clearly delineates functions of the interior, providing residents with privacy, security, and opportunities for socialization.

The artwork at Bakhita Gardens is locally crafted, uplifting in subject matter, and strategically placed to provide interesting views throughout the facility.

Sleeping areas provide each resident with visual privacy and the ability to secure personal belongings in a largely open setting.

projects in the Washington state area by Environmental Works, visit http://eworks.org/.

Design Resources for Homelessness is "a non-profit initiative dedicated to the positive potential of the built environment for healing and recovery." The founder and project lead of Design Resources for Homelessness is Jill Pable, PhD, FIDEC, ASID, and professor in the Department of Interior Architecture and Design at Florida State University. Jill has devoted ten years of research to studying effective built environments for helping homeless persons. For more information about Bakhita Gardens and other housing solutions for the homeless, please visit the Design Resources for Homeless website at: http://designresourcesforhomelessness.org/.

The rooftop terrace includes gardens for the residence to tend while overlooking the city.

and facilities professionals the opportunity to specialize. Most interior designers choose to focus on the ID+C specialty, which includes sections that address location and transportation (LT), water efficiency (WE), energy and atmosphere (EA), materials and resources (MR), and indoor environmental quality (EQ). The LEED system offers several levels of certification for a project based on the degree of sustainability for the overall project—certified (basic), silver, gold, and platinum (LEED, 2018). Professionals must pass the LEED exam based upon specialty and work on LEED certified project in order to become an accredited professional, or LEED-AP.

A relatively new standard that incorporates sustainability ideals while extending beyond the ecological aspects is the WELL Building Standard administered by the International WELL Building Institute (Fig. 4.20). This standard "is a performance-based system for measuring, certifying, and monitoring features of the built environment that impact human health and wellbeing, through air, water, nourishment, light, fitness, comfort, and mind" (Knox, 2015). Each of the seven categories contribute to an overall wellness rating for a project, similar to how the LEED system is evaluated and scored.

Figure 4.20 The International Well Building Institute standards emphasize seven components of well-being in the built environment: air, water, nourishment, light, fitness, comfort, and mind.

Summary

The responsibility of every designer is to create spaces where human well-being is the primary focus. The qualities related to human physiological and psychological well-being dictate how we all use interior spaces and our shared humanity justify the need for equitable access to all portions of the built environment for all users. Scientific developments stemming from observations of the human body and behavior have resulted in actionable data in anthropometrics, ergonomics, and proxemics. Theories of human psychological needs (Maslow's hierarchy of needs), prospect-refuge, territoriality, privacy, and personalization all offer guidelines to help the designer craft space where users can thrive psychologically. Sustainable design and construction practices address the ecological, economical, and health interrelationships found in the built environment. The designer must adopt a holistic view of these topics on spatial well-being in order to craft spaces that are truly human centered.

Key Terms

Aesthetics and beauty	Leadership in Energy and	Prospect-refuge theory	Territoriality
Aging in place	Environmental Design	Proxemics	Touch
Anthropometrics	(LEED)	Safety	Transcendence
Barrier-free, or accessible	Life cycle	Self-actualization	Universal design
Biomimetic	Love and acceptance	Self-esteem	
Building-related illness	Maslow's hierarchy of needs	Sensory disabilities	
Closed-loop	Mobility challenges	Sick building syndrome	
Ergonomics	Personalization	Sight	
Hearing	Phototherapy	Smell	
Knowledge and	Physiological	Sustainable development	
understanding	Privacy	Taste	

Resources

Bromberg, J. (2016, July 14). *How the 5 Senses Help Inspire Workplace Productivity*. Retrieved July 7, 2017, from *http://convene.com/engage-5-senses-inspire-workplace-productivity/*.

Connell, B., Jones, M., Mace, R., Mueller, J., Mullick, A., Ostroff, E., Sanford, J., Steinfeld, E., Story, M., Vanderheiden, G. (1997, April 1). *The Principles of Universal Design*. In *The Center for Universal Design*. Retrieved from https://projects.ncsu.edu/design/cud/about_ud/udprinciplestext.htm.

Dosen, A. S., & Ostwald, M. J. (2016). Evidence for Prospect-Refuge Theory: a Meta-analysis of the Findings of Environmental Preference Research. *City, Territory and Architecture*, 3(1), 4.

Hall, E. T. (1910). *The Hidden Dimension* (Vol. 609). Garden City, NY: Doubleday.

HOK. (n.d.). *Workplace Strategies that Enhance Performance, Health and Wellness*. Retrieved July 7, 2017, from http://www.hok.com/thought-leadership/workplace-strategies-that-enhance-human-performance-health-and-wellness/.

Jaffe, E. (2013, December 23). *Want to Be More Productive? Buy Some Desk Plants*. Fast Company. Retrieved July 07, 2017, from https://www.fastcodesign.com/3021742/evidence/want-to-be-more-productive-buy-some-desk-plants.

Klara, B. (2012, March 04). *Something in the Air*. Adweek. Retrieved July 7, 2017, from http://www.adweek.com/brand-marketing/something-air-138683/.

Knox, N. (2015, April 2). *What is WELL?* Retrieved July 17, 2017, from https://www.usgbc.org/articles/what-well.

LEED. (2018). About LEED. Retrieved from https://www.usgbc.org/articles/about-leed.

McDonough, William. (2002). *Cradle to Cradle: Remaking the Way We Make Things*. New York: North Point Press.

Treasure, J. (2012). Retrieved July 07, 2017, from https://www.ted.com/talks/julian_treasure_why_architects_need_to_use_their_ears. This talk was presented and filmed in June 2012 at TEDGlobal 2012.

World Commission on Environment and Development. (1987, August 4). *Development and International Economic Co-Operation: Environment*. Retrieved July 17, 2017, from https://documents-dds-ny.un.org/doc/UNDOC/GEN/N87/184/67/IMG/N8718467.pdf?OpenElement.

Zhang, T., & Dong, H. (2009). *Human-Centred Design: An Emergent Conceptual Model*. London: Royal College of Art.

Review Questions

1. How do each of the five senses impact the interpretation of the built environment?
2. How does the Americans with Disabilities Act attempt to address mobility and sensory disabilities within the built environment?
3. How can anthropometrics be useful in designing interior environments?
4. What types of spaces and objects within spaces are influenced by ergonomics? If ergonomic data is ignored, what are the possible impacts of users of a space?
5. Describe how the design of the built environment relates to each tier of the eight-tier Maslow's hierarchy of needs. Some answers will connect to users of spaces, while other answers will connect to the design practitioner.
6. Describe how territoriality, privacy, and personalization relate to one another and how they differ from one another in the built environment. Provide situational examples to explain your answers.
7. Describe each of the categories of spatial proxemics in the context of your classroom, or other space that includes each of the four categories.
8. Describe the need to balance ecology and economy in context with sustainability. What are some potential scenarios where one may require more emphasis than the other? What is the designer's role in striking this balance?

Exercises

Senses Exercises

Visit a dining establishment and record your experience with photography, sketches, and writing.

1. Start with your approach of the main entry and analyze each phase of the experience through your senses. Provide photos or drawings as appropriate along with written descriptions detailing each phase of the experience through your senses.
2. Your document should be organized by experiential phase chronologically with subcategories under each phase based on type of sensory experience. As many of the sensory experiences should be described as possible.

Greater Good Exercises

Volunteer for a local charity or service organization, such as homeless shelter, soup kitchen, or Habitat for Humanity, and document your experience.

1. Describe the process of your volunteer experience starting with your initial contact with the organization or coordinator of volunteers and progressing through the completion of the volunteer activity. Analyze your experience in light of the eight-tier Maslow's hierarchy of needs.
2. Your document should be organized by experiential phase chronologically with subcategories under each phase based on the tiers of Maslow's hierarchy of needs. As many of the tiers should be described as possible in connection with your experience.

5

Color Theory

Learning Objectives

As a result of reading this chapter, students will

1. Possess an awareness of the scientific influences on color perception.

2. Possess an understanding of the difference between color as light compared to color as substance.

3. Possess an awareness of color schemes, warm and cool colors, and the psychological impacts of color.

As a result of taking part in the learning exercises at the end of this chapter, students will

1. Demonstrate the ability to identify and analyze color schemes in existing interior environments.

Introduction

Color is a complex aspect of interior design, divided into two primary topics: color as light and as substance. While the two are different from one another, they do interact and inform one another. As color has been analyzed and extensively studied, theorists have developed testable methods to systematically describe color, with the Munsell Color System leading the way. Based on this system, artists and designers utilize the color wheel and the variety of color schemes found within. Alongside the systematic methodology to address color, designers must also understand the influence of sociological and psychological factors that play a role in the way occupants perceive color. Building on these knowledge areas, and the topics addressed in Chapter 1, the designer is called upon to wield color in concert with the breadth of the elements and principles of design. The designer is also expected to consider the longevity of a design due to the application of color and to the transition between spaces in relation to color. Lastly, communicating design intent through color utilizing drawings and samples of finishes and furniture selections is discussed as a primer for Chapter 8, the planning chapter, where visual communication techniques are addressed in more detail.

The designer's mastery of color is proportional to their knowledge of this subject area plus their ability to apply the design thinking process. Beginning with empathy, applied in this context as seeking to understand the client's needs and desires related to color, the designer defines color-related problems, and then begins the ideation process where possible solutions may be found. In particular relation to color, the progression from ideation through prototyping and into testing can require many iterations. Color is often perceived with a certain measure of subjectivity, sometimes the client has difficulty in articulating their preferences. In cases such as these, the designer should strive for patience, which is founded in empathy, as she or he guides the client through the ideation, prototyping, and testing stages of design thinking until a design solution that addresses all color-related design problems can be found.

Color as Light

Color can be described as either light or as substance. While the mechanics of each are somewhat different from one another, the two modes of understanding color depend on one another. For example, without light, color does not exist. The application of light within the built environment is discussed in the lighting chapter (Chapter 11), and here the discussion will focus on the science of light and how color is experienced in the visible spectrum.

A small portion of the electromagnetic spectrum, known as **visible light**, is detectable by the human eye. The visible light spectrum is located between the infrared and ultraviolet rays and ranges from 700 nanometers on the longer wavelength end to 390 nanometers on the short wavelength end (Fig. 5.1). Isaac Newton, in his work Optiks, written in 1671, describes the order of color on the visible light spectrum from long to short wavelength as red, orange, yellow, green, blue, indigo, and violet, or abbreviated ROY G BIV. Today, we tend to replace blue with cyan and indigo with blue resulting in red, orange, yellow, green, cyan, blue, and violet, but the ROY G BIV abbreviation is still useful in recalling the spectrum order of the colors. Daylight, also known as **white light**, contains all the colors of the visible spectrum, which can be demonstrated by passing white light through a prism and viewing the colors on a white surface (Fig. 5.2).

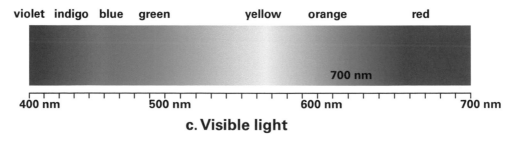

Figure 5.1 Visible light is only a small portion of the entire light spectrum.

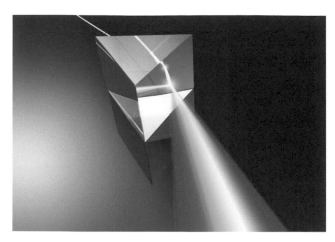

Figure 5.2 White light, such as that generated by the sun, includes all of the colors in the visible light spectrum—red, orange, yellow, green, blue, indigo, and violet.

The **primary colors of light** are red, green, and blue. The **secondary colors of light** are created by mixing two primary colors:

Red + green = yellow

Green + blue = cyan

Blue + red = magenta

This mixing of primary colors by overlapping light colors to create the secondary colors is known as the **additive method** of mixing colors (Fig. 5.3). When all three primary colors overlap one another in equal portions, or intensities, white light will result.

Light can also be described by its relative color temperature, as warm or cool. As mentioned, color as substance relies upon light in order to be visible (Fig. 5.4). As such, the relative color temperature of light influences the

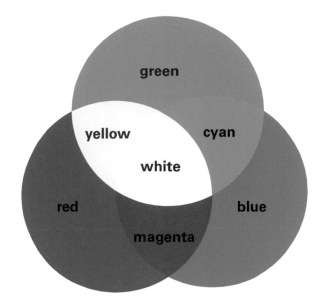

Additive color process

Figure 5.3 The additive method of color mixing applies to light, which overlays two primary colors to create a secondary color. As more light is added, the color becomes white.

perception of an object's color. **Warm light** accentuates warm pigments and neutralizes cool pigments. Likewise, **cool light** accentuates cool pigments and neutralizes warm pigments. A designer has the responsibility to coordinate the selection of color with type of electric lighting source, warm or cool, which is discussed in the lighting chapter (Chapter 11). Daylight also possesses these same qualities of warm and cool, depending on the time of day. Morning light tends to be cool and crisp, accentuating green, blue, and violet tones, while afternoon light is characterized as warm and emphasizes red, orange, and yellow tones.

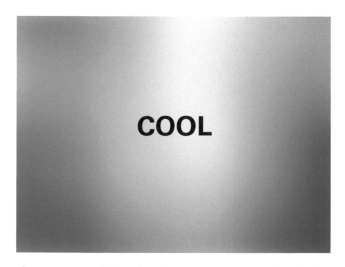

Figure 5.4 Warm light and cool light affects the perception of color.

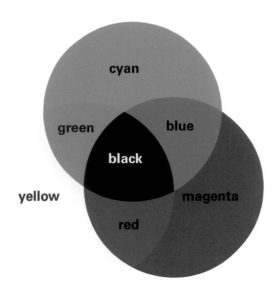

Substractive color process

Figure 5.5 The subtractive method of color mixing applies to substances, such as pigments, which combines two primary colors to create a secondary color. As more is added, the color becomes black.

Color as Substance

Understanding the qualities of color as light is foundational to possessing a clear understanding of color as a substance, or pigment, such as wall paint or textile dyes. With substance, color is understood through the **subtractive method** of mixing colors (Fig. 5.5). As white light strikes a surface, all colors of light are absorbed, or subtracted, with only certain colors of light being reflected and then interpreted by the human eye. For example, a red apple appears red because only the red wavelength of visible light is reflected by the apple's surface. In this method, as more color is added, the mix becomes darker, trending toward black.

To mix pigments, and put the subtractive method of color mixing into practice, one must first understand the primary and secondary colors. The primary colors are magenta, yellow, and cyan, and the secondary colors, red, green, and blue, are created by mixing two primary colors. The color wheel helps to visualize this relationship between primary and secondary colors.

Munsell Color System

Several color systems have been developed spanning several centuries, but it is the Munsell Color System,

published in 1905, that has emerged as the dominant color system standard today. Albert H. Munsell developed the three dimensions of color—hue, value, and chroma—and then visualized the relationship between these three dimensions with a three-dimensional color chart in an effort to describe color in a clear and objective manner that did not rely on subjective color names to describe color (Fig. 5.6). The problem of confusing color names, such as "desert rose" or "sea foam," is only accentuated today as paint manufacturers ascribe names to paint colors

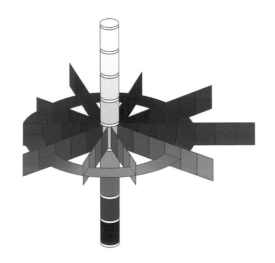

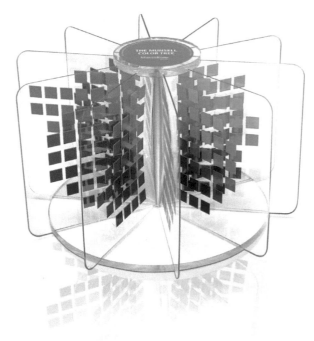

Figure 5.6 The Munsell Color System clearly describes color in terms of hue, value, and chroma.

that do not consistently describe color properties. Using the **Munsell Color System**, hue is measured in radial degrees, similar to pie pieces, around a central vertical axis; value is measured by the central axis on a scale of 0 (black) to 10 (white) from bottom to top; and chroma is measured in distance away from the central value axis, with the more saturated colors at the outer edge and the muted colors at the center close to the vertical axis.

Three Dimensions of Color

The three primaries and three secondaries are considered pure colors, but a full understanding of color, and how to mix colors, requires a more nuanced knowledge base. To fully describe color, one must also grasp three dimensions of color known as hue, value, and chroma. **Hue** describes the basic category of the color based on the three primaries and three secondaries—red, yellow, blue, orange, green, and violet. Colors that fall between the six pure colors are described with combinations of the pure colors, such as red-violet, green-blue, and orange-yellow, with the first hue in this description indicating the more dominant of the two hues in the combination. **Value** describes the brightness of a color, where adding white

will lighten a color to create a **tint** and adding black will darken a color to create a **shade**. **Chroma** refers to the intensity of a color, where adding gray or the complement of a color will result in a **tone** that is muted compared to the fully saturated original (Fig. 5.7). These three qualities—hue, value, and chroma—can be combined in various ways to create millions of colors, and can be expressed numerically, such as with computer graphics software, in order to precisely create and select colors for use in the built environment.

The Artists' Color Wheel and Color Schemes

The standard **artists' color wheel** can be described as the middle layer of Munsell's Color System at maximum chroma, or only including the outermost ring of color divisions (Fig. 5.8). The three primaries of red, yellow, and blue; three secondaries of orange, green, and violet; and also six tertiary colors are included in the artists' color wheel. **Tertiary colors** are the combination of a primary and secondary color such as red and orange to create red-orange. Utilizing the color wheel, an artist or designer can then develop specific color schemes.

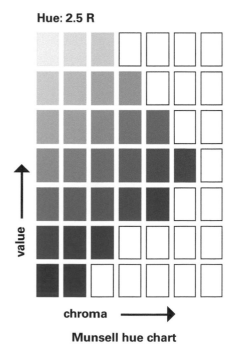

Hue: 2.5 R

value →

chroma →

Munsell hue chart

Figure 5.7 A single hue can possess a variety of value and chroma properties.

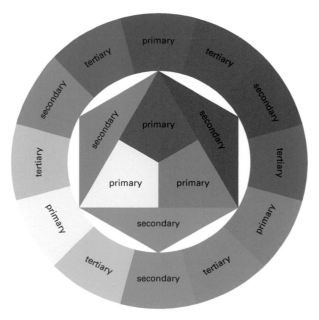

Figure 5.8 The artist's color wheel with primary, secondary, and tertiary colors establishes the basis for color schemes.

All of the colors on the color wheel, and their infinite variants based on the three dimensions of color, can be described as either warm or cool (Fig. 5.9). The **warm colors**, red-violet through yellow on the color wheel, possess characteristics that differ from the **cool colors**, green-yellow through violet on the color wheel. Under balanced lighting conditions, warm colors tend to advance visually compared to cool colors. Designers can use this to their advantage when employing certain design principles in a space, such as hierarchy, contrast, and proportion. Warm colors will tend to make an object appear larger, or a surface appear closer than it actually is. For example, an orange ceiling of high chroma will tend to feel lower because it advances toward the occupant resulting in a proportion that feels compressed, whereas a light blue (tint) ceiling of low chroma will tend to recede slightly, resulting in a proportion that feels lofty. In addition to physical qualities, colors also possess certain psychological and cultural qualities, which will be discussed later in this chapter.

Achromatic color schemes use white, black, and variations of gray (Fig. 5.10). This first color scheme does not use the color wheel, but can be understood by looking only at the vertical value axis of Munsell's Color System. A variation on this type of color scheme integrates an **accent** color, or material such as wood, to draw the eye, adding emphasis (Fig. 5.11).

Monochromatic color schemes focus on a single hue and add variety through tints and shades (varying the value) and intensity (chroma) (Fig. 5.12). The level of variety can

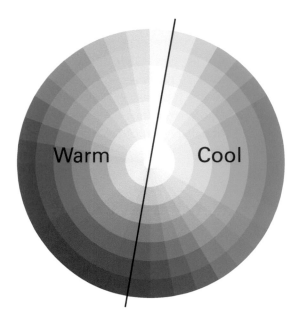

Figure 5.9 In general terms, and no matter the value or chroma, colors can be categorized as warm or cool.

be jarring or very subtle, depending on the degree of change in value and chroma. Monochromatic spaces that utilize bright saturated colors tend to make a strong statement.

Analogous color schemes utilize colors adjacent to one another on the color wheel such as blue, blue-green, and green (Fig. 5.13). These color schemes tend be low in contrast, but carry a dominant warm or cool quality, which can be particularly useful given certain lighting conditions. For example, in a west-facing space that captures warm afternoon sunlight and sunsets, an analogous color scheme of orange-yellow, orange, and red-orange could be very pleasing.

Figure 5.10 This space demonstrates the use of a warm achromatic color scheme.

Figure 5.11 This achromatic color scheme is cool while also integrating a blue-green accent color.

Figure 5.12 This blue monochromatic color scheme utilizes pattern, texture, and asymmetrical balance to achieve a unified and engaging design.

Complementary color schemes encompass several varieties, including direct-complementary, split-complementary, triad, and tetrad. **Direct-complementary** color schemes involve two colors positioned directly opposite one another on the color wheel, such as purple and yellow (Fig. 5.14). **Split-complementary** color schemes utilize a color and the two colors adjacent to its' direct complement, such as blue, yellow-orange, and red-orange (Fig. 5.15). **Triad** color schemes use three colors equally spaced around the color wheel resulting in an equilateral triangle configuration, as can be observed with a primary triad scheme (red, yellow, and blue), a secondary triad scheme (orange, green, and purple), or a tertiary triad scheme (yellow-orange, red-violet, and blue-green) (Fig. 5.16). **Tetrad** color schemes use four colors equally spaced around the color wheel in a square configuration, which can be observed with yellow, red-orange, violet, and blue-green (Fig. 5.17). Direct-complementary and split-complementary color schemes often possess high levels of contrast due to being located on

Figure 5.13 This analogous color scheme utilizes yellow, pink (a tint of red), and orange to create a warm environment.

Figure 5.14 The direct-complementary colors red and green garner the greatest attention in this cafeteria.

Figure 5.15 This composition illustrates a split-complementary color scheme through the warm orange-yellow color of the light fixture, the teal chair, and the violet blanket.

Figure 5.16 The bright sunlight accentuates the yellow and red alongside the blue in this triad color scheme.

Figure 5.17 The orange, yellow, blue, and green found in this lounge demonstrates the application of a tetrad color scheme.

opposite sides of the color wheel from one another, but the contrast level can be lowered by reducing the saturation toward more tonal variations of the hues or by utilizing all tints or shades of the hues. Triad and tetrad color schemes will be naturally lower in contrast between the colors, but this can also be manipulated by using one color that is highly saturated while the others are more muted.

Sociology and Psychology of Color

The sociological impact of color is greatly dependent on an individual's heritage and cultural upbringing, which can shape their personal preferences. A designer must spend time to thoroughly understand the cultural implications of color for the occupants of their spaces if they will practice outside of their home country. For example, red means something different in China (good luck, prosperity, and long life) as compared to South Africa (mourning, sacrifice, and violence). Yellow symbolizes jealousy and weakness in France, while the color is a sign of bravery and wealth in Japan. Blue is considered a masculine color in the United States, but viewed as feminine in China. With each of these contrasting viewpoints, it can be challenging to apply color across cultural lines, but these differences can also be celebrated, adding variety and interest based on cultural differences.

Within many Western cultures, however, some broad impacts of color on the human psyche can be observed. **Neutral** colors, often involving some variation of brown, can lead to a peaceful and calming space that can also embrace visual interest when strategically used in combination with subtle texture variations (Fig. 5.18). Achromatic color combinations of white, gray, and black tend to communicate sophistication, professionalism, or serenity, depending on the emphasis placed on black, gray, or white. Red colors have been found to influence appetite, which is often why many restaurants incorporate some variation of red into their interiors. Yellow is perceived as a very active color, resulting in increased movement and excitability, which can be a problem if used to excess in certain environments such as elementary school classrooms. Blue is associated with calmness, serenity, and focus, making it useful in some work environments. Green is thought to encourage the intellect, making it a potential choice for a classroom or child's bedroom. Violet correlates with opulence and formality for many individuals, which could work well in a corporate conference room. Orange is associated with energy and strength and

Figure 5.18 The neutral, or earthy, color scheme in this lobby space offers the occupants a calm respite from the busy urban environment outside.

Complementary Color Scheme Reinforces a Message of Entrepreneurship

Project: Jim Moran Building

Location: Tallahassee, Florida

Client: Florida State University

Architecture Firm: Architects Lewis + Whitlock

Occupants/Users: University students and faculty, business and industry leaders

Site Characteristics: Urban downtown, compressed site between two existing buildings

Year Complete: December 2017

Cost Estimate: $8.2 million

Facility Size: 20,000 total square feet; three levels

Project Overview

Dedicated to cultivating entrepreneurial growth, the Jim Moran Building is both a downtown Tallahassee extension of Florida State University and an urban hub for connecting students and entrepreneurs with professionals, business mentors, university faculty, and resources. The 20,000-square-foot renovation of a nineteenth-century bank building provides a setting that fosters entrepreneurship and honors the legacy of Jim Moran, a forward-thinking entrepreneur and automotive pioneer, whose story is woven throughout the facility with one goal in mind: inspiring a future generation of entrepreneurs.

The Jim Moran Building brings two groups together: the Jim Moran Institute, located on the third

Approaching from the parking garage, many visitors will experience the impact of the interior architecture.

floor, and the Florida State University Jim Moran School of Entrepreneurship (the nation's first at a public university), occupying the second floor. Jim Moran's business practices, as well as his life, were transparent in so many ways that it became fitting for the facility to reflect that notion of transparency as well. The front and back facades incorporate glass curtain walls over three stories, allowing views into the building from the downtown streetscapes exposing passersby to the impactful use of interior color. Pedestrians are confronted with the multitiered activity of business pitches, lectures, collaborative student activities, events, and a gallery of memorabilia and student works. Inside the building, meeting rooms, classrooms, and offices are designed to be open in plan and divided by glass partitions, where possible, to allow views and natural light to permeate through the building. The transparency adds to the sense of connectivity both within the building and to the surrounding business community.

Partial demolition of the second floor provides for the creation of a two-story event space, accommodating more than 200 people for banquets, lectures, expos, and presentations. The double-height space visually connects first and second floor activities through balconies and glass partitions. Whether it be the first-floor kitchen, the second-floor incubator, or the third-floor lounge, each level also contains collision spaces designed to bring students, faculty, and mentors together.

Challenged with low floor-to-floor heights in the existing building, the design team meticulously coordinated environmental systems and structure to get the most out of every inch of space. Exposed ceilings revealing framing, ducts, and conduit create the appearance of additional height while also celebrating the building systems.

Driving the Design: Weaving the Entrepreneurial Legacy into the Built Environment

The story of this facility evolved through several iterations, which all tie back to the ultimate goal of using architecture and place to inspire future entrepreneurs. Weaving the legacy of the ever forward-thinking Jim Moran with the building's downtown location, the design aims to create a welcoming environment with a dynamic street presence that facilitates both activity and contemplation.

This facility is a place to

- Connect mentors with students.
- Provide transparency of the entrepreneurship process to the community.
- Inspire students through the story and generosity of Jim Moran.

Throughout his life, Jim Moran preached the "three Cs . . . Consideration, Cooperation, and Communication." This facility not only embodies each of the three Cs, but it wouldn't be successful in creating a welcoming place for bourgeoning entrepreneurs without them.

The design of the monumental stair becomes its own piece of abstract art, a beacon to orient the visitor throughout the interior while adding to the story of the design.

Existing Building and Site Context

The existing bank building was vacant, situated on a downtown thoroughfare in the city's densest urban area. The site allows the building to serve as a downtown face for the university in its attempt to strengthen alliances with government and business mentors. The primary public entry is located on the west façade, while the east façade offers student and staff access to parking. Both sides of the building are equally distant from the chain of linear parks that cut through the interior of the city.

Cast stone and copper are found on the main campus as accent materials. For the Jim Moran Building, these materials are used as the primary palette to both tie the building to the university and create a distinctive landmark in downtown Tallahassee. The glass curtain wall of the west façade provides a strong visual connection to the interior for passersby, particularly at night as the red accent on the second floor garners significant attention. The east entry follows a similar strategy to allow the skillful application of the Sinclair green to influence the user's interpretation of the overall building. In this case, the green acts as a beacon, drawing visitors toward the entry from the parking garage. The design team addressed the impact of the predominant eastern sun exposure upon the interior through the use of a copper fin, complementing the green interior wall.

Interior Planning

A primary goal of the design is to allow light and views to penetrate throughout the relatively long and narrow footprint. Interior glass partitions are leveraged whenever possible to maximize transparency from the streetscape through to the interior planning. Beginning with the west entry on the first floor, patrons are greeted with a gallery containing memorabilia chronicling Jim Moran's legacy. The first floor also features a flexible 2,500-square-foot event space, a catering kitchen, a green room, and a lounge that invites informal conversations. The second floor houses the School of Entrepreneurship, which contains a pitch room, student incubator, and office space. The third floor contains a program room, meeting room, a scholar's library, staff offices, and ample informal meeting spaces. Each floor is linked with two stairways, one finished in "Toyota red" and the other "Sinclair green."

Interior Finishes and Color Palette

The interior color palette is largely an achromatic canvas punctuated by complementary red and green accents. Toyota red and Sinclair green, used as accents, are important colors in the legacy of the building's namesake, representing companies that Jim Moran helped to build. Exposed framing is meant to symbolize to students the notion that the entrepreneurship process is always unfinished.

The Toyota red stair carries the greatest visual impact within the project. A continuous wall graphic depicting the time line of the major entrepreneurial milestones in Jim Moran's life wraps the interior of this stair from the first through the third floor. The red backdrop was chosen for its significance with the

Each floor is carefully planned to provide for the functional needs of the organization and users. The stairs act as complementary anchors at opposing corners of the building while serving to tell the story of Jim Moran.

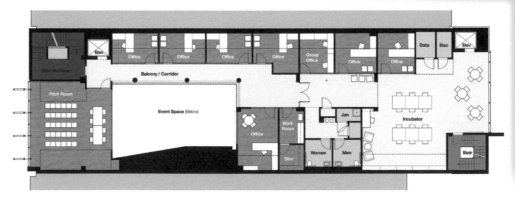

Second Floor

Sinclair Gas Station that he first owned, as well as Mr. Moran's pivotal role in bringing Toyota to the United States.

Following this same complementary color scheme set upon an achromatic backdrop, environmental graphics act as colorful and meaningful accents within the interior. Each piece of wayfinding signage and inspirational graphics is integrated into the design to create engaging spaces that are both easily identifiable and informative. Inspirational quotes in red and green from Jim Moran were selectively sprinkled along wall and glass surfaces in an effort to accentuate axial views and provide moments of visual hierarchy throughout the interior.

Architects Lewis + Whitlock is a full service architecture and design firm in Tallahassee, Florida, specializing in a variety of project types. For more information on the Jim Moran Building and Architects Lewis + Whitlock, visit http://www.think3d.net/.

The interior integrates a largely monochromatic color scheme that, when viewed across the whole of the project, is broadly complementary. The red and green color scheme works to carry the message of the design.

could find positive application in collaborative work environments or places for social engagement. Each of these associations between color and emotion should be treated as a generality, not as a prescription for applying color. The designer is ultimately responsible for understanding the desires and preferences of the client and then working to bring color together in a harmonious manner.

Color Synergies with Other Elements and Principles of Design

Unity, the overarching principle of design, dictates that all design elements and principles of an interior space work in harmony. Color influences each design element (form, pattern, texture, scale, and light), and it is the responsibility of the designer to wield color to achieve a unified design. Under favorable lighting conditions, form can be clarified, or even emphasized, with the use of color. For example, the form of a white curvilinear sculpture is clearly portrayed under daylight conditions, whereas the same sculpture may lose some of the interpretation of form if painted black. Variations of pattern are accentuated by introducing a complementary color scheme to a textile. Subtlety of texture on a wall can be expressed by using a monochromatic or achromatic color scheme. Scale can be communicated by using color to call attention to an object, such as a doorway or a chair, that is intended to communicate that sense of size as being human, large, or small (Fig. 5.19). Light affects all aspects of color, particularly in the pairing of warm or cool light with warm or cool colors—warm light enhances warm colors and neutralizes cool colors, while cool light emphasizes cool colors and neutralizes warm colors.

Color also plays an integral role in creating the various principles of design—proportion, balance, rhythm, hierarchy, and unity (Fig. 5.20). Warm colors have the tendency to advance, while cool colors recede in human vision, which can be used to make a space feel compressed or lofty depending on what color is used on the walls and ceiling. For example, an orange ceiling will cause the apparent proportion within the space to compress. High-intensity colors, such as a saturated yellow, should be used carefully and in low quantities, such as in accessories and accents, in order to maintain balance within a space. Colors used in alternation, sequences, or gradients can create a sense of rhythm within an interior. Hierarchy can be achieved through

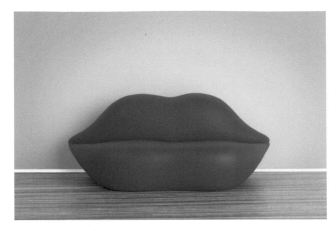

Figure 5.19 The high-chroma color of the lips sofa accentuates the oversized scale of the furniture piece.

careful contrast of color, possibly through one of the several types of complementary color schemes, or through the use of an accent color in conjunction with an achromatic color scheme. Employing several of these design strategies in conjunction with other elements and principles of design can contribute to an interior with strong unity.

Application of Color in the Built Environment

Understanding the science of light and color, the sociological and psychological ramifications of color, and the synergies between color and the other elements and principles of design enables the designer to apply color skillfully within the built environment. In conjunction with these strategies, the designer should also keep in mind that color preferences often follow the fashion of the times, flowing in and out of favor quickly. Knowing this, the designer is well-advised to use trendy colors in a strategic manner that will allow the client to change some of the color applications as style preferences change and at minimal expense of time and funds. Due to the cost and time associated with replacing flooring, it is best to select a flooring material, such as hardwood or a neutral tile or carpet, that will coordinate well with multiple color schemes. Because walls and ceilings are relatively simple to refinish, repainting is one of the more cost-effective methods to freshen a dated interior.

After the primary interior surfaces, furniture and accessories are the next most influential aspects of color within a space. The cost associated with reupholstering

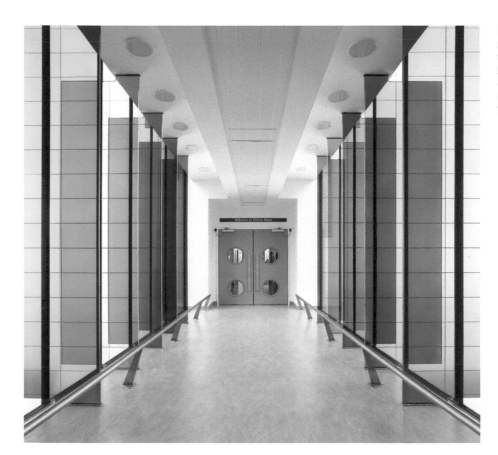

Figure 5.20 The variety of the colored glass partitions found in this corridor stands in strong contrast to the cool gray achromatic background materials and creates a very strong rhythm of progression as an occupant navigates this path.

a piece of furniture can vary widely, and can exceed the original cost of the furniture piece in some cases. As a result, selecting an upholstery that will weather changes in style and can coordinate easily with accessories is an excellent strategy. The ease and relative low cost of changing decorative accessories, including pillows, picture frames, and small items like lamps and candlesticks, allows for the following of fashion trends and making simple changes to a space on a more frequent basis (Fig. 5.21). By taking these cost strategies as they relate to color into account, the designer can build trust and long-term business relationships with their clients. In general, these strategies contribute to the three-part **Law of Chromatic Distribution**:

1. Floors, walls, and ceilings benefit from neutral colors that coordinate easily with many other colors.
2. Primary furniture items utilize a moderate intensity of color, pattern, and texture.
3. Smaller items, such as accessories, utilize strong chroma colors.

In addition to planning for color changes over time, the designer should also plan for color changes between

Figure 5.21 This simple lounge space utilizes warm white tones as background elements (floor, walls, and ceiling) and even continues this simplicity into the furniture, while relying on the small elements, such as pillows and the artwork, to express color.

spaces. When spaces join one another, or are visible from one to the other, the color scheme in each should relate in some way in order to create a harmonious transition between spaces and unify the overall design. One method that could be employed to achieve harmonious transitions between spaces is to begin with an accent color in one

Figure 5.22 This conceptual rendering of a retail environment utilizes simple and quick rendering techniques to imply the impact of color and lighting within the space.

space and then utilize a tint, shade, or tonal variation of that color as background color in an adjacent space.

Communicating Design Intent through Color

Describing the impact of color within a proposed design is a key part of creating excitement and soliciting support from the client. As discussed earlier, the designer will coordinate color with the other elements and principles of design to achieve a holistic and unified design solution. Before the design can become built space, the designer must visually communicate the design ideas and prototypes through the testing step of design thinking in a face-to-face meeting with the client. Visual communication methods include

- Drawings: loose or refined hand sketches in plan, elevation, and perspective; or digitally generated drawings of the same types (Fig. 5.22).
- Finishes: physical samples of materials for the floors, walls, ceilings, upholstery, and window treatments among others;

- Selection Images: furniture, light fixtures, plumbing fixtures, and/or door hardware selections.

Rendered drawings, including plans, loose sketches, and refined three-dimensional perspectives, can quickly communicate the impact of color in context with other elements and principles of design. Finish selections, including flooring samples (wood, tile, stone, carpet, etc.), wall finish samples (paint, wall coverings, wood paneling, etc.), ceiling finishes (paint, acoustical ceiling tiles, wood, etc.), and textiles proposed for window treatments, whether they are loosely displayed on a table for a meeting or formally composed upon a finish board, allow the client to see the finishes, and their colors, in context with one another. Furniture selection images and the finishes that accompany the furniture pieces, including wood, laminate, and metal finishes, along with their upholstery selections, help the client to understand the color impact within the space as well. It is very common for the designer to provide several options to the client in a meeting in an effort to gauge their preferences and speed up the design process. The tools and drawings designers use to present design proposals to clients is discussed in more detail in Chapter 8, Planning.

Summary

The communication and application of color within the built environment is founded on a thorough understanding of color knowledge and the ability to carefully apply the steps of design thinking. Understanding the science of color as light and substance, the Munsell Color System, and the color wheel and color schemes that grow from there is foundational. Overlaying the sociological and psychological perceptions upon color selection will bring a specific contextual relevance to the use of color in any design. Integrating color with the other elements and principles of design will contribute to a holistic and successful design solution.

Key Terms

Accent	Law of chromatic distribution	Tetrad
Achromatic	Monochromatic	Tint
Additive method	Munsell Color System	Tone
Analogous	Neutral	Triad
Artists' color wheel	Primary colors of light	Value
Chroma	Secondary colors of light	Visible light
Cool colors	Shade	Warm colors
Cool light	Split complementary	Warm light
Direct complementary	Subtractive method	White light
Hue	Tertiary colors	

Resources

Holtzschue, L. (2012). *Understanding Color: An Introduction for Designers*. John Wiley & Sons.

Itten, J. (1970). *The Elements of Color*. John Wiley & Sons.

Itten, J. (1973). *The Art of Color: The Subjective Experience and Objective Rationale of Color*. Translated by Ernst van Haagen. Van Nostrand Reinhold.

Jones, L. M., & Allen, P. S. (2014). *Beginnings of Interior Environments*. Pearson.

Long, J. (2017). *The New Munsell Student Color Set*. Bloomsbury Publishing USA.

Winchip, S. M. (2017). *Fundamentals of Lighting*. New York: Bloomsbury.

Review Questions

1. List the primary and secondary colors using the additive method.
2. List the primary and secondary colors using the subtractive method.
3. List the three dimensions of color and define each.
4. List the primary and secondary colors of the artists' color wheel. Identify the warm and cool colors.
5. List each of the color schemes and describe them.
6. In cultures that are not native to the designer, what must the practitioner keep in mind when applying color?
7. Describe the law of chromatic distribution.
8. What communication tools are most effective when describing color in context with the overall design intent of a project?

Exercises

Color Schemes

1. Photograph interior spaces that demonstrate each color scheme (achromatic, monochromatic, analogous, direct complementary, split complementary, triad, and tetrad) described in this chapter.
2. Your documentation should include headings that identify each color scheme and supporting points that critique the application of the law of chromatic distribution in each photo.

6

Professional Practice of Interior Design

Learning Objectives

As a result of reading this chapter, students will

1. Possess an awareness of the role of ethics in the practice of interior design.

2. Possess an understanding of the path to becoming a professional interior designer.

3. Possess an awareness of the different types of legislation affecting the interior design profession.

4. Possess an awareness of the role of interior design professional organizations.

5. Possess an awareness of the various roles within a design firm and specializations available in the practice of interior design.

6. Possess an awareness of the basic types of company legal structures, business relationships within the practice of interior design, and the basic types of legal agreements.

7. Possess an awareness of the various opportunities to procure fees in exchange for design services.

As a result of taking part in the learning exercises at the end of this chapter, students will

1. Demonstrate the ability to engage with designers and fellow students.

2. Demonstrate the ability to conduct an interview with a professional designer(s) and fellow design student(s).

3. Develop an understanding of the state of their local professional design organization(s).

Introduction

Design thinking may not be the first thing one considers when considering professional certification, creating a business, or contemplating the best fee structure for a project. All of the topics discussed in this chapter, however, do work to establish a business environment where design professionals can employ design thinking to reach creative solutions to complex design problems. Put another way, if a designer's mind is occupied with concern and worry over the poor business operations within the design practice, they may not have the capacity to employ design thinking in a project. Furthermore, every business encounters complex problems in accounting and finance, human resources, risk management, technology and information management, and marketing and promotion. The principles of design thinking could be utilized in this context to build a strong business with the greatest likelihood of success. The process begins with gaining a foundational understanding of the variety of topics affecting interior design professional practice. Depth and detail of these topics are left for specialized texts on the practice of interiors, which will differ based on location.

Ethics

Professional ethics impacts all areas of interior design practice beginning with professional preparation, or education. Certification, legislation, and professional organizations offer degrees of third-party oversight to ensure high ethical standards of practice. A firm, or business, is only as ethical as each member of the business, whether they are in a design-related role, a specialization, or a business operations role (Fig. 6.1). The legal structure of the business is established to provide a foundation for an ethical business environment. Each project is founded on professional relationships and a written agreement to outline the ethical practices that will be employed to complete the work, including the financial aspects of purchasing, fee structures, and billing.

Interior designers are expected to abide by the highest standards of professional ethics. The benefactors of these high standards include

- The public.
- Clients.
- Fellow interior design professionals.
- The interior design profession.

Many professional organizations publish a **code of ethical conduct** that follows this same four-part model. In the *public* forum, interior designers must

- Act in the best interest of the health, safety, and welfare of all users.
- Abide by all applicable codes and laws.
- Not sign or seal drawings for a project they were not involved with.

Interior designers must advocate for the best interests of their *clients* by

- Accurately representing their own or their consultants' education, experience, or training credentials.
- Clearly articulating the scope of the project, the fees to conduct the work, and method of payment, and must not change these agreed-to items without the client's full knowledge and agreement.
- Disclosing any conflicts of interest that could jeopardize the designer's ability to impartially render design services (e.g., if a designer has been contracted to design a furniture line and the designer earns royalties on sales of the furniture, then the designer may be inclined to specify that furniture on a project even if it is not the best option for the client).
- Keeping any private information regarding their clients confidential, whether they have specifically requested the designer to do so, or if the disclosure of certain information would damage their client.

Interior designers must respect their *fellow design professionals'* contractual obligations and relationships by

- Advocating honesty and integrity.
- Never plagiarizing another designer's work.
- Only taking credit for work they completed themselves, or was completed under their direction, management, or leadership.

Finally, in relation to the *interior design profession*, designers are expected to

- Conduct business in an ethical manner that reflects positively on the profession.
- Work to expand their knowledge and skill set in order to better serve the public, clients, and colleagues.
- Add to the body of knowledge regarding the profession.

Figure 6.1 The moral compass of the individual and the firm guides every action and decision in practice.

- Work to train up the next generation of designers.
- Represent their professional organization(s) with integrity.

Professional Preparation

The path to becoming a professional interior designer, also termed interior architect in many countries outside the United States, begins with a robust education in an accredited program of an institution of higher education. **Accreditation** relies on a thorough evaluation of the content and approach to education by an unbiased third-party organization, such as the Council for Interior Design Accreditation (CIDA) in the United States (Fig. 6.2). Accreditation is not a one-time occurrence but rather a cyclical process that serves to ensure that programs must *maintain* their accreditation rather than simply obtain the status and then reduce standards afterward. These standards are in place to help prospective and current students, and their families, know that the educational process at a particular program meets basic requirements to properly prepare graduates to become practicing interior designers one day.

Within the discipline of interior design, an ongoing tension exists between interior decoration and interior design as it relates to professional practice. In general, **interior decoration** focuses on the application of finishes and selection of furniture with some consideration to flame spread classification of materials within the built environment, whereas **interior design** includes

these aspects and the more technical aspects of space planning, comprehensive building code compliance, and construction detailing. The Council of Interior Design Qualification defines interior design this way,

> Interior design is a multi-faceted profession in which creative and technical solutions are applied within a structure to achieve a built interior environment. These solutions are functional, enhance the quality of life and culture of the occupants and are aesthetically attractive. Designs are created in response to and coordinated with the building shell and acknowledge the physical location and social context of the project. Designs must adhere to code and regulatory requirements, and encourage the principles of environmental sustainability. The interior design process follows a systematic and coordinated methodology, including research, analysis, and integration of knowledge into the creative process, whereby the needs and resources of the client are satisfied to produce an interior space that fulfills the project goals. (CIDQ, 2004)

Accreditation of interior design education programs and professional examinations, such as the **National Council of Interior Design Qualifications (NCIDQ)** exam, addresses the breadth and depth required in the practice of interior design. With that in mind, interior decorators provide an invaluable service, but nonaccredited degree programs may not be providing the necessary education and training that will allow an individual to become a credentialed interior design professional.

Figure 6.2 Accreditation in design education is a foundational component to becoming a practicing designer.

Certification

One of the primary interior design certification bodies in the world, and the only one in the United States and Canada, is the **Council for Interior Design Qualification (CIDQ)** which oversees the NCIDQ examination (Fig. 6.3). Several paths exist in order to be eligible to sit for the NCIDQ exam, but all require some combination of higher education and work experience in the profession. The exam is offered in two phases, a written portion and a practicum portion. The written exam content addresses several content areas, including building codes, FF&E specification, interior environmental systems, basic construction practices, contract administration, consultant coordination, and professional practice. The written exam can be taken upon completion of the education requirements for eligibility, referred to as the Interior Design Fundamentals Exam (IDFX), or upon completion of the education and work experience requirements, referred to as the Interior Design Professional Exam (IDPX). The practicum portion of the exam requires the participant to draft solutions to seven separate exercises that address space planning, lighting design, egress, life safety, ADA restroom planning, environmental systems, and custom millwork. The practicum can only be taken upon completion of the education and work experience requirements.

With the NCIDQ examination providing the foundational method of measuring competency in the profession, interior designers can also choose to seek certification in a variety of specialty areas in an effort to distinguish themselves from their peers. Designers who utilize the process of evidence-based design (EBD) in conjunction with health care design may benefit from the Evidence-Based Design Accreditation and Certification (EDAC) examination. For those seeking to focus on project management, many university programs offer higher degrees or certificate programs in project management specifically for designers. The Construction Specification Institute (CSI) offers several certifications for designers who specialize in construction documentation preparation and specification writing among others. The United States Green Building Council (USGBC) provides design professionals with the opportunity to become accredited in Leadership in Energy and Environmental Design (LEED) as they seek to complete LEED-certified projects. The International Well Building Institute (IWBI) offers accreditation

Figure 6.3 Written certification examinations, such as the NCIDQ, seek to set minimum qualifications for certified interior designers.

for designers who desire to specialize in designing spaces that promote health and wellness for the building occupants. Specialized certifications and accreditations often become necessary for design professionals as they advance in their career.

Legislation

Each nation, state, or province will consider the practice of interior design, or the title of interior designer (or something similar), in a different way. The jurisdiction of the regulation is within the district of the project location, not where the professional resides (Fig. 6.4). It is the responsibility of a practicing professional to understand the regulations that impact the location of the project in order to be sure that they can lawfully offer design services there. Some jurisdictions do not regulate interior design at all, while others employ a Practice Act, and others use a Title Act. A **practice act** requires that an individual be licensed to practice interior design, and declares it unlawful to practice without a license. A **title act** controls the use of a title, such as "Certified Interior Designer," in order to help the public understand which individuals have met the requirements to use the title as outlined by the governing body. A title act does not regulate the practice of interior design, nor does it prevent someone from performing such services, it simply controls the use of specific titles, which can vary from one jurisdiction to another.

Figure 6.4 Interior design legislation, in the form of a practice act or title act, will vary between nations and states/provinces within nations.

forty-seven chapters spread across the nation. ASID also reaches out to students offering student memberships, design competitions, and networking opportunities with professionals. The British Institute of Interior Design (BIID) is the oldest professional organization dedicated to the interior design profession within the UK. BIID serves the interior design profession within the UK through published business resources, networking, and promotion of work to potential clients. BIID is also affiliated with the International Federation of Interior Architects/Designers (IFI). IFI was founded in 1963 in Copenhagen, Denmark, and includes members from 110 countries across the globe. Currently headquartered in New York City, "IFI exists to expand, internationally and across all levels of society, the contribution of the Interior Architecture/Design profession through the exchange and development of knowledge and experience, in education, practice and fellowship" (IFI, 2017). IFI is also the founder of World Interior Day, an annual event on a global scale that brings the impact and value of interiors to the forefront of people's minds.

Joining a professional organization can provide many benefits. First, the professional community that an organization provides allows designers to share ideas and support one another through the regular challenges that many designers regularly face. Second, a professional organization provides individuals with networking opportunities

Professional Organizations

Several **professional organizations** serve the interior design community in an effort to unite design practitioners, share best practices, and enhance the role of interior design in society (Fig. 6.5). The International Interior Design Association (IIDA) seeks to provide its members with connections to other designers, clients, and educators; offers continuing education and timely research resources; and advocates for design across national boundaries. Spread across more than five countries in North, Central, and South America, with thirty-six chapters, the membership base is broad and includes practitioners, educators, and students alike. The American Society of Interior Designers (ASID) is the largest organization for interior designers within the United States with

Figure 6.5 Professional interior design organizations provide many benefits to members by offering networking among members, advertising to potential clients, advocacy for the profession, and access to research.

that can lead to improved employment opportunities. Third, professional organizations can be politically active depending on the status of design practice legislation in a given state, province, or nation. Depending on the jurisdiction, designers may face certain legislative hurdles to practice, and professional organizations can pool resources to lobby legislators and advocate for improved legislation in support of the profession. Most interior design professional organizations are locally organized with support from the national/international organization infrastructure. This local rooting allows each chapter to recruit members and address issues that are most relevant to their community of professionals.

Design-Related Roles within a Firm

Designers can play a variety of roles within a firm that range from entry-level positions to firm owner (Fig. 6.6). A strong education and professional certification and experience open opportunities for the designer to advance in position within a firm. Upon entry to the profession, a student begins as an **intern designer**, functioning in a supporting role on design projects. Intern positions can be paid or unpaid, depending on the situation and agreement between the intern and employer. A **junior designer** is someone who has completed their education and is logging work experience hours as they complete a variety of tasks in a support role on projects.

Once the NCIDQ exam requirements are met and the individual passes all parts of the exam, it is customary for a firm to advance the individual to a higher position of leadership on projects. As a **project designer**, the individual will likely be working on small- and medium-sized projects with some peripheral input from a senior leader in the firm, or with a team of designers on a large project. Depending on the size and completion schedule of a project, project designers may work on multiple projects simultaneously. Multitasking is part of being a successful designer, as it is rare for one project to complete and another to begin in perfect synchronicity.

Figure 6.6 Internal design team members, including design leaders and those in support roles, often brainstorm ideas and prototype design solutions together.

Project designers continue to gain experience on projects that increase in size, scope, and budget as they garner the trust of the firm's leadership and many interior designers will direct the design of projects, or choose to focus on managing the design team personnel. **Senior designers** often direct the design decisions of multiple projects simultaneously and direct the design of large, high-profile projects where several project designers may be responsible for some portion of the work. **Project managers** are seasoned interior designers that focus more on the operation and function of the design team, management of the design process schedule, coordination of consultants and specialists, and coordination of communication with the client. In an increasingly global community, designers may work on projects in a variety of countries, which will require the use of advanced technology for communication and transmission of design documents, knowledge of international cultures and building codes, and the ability to travel, sometimes for long periods of time. On occasion, design teams will temporarily relocate to be closer to the project site.

In small firms, a new designer can experience these various roles much earlier in their career than in large firms, but small firms tend to offer lower salaries. This tension between gaining experience quickly and higher compensation is a common issue for designers early in their careers, but as designers advance into leadership roles, the salary concern tends to resolve itself. Leaders in design firms set the direction for the company, mentor the less-experienced employees, manage firm finances, and make the hiring decisions. A firm leader can be strong in design, technical detailing, contract administration, managing projects, fostering client relationships, or business administration. In small firms, the owner is typically the leader in the firm and needs to have skills in each of these areas, while leaders in large firms can specialize in one or two areas.

Specializations

As described in the prior section, designers can specialize based on their roles in the areas of project design, project management, technical detailing, and other areas. The degree of specialization is sometimes determined by the size of the firm, as individuals in small firms tend to be generalists by role. Specialization can also develop based on project type, however. Individuals within firms can focus on residential, hospitality, retail, health care, corporate workplace, and many other project types. Small firms will occasionally specialize as well, focusing on one or two project types as they develop a reputation as specialists in certain areas. No matter the project type, the various roles described in the previous section will continue to exist.

Specializations can become very focused, such as with **kitchen and bath design**. Interior designers that are particularly well versed in designing kitchens and baths will complete the space plans and specify all of the intricate components, including finishes, millwork, appliances, hardware, and lighting. The National Kitchen and Bath Association is a trade organization that seeks to enhance the kitchen and bath industry through resources and certification for designers, standards for trades and installation, and awareness for and promotion toward consumers.

Many designers also choose to specialize as sales representatives of product manufacturers to designers, or specifiers, working in design firms. **Sales representatives** understand the design process intimately and have well-established contacts with other designers in firms, which makes them the perfect liaison between the product manufacturer and the designer who specifies the finishes, furniture, or lighting fixtures (Fig. 6.7). Sales representatives are assigned to a geographical area and visit firms within their territory to foster relationships and act as a resource to designers with the intention of increasing sales, or specifications, for their employer.

Figure 6.7 Design professionals can pursue a variety of design specializations, including becoming a sales representative for finish manufacturers.

Business Operations

Operating a thriving design practice requires great designers and personnel specializing in business operations. Operating a design practice can be divided into two categories: administration and project management. The administration arm of a design practice relies on a wide range of expertise, including accounting and finance, human resources, risk management, technology and information management, and marketing and promotion. It is important to note that these roles are considered part of **overhead costs**; they do not directly generate revenue for a firm, and, therefore, individuals dedicated to any of these roles will only be hired as the firm grows large enough to support them. Small firms also need these expert services, but they may be fulfilled by one person or some of these areas may be outsourced to a professional services firm. At some point, the designer who is operating a successful practice must learn to understand their own limitations and also to focus their time and effort where they can grow their business most efficiently. This is the time where a designer will begin hiring support personnel, or begin to solicit services from practitioners who specialize in these fields.

The administrative roles within a design practice often work in tandem with one another as they seek to provide a strong business operations foundation for the practice of design. **Accounting and finance** personnel provide a twofold role in overseeing the finances of a firm. First, they track the financial health of the firm as they ensure that monies are on hand to pay employees, provide payment for health insurance coverage, pay for malpractice insurance coverage, purchase new computers and software, and pay rent and utilities for the operation of the office space among many other things. Second, accounting and finance personnel work alongside design project managers to ensure that clients' fees for individual projects are being properly tracked so that the firm does not spend more time on a project than they will be paid for—this is how a firm stays profitable. **Human resources** personnel are experts in managing people, beginning with recruiting and hiring new personnel, analyzing options for employees' compensation and fringe benefits, conducting performance evaluations, and evaluating the grounds for employment layoffs and termination (Fig. 6.8). **Risk management** is a process that seeks to minimize the firm's exposure to legal risk, which starts before a

Figure 6.8 Human resources is one portion of the business operations team that is invaluable in assembling the best employee base for the firm.

designer begins work on a project, includes the writing of fair contracts, hiring competent and conscientious employees, purchasing appropriate insurance coverage in the event a suit is brought against the firm, and then appropriately managing disputes if and when they occur through mediation, arbitration, or litigation. The most expensive portion of risk management is the litigation portion, but this can be avoided if the early steps of the process are carefully employed. Most firms hire legal counsel from outside of the firm to vet their contracts prior to clients signing them and to represent them in the event of a suit or dispute, but some very large firms have internal risk management personnel. **Technology and information management** has grown in importance for designers through the digital revolution of the 1980s and 1990s and has grown more complex with the proliferation of mobile technology. Designers utilize graphically intense software that places stress on computer hardware that requires specialized knowledge to coordinate. As firms grow, access to information by multiple employees in diverse locations through a secure server becomes a must to complete projects on a global scale. **Marketing and promotion** personnel work to expand the business of the design firm by purposely seeking out the next client and developing relationships with them, fostering long-lasting relationships with current clients, and maintaining positive contact with past clients in an effort to secure repeat business. Part of achieving these goals includes digital communication tools such as e-newsletters and promotional email, a well-branded web presence through an engaging and informative website, and print media including postcards and pamphlets. The most valuable tool in a marketing and promotional effort is a satisfied client who will come back to the firm for future business and promote their satisfaction in the design personnel and final design to their business contacts. The business administration arm of a firm is complex, particularly in large multinational design firms, but can create a business environment that will allow the design process to operate smoothly.

The second portion of business operations, **project management**, acts as a bridge between the business administration side and the design side of a firm. A project team consists of a diverse set of members, including the client, design firm administrative personnel, the internal design team, the external consultants, and the contractors. A **project manager** (PM) serves to ensure that this team can work together effectively toward a successful end to a project (Fig. 6.9). The successful completion of a project requires the PM to have strong communication skills to uncover the client's definition of success for the project, strong leadership skills to motivate the internal and external team members to work together, the drive to complete project milestones on time and within the project budget, the ability to delegate responsibilities and tasks to the appropriate team members based on their skill level and drive to succeed, and a working knowledge of contractual obligations to ensure that project scope remains within the guidelines of the contract. Project management is foundational to achieving success on projects and it is no surprise that successful project managers often move on to positions of authority, influence, and ownership within design firms.

Business Legal Structures

Business legal structures vary widely based on strategy, number of owners, and exposure to liability in the event of malpractice (Fig. 6.10). For purposes of brevity, this discussion will introduce the legal structures of a sole proprietorship, partnership, corporation, and limited liability company. A **sole proprietorship** is a company owned by one person where the financial assets and liabilities are conjoined with the owner's personal finances. Positives of this business structure include the lack of certification requirements upon the owner, resulting in increased flexibility, the ability to make immediate decisions by the owner as the sole decision maker, and possibility of high profits and personal gain in times of business growth and success. Negatives include high risk due to the exposure of personal assets to claims in the event of a malpractice lawsuit or bankruptcy of the company during economic downturns, raising capital for expansion is restricted to the owner securing a loan on personal assets or making a higher investment from personal assets, and the business itself is not transferable to another owner in the event of the owner's death or retirement.

A **partnership** is an agreement between two or more individuals to own and operate a business and is much more complicated than a sole proprietorship. Business partners should clearly describe in writing the financial investment of each partner, authority and responsibility of each partner, the means to distribute profit and loss, the admission process of new partners, and the means to dissolve the partnership for any, or all, involved. Positives of this model include the relative distribution of liability when compared

Figure 6.9 A project manager is responsible for organizing all members of the design team in an effort to complete design projects to the highest level of craft on time and within budget.

Figure 6.10 The company legal structure provides the foundational elements that are used to operate a design firm over the long haul.

to a sole proprietorship, the freedom to offer a variable class of partnership where higher investment brings higher profit shares, and the business lives on in the event of a death or retirement of one of the partners. Negatives include a high risk factor compared to corporations and limited liability companies; raising capital for business expansion and operations is restricted to investment by the partners; and decisions can only be made through the agreement of the partners, which can limit flexibility somewhat compared to a sole proprietorship.

A **corporation** is a stand-alone legal entity, separate from the shareholders who own it, able to file a lawsuit and be sued by individuals or other corporations, and shields owners from personal risk beyond their initial monetary investment. Laws governing the establishment and operation of corporations will vary slightly from one state to another, which can result in a corporation possessing separate subsidiary corporations from state to state that report to the parent organization. Positives of this legal structure focus primarily on the ability of

the owners or managers to shield their personal wealth from claims against the company and the ability to raise capital through the sale of stock or bonds in the company. Negative aspects include the slow ability to implement changes into the corporate structure or to the methods of conducting business because primary business decisions are made by a board of directors.

A **limited liability company** (LLC) structure is a blend between a partnership and a corporation offering some benefits from each type. Laws governing the formation of an LLC vary by state, with particular restrictions occasionally in force for those offering professional services such as interior design. In some states, for example, the personal assets of an owner of an LLC may not be shielded from a suit or bankruptcy. In some states anyone can be an owner in an LLC, but other states require the formation of a PLLC, or professional limited liability company, where at least 50 percent of the owners are licensed to practice in that state. A designer must understand the laws governing LLC legal structures in relation to licensing within each state that the company intends to practice, as this could make it difficult, or impossible, to cross state lines in practice.

Professional Relationships and Agreements

The practice of interior design relies on a variety of agreements between the design firm and the members of the larger design team—primarily the client but also the consultant group and contractor (Fig. 6.11). These agreements are founded on strong professional relationships between the design firm and these external team members. The **designer and client relationship** is based on the designer acting as an advocate for the client, representing their best interests in all matters related to the design. Depending on the project type, the designer may become very familiar with the client's personal life, especially in context with residential design. The relationship should always remain professional, however, relying upon the written agreement established prior to beginning work.

The **designer and consultant relationship** is hierarchical in nature, where the consultants answer to the designer. Mechanical, electrical and plumbing (MEP) engineers, structural engineers, artwork consultants, commercial kitchen designers, acoustical designers, and lighting designers are common consultants to interior designers depending on the scope and complexity of a project. At times, the interior designer can act as a consultant to an architect if the architecture firm does not offer in-house interior design services, which alters the hierarchy of the relationship.

The **designer and contractor relationship** relies on the client as the central figure. The contractor is formally recognized as a general contractor (GC), particularly in the case of a competitive bid process where multiple GC companies are competing to win a project, or a construction manager (CM) in cases where a construction professional provides construction review services during the design process that offer suggestions to improve the construction efficiency of the design and also conduct cost estimations prior to construction bidding. A construction manager may then conduct the competitive bid review process by hiring the subcontractors. The designer and the GC or CM both work toward the completed construction of the project, which can occasionally include unforeseen problems or the need to reduce costs resulting in changes to the design. In these cases, the designer and GC or CM both make proposed changes to remedy the issue and the client chooses which solution to execute. This process is often complex, requiring the client to rely on the designer to advocate for their best interests and preserve the original intent of the design. In an ideal setting, when the relationship is strong between the designer and contractor, the GC or CM will be integrated into the design process shortly after schematic design is complete to offer feedback on ways to streamline construction and conduct cost estimates.

Interior designers utilize a letter of agreement or a contract to formalize the agreement with the client (Fig. 6.12). A **letter of agreement** is a short-form binding

Figure 6.11 Professional relationships are built on trust, work ethic, and camaraderie.

Figure 6.12 Written agreements are a critical component to creating clear expectations in any design business transaction of services.

Designer to Entrepreneur

Firm:	Studio M
Founder, President, Lead Designer:	Michelle Jennings Wiebe, ASID
Location:	Tampa, Florida
Established:	1991
Business Structure:	S-corporation
Project Types:	Luxury single-family residential (75 percent) and contract (25 percent; multifamily residential, student housing, residential clubhouses and sales centers, offices, restaurants)
Project Location:	Across nine states in the United States, mostly Florida
Project Size Range:	Single-family residential: average at 10,000 square feet, and over $5 million maximum at 36,000 square feet and $25 million
Contract:	Varies

The author engaged Michelle Jennings Wiebe in a long-distance interview in an effort to provide a candid description of her design practice from its founding through anticipated future endeavors.

Please tell the story of founding your firm.

I was young and didn't have too much to lose, so I just did it! My goal was to own my interior design firm five years after college graduation, but I had an opportunity come my way sooner than expected. I had worked as a design assistant for an interior designer in my hometown of Clearwater, Florida, during college (summers and holidays). She really wanted to hire me full-time after graduation, but she couldn't afford it. I was interviewing with several other firms in the southeast US, but it was during a bad recession causing many interior design firms to reduce staff rather than expand.

Long story short . . . the interior designer I had worked for as an assistant challenged me to go out on my own, and she would provide me with free office space and access to all her wholesale vendor accounts, samples, etc. In exchange, I would help her with her clients while developing my own clientele.

So I moved into her interior design studio, while borrowing $1,200 from my mother's employer. I bought business cards, letterhead, and a good typewriter! It's crazy to think back . . . this was before the internet and cell phones were rare. My old boss actually had a cell phone attached inside her BMW. She would occasionally let me borrow her car, and I thought I was big time driving her car and talking on that cell phone! I also spent some of the startup business loan on forming an S-corporation and obtaining business licenses. I paid back the original loan at $100 per month plus interest within 12 months and the wonderful person who loaned me the money also became one of my first clients!

This arrangement was in effect for the first four years of my business until she sold me her business due to her move to Chicago. I purchased her book of business and her vendor accounts, merging her business with mine.

How did your education and early training prepare you to become a business owner?

I loved my business practices course in college. As I was quite entrepreneurial by nature, I looked forward to this class. I referred to my handwritten notes (of course all in architectural lettering!) in my spiral notebook a lot as I was forming my business.

My education also provided me with confidence, because I graduated with honors from one of the top five interior design programs in the nation. My business minor provided some accounting and marketing classes that also gave me exposure to the world of business. My course load was rigorous, and I felt prepared design wise, especially coupled with my real-world experience of working for a design firm during college.

Side note: I highly recommend internships during college! At Studio M, we almost only hire those that have completed internships with interior design or architecture firms, as it is so helpful to have new hires with practical experience.

In the early years of your firm's history, what were some of the challenges that you faced?

Business owners have personal crises like everyone else and mine came right after starting my business. I began my firm in April 1991, and my mom was murdered in

June of that same year. Not only had I lost my beloved mother, but had a murder trial to deal with and became guardian of my 11-year-old brother. But, I didn't let any of these very trying and difficult times keep me from loving and growing my business. I flew home from my mom's funeral dedicated to making this new "normal" work in the face of the most challenging time of my life.

Professionally, the biggest challenges were obviously finding good clients, learning about revenue and expenses, and just keeping it all afloat.

Studio M specializes in high-end homes.

The selection of large, statement artwork coordinates with the cabinets.

As your firm gained a foothold, was there a point where you knew that your firm was going to "make it"?

Hmmm, I always knew it would work. I can't recall a day when I questioned that, even during the loss of my mom. I knew I wanted to own an amazing interior design firm, so I've been thankful and hard working from 'Day One'. I will say that the past five years have brought new and fun opportunities that made me feel like Studio M has risen to a new level, but we have so much more to achieve, and so many more fun clients to serve! I keep telling our team to stay hungry and to stay humble.

Did you have any employees when you first started, or did you add personnel later?

It was later. I actually taught a college class once or twice a week in the evenings during several years in the mid to late 90s. One of my drafting students said, "I want to work for you!" I told her that was sweet, but I had no positions (nor really the money to hire). She kept on asking. Then after several persistent months, she came in to class one Monday evening and stated that she had quit her other job, and she was starting for me that week.

Dumbfounded, I agreed, and she became my first part-time assistant! She worked for me for several years.

Fast forward . . . many years later, she went to artisan school to learn how to craft specialty artistic interior finishes. She now does work as an independent contractor for Studio M, creating unique finishes in our clients' homes.

How did you know when it was time to hire people?

Following my first employee, I would always have one or two assistants then gradually moved to hire a senior designer in 2003 when I was having our second baby! We were designing a large-scale commercial project at the time, plus many homes, and finally decided I needed HELP in a big way! From then on, our team would slowly begin to build.

In 2007, my husband Tom and I made the decision for him to join Studio M. He had been with a global investment firm for the first decade of our marriage, but he was traveling more and more with every promotion. We had two small sons at the time, and my business was getting very busy. So, we knew that one of us had to make some changes. At the suggestion of some relatives and many months of thinking about it, we decided to grow

Studio M into a larger firm with him coming on board. We quickly hired a marketing company to redesign our logo and marketing materials and launched our first website. We also hired an office manager along with several other designers. Since 2007, and even during the recession in 2009, we continued to hire more people and have never had one layoff!

When you consider hiring new personnel, what are some qualities you look for?

The candidate that excites us is someone eager to learn, passionate about design, and will mesh with our existing team. We have a wonderful team culture, so it is important not to bring in anyone who will disrupt this. We value prior experience (even if from an internship), and we desire someone who has a twinkle in their eye during the interviews. Speaking of which, we never hire off one interview. We have a series of meetings (three to four) with different existing team members, then typically a dinner before we extend an employment offer. We are looking for people who want to be with us long term and bring their best game every single day!

As you assess your firm's current standing, what are your goals for the next ten years?

Last year, one of our firm's goals was to "expand our borders" over the next ten years. We now have completed, or in process with, interiors projects in nine states! We plan to keep expanding in the US and internationally.

A second goal is to serve our clients with a "luxury client experience." This includes VIP client service, excellent design, 3D renderings, new technologies, and hopefully a new office building that represents our brand, fosters creativity, and helps our team operate more efficiently and creatively.

Other Ten Year Goals:

- We keep becoming more selective in what projects we take. For residential, we focus on large construction budgets of $400 per square foot and up, and a reputable architect or builder must be involved.
- Design a series of boutique hotels.

- Launch an online design media site.
- Continue to grow the team.
- Consider opening offices in other cities.
- Personally, I would like to write three to five design books within the decade.

What are some challenges that you expect to face, and how do you plan to address them?

We need to address practical needs, including time and money. I feel there is not already enough hours in the day, so I'm trying to delegate more responsibilities and tasks to my team in order to focus on some of the above goals and big picture items. Moneywise, we really don't like to take out loans. I've had minimal or no loans from the beginning, so my goal is to continue operating with minimal or no debt. We have grand goals and ideas, so this will certainly be a challenge! A second challenge is finding the right new team members. Right now, the economy is strong and it's difficult to find "A game" people. Lastly, fast-changing technology presents challenges, since it can be difficult to stay up on new software implementation, social media trends, etc.

The blue flowers coordinate with the upholstery to provide a pop of color in this monochromatic kitchen.

What aspects of your business structure appeal to you?

An S-corporation helps shield us from personal liability and to date has offered a good tax structure. We have also developed a good team structure. For our design team, we have a principal designer, director of design, senior designers, junior designers, design assistants, and interns. We also have an office manager, executive administrator, and several expeditors who handle the ordering process.

How do you manage risk?

Obviously, we carry insurance (general liability, errors and omissions, worker's comp, etc.). We also try to make good design decisions and good business decisions. My husband and I are always thinking through risk and liability in everything we do, including which projects we choose to take. We create a customized letter of agreement for each project that details our definite scope of services. It is important for each of our clients to know what they are paying for and what is excluded.

What are some strategies you employ to balance overhead costs with positive revenue streams?

First and foremost, we require a nonrefundable retainer (roughly 10 to 15 percent of the entire fee) up front with a signed letter of agreement. We begin *no* design work without these two items. The retainer is nonrefundable because we begin allocating team resources to the project, and may pass up on other work. We only take on so many new homes or projects a year.

Starting three years ago, we began asking for a 100 percent deposit on all merchandise (furnishings, lighting, area rugs, etc.). Before then, we had asked for 50 percent, but we found construction schedules were going over in length, and we had a warehouse full of furniture that Studio M had paid for, but not the full payment by the clients. This change has helped tremendously with cash flow and making sure we get paid in full.

The financial health of the firm is definitely a team effort. On an ongoing basis, I study what typical design fees and product pricing should be to make sure we are competitive. My husband oversees securing the best wholesale pricing from each of our hundreds of vendors. Our preferred buying power gives us higher profit margins and better prices for our clients. Our executive administrator secures credit from our vendors and oversees the daily data entry. We have several expeditors who handle our ordering process, and they are tasked with ensuring there are no errors.

On a big picture, we prepare an annual budget and stick to it. We watch expenses and try to maximize efficiency as we can. We have a CPA who prepares our taxes and gives us advice on larger financial decisions. I have been working with the same accountant since our founding! We also hired a third-party bookkeeper about four years ago who only works with interior design firms. This has been one of our best decisions. They now prepare critical monthly and quarterly reports, file our sales tax in several states, reconcile our accounts, and generally keep us aware of our financial standing.

What have you learned about yourself as a designer and business owner?

I have learned that hard work pays off and that passion matters!! You must want to get up every day and do what you are doing because you love it! After 27 years, I still *love* design and owning a business. I stay curious, and am always learning and asking questions. I've learned to tweak and expand my business with technology and new practices. I can't rest on what has worked in the past; I've become very forward focused.

My husband and I also invest in our team members by training and helping each of them discover what they do best. We have found that our team members do their top work when they are each working in their talents and strengths. It is a team effort, and we are very thankful for our entire Studio M team!

Studio M is a full-service design firm in Tampa, Florida, that specializes in residential design while offering contract design services as well. For more information on Studio M, visit http://interiorsbystudiom.com/.

agreement written in language that is more user-friendly to non-attorneys. A **contract** is a long-form agreement outlining in extraordinary detail all of the legal arrangements and binding relationships for all the parties involved. Both types of written agreements address the following areas:

1. Project scope.
2. Schedule of completion.
3. Parties involved and responsibilities.
4. Services to be provided.
5. Third-party involvement, such as consultants, and their services.
6. Price and payment process.
7. Intellectual property and photography of completed work.
8. Method to resolve disputes.
9. Terms for terminating the agreement.
10. Signatures and dates.

Professional organizations, such as ASID or the American Institute of Architects, offer form agreements for interior design services. Depending on the country of practice, it is wise for the designer to understand the legal ramifications of contracts in various nations and states or provinces. It is also advisable to solicit the services of an attorney specializing in contract law to review any standard or form contracts prior to using them. The primary written agreement for the designer is with the client, but designers also enter into written agreements with consultants. Because the relationship with the contractor is typically through the client, a formal written agreement between the designer and contractor is often not used. Clauses within the written agreement between the designer and client will often outline the responsibility the designer has to communicate with the contractor and to review the construction process on behalf of the client.

Purchasing

A designer may also be called upon by the client to handle the purchasing of goods, particularly furniture, appliances and other equipment, and accessories. In this case, the designer will need to clearly outline the method of purchasing, delivery, and payment structure in the letter of agreement or contract. In performing this service, the designer works with the client to select the goods, and any upholstery in the case of furniture, and the vendor(s)

to purchase the goods. Delivery to the project site is often handled by two distributors or shipping companies, from the manufacturer to a storage facility, and then storage facility to project site. Vendors typically offer designers a large discount on furniture, up to 50 percent below the retail price. The designer purchases the furniture and then sells the furniture to the client at a markup rate that is agreed upon between the client and designer. Due to the cost of storing the goods, it is in the best interest of the designer to strategically schedule the purchasing and delivery of any goods to coincide as closely as possible with the installation of the goods in the space.

In order for the designer to provide purchasing services, to act as a merchant in other words, certain applications must be filed with government agencies based on the local, state, and national laws of the project location. Generally, a certificate of authority is issued to the designer that allows the professional to purchase goods, resell them, and collect tax on the sale of the goods. The designer then transmits the tax payment to the government authorities, which could be multiple.

Fee Structures

Time is a precious commodity for designers as they provide their services to clients and a variety of structures can be employed to procure payment for these services, including hourly fee, a fixed fee for the entire project, an area fee on a per-square-foot or per-square-meter basis, or a cost-plus fee (Fig. 6.13). Hourly, fixed, and area fees are utilized for design services and cost-plus fees are used for purchasing services. Design services at their most fundamental levels are based on an hourly billing rate for each team member that is assigned to work on the project with more experienced team members, such as a project manager or project designer, commanding higher billing rates than those who are less experienced, such as a draftsperson. The **hourly fee**, and by extension the hourly billing rate, must cover the salary and fringe benefits of the design team member plus cost of the administrative team, because these team members do not generate revenue for the firm, and overhead costs of the firm such as technology, utilities, and rental costs for office space. These expenses can be expressed as a formula known as **direct personnel expense** (DPE), which is typically between two and a half and three times

Figure 6.13 Designers seek to be fair with their fee structures as they strike a balance between remaining competitive in the marketplace and making a profit. The designer's fee, including that of consultants, is part of the overall cost of the project.

the hourly salary of the design team member. In the case of a draftsperson who earns approximately $20 an hour, their hourly fee would be $50 to $60 per hour, or a project manager earning $40 an hour would command a $100 to $120 hourly fee. Design professionals often work on multiple projects in the same month, or billing cycle, which requires that each employee carefully tracks their time, often in quarter or half hour increments.

Flat fee structures utilize a fee amount that both the design firm and client agree to in the contract phase prior to beginning work on a project. Flat fee structures provide the client with a peace of mind in knowing what they will be paying in design fees, while the designer has the opportunity to increase profit margins compared to the hourly fee structure, or the firm could experience lower than normal profits, or even lose money on the project. The key to making flat fee projects financially successful is accurately projecting the number of hours that will be necessary to complete the project for all team members involved. Underestimating the required hours to complete the work could result in financial losses for the firm. To be correctly estimated, the flat fee structure relies on the DPE formula.

The **area fee** structure charges the client for design services based on the quantity of area that will be designed. This fee structure works well for firms that complete many projects of a certain type, such as workplace projects, so that they have extensive knowledge to draw upon when planning the fee structure in the written agreement with

the client. Similar to the flat fee, this structure relies on the DPE for accurate estimates of time and cost-per-area fees in order for the firm to make a profit on the project.

The **cost-plus** fee structure places a greater emphasis on purchasing services for the client by applying a markup to furniture costs. Furniture sold at trade shows or retailers that cater to the design industry offer large discounts to interior designers. For example, a sofa that a designer purchases for a residential client may have a retail price of $3,000, but the cost to the designer may be 50 percent below retail, or $1,500. Based on the agreement between the designer and client, the designer may charge a 25 percent markup above cost, resulting in a total cost to the client of $1,875. Under this fee structure, the client receives the expert services of the design professional and the furniture at a cost below retail. Residential projects are commonly organized this way with the designer's fee relying on a 25 to 35 percent markup above the discounted designer's cost, but contract projects that only involve furniture purchasing often have a much lower markup, approximately 8 to 15 percent, due to larger volumes of furniture purchases. Projects that involve a combination of space planning, new interior construction and finishes, as well as furniture purchasing may operate under two different fee structures.

A fee structure is selected based on the unique circumstances of the project, the comfort-level of the client, and the risk tolerance of the firm. Hourly fees are the safest for the firm with a low to moderate level of profit built into the hourly fee, but clients can view this structure as potentially costing them more in the end if the process gets drawn out. To provide a safety mechanism for the client, a "not to exceed" maximum fee amount will be stated in the contract, but this can put the designer in a difficult position financially if the contract does not clearly describe the scope of services. Any time the scope of services is about to be exceeded, the designer should notify the client so they are aware of the added costs associate with such an action. The flat fee is advantageous for the client as they will know with relative certainty what they will be billed for design services, but the design firm must be accurate in estimating the time in hours to complete the work in order to be profitable. The area fee is similar in that it allows the client to know with certainty what they will be paying for design services, but the design firm must have accurate metrics by which the fees can be established in order to ensure profitability. The cost-plus structure is useful on projects that emphasize furniture purchasing and provides the client with design services and furniture below a retail price point.

Billing Processes

Billing for design services can be a complicated process with the variation in fee structures, as the design firm must balance paying their employees and covering overhead costs with income from billings (Fig. 6.14). It is common for the beginning of projects to be particularly troublesome financially as the designer obtains a signed agreement with the client and begins work, but the billing cycle will not begin for at least thirty days after the project begins. Combine this with the standard billing arrangement where the client has thirty days to complete the payment for the first bill, and the designer may not receive payment until they have already been working on the project for sixty days. This is where a

Figure 6.14 Billing and receiving payment in a timely manner is a delicate balance for designers. The overall project fee is typically not billed or received in a lump sum but in installments as the project work is completed.

retainer, or an advanced payment to the designer at the time the client signs the agreement, is so valuable. The amount of the retainer will vary but will approximate the cost of services for the first thirty days of work.

Depending on the written agreement terms, the design firm may also be paid for reimbursable expenses. **Reimbursable expenses** include travel expenses for long trips or overnight meetings, and printing costs for large-scale drawings or photocopies. Ideally, reimbursable expenses should be integrated into the normal billing cycle in order to avoid "sticker shock" for the client if all reimbursable expenses are billed at the end of a project.

The written agreement will also dictate the **billing cycle**, or period for soliciting payment for design services from the client. The billing cycle could be on a thirty-day schedule, which works well for large and lengthy projects, or it could be based on the completion of project phases (schematic design, design development, construction documentation, and contract administration are common billing cycles by phase), which works well for small- and moderate-sized projects. Either way, it is standard practice for the client to complete the payment within thirty days of the date of the bill being issued. If this is stated in the written agreement, but the client does not abide by this clause, they will technically be in breach of the agreement. The agreement also should outline what recourse the designer may have if this happens, such as charging interest on late payments, or stopping the work until all payments and interest have been brought up to date.

Summary

The practice of interior design is founded on an ethical understanding that prioritizes the health, safety, and welfare of those who will use the space and the fiduciary, or financial, responsibility that designers have toward their clients. Complex problems that require creative solutions are not limited to the design of spaces, but they also arise in running a business. Designers, as business professionals, can also use their design thinking expertise to create the optimum business environment that will enable the design of great places. The following chapters, focusing on contextual factors for the built environment, planning, finishes, furnishings, lighting, and support systems, all rely on ethical business practices to be successful.

Key Terms

Accounting and finance

Accreditation

Area fee

Billing cycle

Code of ethical conduct

Contract

Corporation

Cost-plus

Council for Interior Design
   Qualification (CIDQ)

Designer and client relationship

Designer and consultant relationship

Designer and contractor relationship

Direct personnel expense

Flat fee

Hourly fee

Human resources

Interior decoration

Interior design

Intern designer

Junior designer

Kitchen and bath design

Letter of agreement

Limited liability company

Marketing and promotion

National Council of Interior Design
   Qualifications (NCIDQ)

Overhead costs

Partnership

Practice act

Professional ethics

Professional organizations

Project designer

Project management

Project manager

Project manager

Reimbursable expenses

Retainer

Risk management

Sales representative

Senior designer

Sole proprietorship

Technology and information
   management

Title act

Resources

CIDQ. (2004). CIDQ l NCIDQ EXAMS l Definition of Interior Design. Retrieved from https://www.cidq.org/definition-of-interior-design.

Demkin, J. A. (2006). *The Architects Handbook of Professional Practice: Update 2006*. Hoboken, NJ: John Wiley & Sons.

IFI. (2017). About IFI. Retrieved June 21, 2017, from https://ifiworld.org/about/.

IIDA. (n.d.). IIDA Code of Ethics for Professional and Associate Member Conduct. Retrieved December 15, 2017, from https://www.iida.org/resources/content/6/3/6/0/documents/IIDA-Code-of-Ethics_Designer.pdf.

NCIDQ Certified Interior Designers. (n.d.). Retrieved December 15, 2017, from https://www.cidq.org/find-ncidq-certified-int-designer.

Piotrowski, C. M. (2001). *Professional Practice for Interior Designers*. John Wiley & Sons.

Winchip, S. M. (2012). *Professional Practice for Interior Design in the Global Marketplace*. New York: Fairchild.

Review Questions

1. List the four parts commonly found in professional organizations' ethical code of conduct.
2. Describe the importance of educational accreditation for the interior design profession.
3. Describe the importance of professional certification for the interior design profession.
4. Describe the difference between a practice act and a title act.
5. List the design-related roles within a firm.
6. List roles of design specialization.
7. List business operations roles within a firm.
8. Describe the three business legal structures.
9. Describe the three types of relationships involving an interior design.
10. List the sections of a written agreement between the designer and client.
11. How does a designer make money by offering purchasing services?
12. Describe the relationship between hourly fee and DPE.
13. Describe the importance of a retainer and the importance of collecting reimbursable expenses from a client.

Exercises

1. Identify the interior design professional organizations in your district and determine which ones offer membership to students.

2. Contact your interior design student organization, if one exists, and establish contact with a more experienced group of students. Develop a list of interview questions that will help you decide the best course of action as you evaluate the positives and negatives of joining a local chapter in a professional organization. Interview at least one student. Consider joining the interior design student organization if one exists.

3. Contact a local firm that offers design services and establish contact with a designer. Develop a list of interview questions that will help you decide the best course of action as you evaluate the positives and negatives of joining a local chapter in a professional organization. Interview at least one professional designer.

4. If you do not have an interior design student organization at your university, consider starting one. If a professional interior design organization does not have a presence in your area, reach out to one and determine what is needed to establish a presence in your locale.

5. Document each step of your work and summarize the action steps and findings. Document your reflections on your findings and describe your intended future actions on the matter.

7

Contextual Factors of the Built Environment

Learning Objectives

As a result of reading this chapter, students will

1. Possess an awareness of the role of user demographics as an influencer of design outcomes.

2. Possess an awareness of the importance that a project location can have on the design of the interior.

3. Possess an awareness of the different types of construction systems, including wood, concrete, and steel construction.

4. Possess an awareness of the ideas that contribute to anticipating future design needs, both functional and aesthetic.

As a result of taking part in the learning exercises at the end of this chapter, students will

1. Demonstrate an understanding of the potential impact that location can have upon the success of an interior design.

2. Demonstrate the ability to evaluate possible locations for a project based on demographic and location factors.

3. Demonstrate the ability to observe a construction project.

4. Demonstrate the ability to identify the relationship of an interior space to grade, basic structural system types, and load-bearing components.

133

Introduction

Every interior environment has a complex set of contextual factors that influence the design process and outcomes. These factors include population and cultural influences of the people who will use the space, environmental impact related to the location of the interior space, and structural characteristics of the building that will contain the space. Each of these contextual factors are addressed in the design thinking process, as the designer seeks to empathize with the client and users, define the design problem, seek ideas for design solutions, prototype those ideas, and finally test and revise the design solutions.

Figure 7.2 Blurring boundaries between stages of life and age factors in combination with freedom for the mobile worker creates new and interesting design challenges such as child care in a workplace context.

Demographic Factors

Every built interior exists within a broader cultural context that must be taken into account by the designer when seeking to understand and empathize with the client. Cultural influences tied to a specific people group and location can help to inspire aesthetic and functional solutions for any design. On the other hand, if cultural influences are ignored, it can become very challenging for users to live, work, or play within an interior. The spiritual practices of a family, for example, profoundly influence the design of their home, which if not taken into account during the early stages of the design process can negatively affect the usability of the interior (Fig. 7.1).

Generational factors and an individual's personal or professional **stage of life** are also very influential in

Figure 7.1 Spiritual practices, such as celebrating Passover, are among many cultural influences that the designer must take into account when designing any space, whether private or public.

determining what functional qualities someone will need in a new design or renovation. In a workplace environment, individuals who are single, without children, and freshly graduated from university in an entry-level position will likely have vastly different needs and wants from their work environment when compared to those who are married with children and in a position of middle to upper management (Fig. 7.2). Recent studies are also demonstrating that the clean divisions of generational boundaries are not as useful in understanding the needs of users as collecting data on stage of life can be. Generational boundaries, or age, are not predicting when people go to college, get married, and have children as accurately as they used to. These traditional milestones are happening later in life for many people, which, when coupled with many people retraining for a new career, can further throw off the traditional assumptions of generation and age boundaries. The world is becoming more complex in relation to demographic factors, and designers need to develop improved ways of understanding their clients in an effort to create design solutions that solve their clients' problems.

Location Factors

Location factors include a variety of influential aspects, including the level of urban density and climate. Urban density can be categorized as either urban, suburban, or rural in order of population density from high to low. The U.S. Census Bureau defines **urbanized areas** as having

50,000 inhabitants or more, and **urban** as possessing 1,000 or more people per square mile. In lay terms, urban zones are often characterized by multistory buildings with a variety of uses (multifamily residential, business, entertainment, etc.) in close proximity to one another with significant infrastructure in place to address transportation and utility needs. The term suburban is not strictly defined by the U.S. Census Bureau, but is often characterized as containing mostly single-family residential structures with some economic activity clusters interspersed throughout. Suburban areas are often located around the edges of urban centers and developed in the 1900s as a result of improved rail services and roads for vehicular traffic allowing people to dwell in the suburbs and commute into the urban city center for work. **Rural** is defined by the U.S. Census Bureau as possessing less than 1,000 people per square mile. Visions of small towns, agriculture, wilderness, and forests typically characterize rural zones.

Figure 7.3 Urban and rural locations each have their benefits, which the designer must take into account when designing an interior.

Urban density influences interior design in a variety of ways (Fig. 7.3). First, real estate costs are often higher in dense urban zones, which translates into more efficient space planning in an effort to keep rental costs lower. In other words, apartments are smaller and more expensive in New York City compared to Erie, Pennsylvania. Access to amenities such as grocery stores, restaurants, dental offices, child care and schools, and entertainment hot spots can greatly impact where people choose to live and work. These amenities will likely be located more closely to one another in urban settings, which makes a big difference for office workers in varying stages of life—think back to the demographic factors discussed earlier. Another very important amenity is access to transportation, mass transit, and parking, which will also differ depending on urban density (Fig. 7.4. Views from the interior toward the exterior will vary widely based on urban density as green space comes at a premium the more densely configured an area becomes.

While not obvious on the surface, the project location's climate influences the design of the interior in several important ways. First, temperature, humidity, and pollution levels of the outdoor air will influence how often doors and windows can be left open. In excessively hot, cold, humid, or polluted areas, the doors and windows must remain closed, which affects the degree to which occupants can adjust their interior surroundings (Fig. 7.5). Second, outdoor noise will also influence the operability of doors and windows, and, in extreme cases, may warrant nonstructural improvements to the building envelope to reduce the amount of noise reaching the interior.

Third, sun exposure directly impacts the specification of window treatments to reduce heat gain within the space (Fig. 7.6). Direct exposure to the sun can also influence the selection of interior finishes, which could lead to discoloration from excessive UV light. Sun exposure will vary by location based on the latitude of the building location. The further away the project site is from the equator, the greater the swings in sun exposure in the winter and summer months. For example, locations far to the north, near the Arctic Circle, will receive little to no sunlight on days in the depths of winter while experiencing days almost entirely of sunlight at the height of summer. Project sites located in the northern hemisphere will receive more intense sun exposure on the southern face of the building and projects in the southern hemisphere will receive more intense sun exposure on the northern face of the building. For locations close to the equator, the sun can have a very

Figure 7.4 Access to a variety of urban amenities, including mass transit, will often impact the location a client chooses for their home or business.

Figure 7.5 Outdoor air quality is one of many existing factors that will impact the design of an interior space.

intense warming effect on spaces fronted in all glass nearly all year round if not protected. In any of these cases, the interior designer must take note of the existing conditions regarding the location, climate, and architectural features of the building to appropriately design window coverings and select interior finishes that may receive direct sunlight. The designer will also need to coordinate with mechanical engineering consultants to be sure that spaces can be appropriately conditioned and controlled.

Other location factors, including multi-tenant scenarios, architectural style, and building codes exert influence on the design of an interior. Designing a space for a single tenant of a multi-tenant building requires some special considerations and planning on the part of the designer, including concerns surrounding visual and acoustical privacy. In the case of a multistory and multi-tenant residential building the floors, ceilings, and walls that divide tenants must be designed for acoustic separation. Office buildings often have multiple tenants and these tenants will share certain spaces, including stairwells, elevators, restrooms, and centrally located amenities such as an exercise facility or coffee kiosk.

Architectural style and possible historical designation of a building will impact the design of an interior. In cases where a building is designated as historically protected or significant, the designer will likely need to take measures to respect the architectural bones of the building while making contemporary design interventions. This process will require delicacy and knowledge in historical preservation. In cases where an old building is being adaptively reused for a new purpose, the building was once a factory and is being converted into a restaurant and shopping venue for example, the designer has the opportunity to embrace the story of the prior use while beginning a new chapter in the life of the building (Fig. 7.7). In cases where an architectural style is applied in a unique manner in a particular place, a **vernacular** develops. An architecture or design vernacular contributes to the identity of a community and a place, which can be highly influential on new design projects.

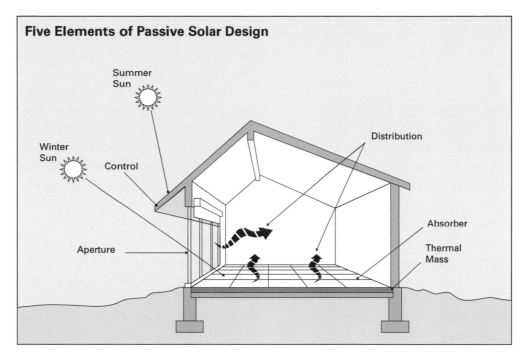

Five Elements of Passive Solar Design

Summer Sun

Winter Sun

Control

Aperture

Distribution

Absorber

Thermal Mass

Figure 7.6 Sun exposure of a building greatly influences the design of the interior, including finish selections and views toward the exterior.

Figure 7.7 This example of an adaptive reuse interior was once a church, but now functions as a nightclub.

Building codes will vary by country and even by municipality within one country. **Building codes** are regulations adopted by local municipalities that govern the design and construction of buildings in order to protect the health, safety, and welfare of the public. Codes provide requirements for space planning with a particular emphasis on **egress**, or the means to exit a building in the event of an emergency. In relation to finishes, codes provide minimum requirements for performance in context with fire safety in an effort to reduce damage to life and property in the event of a fire. Codes also govern the extent of planning for plumbing facilities, such as the quantity of toilets and lavatories in the restrooms of a school. Each new design project requires a code study to be performed, which will increase in complexity as the project scope and size increases. In renovation projects that have multiple use classifications, or where the use classification is changing, the code implications are complex, sometimes requiring additional fire-rated separations between spaces and tenants, or requiring additional restroom facilities to be added to meet code requirements.

Closely related to location are the methods used to construct a building. From one climate to another, one country to another, construction methods vary widely across the globe. As nations advance technologically, more countries are creating basic building standards that guide designers. The following discussion offers a very simple introduction to the most basic of construction methodologies.

Existing Construction Factors

In order for the interior to be properly designed, the existing architectural conditions must be thoroughly understood. The interior designer must also be aware of the professional boundaries that exist between interior design and architecture, and one important aspect of understanding this boundary is awareness of the various structural components of a building (Fig. 7.8). Broadly speaking, buildings can be divided into two broad structural categories: substructure and superstructure. The **substructure** includes those portions of a building that are constructed partially or fully below **grade**, or the ground plane, and include footings for load-bearing walls and columns, below-grade columns, and pilasters, foundation walls, and below- and on-grade slabs. The **superstructure** consists of all above-grade construction and includes above-grade floor and subfloor structures, walls, columns, and roofs and all the materials associated with these components.

Each structural component is designed, engineered, and constructed to resist **load**, the forces exerted by gravity and the natural elements, including wind and snow/ice,

upon a building. The primary loads can be divided into two categories: vertical loads and lateral loads. **Vertical loads** result from the forces of gravity and are categorized as **dead load** (DL), or the unchanging force that the structure places upon itself by the simple massiveness of the structure, and **live load** (LL), or the movable sources of load, such as mobile equipment and people within the building and the changing loads of nature, such as snow and water that can collect on a roof. **Lateral loads** are horizontal loads, place pressure on buildings from the side, and often originate from wind or shifting soils. Soils can move due to seismic action or during the freeze-thaw cycle when soils expand and contract with changing temperatures. To counteract lateral loads, engineers may include a shear wall within the structural design of a building. An interior designer must know the location of all load-bearing components, whether these components bear vertical or horizontal loads, in order to not compromise the structural integrity of a building.

Techniques and Materials for Load-Bearing Floor, Wall, and Roof Structures

Floor, wall, and roof structures can be constructed utilizing multiple construction techniques, including light framing, heavy steel, and concrete. The type of construction is determined based on building code requirements for flame spread ratings, required building height, and span capabilities of floor structures as required by column placement for interior planning strategies. Light framing in wood or steel can be executed in a balloon-frame or platform-frame technique (Fig. 7.9). **Balloon framing** utilizes continuous studs running up more than one story from foundation to roof structure. **Platform framing** is achieved by supporting the floor structure (the platforms) with wall framing and then building the next level wall framing on top of the floor structure (Fig. 7.10).

As mentioned, either light framing technique can be achieved with wood or light-gauge steel studs, with steel having the added benefit of fire resistance over conventional wood studs. Wall studs are typically spaced at 16-inch intervals and vary in size depending on how much load they will carry, the height of the wall, and how much insulation is needed inside the wall. Wood studs are described as "two by framing" (2×4, 2×6, and 2×8 nominal sizes are typical for walls) meaning

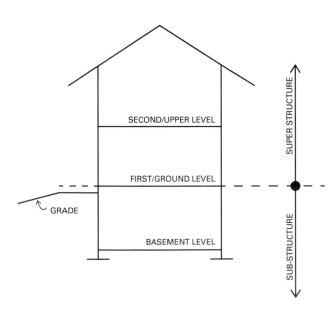

Figure 7.8 Understanding the impact of substructure and superstructure spaces will help a designer make informed design decisions regarding space planning, finishes, lighting, and furnishings.

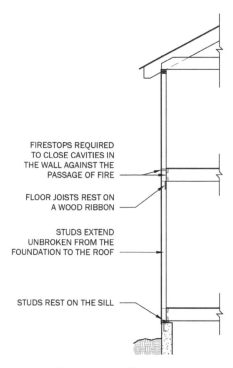

FIRESTOPS REQUIRED TO CLOSE CAVITIES IN THE WALL AGAINST THE PASSAGE OF FIRE

FLOOR JOISTS REST ON A WOOD RIBBON

STUDS EXTEND UNBROKEN FROM THE FOUNDATION TO THE ROOF

STUDS REST ON THE SILL

Figure 7.9 This wall section illustrates how the wall studs in a balloon-framed building run from the foundation to the roof structure.

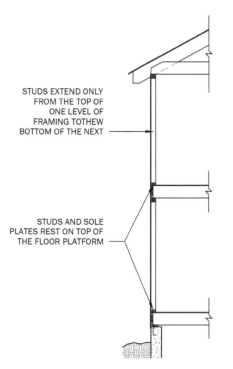

STUDS EXTEND ONLY FROM THE TOP OF ONE LEVEL OF FRAMING TOTHEW BOTTOM OF THE NEXT

STUDS AND SOLE PLATES REST ON TOP OF THE FLOOR PLATFORM

Figure 7.10 This wall section illustrates how the wall studs in a platform-framed building stop at each floor structure.

Table 7.1 Nominal Sizes and Actual Sizes of Wood Studs. Wood studs are identified by their nominal size, 2 x 4, 2 x 6, etc., but their actual sizes are a fraction of an inch smaller.

Nominal Size (In Inches)	Dressed Size (In Inches)
1 × 3	3/4 × 2 1/2
1 × 4	3/4 × 3 1/2
1 × 6	3/4 × 5 1/2
1 × 8	3/4 × 7 1/4
1 × 10	3/4 × 9 1/4
1 × 12	3/4 × 11 1/4
2 × 4	1 1/2 × 3 1/2
2 × 6	1 1/2 × 5 1/2
2 × 8	1 1/2 × 7 1/4
2 × 10	1 1/2 × 9 1/4
2 × 12	1 1/2 × 11 1/4
3 × 8	2 1/2 × 7 1/4
3 × 12	2 1/2 × 11 1/4
4 × 12	3 1/2 × 11 1/4
4 × 16	3 1/2 × 15 1/4
6 × 12	5 1/2 × 11 1/2
6 × 16	5 1/2 × 15 1/2
6 × 18	5 1/2 × 17 1/2
8 × 16	7 1/2 × 15 1/2
8 × 20	7 1/2 × 19 1/2
8 × 24	7 1/2 × 23 1/2

they are 2 inches thick by their corresponding depth. The nominal size description for wood framing is not the actual size of the framing member. Table 7.1 provides a comparison between nominal and actual sizes of wood framing. In substructures, the floor is typically a concrete slab supported by poured-in-place concrete or concrete masonry foundation walls while superstructure floors are constructed of wood or light-gauge steel. Light frame superstructure floors will be covered with sheathing, which provides added lateral load strength as well as support for flooring finishes.

Light framing is reserved for buildings of lower stature (Fig. 7.11 and 12), but heavy steel and concrete structures are required for high-rise buildings. Heavy steel uses a system of columns connected by heavy girders with intermediate beams or open web trusses linking the girders together (Fig. 7.13). Floors in steel structures involve a concrete slab that is supported by a steel corrugated pan over the steel beams. Poured-in-place concrete structures follow a similar strategy as steel only using concrete columns, girders, and beams. Concrete is incredibly strong in compression, but weak in tension, whereas steel is equally strong in both compression and tension (Fig. 7.14). Due to the weakness of concrete in tension, concrete slabs,

Figure 7.11 Wood stud framing, trusses, and sheathing are used to construct this residence.

Figure 7.12 Using light-gauge steel framing in place of wood framing provides enhanced fire protection.

Figure 7.13 The heavy steel columns (vertical) and beams (horizontal) also rely on cross bracing (angled) to protect against lateral loads.

girders, and beams are reinforced with steel bars, or **rebar**. Concrete columns are also reinforced with steel to prevent them from cracking under lateral loads. Interior walls in heavy steel and concrete structures are typically not load bearing and are constructed with light-gauge steel framing.

Concrete masonry can also be used as a structural material. Concrete masonry units, or CMU, are modular pieces used for wall construction only, can be used in either substructure or superstructure conditions, and are fire resistant (Fig. 7.15). Concrete masonry relies on poured-in-place concrete for substructure floors and light framing or heavy steel for superstructure floors and roofs. Historically, clay masonry, or brick, has also been used as a load-bearing material, and the interior designer is well-advised to be aware of the presence of load-bearing brick walls in any historical preservation or adaptive reuse projects.

The primary function of roofs is protecting the interior from rain, snow, and ice, and it is this functional imperative

Figure 7.14 Concrete columns (vertical) and beams (horizontal) make up this exposed concrete structure.

that can often drive the form of the roof (Fig. 7.16). Roof forms are broadly described as pitched or flat and can incorporate overhangs or not. Pitched roof forms include shed, simple and compound gables, hip, gambrel, and mansard (Fig. 7.17). The structure supporting pitched roofs can be light framing in wood or steel or heavy steel and will be achieved using beam rafters or open trusses. Pitched roofs have the possibility to greatly impact the interior with sloped ceiling forms in which case rafters or a scissor truss is required. Flat roofs are not literally flat, as they must shed water with a minimal slope and include overhang or parapet form varieties. Flat roof structures can be constructed of light framing, heavy steel, or concrete slab. In each case, the roofing material will be sloped with either a slightly sloped roof structure or a flat structure with built-up insulation that will create the slight slope toward roof drains, which will conduct water to drainage pipes dispersed throughout the roof or scuppers that allow water to drain off the edge of the building. In the case of

drainage pipes, these pipes will be located to run vertically along columns that will then run below the building and deposit rainwater into a retention pond located on the site, a municipal waste system, or a cistern where the water could be used for irrigation or flushing toilets.

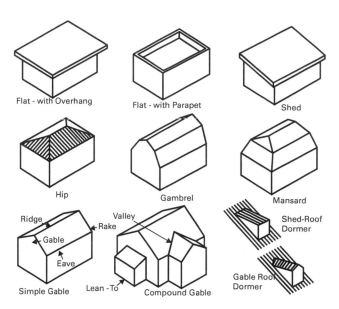

Figure 7.16 A variety of roof forms are possible and each can potentially influence the design of the interior through form or the admittance of daylight.

Figure 7.15 Concrete masonry units are laid one row, or coursing, at a time, and mortar seals the joints between each block. The voids are often filled with mortar and steel rebar for added strength to resist lateral loads.

Figure 7.17 Roofs are complicated systems that protect the interior from the natural elements. In this case, roofing installers must take special care to properly install clay roofing tiles around a skylight.

Design Trends: Anticipating Future Aesthetic and Functional Factors

A full and well-rounded understanding of the demographic, cultural, location, and climate factors, along with an awareness of architectural construction types, sets the stage for creating lasting interiors with the best opportunity to meet the user's needs for many years to come (Fig. 7.18). These areas of influence are only discovered through research, visiting the proposed project site with careful observations of all existing structural components, and observation of the client and their needs. Forward-thinking design strategies that seek to understand the client's future goals for the space play a significant role in planning a home for changes in family structure as children age and leave the house or to plan for the process of aging-in-place. In corporate design, companies rarely maintain the same employee base for very long as they intend to grow, or the economy forces them to shrink their employee base. With any project, the designer has the opportunity and responsibility to plan for the client's intended future accordingly, and, by doing so, will create a design with an extended life span.

Significant emphasis is also placed on forecasting aesthetic design trends. Interior designers can occasionally create a design trend, but most trends originate from outside of the design firm. It is the designer's responsibility to be aware of current trends and the best guesses of experts regarding future trends. Color forecasting is one example of a design trend that does not typically originate within the field of interior design. Fashion design, and more specifically textile design, relies heavily upon color forecasting by such organizations as Pantone, the Color Marketing Group, and others to aid in research and development directions for new products. Interior designers, through paint manufacturers, such as Sherwin-Williams, PPG, and others, also seek to remain current with color trends, but interior design renovations tend to cost more than a new wardrobe. It is this sense of economic risk in chasing a potential fad that gives the designer and client pause in trying something new. The lure of being on the forefront of a new style or technology is very powerful, however. Time is the only test able to determine if a new idea will have lasting impact.

Cutting-edge ideas are often on display at trade shows that highlight new furniture, finishes, and accessories for interiors. Some shows are so large that they draw an international audience such as at NEOCON in Chicago or the Milan Furniture Fair in Italy (Fig. 7.19). Style and technological innovations are displayed side by side, offering both a feast for the eyes and functional innovations in one place. Many designers will attend at least one trade show per year in order to remain knowledgeable regarding the latest design trends as they come to market.

Technology and ecology have been two strong drivers of emerging design trends in recent years (Fig. 7.20). Digital technology affects every area of life as contemporary society has become fully integrated with technology. Providing mobile digital technology with power access as well as integrating digital technology into everyday products has become one area of design innovation. Simultaneously, the design industry is witnessing a

Figure 7.18 Client meetings typically happen face-to-face so that the designer and client can examine the needs of a project and the designer can test design ideas. The care and attention given to topics of conversation in these meetings has an impact on the longevity of the built space.

Figure 7.19 The Milan Design Week attracts designers and buyers to one large exposition that highlights countless furniture, lighting, finish, and accessory manufacturers from around the world.

backlash against mobile digital technology in some cases, as designers are seeing a desire by clients to unplug, and manufacturers are answering. Technological trends in design have been met with mixed reviews, which is

Figure 7.20 Hardwired and wireless devices permit flexibility in where work is accomplished, but this also creates planning challenges for designers and clients as electricity and access to wireless internet must be accommodated.

typical of many trends as they either become fads or are integrated into new design styles.

Ecology has been a growing area of focus since the energy crisis in the United States of the 1970s. Rising fuel costs opened the eyes of many to the economic impacts of inefficient living, working, and manufacturing practices. As the ideology of climate change has grown and taken hold, many clients and designers will only purchase and specify products or materials made using sustainable practices. Today, the economics and ideological arguments in favor of ecologically sound design practices have created a movement that extends far beyond a temporary trend and will continue to stand the test time. It is important for the designer to be able to distinguish between the underlying issues at work, in this case sustainability, and some of the aesthetic trends that can emerge. The two are not intrinsically linked, as the sustainable priorities will persist, but the aesthetic manifestations will continue to evolve (Fig. 7.21).

Figure 7.21 A planted wall is one example of how a sustainable feature, or focal point, can make aesthetic and functional impacts within interior spaces.

Setting Creativity Ablaze through Contextual Design Challenges

Project:	Kotler-Coville Glass Pavilion at the Ringling Museum of Art
Location:	Sarasota, Florida
Client:	Florida State University
Architecture Firm:	Architects Lewis + Whitlock
Occupants/Users:	Museum patrons and curatorial staff
Site Characteristics:	Historic museum campus
Year Complete:	January 2018
Cost Estimate:	$3.6 million
Facility Size:	5,500 total square feet; two levels

Project Overview

Modest in size but packed with program, the Kotler-Coville Glass Pavilion is the latest addition to the John and Mable Ringling Museum Campus. The design of the Glass Pavilion continues the Ringling tradition of creating innovative architecture that serves the arts. This signature gallery offers a contrasting modern backdrop to the historic gatehouse that greets visitors coming to experience the wide-ranging art collections offered at the Ringling. The

5,500-square-foot addition to the visitor's pavilion houses the museum's glass art collection, serves as the reception lobby for the historic Asolo theater, and provides a dance rehearsal studio and dressing rooms for the theater.

The floor plan is largely dictated by a constricted site location which includes the existing visitor's pavilion to the west, the historic Ringling driveway to the south, and the adjacent historic gatehouse and wall to the east. Inspiration for the project is derived from the interaction of air, water, sand, and the resulting ripples found in nature, both on the beach and in the shallow waters just offshore in the Gulf of Mexico. The ripples on the beach are manifested as vertical shade fins that define the eastern facade, controlling morning sunlight and creating a dynamic architectural statement that complements the world-class art collection it houses.

Project Design Goals

At the beginning of the design process, the design team worked with the client to identify five key goals that the project should meet.

1. Display the world-renowned glass art collection for the enjoyment of campus patrons.

2. Balance delicate control of natural light with the client's desire to maximize views into the building from the campus entry path.

3. Engage the existing visitor's pavilion to provide theater pre-function, event, and intermission spaces.

4. Incorporate theater backstage support (improved circulation, private dressing rooms, rehearsal studio).

5. Improve the museum entry sequence and admission experience while respecting the historic gatehouse.

Context: Inspiration through History, Culture, and Location

Each substantive project stretches the realm of possibilities within which creative inspiration can materialize. Tight parameters and a collection of conflicting problems to solve do not dampen creativity but set it ablaze. The Kotler-Coville Glass Pavilion is a prime example of a project that, through its own complex context, awakened design possibilities. Grappling with contextual challenges produces solutions that are beautiful, unique, and responsive. This project exemplifies innovation inspired through limitation and constraint.

The sunshade fins immediately garner visual attention as one approaches the pavilion from the street.

Sarasota, Florida, has a rich art, design, and architectural history deeply influenced by a modernist design movement beginning in the 1950s that became known as the Sarasota School of Architecture. This valued legacy is part of Sarasota's identity, and continues to be integrated into the community's design culture. Values of Sarasota modernism include creative originality, pursuit of design excellence, human scale, and a responsiveness to the environment.

Context: Inspiration through Natural Materials

With the understanding that sand is the principal ingredient in the creation of glass, the design team focused on the natural material as a way to inform the design process. This inspiration began with the exploration of Sarasota's coastal environment along Siesta Key. Sand bars, typically located a hundred yards or more offshore, constantly shift with the tide and seasons while collecting artifacts and providing a place of rest and contemplation. The sand bar and art museum share a common role in this way as artifact collectors and a place for reflection.

With the emphasis on sand and its role in the coastal environment, the design team was drawn to experience the beautiful beaches that the area has to offer. The beaches are known for crystal clear water and low-sloping shorelines that allow the beachgoer to often wade out hundreds of yards without the water rising above the waistline. When viewing the beach sand in these

conditions, the sand's ripples appear mostly parallel, interspersed with wiggling curves in natural artful display. The design team interpreted these sand ripples through sketches depicting the abstracted lines created by the topography. The team studied the sand's ripples in cross section to see how water and air formed them and began to realize their potential for the building façade as a means to filter the predominant eastern sunlight that would dominate the new gallery in the morning hours.

Context: Meeting the Needs of the Interior While Addressing Site Constraints

The design team applied this information to the project's façade, manipulating the sand ripple profile in such a way as to protect the glass art collection and patrons from the severe sun exposure. The resulting "fins" allow soft light and views to permeate from the north serving to improve the interior environment and to create a defining architectural feature on the eastern facing facade. Extended overhangs serve to further protect the interior from direct angles.

The interior finishes acknowledge the natural context of the project while placing the emphasis upon the art collection. Concrete, which contains sand as a fine aggregate, serves as flooring while the white walls recall the pure silica content of the Siesta Key sand. Building systems were carefully coordinated to result

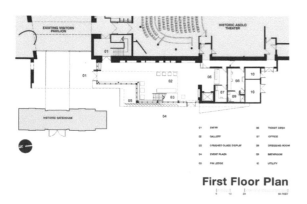

First Floor Plan

The gallery is relatively small in size but strong in terms of influence, as it provides exhibition space for the glass art collection at the Ringling and support space for dance recitals that will be performed in the Asolo theater of the existing building.

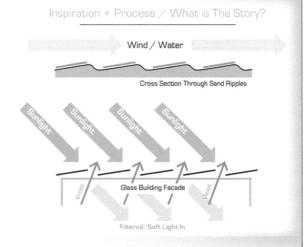

The design team took inspiration from the surrounding natural conditions, the ripples of sand created by ocean currents, to inspire the design of the building façade that would serve to selectively allow daylight to penetrate the interior while protecting the art work.

The vertical sunshade fins protect the art from harmful UV light while allowing soft northern light to filter to the interior.

The proportion, lighting, color, texture, and lines of the interior draw the eye upward, encouraging the visitor to engage with the art.

in a minimalist ceiling design to further reduce distractions and visual clutter.

Taking into account the nearby functions surrounding the glass pavilion, the design team addressed programmatic needs and embraced views from the exterior. The pavilion is immediately adjacent to the visitor's pavilion and the Asolo theater to the west, the historic gatehouse to the south, Bay Shore Road and a new event plaza to the east. The ground floor incorporates a two-story art gallery, which is versatile enough to also serve event ticketing and theater access functions. Located on the north end of the addition is a dressing room for theater performers as well as building utilities. The second floor art gallery space is composed of a mezzanine overlooking the ground floor. Ground-floor exhibit space is maximized by suspending the second-floor mezzanine, thereby eliminating ground-floor columns. Additionally, the art display cases on the second floor are recessed between structures on the western edge of the space to maximize floor space. A dance rehearsal room serving as warm-up space for the adjacent Asolo theater is also incorporated to the north. A 14-foot glass wall looking east allows for views into the rehearsal room from the street below for an active and engaging façade.

Architects Lewis + Whitlock is a full service architecture and design firm in Tallahassee, Florida, specializing in a variety of project types. For more information on the Kotler-Coville Glass Pavilion and Architects Lewis + Whitlock, visit http://www.think3d.net/.

Summary

In the hands of a thoughtful and talented designer, knowledge of demographics, location, and climate influences in combination with construction techniques and design trends can serve to create design solutions with longevity.

Design is the combination of many knowledge areas applied in a creative manner to solve problems for the client and users of a space. Great designers do the heavy lifting of integrating these knowledge areas into their design processes because they seek to improve their clients' quality of life for the long term.

Key Terms

Balloon framing	Live load	Substructure
Building codes	Load	Superstructure
Dead load	Platform framing	Urban
Egress	Rebar	Urbanized areas
Grade	Rural	Vernacular
Lateral load	Stage of life	Vertical load

Resources

Allen, E., & Iano, J. (2017). *The Architect's Studio Companion: Rules of Thumb for Preliminary Design.* John Wiley & Sons.

Ching, F. D. (2014). *Building Construction Illustrated.* Hoboken, NJ: John Wiley & Sons, Inc.

Kennon, K. E. (2018). *The Codes Guidebook for Interiors.* John Wiley & Sons.

Tucker, L. M. (2015). *Sustainable Building Systems and Construction for Designers.* New York: Fairchild Books, an Imprint of Bloomsbury Publishing Inc.

United States Census Bureau. (2012, September 1). 2010 Census Urban Area FAQs. Retrieved December 15, 2017, from https://www.census.gov/geo/reference/ua/uafaq.html.

Review Questions

1. What demographic factors should the designer consider that could positively impact design outcomes?
2. What factors regarding an urban location could impact the design of the interior?
3. What factors regarding a rural location could impact the design of the interior?
4. How might the relationship between a space and grade, for example, substructure versus superstructure, impact the outcome of an interior design?
5. What types of structural systems are typically reserved for low-stature buildings? For tall buildings? What is the primary advantage of light-gauge metal framing over wood framing?
6. What are some ways a designer can anticipate future functional needs of a client? What are some ways a designer can plan for future aesthetic desires of a client?

Exercises

Demographic and Location Needs

1. Imagine that a client has hired you to design a new workspace for their graphic design and marketing firm of thirty employees. Their business has been growing and they are in the process of hiring more people, but they will soon outgrow their current location at the edge of the city. They want to move closer to the city center where most of their clients are located. Before designing anything for the interior, they are hiring you to consult with them on the best location for their new space. Simply in terms of relationship and family status, demographics of the firm include
   a. 20 percent single with no children.
   b. 10 percent single with children.
   c. 40 percent married/committed with children.
   d. 30 percent married/committed with no children

2. Select an interesting urban location, and specifically select three diverse addresses that could suit their needs. Evaluate each location in terms of its access to
   a. Mass transit.
   b. Child care and schools.
   c. Housing and grocery.
   d. Social venues, coffee shops, restaurants, and entertainment.
   e. Green spaces or parks.
   f. Health care and exercise.
3. Provide the client with pros and cons for each location and make a recommendation on the preferred location. Present your work in an organized printed document, or digitally.

Construction Techniques

1. With the help of your instructor and a local contractor that is willing to host you and your classmates, visit a construction site. Preferably the construction project should be large enough and at a stage in the process to see a variety of work in progress.

2. Document your observations through writing, photography, and sketching. Describe the following:
   a. What type of project is this? Who is the client and who are the users? What issues influenced the design and now the construction of this project?
   b. What is the relationship between the space and grade?
   c. What type of framing system is used?
   d. Locate all of the load-bearing elements.
   e. How many levels are in this building? How many levels does this project include, if it is only a portion of the overall building?
   f. Describe the roof if this space is directly beneath it.
   g. Describe other points of interest regarding the project.
3. Present your work in an organized printed document, or digitally.

8

Planning

As a result of reading this chapter, students will

1. Possess an awareness of the relationship between design thinking and drawing.

2. Possess an awareness of the various drawing types and their individual purpose.

3. Possess an awareness of occupied and circulation space and how they are used to define the interior.

4. Possess an awareness of the types of circulation space and the qualities that each possess.

5. Possess an awareness of wayfinding and wayfinding strategies.

6. Possess an awareness of stair design.

As a result of taking part in the learning exercises at the end of this chapter, students will

1. Demonstrate the ability to identify and analyze occupied space and circulation space.

2. Demonstrate the ability to complete a stair calculation.

Planning Process

Successful interiors do not happen by accident, but are the result of careful planning that relies upon the design thinking process. As discussed in Chapter 1, design thinking starts with the designer building empathy for the client and users, defining the problems that the proposed design will seek to solve, developing multiple ideas that could solve those problems, creating prototype solutions, and then testing those solutions by presenting them to the client and gauging their reaction (Fig. 8.1). As discussed in Chapter 3, the design process utilizes the steps of design thinking in cycles in order to efficiently progress through each of the design process steps: pre-design, concept development, schematic design, design development, construction documentation, and contract administration (Fig. 8.2).

The design thinking steps span multiple phases of the design process, and will recur in cycles, but certain phases in the design process will be dominated by certain steps of design thinking. Loosely, pre-design tends to focus more heavily on empathy and problem definition, while schematic design, design development, and construction documentation will utilize ideation, prototyping, and testing in frequent cycles. Contract administration is where the designer is playing a role in executing the design decisions that were made in the earlier phases. Notice that the five-step design thinking process does not strictly fall in line with the traditional five-step design process boundaries, but is much more fluid, such that ideation also occurs in the construction documentation phase where the designer is creatively seeking solutions to technical design challenges.

The planning process grows in complexity as project scope increases in size, relying on the designer to manage multiple disciplines, including engineers and specialty consultants, as discussed in Chapter 6. While the designer views the entire process holistically, a consultant is responsible for only a small portion of the design, such as door hardware, HVAC, or engineering the elevator machining. The designer coordinates the needs of each of the consultants, making sure that any conflicts get resolved with little to no compromise in the design integrity of the overall project. To do this, the designer begins with a plan that is both aesthetically pleasing and functional. With small projects that may not involve a team of consultants, the designer still starts with a strong plan.

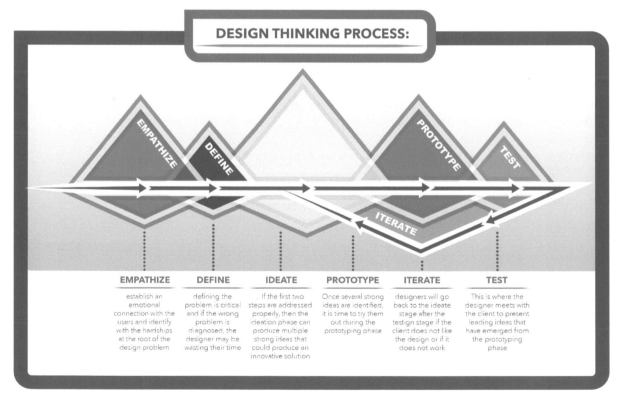

DESIGN THINKING PROCESS:

EMPATHIZE	DEFINE	IDEATE	PROTOTYPE	ITERATE	TEST
establish an emotional connection with the users and identify with the hardships at the root of the design problem	defining the problem is critical and if the wrong problem is diagnosed, the designer may be wasting their time	. If the first two steps are addressed properly, then the ideation phase can produce multiple strong ideas that could produce an innovative solution	Once several strong ideas are identified, it is time to try them out during the prototyping phase	designers will go back to the ideate stage after the testign stage if the client does not like the design or if it does not work	This is where the designer meets with the client to present leading ideas that have emerged from the prototyping phase

Figure 8.1 The design thinking process is a rhythmic process of gathering information in an outward focused manner in the steps of empathy, ideation, and prototyping, to focusing inwardly as in problem definition and testing. The process also embraces iteration as testing can often expose problems in a design prototype.

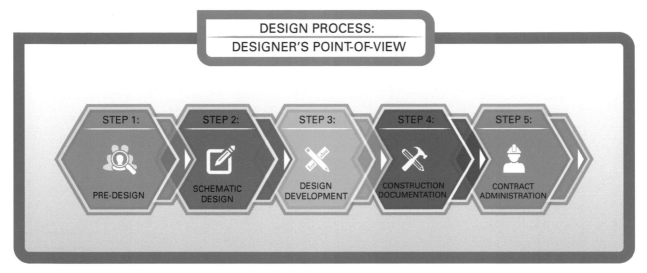

Figure 8.2 The design process from the designer's point of view begins before a contract is signed, and continues after construction is complete.

Purpose of Drawing

The planning process relies on a variety of drawing types to aid the designer in developing design solutions and to visually communicate proposed solutions to the client for approval, and to contractors, fabricators, and installers for implementation. The act of drawing is a manual or digital process that is integral to the design thinking process for designers. Designers process visually, so not only are drawings communication tools, but they are also evidence of design thinking. Drawings can also be used to measure the phases of the design process as certain types of drawings must be completed in order to convey schematic design, design development, and construction documentation.

Figure 8.3 A designer uses a variety of tools to draw, including pens, pencils, drafting equipment, and a computer with CAD software.

Designers use a variety of tools to draw based on which design thinking step they are engaged in (Fig. 8.3). For example, when the designer is engaged in ideation, no matter if it involves developing quick ideas on paper for space planning options during schematic design, or if developing ideas for a construction detail option during construction documentation, it is common to use a pen or pencil. The designer typically uses digital tools when finalizing space plans for schematic design renderings, or finalizing details in construction documentation, which could both be considered the prototyping steps in design thinking.

Drawing Types

Drawings are to scale two-dimensional representations of three-dimensional spaces and masses. A **floor plan** is a top-down view showing all elements that are within 4 feet of the floor plane (Fig. 8.4). These elements include walls, doors, windows, stairs and handrails, elevators, floor finishes, furniture, fixtures, equipment, and accessories. Floor plans can vary in scale based on the project size, with residential floor plans typically drawn at 1/4 inch = 1 foot (1:50) and nonresidential floor plans at 1/8 inch = 1 foot (1:100), with some occasion to vary the scale based on the composition of the drawing on the paper. A **reflected ceiling plan** (RCP) illustrates the design of the ceiling as if a mirror was placed on the floor and shows walls, windows, door openings, ceiling finishes, changes in ceiling height, skylights, openings in

Figure 8.4 This rendered floor plan of a hotel restaurant shows interior architectural components, floor finishes, and furniture while demonstrating a clear delineation between occupied and circulation space.

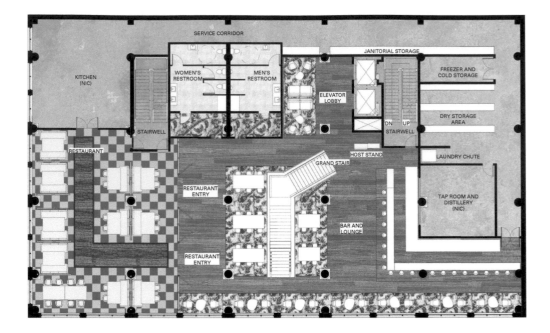

Figure 8.5 This RCP accompanies the preceding floor plan and demonstrates how lighting and ceiling heights reinforce the space planning.

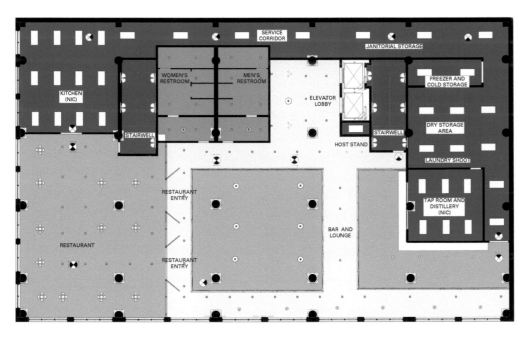

the ceiling or floor above, light fixtures, HVAC diffusers and returns, and fire suppression components (Fig. 8.5). The RCP matches the scale of the floor plan in any set of drawings to make coordination between the two drawings as intuitive as possible.

Floor plans and reflected ceiling plans illustrate the horizontal planes of a space (floors and ceilings), while sections and elevations illustrate vertical planes of a space (walls). **Sections** illustrate a vertical cut through layers of materials and components and through volumes.

Building sections are cut through the entire building, the multiple levels of a design, and show the relationship between floor levels, ceiling planes, and large volumes, typically matching the scale of the floor plan (Fig. 8.6). Detail sections cut through specific portions of a design to illustrate how materials and components connect to one another and are much larger, at scales of 3/4 inch (approximately 1:20), 11/2 inch (1:10), 3 inches (1:5), and 6 inches = 1 foot (1:2), or full size (1 inch = 1 foot; 1:1; metric scales are approximate conversions) (Fig.

8.7). **Elevations** are two-dimensional projections of a vertical surface that do not show thicknesses of adjacent components, such as walls, floors, and ceilings (Fig. 8.8). Exterior elevations show an exterior view of the exterior walls, roof, and grade level of a building and typically match the scale of the floor plan. Interior elevations focus on individual walls and the components immediately in front of them, at a scale larger than floor plans but less than detail sections, typically 1/4 inch (1:50), 3/8 inch, or 1/2 inch = 1 foot (1:25). Each of these drawing types described here are two-dimensional planar views of a three-dimensional design, but three-dimensional drawings play an important role in the design process, especially in communicating future design outcomes to clients who may not be skilled in comprehending two-dimensional drawings.

Figure 8.6 This one-point section perspective of a hotel design shows the stacking of spaces, including the public zones (hotel lobby, restaurant, and lounge) on levels one and two with their strong connections to the street life, and the private guest rooms on the upper levels leveraging their use of prospect-refuge theory.

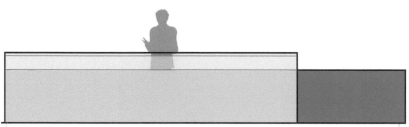

Figure 8.7 This section is rendered to show the materials and ergonomic features of a hotel registration desk.

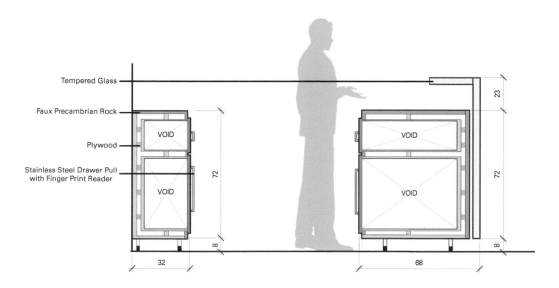

Tempered Glass

Faux Precambrian Rock

Plywood

Stainless Steel Drawer Pull with Finger Print Reader

VOID

VOID

VOID

VOID

23

72

72

8

8

32

68

Figure 8.8 Rendered elevations can be a very effective way to show the design intent of intimate spaces or long corridors.

Figure 8.9 Perspectives are often the most effective way to demonstrate the design intent of an interior space to a client. This example demonstrates careful composition of fore-ground, mid-ground, and back-ground views, creating a dynamic depiction of the design proposal.

Three-dimensional drawings consist of perspective and isometric drawings. A **perspective** is an accurate three-dimensional drawing (on a two-dimensional sheet of paper or screen) of a space from a specific point of view looking at a specific point in space (Fig. 8.9). Perspectives include one-point, two-point, and three-point varieties, which references the number of **vanishing points**, the points where lines converge off in the distance. Drawing accurate perspectives is a learned skill requiring practice and much care, but quick perspective sketches, while lacking accuracy, are very descriptive and useful in ideation. Isometric drawings are one drawing type in a broad category referred to as axonometric drawings. **Axonometric** drawings show three sides of an object,

show vertical edges straight up and down, and show the receding sides with parallel angled lines so there are no vanishing points. Specifically, **isometric** drawings portray three sides of an object with equal foreshortening to each side of the central vertical edge line where the angled sides are drawn at 30 degrees from horizontal (Fig. 8.10). Other types of axonometric drawings follow the same common rules for axonometric drawings (*show three sides of an object, vertical edges are straight up and down, and receding edges are shown parallel to one another*) but they do not foreshorten the receding sides equally, which results in showing one side more prominently than another.

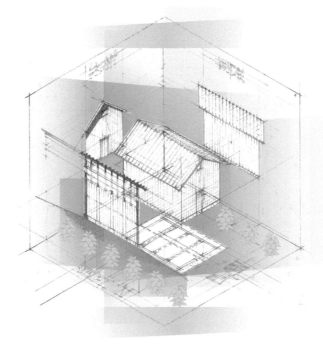

Figure 8.10 This isometric view drawing incorporates several views into one composition.

Space Planning Categories

Creating a new layout for an interior space, referred to as **space planning**, involves two broad categories of space: occupied space and circulation space. **Occupied space** can be described as floor area that is consumed by architectural elements, including walls, columns and doors, and interior components such as furniture, millwork, or equipment. **Circulation space** is the open floor area that allows users to travel within a space in order to navigate around, or through, architectural elements and to use interior components. In an abstract sense, occupied space can be considered the positive space, while circulation is the negative space of the overall design composition.

Occupied spaces can also be thought of as functional destinations, or clusters, within a larger space that are linked together by circulation spaces (Fig. 8.11). Commonly, spaces are grouped with one another by function, such that adjacencies are logical based on what role the space serves, or the role of the people within those spaces. The function of occupied spaces will vary from one project type to another. For example, occupied spaces within a residence include sleeping, dining, and sitting areas while occupied spaces in an airport terminal include ticketing, security, and waiting spaces. These spaces tend to be grouped together for convenience, security, privacy, or some other functional reason.

The categorization of spatial types occurs in the programming step of pre-design where occupied and circulation spaces are quantified. The relationship between the types and quantity of occupied space and circulation space based on project type is an important part of the programming phase within pre-design. As designers become highly experienced in specific project types, they learn to utilize basic rules of thumb in estimating area quantity during programming, such as private offices, conference rooms, and open workstations for a workplace interior, and in estimating necessary clearances for circulation spaces. For example, a simple single-family residence will function well with 3 feet 6 inch (105 centimeter) hallways between bedrooms, whereas corridors and aisles in an office environment function better with widths between 4 feet 6 inches and 6 feet, and airport terminals can require corridors 20 feet (6 meters) or more in width connecting the gates and waiting zones.

A variety of needs particular to a project type will influence the space planning process as well. For example, consumer behavior and retail marketing strategies will

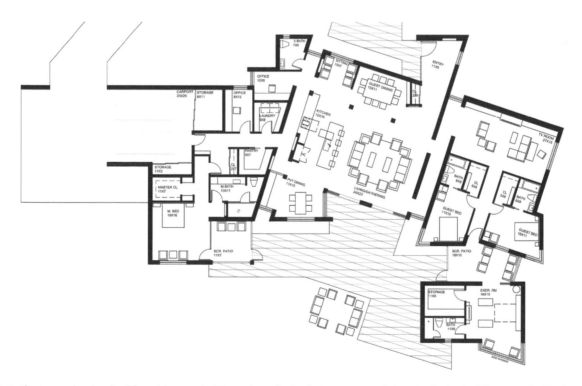

Figure 8.11 The space planning for this residence prioritizes privacy for the homeowners and views to the back of the property. The home is divided into the private entry and sleeping quarters to the west, a social zone in the center, and guest sleeping quarters coupled with exercise and entertainment to the east. (Design/drawing by author.)

influence the planning process of a retail establishment in an effort to encourage the customers to remain in the store as long as possible in the hope they will purchase more goods. The space planning of health care environments is driven by disease prevention, visitor wayfinding, and laws including HIPAA (Health Insurance Portability and Accountability Act) in the United States. HIPAA was enacted to preserve patient privacy. This law calls for visual privacy of all patient records, such that no prying eyes can easily view records in print or on screen and the act requires that audible privacy for patients be maintained wherever possible so that confidential information is not overheard by those nearby.

These rules of thumb for circulation and project typology influences help to get the planning process moving, while the exact size and configuration of a space will become settled as the plan is finalized. The graphic representation of the program in the adjacency matrix, bubble diagram, and blocking diagram allows the designer to carefully consider each of the spatial types and categories in terms of their adjacency to one another, along with other considerations unique to each diagram. These diagram types are described in Chapter 3, which may be worth revisiting to see how the occupied and circulation spaces are described in the program table and in each diagram.

Horizontal Circulation

Horizontal circulation is typically the first consideration when discussing means of travel throughout a building interior. Horizontal circulation includes all means of traversing an interior whether on foot or by some assisted means, such as a wheelchair, and can be very strictly *defined* (Fig. 8.12), such as the case with a hallway lined by fixed partitions; *flexible* (Fig. 8.13), as is the case when furniture placement defines a path; or *undefined* (Fig. 8.14), such as in large unfurnished gathering spaces where paths are defined by clusters of people and can change at a moment's notice.

A certain measure of control should be understood by the designer with each type of path in terms of who exercises the control and for what reason. Defined paths are controlled by the designer, flexible paths are controlled by the client with input by the designer, and undefined paths are controlled by the users of the space. Many designers like to think that a client will never change a furniture arrangement, or that users will behave exactly

Figure 8.12 This example of a defined circulation space utilizes one wall to display artwork and the opposite wall to orient users using a view to the exterior.

Figure 8.13 The circulation zone in this workplace is flexible, allowing users to traverse the space, gather for conversation and collaboration, or slightly reconfigure furniture for a sit-down meeting if needed.

as they intend them to in a space, but this is simply not the case—both clients and users will exercise freedom within the built environment as they see fit.

Some instances do exist, however, when circulation must be tightly controlled for the health, safety, and welfare

Figure 8.14 The circulation in this hotel lobby space is largely undefined, allowing large groups to gather. This space also functions as a node of intersecting circulation paths that is reinforced visually through the furniture placement, lighting, and floor finishes.

of the occupants. In cases where code dictates that a path of egress must maintain a minimum width, then it is a wise decision to utilize objects that are difficult, or impossible, to move to define that path, such as built walls, systems furniture partitions, or heavy furniture. It is also worth noting that simply because a path is defined with built walls, does not mean that it has to be dark, confusing, or uninteresting. Part of the designer's responsibility in exercising control over circulation is to also make it functional and visually appealing through lighting, purposefully placed finishes, and by controlling the height and transparency of partitions to increase visibility while controlling the path.

Wayfinding Strategies

Designers also control circulation in an effort to help users navigate a complex space, referred to as **wayfinding**, through a variety of techniques. Certain project types, such as transportation terminals, hospitals, and education buildings, are inherently more challenging to navigate than others. As these buildings are expanded and renovated, the system of circulation can become confounded even

further. The first remedy that many clients and designers will go to is signage, which is very useful, but signage is only one part of a wayfinding strategy (Fig. 8.15).

The first wayfinding strategy for building occupants is helping them see where they are going, or making their destination visible from their current location. If that is impossible, where the destination may be seven floors above the main entry, for example, then functional nodes,

Figure 8.15 Signage is an important part of wayfinding, especially in large buildings such as an airport, but it is not the only wayfinding strategy available to designers.

Effective Space Planning Reflects the Working Process of a High-Tech Company

Project:	Vectorform Headquarters Office
Location:	Royal Oak, Michigan
Client:	Vectorform
Architect/Designer:	O|X Studio
Project Type:	Workplace
Site Characteristics:	Former retail space, urban setting
Year Complete:	2014
Cost Estimate:	$1.8 million
Facility Size:	Tenant space: 19,646 square feet; primarily on the second level

Design Goals

Previously housed in a nondescript commercial office space, the young tech company was looking for a new home to reflect its creative work environment and its fun, vibrant culture. The goals of the design included

- Transform the vacant two-story urban retail space into an inspiring headquarters office environment.
- Design an interior space that embodies the fluid work process of the young, creative, technical, and design-oriented personnel that work for the high-tech firm.
- Provide a vibrant branded environment that enhances the client experience and increases client engagement.
- Create an emphasis on connectivity to the urban character of their new setting and promote activation into the community

Design Process

The design team at O\|X Studio worked with the client user group of sixty-five employees in order to empathize with their needs and accurately identify the problems that a new space could help to solve by conducting an immersive series of programming charrettes with

the staff. The design team went beyond the typical observations of how people work to uncovering how the firm views itself from a branding and core values perspective. The design team utilized several methods of information gathering to do this:

Discovery Homework

- Bring an image or object that best describes your
  - Perception of your brand personality today.
  - Desired perception of your brand identity.
  - Brand position within professional markets.
  - Thinking around technology integration as part of the core experience.
  - Thinking about your local community.

Solution Group Questions

- How are projects initiated?
- Describe the type of projects you work on and their life cycles.
- What dedicated disciplines (assets) are needed for your projects?
- What are the disciplines that make up the project group?
- What are the skill sets per group and what are their needs?

The design team utilized a robust diagraming process during pre-design to identify priories that the design needed to solve.

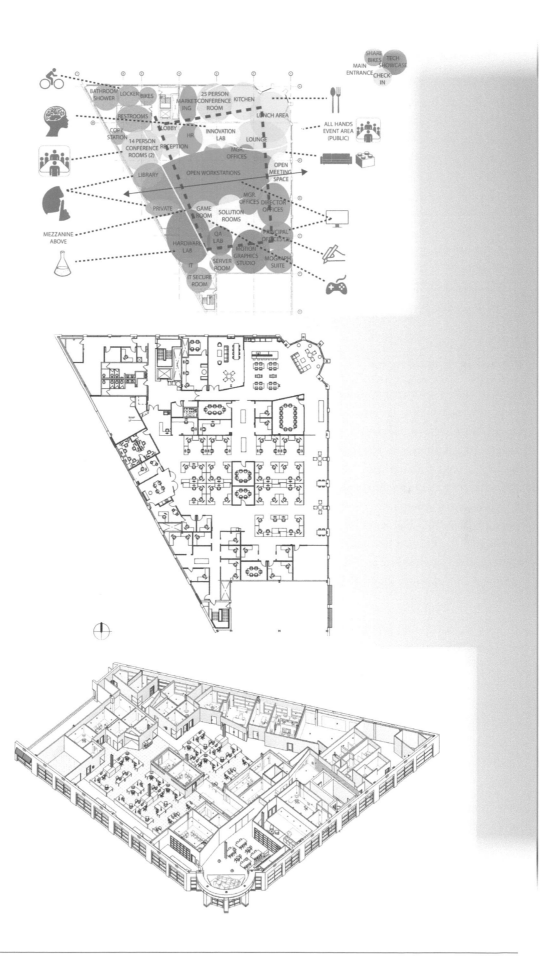

From this process, the following needs were identified:

- A flexible and open office environment design that includes dedicated meeting rooms and breakout spaces would allow the users to work together on a variety of complex projects in many different ways based on the needs of the team members and the stage of work that each project was in.
- A work environment that offers the employees a variety of choices on how and where they will complete their work on a daily basis.
- A palette of raw material finishes and high-tech accents were identified as the preferred method to showcase the company's youth, vibrancy, and energy.

Planning Challenges

Even though Vectorform was made up of a youthful, energetic, and highly creative group of people, their former work environment did not reflect this. The paramount challenge of the project was to abandon the old, compartmentalized, and fragmented office workspace in order to match the culture of this visionary, design-oriented company. There was a necessity to de-emphasize the segmentation of their daily work experience to enhance how they truly functioned as a collaborative, nonhierarchical team. The client had a variety of varying work modes:

- Dedicated work areas for acoustically sensitive graphic and sound production
- Quiet and dark open work environments for hardcore programming
- Open, collaborative settings for ideation and brainstorming
- Breakout space for small group gatherings
- Flexible and fluid spaces for large "all hands on deck" meetings

The all-encompassing variety of spaces incorporated acknowledges not only their aspirations for a definable work environment but becomes a statement for the establishment of their overall culture and ethos.

Planning and Design Solution

Specific concentration was given in the design to establishing linkages to the urban context. The "main street" zone within the space was defined as the central hub of the workplace, with direct visual connectivity to the exterior streetscape. This zone was designed for spontaneous interaction between clients and employees while allowing daylight to penetrate deep into the interior space.

The final layout and floor plan established a perimeter system of specialized rooms and communal spaces that provides a dedicated path for introducing both new employees and clients alike to the nature of the company through a series of branded environments. Each reflects elements of key spatial activators that introduces the varying elements that define the company brand.

From a design perspective, the team utilized materials in the space that would reinforce the nature of the firm's work, brand, and style, which included a combination of raw material finishes and high-tech accents. In the ceiling, the structure and environmental systems in the ceiling plane were exposed to create a loft-like space. The use of polished concrete floors and reclaimed wood finishes as key focal features gives a utilitarian feel. The contemporary lighting and brushed aluminum accents were used throughout the offices to give an appropriate tech vibe, including the installation of color-changing LED strips in floors and walls that heighten the dynamic energy of the workspace.

Long-Range Impact and Benefits

The enhancement of employee productivity is arguable the most significant benefit realized from the design of the space. The firm's human resources coordinator believes the space is a perfect fit for the entrepreneurial staff. "Everyone has so many fabulous ideas that allowing them to work and function in this type of workspace is ideal for them." A senior interactive developer said that employees spend a lot of time in the office and not just because they have a lot of work, but because they enjoy being there. "They play foosball; they just have a good time. I think that's really important and it helps bring out the best in each of us and makes us more productive."

A second key benefit is that the space is used as a recruiting tool. Michigan is home to the fourth largest high-tech workforce in the United States and the need for talent continues to grow. A senior program manager who was being recruited made his decision to join the firm, in part, due to the office environment. "Seeing that management was very much committed to having a cutting edge space for their employees very much influenced my decision to come here." In addition, the layout of space and the variety of spaces that are designed to accommodate the collaborative environment helps ensure the longevity and relevancy of the space from an efficiency standpoint as the company evolves and workplace trends and technology changes.

Front-End/Reception		W x	L	Area	Total Number	Closed Offices	Open Offices	Private Work Rooms	Admin	Lab and Studio Space	Conference Rooms	Collaboration Space	Living Space	Facilities	Totals
	Reception	(8' x	10')	80	1	0	0	0	80	0	0	0	0	0	
	Lobby	(10' x	15')	150	1	0	0	0	150	0	0	0	0	0	
	Bike Storage	(10' x	20')	120	1	0	0	0	0	0	0	0	0	120	
	Restroom	(10' x	30')	300	1	0	0	0	0	0	0	0	0	300	
Conference/Meeting Space															
	Large Conference Room	(20' x	30')	600	1	0	0	0	0	0	600	0	0	0	
	Medium Conference Room	(14' x	20')	280	2	0	0	0	0	0	560	0	0	0	
	Solution Room	(14' x	20')	280	4	0	0	0	0	0	0	1120	0	0	
	Open Meeting Space	(10' x	12')	120	3	0	0	0	0	0	0	360	0	0	
Laboratory Space															
	Electronic Lab	(15' x	20')	300	1	0	0	0	0	300	0	0	0	0	
	Motion Graphics Studio	(20' x	30')	600	1	0	0	0	0	600	0	0	0	0	
	Quality Assurance Lab	(10' x	20')	200	1	0	0	0	0	200	0	0	0	0	
	Innovation Lab	(20' x	20')	400	1	0	0	0	0	0	0	400	0	0	
Workspace															
	Principals Office	(12' x	15')	120	2	360	0	0	0	0	0	0	0	0	
	Director's Office	(8' x	9')	72	13	536	0	0	0	0	0	0	0	0	
	Project Managers	(10' x	10')	100	5	500	0	0	0	0	0	0	0	0	
	Motion Graphics Editing Suite	(10' x	10')	100	3	398	0	0	0	0	0	0	0	0	
	Developers	(6' x	5')	30	54	0	620	0	0	0	0	0	0	0	
	Designers	(6' x	5')	30	12	0	360	0	0	0	0	0	0	0	
	Interns	(8' x	5')	30	5	0	150	0	0	0	0	0	0	0	
	Architects	(6' x	5')	30	3	0	90	0	0	0	0	0	0	0	
	Misc.	(6' x	5')	30	4	0	120	0	0	0	0	0	0	0	
	Admin	(6' x	5')	30	3	0	90	0	0	0	0	0	0	0	
	HR	(10' x	15')	150	1	150	0	0	0	0	0	0	0	0	
	Mrketing	(10' x	10')	100	2	200	0	0	0	0	0	0	0	0	
	QA Assurance	(10' x	10')	100	1	100	0	0	0	0	0	0	0	0	
	IT	(8' x	9')	72	1	0	0	0	0	0	0	0	0	0	
	Hackathon/Library	(10' x	10')	100	2	0	0	200	0	0	0	0	0	0	
	Private Room	(8' x	8')	48	4	0	0	192	0	0	0	0	0	0	
Shared and Support Spaces															
	Kitchen	(9' x	20')	180	1	0	0	0	0	0	0	0	180	0	
	Lunch Area	(30' x	30')	900	1	0	0	0	0	0	0	0	900	0	
	Lounge	(8' x	12')	96	2	0	0	0	0	0	0	0	192	0	
	Kitchenette	(6' x	8')	36	1	0	0	0	0	0	0	0	36	0	
	All Hands Area/Event Space	(30' x	40')	1200	1	0	0	0	0	0	1200	0	0	0	
	Game Room	(12' x	14')	168	1	0	0	0	0	0	0	0	168	0	

The spatial program quantifies the basic physical needs of each space.

O|X Studio

O|X Studio is a full service architecture and design firm located in Ann Arbor, Michigan, with a broad base of experience in many project types. For more information on the Vectorform Headquarters Office or O|X Studio, visit http://oxstudioinc.com/.

The design of the interior, lighting, material selections, furnishings, and overall planning strategies reinforces the creative process of the client and the technical services that they offer to their clients.

such as a bank of elevators, should be clearly visible from their current location that will take them up to their desired floor where they will then be able to see the front door of the office suite that they are seeking. A **node** is a place where multiple paths intersect, an intermediate destination, or a hub of activity along a path (Fig. 8.16). In some cases, several nodes may need to be linked by well-defined paths that help a user navigate a long distance from one location to another within a large building complex or campus.

Another wayfinding strategy involves clearly defining a path and current location through some kind of orienting device (Fig. 8.17). Embracing views to the exterior from an interior path is one way to achieve this, allowing users to orient themselves to an easily recognizable exterior view of mountains, a city skyline, or a courtyard, for example.

Figure 8.16 This circulation node works well due to its placement at the intersection of multiple paths, and strategic use of finishes and color.

Figure 8.17 The expressive color and lighting design calls attention to this circulation connection between two spaces, providing users with an intuitive wayfinding mechanism.

This same strategy can also be employed through well-defined paths, and purposeful lighting strategies and finish selections. Circuitous hallways that are all the same width or that circle back on themselves can be particularly disorienting for occupants. Instead, seek to create a hierarchy for primary paths versus secondary paths by making the primary paths wider, and limit the use of dead-end corridors and corridors that circle around on themselves. The selection of finishes and lighting can be used in wayfinding by selecting the same flooring, ceiling materials, and light fixtures to define all primary circulation zones and contrasting those finish and lighting selections with others in adjacent spaces. Selecting an accent material and decorative light fixtures to call attention to nodes is also very helpful in creating a space that is user-friendly and easy to navigate.

Vertical Circulation

The success of a space plan can often hinge on the quality of the circulation spaces and the interior architectural elements that enable circulation, such as stairs, ramps, elevators, and escalators. Vertical circulation elements can be aesthetic focal points in a large interior volume, helping to orient users as they seek to navigate a large building. These elements can be sculptural and elaborate, or very simple in their design and construction. The planning of vertical circulation elements requires detailed consideration by the designer due to their safety requirements, which are dictated by building codes, frequent use, and high construction cost. By their nature, vertical circulation elements often cut through, or navigate around, building structural components, and the design of these items will require the input of a structural engineer, architect, and special consultants in the case of elevators and escalators.

Stairs

Stairs can be designed with a variety of forms in mind, including linear, switch-back, circular, spiral, or free form, which can influence the type of materials used to construct the stairs (Fig. 8.18). Most often, the structure of the stairs will mimic the structural materials of the rest of the building to include wood, concrete, or steel. The finish materials of a stair can blend in with the surrounding floor and wall materials of the rest of the space. Stairs can also be pre-engineered based on a given height and form, which includes spiral stairs, often favored for tight spaces.

Stairs are always designed to allow users to safely ascend or descend between levels in a building and for aesthetics, especially in the case of monumental stairs such as those found in hotel and office building lobbies, transportation centers, high-end homes, and other grand spaces (Fig. 8.19 and 20). Whether a stair is utilitarian or monumental in stature, all stairs are comprised of a variety of components (Fig. 8.21). A **tread** is the portion of each step that supports the foot and the **riser** is the vertical face between treads. In cases where the riser is missing, the stair is described as an "open riser" staircase. The ideal depth for a tread is 11 inches (approximately 27 centimeters) and ideal height for a riser is 7 inches (approximately 17 centimeters). A **nosing** is the portion of a step where the tread transitions to the riser that projects out beyond the riser. A **landing** is an intermediate platform in a stairway that allows the stair to change direction (e.g., in a switchback or U-shaped stair), allows users to rest as they ascend, and protects users from excessive injury if they happen to trip and fall. Building code will dictate the maximum vertical height that a stair can traverse before needing a landing and the designer should be aware of code requirements for the project location. **Guardrails** prevent a user from falling over the edge of a stairway or opening in a floor, such as in an atrium. They are approximately 40 inches in height and can be constructed of glass, steel, aluminum, or wood. **Handrails** provide a user something to grip to steady themselves while ascending or descending a stair (Fig. 8.22). They are 30 to 34 inches above the stair tread, and are 11/2 inches in diameter for ease of grip. Openings in a stair system,

STAIR TYPES

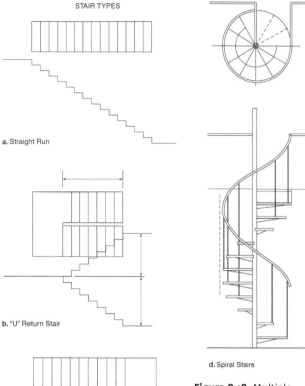

a. Straight Run

b. "U" Return Stair

c. "L" Stair

d. Spiral Stairs

Figure 8.18 Multiple form configurations are available for stairs, each with their own positives and negatives that relate to the amount of space occupied in plan, vertical clearance requirements in section, code compliance requirements, and also form expression.

Figure 8.19 Monumental stairs take on many forms, as shown in this modern, sinuous, and sculptural example.

including the guardrail, must not have any openings larger than 4 inches due to code requirements, as this prevents young children from putting their heads through and falling.

Stair Design Rules

Ten rules are used to guide the design process of stairs:

1. Every stair has one less tread than risers.
2. The stair tread material must be slip-resistant.
3. Risers should not be too *tall*.
   - Maximum riser height = 7.5 inches.
   - Ideal riser height = 7 inches.
4. Treads should not be too *small*.
   - Minimum tread depth = 101/2 inches.
   - Ideal tread depth = 11 inches.
5. Due to ergonomics, the ratio of the size between the riser and tread should meet the ergonomic ideal, which is expressed in the following equation:
   - $2r + t = 25$ inches
   - (r = the dimension of the riser; t = the dimension of the tread)
6. All risers should be the same size within a stair design.
7. All treads should be the same size within a stair design.
8. Stairs along a path of egress must meet the minimum width requirements for egress as dictated by building code.
9. Stairs that have a clear width greater than 68 inches must have a third handrail dividing the stair width (typically in half).
10. Stairs must have a minimum vertical clearance of 80 inches, measured from the stair nosing to any obstruction overhead.

The design of stairs requires a significant effort in planning due to the level of detail required to successfully execute a stairway. First, the overall **rise** of the stair, or the finished floor to finished floor height, must be exactly determined through the use of architectural drawings and field measurements. Once the rise is determined, calculations must be conducted that will determine the overall **run** of the stair, or the horizontal distance from the top nosing to the bottom nosing including any landings.

In regard to stair form, the determining factor may be the space available on the floor plan. If space is tight, then a more compact stair layout may be necessary. Where the total rise is greater than 12 feet, a landing is

Figure 8.20 Monumental stairs can also be very simple in form while elaborate in the details, as shown in this more traditional approach to a monumental stairway.

Figure 8.21 Stairs possess many parts that all work together to create a stair that is safe, functional, and attractive based upon the design intent of the stair.

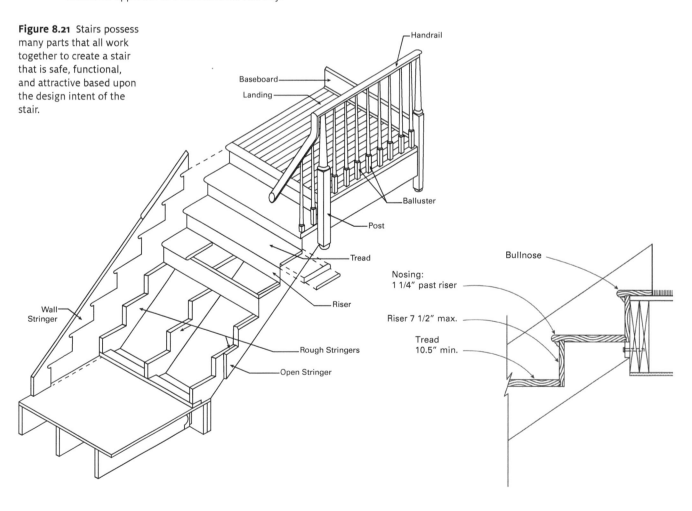

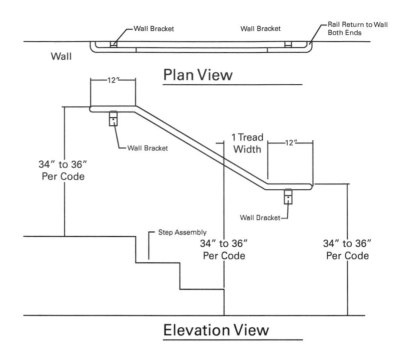

Figure 8.22 Code dictates the heights of guardrails and handrails to ensure that basic safety is provided and so that the greatest number of people can use the stairway.

Plan View

Wall

Wall Bracket — Wall Bracket — Rail Return to Wall Both Ends

12"

34" to 36" Per Code

Wall Bracket

1 Tread Width — 12"

Wall Bracket

Step Assembly

34" to 36" Per Code

34" to 36" Per Code

Elevation View

needed, which will add to the overall footprint of the stair. For purposes of figuring the number of risers and treads (see the first rule under preceding Stair Design Rules), think of the landing as one large tread.

Ramps

Ramps are used to allow for small vertical changes in floor height, such as the case in an office setting that moves from a concrete floor slab to a raised flooring system that carries electrical and/or conditioned air underneath. More often, however, ramps are used to meet barrier-free design requirements, as they allow persons with physical disabilities to traverse a change in floor level gradually. In many cases, building codes limit the slope of a ramp to 1:12, or 1 foot of rise for every 12 feet of run. This minimum code stipulation does not actually help some individuals in wheelchairs, as the force required to travel up a 1:12 ramp is too great. A 1:20 slope is a preferred ratio when universal design is made a priority by the designer and client.

While properly designed ramps enable more users to navigate vertical changes in level more easily, they do have some drawbacks. One drawback of ramps is that they consume a large amount of floor area. A ramp 5 feet in width that travels 1 foot vertically requires 60 square feet of floor area in addition to the clear floor space at the top and bottom of the ramp for circulation, whereas a stair of the same width and rise would only consume 10 square feet in

addition to the clear floor area at the top and bottom of the stair. Second, ramps frequently are designed as a retrofit, or as an afterthought, to the rest of the design, resulting in a disjointed appearance. Third, ramps tend to segregate the physically disabled from other building users, resulting in an emphasis on the disability. Despite these drawbacks, ramps can be an integral and successful aspect to a building interior if the designer considers the requirements of a ramp early in the design process (Fig. 8.23).

Elevators and Escalators

Elevators and lifts are the most efficient means to provide vertical circulation in terms of floor area, and they are barrier-free if large enough to accommodate a wheelchair (Fig. 8.24). In addition to adequate floor area, barrier-free elevators also require Braille lettering at the call buttons outside the elevator and at the floor command buttons inside the elevator, and benefit from an audible notification of the current floor number when the doors open. Building codes dictate that elevators are required in non-single-family residential buildings above a certain number of stories, which can vary based on occupancy classification and occupancy load. Where universal design is a priority, however, elevators, or lifts, are the preferred solution due to ease of use.

In addition to transporting users, elevators are also used to transport freight. Dedicated freight elevators are a common amenity in high-rises, hotels, education buildings,

Figure 8.23 A ramp can be a celebrated design element in an interior space, such as the one in the Reichstag in Berlin, Germany, by Foster + Partners.

Figure 8.24 Elevators, when creatively highlighted, can be a wayfinding element in an interior space in addition to providing safe and functional travel between levels in building.

and hospitals. Freight elevators are used to transport large equipment, construction materials, and furniture to the upper floors of high-rise office and residential buildings and provide convenient access for cleaning staff in hotels and education facilities. In hospitals, the majority of elevators are the size of freight elevators, as they are meant to accommodate gurneys to transport patients between floors (Fig. 8.25). During the design process of an upper level of a building, it is strongly advised to measure the door opening and overall size of the elevator to be sure that all furniture, materials, and other components can be transported up to the space in question prior to specification and purchasing.

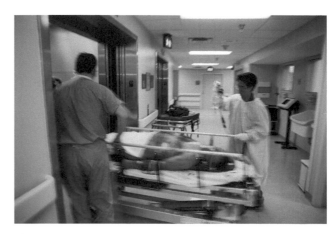

Figure 8.25 Elevators are sized to accommodate specific purposes, such as transporting patients on gurneys between levels in a hospital.

Figure 8.26 In large open volumes, escalators can be used to emphasize the connection between floors providing users with an open view of their destination.

Design considerations in relation to elevators and lifts are both aesthetic and technical. Elevator cab interiors require thoughtful attention to flooring, wall panels, lighting, and chair rails, as these items receive a significant amount of wear and tear. Technical considerations include the location of the machine components that power the elevator and the clearance around the elevator cab within the vertical shaft that runs through the building. Elevator shafts run continuously up through a building, requiring that nothing penetrates horizontally through the shaft, including structural components. An architect, engineer, and elevator consultant are needed to address these technical matters.

Escalators possess characteristics in common with both stairs and elevators (Fig. 8.26). Similar to stairs, escalators have a tread, riser, guardrail, and handrail, but escalators are not required to abide by the same rules of proportion in the treads and risers, nor are landings required. Escalators typically are designed with a 30 percent slope proportion, but can be steeper if necessary.

Similar to elevators, escalators have heavy machinery to power them, which requires maintenance and access for repair workers and have significant structural requirements to support them. As a result, the planning and design of escalators also requires the input of an architect, structural engineer, and specialty consultant.

Summary

The planning process is complex in all that it intends to achieve, but the design thinking process ensures a high level of quality in the finalized design. The drawings used to articulate the design thinking process are also used to convey design ideas to the client and intent to contractors and fabricators for construction. Two-dimensional drawings include floor plans, reflected ceiling plans, sections, and elevations. Floor plans and reflected ceiling plans show the horizontal surfaces (floors and ceilings) of a space while sections and elevations show vertical surfaces (walls) and volume. Spatial types encompass both the occupied portions, which serve a specified function, and the circulation portions that allow users to travel between occupied spaces. Circulation can be horizontal, which is described on floor plans, or circulation can be vertical, articulated through sections or elevations. The designer, in collaboration with architects, engineers, and specialty consultants orchestrates the planning process from beginning to end through well-crafted drawings to ensure the design intent is achieved.

Key Terms

Axonometric	Landing	Riser
Circulation space	Node	Run
Elevation	Nosing	Section
Floor plan	Occupied space	Space planning
Guardrails	Perspective	Tread
Handrails	Reflected ceiling plan	Vanishing points
Isometric	Rise	Wayfinding

Resources

Aspelund, K. (2014). *The Design Process*. Bloomsbury Publishing.

Brown, T. (2008, June 1). *Design Thinking*. Retrieved December 16, 2015, from https://hbr.org/2008/06/design-thinking.

Ching, F. D., & Binggeli, C. (2017). *Interior Design Illustrated*. John Wiley & Sons.

Crash Course. (2016). Retrieved April 14, 2016, from https://dschool.stanford.edu/resources/virtual-crash-course-video.

Rengel, R. J. (2014). *Shaping Interior Space*. Bloomsbury Publishing.

Rengel, R. J. (2016). *The Interior Plan: Concepts and Exercises*. New York: Bloomsbury, Fairchild Books, an imprint of Bloomsbury Publishing Inc.

Seidler, D. R. (2017). *Revit® Architecture 2018 for Designers*. New York: Fairchild Books, an imprint of Bloomsbury Publishing Inc.

Review Questions

1. Describe the purpose and benefits of drawings for the designer and the client.
2. List the types of two-dimensional drawings and purpose for each type.
3. List the types of three-dimensional drawings, the purpose for each type, and how they are different from one another.
4. Describe the two broad categories of space.
5. Describe the different types of horizontal circulation.
6. Other than signage, describe two wayfinding strategies.
7. What are the three primary means of vertical circulation? List planning concerns for each.

Exercises

Occupied and Circulation Space

1. Find two floor plans:
   a. One should show a building floor plan with multiple rooms, such as the floor plan of a classroom university building.
   b. Another should show a lobby or waiting space with numerous seating clusters, such as the floor plan of an airport terminal or lobby space of a performance venue.
2. Overlay each plan with tracing paper and outline the occupied zones with black marker, then fill them in solid. The result should be two "positive-negative," or "figure-ground," drawings that clearly delineate occupied space.
   a. For the classroom building floor plan, the occupied zones are the rooms.
   b. For the terminal or lobby floor plan, the occupied zones are the seating clusters.
3. Provide a second tracing paper overlay and outline the circulation zones with black marker and render them in green for horizontal circulation, or blue for vertical circulation. The result will be a rendered drawing that clearly delineates circulation types.
4. Overlay the occupied and circulation drawings for each plan and observe the patterns of occupied space and circulation.

9

Finishes

Learning Objectives

As a result of reading this chapter, students will

1. **Possess an awareness of the floor, wall, and ceiling finishes as being a part of a larger system.**

2. **Possess an awareness of the three categories of floor materials (hard, resilient, and soft) and the types of flooring finishes that fall into each category.**

3. **Possess an awareness of the types of wall finishes.**

4. **Possess an awareness of the types of ceiling finishes.**

As a result of taking part in the learning exercises at the end of this chapter, students will

1. **Demonstrate the ability to identify and select a variety of finishes for a simple interior space.**

2. **Demonstrate the ability to compose and/or craft a finish selection board.**

Introduction

Finishes affect the user's experience of a space by involving all five of the physiological senses. Finishes are the surfaces that we can see and touch within a space. Finishes affect the way we hear in a space, and even how we experience the sensations of smell and taste. As discussed in Chapter 4, the spatial well-being chapter, finishes also have the potential to profoundly impact an individual's mental and emotional well-being within a space. Consider your last visit to a restaurant. How did the colors, patterns, and textures within the space affect your enjoyment of the cuisine, or the company you were with?

When a designer is involved in the earliest phases of design thinking, such as building empathy for the client and defining the design problem, it is only natural to consider the impact that finishes will have in the eventual design solution. When a designer is conducting the earliest phases of conceptual development and schematic design, she is thinking about the quality of the surfaces in a space. As the process progresses further into schematic design, her ideas about finish qualities become proposed selections to the client. As the proposed finishes become determined, then the detailing process can begin in design development and become finalized in the construction documentation. Finishes are installed during construction, as the designer observes progress, making sure the original design intent is realized and addressing any questions from the contractor as they arise. The construction process is critical in understanding the successes and failures of finishes.

The best interior designers see finishes as part of a larger system. The three primary interior finish systems include floors, walls, and ceilings. Interestingly, this categorization structure of finishes reinforces the assumption that finishes are planar in nature, but they do not have to be executed in this manner. In fact, as the designer becomes well versed in the capabilities and limitations of various finishes, he can use them in a volumetric sense, creating masses at will within a larger space.

Floors

Of all the primary finish systems, floors require the highest degree of durability. Whether the space is a residential living room, a hospital corridor, a cross-training exercise facility, a mosque prayer space, or an automotive dealership showroom the floor finishes and underlying substrates are critical to the success of the space. **Substrates** are the construction materials under the finishes themselves (Fig. 9.1). For example, residential carpet has a pad underneath that is glued or stapled to a subfloor made of plywood or concrete. Sometimes, the interior designer can decide what the substrate will be, and other times will have to use whatever is already there.

Long-term maintenance and cleanability should also be considered by the designer, because flooring finishes receive the most wear and are quickly soiled compared to walls and ceilings. If a flooring material requires costly or labor-intensive maintenance, the designer must make sure the client is aware of this fact. Of the three primary categories of finish systems, floors are the most disruptive to replace, so it is especially important to consider the longevity of any flooring finish and the quality of the underlying support system. National and local codes must also be considered in relation to flooring and the type of project at hand. The International Building Code, applicable to projects in the United States, classifies finishes into three Classes, A, B, and C, where A is the most stringent qualitatively.

Floors significantly impact the physical and psychological experience of the user in the space. Acoustics, thermal comfort, perceived cleanliness, and safety influence the selection of a flooring material. In the case of acoustics, the ability of a flooring material to decrease the amount of unwanted sound is very important. For example, carpet is often used in open office environments to reduce the amount of noise in the space, which results in an increase in concentration and productivity for the workers. By contrast, when designers are working on a space high in foot traffic, such as airport terminal corridors, they are not as concerned with reducing the amount of noise in the space as they are in cleanability, safety, and durability so a material such as terrazzo is more desirable. These flooring materials, and many others, fall into three primary categories: hard, resilient, and soft.

Hard Flooring

Hard flooring materials have many positive attributes, including high strength and durability. They are relatively resistant to soiling and staining, easy to maintain and clean, and they are versatile and adaptable to both formal

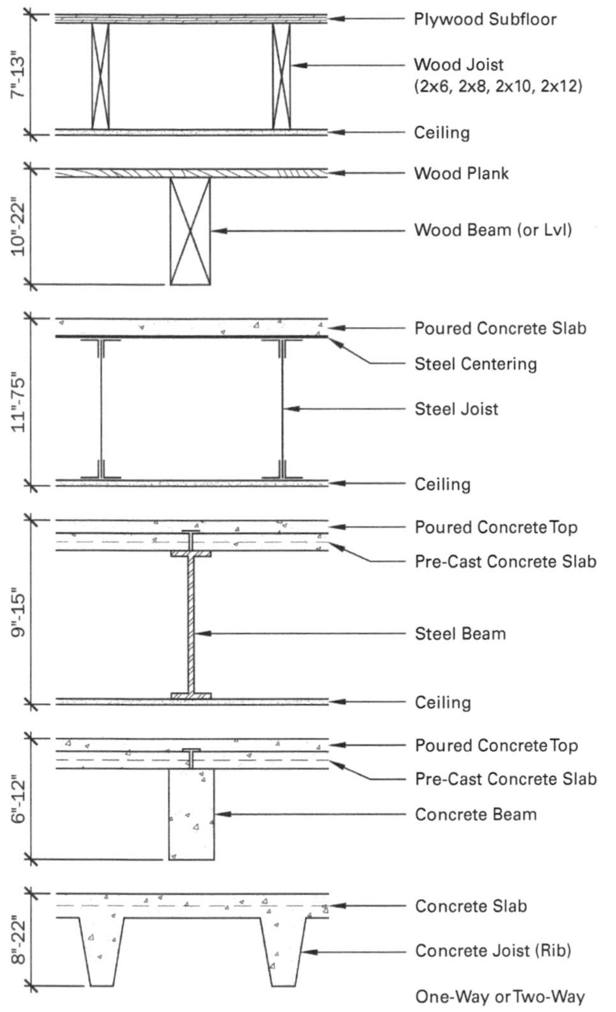
Plywood Subfloor
Wood Joist
(2x6, 2x8, 2x10, 2x12)
Ceiling
7"-13"
Wood Plank
Wood Beam (or Lvl)
10"-22"
Poured Concrete Slab
Steel Centering
Steel Joist
Ceiling
11"-75"
Poured Concrete Top
Pre-Cast Concrete Slab
Steel Beam
Ceiling
9"-15"
Poured Concrete Top
Pre-Cast Concrete Slab
Concrete Beam
6"-12"
Concrete Slab
Concrete Joist (Rib)
One-Way or Two-Way
8"-22"

Figure 9.1 These floor systems utilize a variety of materials, including wood, steel, and concrete.

and informal uses. Some disadvantages include their high initial cost, the need for extensive subfloor preparation, poor safety factor due to possible slips and falls, their chilly tactile temperature, and their tendency to amplify noise within a space. Hard flooring materials include masonry (stone, brick, and tile), concrete, terrazzo, and wood.

Masonry

Masonry refers to stone, brick, or tile assembled in modules and installed with mortar and/or grout or dry-laid. **Mortar** is used to secure the masonry pieces to a substrate, such as a concrete slab or cement fiberboard backing, and **grout** fills the gaps between modules. Certain types of masonry can be dry-laid where mortar or grout is not needed. While typically rectangular, masonry can be any shape, and its modular nature allows for tightly controlled seams or joints and produces little waste. Masonry can be **quarried**, cut directly from the earth and includes stone slabs or tiles (Fig. 9.2), or **fabricated**, made by human hands or industrial processes and includes brick, and ceramic, porcelain, and clay tile. The modular nature of masonry can be manipulated by the designer to impact the perception of space through the regular patterns that emerge in the rhythm of material.

Stone

Stone is versatile, durable, and sought after for its natural beauty. The material has a wide range of textures from rough, or granular, texture to a polished surface. The colors and veining of stone vary widely based upon the mineral content in the ground of a particular quarry. Once quarried, stone can be cut into a variety of geometric or naturally random shapes.

Stone is long-lasting and easy to maintain, but it is difficult to repair if damaged and relatively expensive compared to other materials. Stone can contribute to sound reverberation and can be chilly to the touch, a negative quality in cold climates. Alternatively, if the stone floor is dark in color and located in a space that receives direct sunlight, the surface can absorb heat and slowly release it into the space at night contributing to a passive solar design strategy.

A designer selects a specific type of stone with certain design outcomes in mind based on the qualities of the stone. All stone is heavy compared to other flooring materials and certain installation methods, such as a thick-set mortar, can add substantial weight to a floor system in existing spaces. The designer should consult a structural engineer prior to proposing a flooring solution that could add substantial structural load to the building. For the purposes of this discussion, marble, granite, travertine, and slate will be described. The finish of a stone floor is important in reference to safety, maintenance, and aesthetics. Polished finishes become very slippery when wet and should therefore be used with caution. A honed finish is generally a preferred choice due to its dull sheen without reflections and better performance in the presence of moisture. Whenever a designer is considering a natural material, stone or otherwise, it is a good idea to request a large sample size from the manufacturer due to the variety of colors and patterns in the stone.

Figure 9.2 Marble, granite, travertine, and other types of stone are extracted in large blocks from the earth in a stone quarry and then cut into slabs prior to being installed in a building interior.

Marble, Granite, Travertine, Slate

Marble is a very hard type of limestone formed under extreme heat and pressure. Even though marble is very hard, the stone is somewhat porous, requiring an annual sealant application when used in wet locations such as in kitchens, baths, or near building entrances (Fig. 9.3). Marble is selected for its expressive veining and color, with notable types including the white or blue/gray Carrara marble from Carrara, Tuscany; the white Makrana marble from Makrana, India; the gray/brown Purbeck marble from the Isle of Purbeck, UK- the semi-translucent white Penetic marble from Mount Pentelicus, Greece; and the pure white Yule marble from Colorado, US. Marble is often the standard by which other stone materials are measured.

Granite is an igneous rock with a tight granular appearance and can be found in a variety of colors, including white, gray, pink, and green, depending on its mineral composition. This stone type is much harder than marble and is often used where both durability and a luxurious appearance are valued. Granite also finds extensive use as a countertop material.

Travertine is a type of limestone like marble but differs in that it is found near natural springs, resulting in a softer stone that has many voids in its surface. When used as a flooring material, it is necessary to fill these voids, or dirt can collect and mar the surface. Travertine characteristically varies in color between white, cream, and tan, and the majority of travertine is sourced from Italy. Notable uses of travertine include the Colosseum in Rome and The Getty Center in Los Angeles.

Slate is cleaved from sedimentary rock shale and is characterized by its tightly compressed layers that results in natural variance in thickness. Slate possesses a multitude of colors, including light and dark grays, green, purple, and rusty oranges and reds (Fig. 9.4). Natural slate flooring, whether in slabs or tiles, can have a textured surface, which should be taken into account by the designer when considering furniture placement, particularly in areas where the furniture will be moved frequently, such as a dining room. It is especially important with slate that the designer should order multiple large samples to show to the client in order to demonstrate the range of color and texture that should be expected in the material.

Brick Pavers

Brick is fabricated clay masonry and is known for high durability and low maintenance. Brick pavers can be arranged in a multitude of patterns, including

Figure 9.3 Marble is often used as a flooring material for its beauty and durability, but it also works very well as a countertop material if properly cared for.

Figure 9.4 Slate is known for its wide range of color and expressive texture.

Figure 9.5 Brick pavers can be arranged in many types of patterns such as a basket weave, shown here.

a bond pattern, basket weave (diagonal or square), and herringbone (Fig. 9.5). The installation of brick flooring will greatly impact the appearance and performance, whether it is dry-laid or mortared and grouted into place. Brick color also varies widely, based on mineral content of the clay used to fabricate the brick. Left unfinished, the material has a naturally rough surface that can provide an inherent slip-resistance, but is prone to absorbing stains. If sealed, the brick surface will resist stains, but could also become slick when wet.

Tile

Tile is a durable manufactured material that can be made from stone, clay, ceramic, porcelain, concrete, glass, or metal. The oldest tile examples are made from clay and originated in Egypt around 4000 BC. Tile crafting has been recognized with pride by many cultures throughout history, including the Assyrians, Babylonians, Chinese, Mesoamericans, Greeks, Romans, and, later, the Italians. The artistic decorations and glazing techniques of each group of artisans tends to characterize ceramic and porcelain tile. The names given to these tiles link back to the geographic origin of the artisans and include Faience tiles (Faenza, Italy), Majolica tiles (Majorca, Spain), and Delft tiles (Delft, Netherlands) to name a few (Fig. 9.6). Today, Italy continues to be a leader in tile making, but the techniques perfected there have spread to many other artisans and manufacturers worldwide.

The manufacturing process of tile directly impacts the aesthetic and functional performance of the material. Tile can be made by hand, resulting in slight differences between each tile, manufactured by machine press or extrusion resulting in a very consistent appearance from one tile to the next, or created digitally with a three-dimensional printer, currently in the experimental stages of development in the tile industry. In order for tile to harden and cure the surface glaze, it is typically exposed to heat, either by direct sunlight or fired at very high temperatures in a kiln. Tile can have a variety of finishes and textures created by the extrusion process, firing temperature, chemistry of the clay, artistic effects, and type of glaze applied to the tile. When used in flooring, tile should not be highly glazed due to slipping. It is better for tile flooring to have a bit more texture, referred to as a higher **coefficient of friction** in the practice of interiors.

Clay tiles come in many varieties including terracotta and Mexican tiles. Terracotta was used extensively in the Roman Empire and paired with a unique form of radiant floor heating (Fig. 9.7). Terracotta can be painted with intricate designs or left to its natural orange clay color and simply glazed. Mexican, or Saltillo, tile utilizes clay harvested directly from the ground with little attention given to precise proportioning of ingredients and it is the imperfections that result from this process that make this tile appreciated.

Much of the historical discussion on tile in general applies to ceramic tile. Modern ceramic tile can be hand-made, but is typically manufactured in mass quantities through either a pressed or extruded industrial process. Ceramic tile is available in solid colors, and subtle or bold patterns—limitations are few when it comes to the

Figure 9.6 Many ceramic tiles are associated with a specific group of artisans practicing their craft in a certain place, such as Majorca, Spain, where Majolica tile is made.

Figure 9.7 Terracotta tile dates to ancient civilizations, encompassing a wide range of cultures, and is still in use today, although the tile is manufactured utilizing modern methods.

visual possibilities with ceramic tile. Ceramic tiles are less durable than porcelain, and, when used for flooring, are typically reserved for residential applications. In comparison to ceramic, porcelain tiles are significantly harder and, therefore, have higher degrees of moisture and impact resistance. In addition, porcelain is consistent through the tile thickness while the finish for ceramic is only on the surface. The same range of visual and finish options are available in porcelain that are available in ceramic tiles, making the design possibilities enticing.

Mosaic tile has been used for centuries, reaching back to the eighth century BC in Greece. Many cultures embraced the craft of mosaic tile, including Native Americans with Pueblo turquoise plaques and Mexican mosaic masks. The beauty of mosaic tile rests in the detail of the designs and the large-scale pictorial scenes and patterns that otherwise could not have been achieved using other materials. Christian artisans during the Antique and Early Medieval Roman periods embraced the mosaic craft which quickly spread throughout Europe. Mosaics are highly prized and still in use today. Ceramic mosaic tile is classified by size; each individual tile is less than 6 square inches in face area. Tiles are 1/4 inch to 3/8 inch in thickness and are manufactured such that the color is typically throughout the tile, not simply on the surface. For centuries, mosaics were laid one tile at a time, but today mosaic tiles are laid in sheets with fabric or a plastic grid holding the individual tiles together ensuring a uniform spacing. This innovation in modern mosaics allows for a lower cost of installation and for the beauty of the material to be enjoyed in the homes of the middle-class rather than only the wealthy (Fig. 9.8).

Glass tiles are common on walls, but they can also be used on floors. Modern glass tile has the benefit of utilizing the top and bottom sides of the material to maximize durability while preserving the visual qualities of the design. Glass is highly durable and resistant to scratching, but the film that gives glass tile its color is not typically durable. As a result, the decorative finish of glass tile is applied to the underside of the tile to preserve its appearance. This fabrication process results in a tile that has visual depth accentuated by subtle shadows cast by the tile thickness upon the decorative finish at the bottom of the tile. Pairing unsanded grout with glass tile is critical to preserve the characteristic high-gloss surface of glass tile.

Figure 9.8 Mosaic tile materials can be combined, such as glass and ceramic in this example.

Concrete

Concrete is a composite material made of coarse aggregate (stones or pebbles), fine aggregate (sand), cement, water, and possibly other additives for specialty uses. These components are mixed together into a fluid composition that can be formed into virtually any shape and will then harden over time. Within the mix, the cement is the binder, holding the aggregates and additives together, which is activated by water. The quantity of water is a somewhat delicate issue, as more water will allow the concrete to flow more easily, but less water will result in a stronger finished concrete. Additives can improve a variety of concrete characteristics, including reduced hardening time, the ability to harden in cold temperatures, and the color.

Concrete has purposefully been used as a building material for centuries, with the Romans providing major advancements in the technology as they worked to perfect the material from 300 BC to AD 476 and utilized an improved mix as a core material and then clad it with stone. Such structures as the Pantheon in Rome and the aqueducts at Ponte du Gard were constructed in this manner. The medieval era (sixth century to fourteenth century) witnessed a significant decline in the use of concrete but the technique was rediscovered prior to the Industrial Revolution and the material contributed to significant changes in architecture of the late nineteenth and early twentieth centuries. During this time, concrete reached new heights (literally) with the advent of Portland cement by Joseph Aspdin in 1824. As one looks back at the historical development of concrete it is evident how the material became a structural replacement for stone, often mimicking the arched, vaulted, and domed forms of the ancient and medieval eras. Stone was preserved as a cladding material to keep the aesthetic, functional, and tactile qualities of those beloved stone varieties. Stepping into the modern era, however, one can see the revolution in formal qualities as well.

Concrete is strong in compression but weak in tension, while steel is very strong in tension. As a result, concrete slabs, beams, and even columns, are constructed with steel bars set in place at the time of pouring the concrete. When the concrete hardens, the steel reinforcing bars, known as **rebar**, increase the tensile strength of the concrete and help prevent it from cracking. Another advancement in concrete has come with the use of additives. Many additives exist that can increase the ease of working the concrete, speed of the hardening time, increase the tensile strength, or add to the aesthetic value of the finished slab such as glass or stone aggregates.

Figure 9.9 Polished concrete floors are durable and can add visual interest to a variety of interior spaces.

Contemporary concrete flooring builds on the technological advancements of the material while also leveraging improved finishing techniques which includes color (Fig. 9.9). If the slab is existing, a topical stain can be added to the concrete, or if the concrete slab is new then the coloration can be included in the mixture as an additive. Through-color concrete mixtures are superior due to their ability to hide chips or gouges more effectively, but most colored concrete is stained after installation. Concrete can also be textured to resemble other materials such as brick or cobblestone through a pattern-stamping process while the concrete is still pliable. Many concrete floors are also sealed and polished to preserve the underlying finish, slow down the absorptions of unwanted stains, and improve the cleanability and longevity of the finish. Similar to stone, concrete floors contribute to sound reverberation in a space, which must be taken into account with any active interior.

Terrazzo

Similar to concrete, terrazzo is a composite material, but terrazzo differs in that it possesses a much higher quality finish surface (Fig. 9.10). Terrazzo ingredients can include marble, granite, quartz, or glass chips in combination with a cement binder. This flooring material can be **cast in place** (poured on site) or **precast** (created in a factory, then delivered to the construction site). The traditional form of terrazzo, developed by sixteenth-century Venetians, is thick, involving a 4-inch concrete slab with a minimum 1-inch terrazzo slab on top, is very heavy, requiring additional structural support compared to other flooring materials, and can be used in either exterior or interior applications. Newer versions of terrazzo occasionally use an interior-grade thin-set method that involves a 1/4-inch to 3/8-inch thickness of terrazzo sheet over an existing concrete slab reducing the overall thickness and weight of the system. Terrazzo slabs can be designed with any color scheme in mind, can achieve very intricate details in form, and rely on metal strips to separate the varying colored slabs from one another.

Wood

Wood is the most versatile of all flooring materials and is well-known for many pleasing aesthetic and functional qualities including its natural beauty, visual warmth, and variety in visual texture. It is also readily available in

Figure 9.10 The Colorado History Museum utilizes an intricate terrazzo floor depicting a map of the state in the main lobby.

many parts of the world with strong connections to local history and culture. The material is durable, relatively resistant to temperature change, and simple to maintain.

Wood species can be divided into two broad categories, softwood and hardwood. **Softwood** is typically used for wood framing, including studs, joists, and rafters, and for sheet goods, such as plywood. Species of softwood include Douglas Fir, Southern Yellow Pine, Western Red Cedar, and Yellow Cedar, among many others. **Hardwood** is reserved for finish surfaces such as flooring, furniture, and millwork. Species of hardwood are numerous and include White Oak, Red Oak, Black Walnut, Cherry, Pacific Coast Maple, and Yellow Birch. While a species of wood flooring is often selected first based on appearance, the hardness rating can also be a determining factor. It is also important for the designer to know that quality and hardness can fluctuate from one manufacturer to the next.

The appearance of any wood product depends on how the wood is cut from the tree (Fig. 9.11). When logs are processed, lumber mills use four different methods to saw logs: plain sawn, quarter sawn, rift sawn, or live sawn; each of these sawing methods produce a different grain pattern (Fig. 9.12).

- **Plain sawn**: soft, consistent cathedral pattern in the wood grain; most common and widely used sawing types; medium to large size boards; low to moderate in cost.
- **Quarter sawn**: linear grain pattern with periodic diagonal flecks; occasionally specified as an upgrade to plain sawn; medium to narrow size boards; relatively high in cost.

- **Rift sawn**: very tight linear grain pattern often highly prized in modern wood finishing applications; rarely used; narrow size boards; very high cost.
- **Live sawn**: variety of grain patterns incorporating characteristics of plain, quarter, and rift sawn; least desirable in appearance; often painted due to the range of the grain pattern; largest size boards; low cost.

Each of these sawing methods has its own positives and negatives and should be carefully considered in conjunction with the species of the wood.

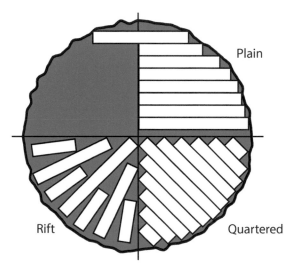

Figure 9.11 This diagram shows how a wood log can be milled to achieve certain grain patterns.

Figure 9.12 The appearance of wood flooring depends on the tree species, method used to cut and process the wood, and any stain and finish applied to the surface.

Figure 9.13 Wood flooring adapts to its context, communicating a sense of traditional warmth or cool modernity.

Bamboo, while actually a type of grass, is often grouped with wood because it can be used as a flooring material and exhibits a range of color that can loosely be characterized in similar terms as wood. Bamboo, when processed properly, can be very hard, demonstrates a very linear graining pattern, and is available in a variety of light to dark colors. Bamboo grows very quickly, which can make it a very sustainable material depending upon its place of origin in relation to the location of the project. The designer should consider the ecological and economic sustainability implications of all material choices, including the energy expended in transportation, prior to selection and presentation to a client. It is also the responsibility of the designer to update their knowledge base as domestic production of certain sought-after materials, such as bamboo, becomes more readily available.

Wood flooring can be arranged in a variety of patterns. The most common of these patterns is in a straight **strip**, 21/4 inches wide, or **plank** pattern, 3 to 8 inches in width (Fig. 9.13). **Parquetry** flooring is a simple geometric pattern of wood flooring utilizing shorter strips or planks of wood and can include checkerboard, basket weave, and herringbone variations (Fig. 9.14). **Marquetry** involves elaborate curvilinear patterns, involving some measure of inlay in many cases. Today, marquetry benefits from the use of laser cutters and digital drawing methods to produce these elaborate designs in wood flooring. In the case of wood strip, plank, and parquetry, the flooring pieces are held together via a tongue-and-groove joinery connection between the pieces of wood.

Tongue-and-groove involves the protruding profile of one piece of wood fitting into the slotted receiving profile of the neighboring piece of wood.

Wood flooring is available in three basic construction compositions: solid, engineered, and laminate.

- **Solid wood flooring**: characterized by species, such as Black Walnut; typically 3/4 inch thick; finished with several layers of polyurethane or an acrylic; able to be sanded and refinished several times during its life cycle; higher initial purchase cost; susceptible to warping if it becomes saturated in water or exposed to high levels of humidity.
- **Engineered wood flooring**: characterized by species which will only consist of the top layer while the bottom layers made of plywood; thickness can vary between 3/8 inch and 3/4 inch in thickness depending upon quality; thicker products can be sanded and refinished while thinner varieties may not provide this option; less expensive initially; performs relatively well in the presence of moisture and useful in subgrade spaces where humidity levels are often higher.
- **Laminate flooring**: contains little to no hardwood; printed paper layer resembles wood with a protective coating for wear; poor moisture resistance due to a particleboard under-layer; low cost.

The designer is faced with taking each of these basic types of wood flooring products into account when evaluating the best flooring options for a design.

Figure 9.14 Wood can be installed in a variety of patterns, including a geometric parquetry as shown here at the Palace of Versailles.

Resilient Flooring

While wood flooring is considered a type of hard flooring, it also exhibits many characteristics of resilient flooring. **Resilient flooring** materials are characterized by their dimensional memory, or the material's ability to return to its normal size and shape after receiving pressure. Materials in this category can be either natural or synthetic, and vary in size, available as rolled sheets, or modular tiles. Resilient flooring comes in a multitude of styles, textures, and colors, but they tend to be unified in their somewhat casual nature—these flooring materials are not used in highly formal spaces, such as the dining rooms of five-star restaurants, but rather find common uses in educational facilities, exercise spaces, kitchens and bathrooms, transportation terminals, and health care facilities. By nature, these materials are firm, but they also have a degree of softness that serves to protect occupants in the event of a slip and fall, and reduces noise generated by foot traffic. The most common resilient flooring materials include cork, linoleum, rubber, and vinyl.

Cork

Cork comes from the bark of the *Quercus suber*, or the evergreen cork oak tree. These trees primarily grow in Spain and Portugal near the Mediterranean Sea and are grown specifically for their bark, which is harvested without killing the tree. This harvesting process can be completed approximately twelve times during the 150- to 250-year lifespan of the tree, making cork a very sustainable material.

Used primarily as cork stoppers for wine and champagne bottles, the material possesses a natural resistance to moisture, making it an intriguing choice as a flooring material. In addition, cork flooring is pleasant to walk on, especially in spaces where users are on their feet for long stretches of time (Fig. 9.15). The material is available in rolls, necessitating an adhesive for installation, or as tiles/planks which can be installed without adhesive. The tile or plank version is a composite material where the cork is adhered to a plywood or particleboard backing and then

Figure 9.15 Cork flooring is available in a variety of textures and colors.

installed with a tongue-and-groove joinery method much like wood flooring. The material is prized for its comfort and its expressive figuring in the grain which are available in many combinations.

Linoleum

Linoleum is a natural flooring material made of linseed oil, cork dust, wood flour, and rosins with a burlap backing. The material was invented in 1860 by Sir Frederick Walton near London, England. Today, the quality and durability of linoleum varies significantly with the most durable products consisting of inlaid solid linoleum sheets and the lesser versions utilizing thinner layers of linoleum with a patterned print wear layer on top. Linoleum is prized for its natural content, durability, no volatile organic compound emissions, natural bio-degradability, anti-static and anti-allergenic properties, and ease of maintenance. Linoleum sheets are available in a variety of colors and the sheets can be cut to fit any configuration. The seams between sheets are welded using a color-coordinated rod to match the adjacent flooring color while creating a durable bond between the sheets of linoleum.

Rubber

The use of natural rubber flooring began in the mid-1800s with an increase in use following the invention of an innovative system of interlocking tiles by Frank Furness in 1894. Today, rubber flooring is synthetic due to technological advancements during World War II when the product was improved to increase durability, improve texture and color uniformity, and decrease problems related to oxidation that frequently occurred in natural rubber products. Rubber flooring is valued for its vibrant color options, durability, acoustic properties, safety related to slip-and-fall potential in wet locations, and simple installation (interlocking tiles or sheets). While rubber flooring is stereotyped as useful in exercise facilities, particularly weight rooms, it is also gaining in popularity anywhere that people may be on their feet for long stretches of time where durability and ease of maintenance are valued (Fig. 9.16).

Figure 9.16 Rubber flooring is also commonly used in exercise facilities.

Vinyl

Vinyl is an entirely synthetic material and was first introduced as a flooring tile in 1933 at the Century of Progress Exposition in Chicago where it was very well received due to its vibrant color choices. Vinyl is most commonly used as a tile (12 × 12 inches is most typical, but other sizes are available), and, in its standard quality form, is referred to as vinyl composition tile (VCT). High-end versions are referred to as luxury vinyl tile (LVT). In sheet form, vinyl is selected for its durability and ease of maintenance due its low frequency of seams. Overall, vinyl flooring is typically less expensive than other flooring materials, easy to install and maintain, possesses high durability, can withstand strong cleaning agents, and has a wide variety of patterns and colors. Vinyl flooring often has a flecked appearance with slight variations in the visual texture of the product, but it can also involve a highly durable printed layer to mimic wood, stone, or concrete. Potential problems include low impact resistance and poor acoustic properties. Some controversy has surrounded vinyl flooring products in and around 2015 where many tested positive for phthalates, which can cause cancer. Significant efforts have been made to phase out products that include phthalates, but it is the designer's responsibility to avoid specifying products that are known to cause health or environmental problems.

Soft Flooring

Soft flooring finishes consist mainly of carpets and rugs and contribute in significant ways to the overall quality of a space. Due to its soft qualities, carpet can absorb ten times more sound than hard flooring materials, greatly improving the psychological atmosphere of a space. The material can also add thermal insulation at the floor surface contributing physical and psychological warmth to a space. The cushioned nature of carpet also increases safety in high-traffic areas and at the base of stairs, and increases comfort for users as that spend long durations on their feet during working hours.

The nomadic tribes of Turkey and Persia are considered the first developers of rugs. The natural fibers used to make early rugs degrade easily, resulting in very few rugs from before the fifteenth century surviving as examples today. Due to the lack of historic rug and carpet examples, the majority of carpet knowledge is based on findings dating from the 1600s and forward to modern day. Europeans, particularly the French and English, exercised a considerable influence on carpet and rug design and construction through advancements in the types of weaves and tools used by weavers. One of the most influential inventions was a mechanical loom by Thomas Witty in England in the 1700s, and then another in Lyon, France, by Joseph-Marie Jacquard in 1804 (Fig. 9.17). Witty's loom would be used to create Axminster carpets, one of the most successful carpets of the day and still prized for their beauty. The European advancements had great influence on carpet and rug makers in the United States with the first US carpet mill established in Philadelphia in 1791, and, later, Erastus Bigelow took the mechanical loom to new heights by adding power in 1841. These advancements laid the foundation for the modern-day carpet industry, which is largely concentrated in the United States.

The construction of rugs and carpets is very similar, with size as the primary difference. Rugs are available in standard sizes (4 × 6 feet, 5 × 8 feet, 8 × 10 feet, 12 × 15 feet, etc.) or can be customized to fit specific spatial needs. Carpet is available in rolls, referred to as broadloom, or as

Figure 9.17 A Jacquard loom utilized a series of punches to create complex weaving patterns.

Figure 9.18 Carpet tile is a modular product with integral pad.

tiles. **Broadloom carpet** is typically 12 feet wide, but also 6 feet or 15 feet widths are available. **Carpet tiles** can vary in size, but are commonly available in 24-inch squares or rectangular modules (Fig. 9.18). A variety of construction methods exist including tufted, needle punch, and woven with the vast majority of carpet being tufted. The tufting process is fast and economical; it involves adhering the yarn to a durable primary backing fabric.

The most important aspect of any carpet is the type of fiber that is used to weave the yarn for the carpet. The most common natural fiber is **wool** and has historically set the standard by which all other carpet fibers are judged. Wool is valued for its aesthetics and inherent resilience to wear, but it is prone to static and does not clean as easily

as the synthetic fiber, **nylon**. Other synthetic fibers exist, but nylon is the most common due to its excellent abrasion resistance and its ability to repel fluids. Both natural and synthetic fibers are dyed, which greatly impacts durability and the ability of the fiber color to resist fading over time. **Stock dyeing** is used for either natural or synthetic fibers, and involves applying color to fibers that have already been made, resulting in a fiber whose color is superficial much like the red rind of a radish. The **solution dyeing** process is only possible with synthetic fibers, as the color is added when the fiber is still in its liquid state. The solution dyeing process results in a through-color fiber, much like an orange carrot. These two dyeing processes result in fibers that differ greatly in quality and durability where the solution dyeing method can better resist fading and staining.

The **carpet pile** is the tufted natural or synthetic carpet yarn that tends to characterize the appearance of the carpet (Fig. 9.19). Carpet pile can be tufted and sheared into several different types, including

- **Loop pile**: the surface consists of uncut loops of twisted yarn that can vary in height and color.
- **Cut pile** (plush): can be made from firm or frizzy yarns and appears more luxurious than loop pile, but also shows wear sooner than loop pile.
- **Frieze pile** (hard twist): this is a variation of cut pile that uses highly twisted yarns set in a snarled configuration that will hide footsteps much better than cut pile.

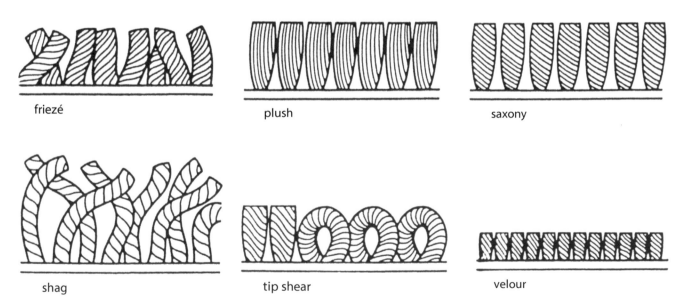

Figure 9.19 Carpet pile type is a very influential characteristic that the designer must consider carefully when specifying carpet.

- **Semi-shag pile**: a soft cut pile that is shorter than shag where the yarns still stand up.
- **Shag pile**: also a soft cut pile with long yarn that tends lay down, exposing the side of the yarn.
- **Tip-sheered pile** (random shear): consists of a loop pile with some loops sheered creating a combination loop and cut pile.
- **Berber** (multilevel loop): generally a coarse loop pile but is also available in a cut pile and shag. This pile type is named after handwoven wool squares made by North African tribes; now machine made.

Onc last aspect of carpet and rugs for the designer to consider is the padding. The importance of padding reinforces the need for interior designers to think of finishes as part of a larger system, as padding provides the foundation for carpet, enhances overall foot comfort, adds thermal insulation, reduces noise, and can greatly extend the life of the carpet. Thicker and softer carpet generally benefits from a firm pad of 7/16-inch thickness or less, while thinner or firmer carpet needs a thicker pad of 3/8 inch or more.

The wide variety of flooring materials available to an interior designer makes the selection of these materials a highly detailed process. The designer makes flooring recommendations to a client based on aesthetics, performance, and the impact that the finish will have on the functionality and psychology of a space over the life of the material. Flooring finishes are particularly reliant upon the substrates below them due to the heavy use that all flooring receives. Any problems that exist in the substrates below will impact the ability of the flooring material to function properly.

Walls

Interior walls receive far less abuse compared to floors, and, as such, the finishes of an interior wall system can be less robust than their flooring counterparts. As a general rule, it is permissible to use a flooring material on a wall, but not a wall material on a floor. For example, wood flooring may wrap up a wall and across a ceiling, but the floor material has stricter requirements than the wall or ceiling versions of the material, as it will likely be thicker, involve a more robust method of installation, and require more detailed considerations in relation to cleanability and maintenance (Fig. 9.20).

Walls are divided into two basic types: load bearing and non-load bearing. **Load-bearing walls** support their own weight and additional weight above that could include a higher level of the building or the roof. Altering the structural integrity of a load-bearing wall in any way, including adding a door or window opening or moving the wall, requires the input of an architect and/or a structural engineer. **Non-load-bearing walls** simply support their own weight and serve to divide larger interior volumes for functional or aesthetic purposes. Interior designers may make simple aesthetic changes to load-bearing walls, such as painting or adding wall covering, and change non-load-bearing walls at will.

All walls involve some type of light framing or heavy material internal construction. Light framing can be wood (Fig. 9.21), in cases where fire code requirements are not especially stringent such as a single-family residence, or light gauge metal framing in cases where fire code requirements are stricter, such as in a hospital, large

Figure 9.20 This space utilizes wood on all surfaces, with the stair treads and right-hand wall embracing the same wood flooring material and the left-hand wall and ceiling utilizing highly textured bands that could not be used as a flooring material.

retail mall, or multi-tenant residential high-rise building. Heavy construction in the form of concrete masonry units (CMU) can also be used to build walls that are highly fire resistant and provide improved acoustical separation and security between neighboring spaces. Occasionally, CMU walls will separate neighboring tenants of a larger building while walls within a single tenant space will be built using light gauge metal framing. Each of these wall construction types can be finished using a variety of wall finishes.

Stone

Historical uses of stone and methods of quarrying in relation to floors also apply to walls. When stone is used in a wall application it will typically be a relatively thin veneer, 1/2 inch or thicker for slabs or 1/4 to 1/2 inch for tiles. Whether marble or granite, the finish can vary from a rough texture to a very smooth surface with a high gloss. When travertine is used on walls, the voids can remain unfilled. When small- to medium-sized pieces of stone are used, they must be laid in a coursing pattern. Stone coursing types include

- **Rubble**: uncut irregular sizes and shapes of stone.
- **Ashlar**: precut rectangular shapes.

These two categories can be either random, resulting in little or no horizontal grout alignment, or coursed, where the horizontal joints align with one another. These attributes can be combined to result in the four most common types of stone coursings: random rubble (Fig. 9.22), coursed rubble, random ashlar, and coursed ashlar.

Figure 9.21 Light framing, in this case wood, is the most common method of constructing walls.

Figure 9.22 The uncoursed rubble stone wall offers a rustic counterbalance to the refinement of this contemporary interior.

Brick

Brick has been in use for thousands of years due to widespread access to clay, its ease of fabrication, and the high durability that brick provides as people seek protection against the natural elements. The earliest found examples of brick date from approximately 7,500 BC at Tell Aswad near modern day Damascus, Syria, and the earliest recorded brick-making is by the Israelites found in Exodus 1:4. Early uses of brick involved a natural drying process where the bricks were set to bake in the sun, but between 2500 and 2000 BC kilns were introduced in India to fire brick. Kiln-fired brick, with its greater strength and durability, is far superior to the dried varieties and provides the technological basis by which bricks are made today.

Bricks are fabricated today utilizing standard sizes adopted by the brick-manufacturing industry. The most widely used brick is the **modular brick** (3 5/8 inches W × 7 5/8 inches L × 21/4 inches H). When coupled with a typical mortar joint of approximately 3/8 inch thickness, the modular brick adopts an 8-inch module in length

(7 5/8 inches + 3/8 inch) and approximately 8-inch height for every third coursing ([21/4 inches + 3/8 inch] × 3). This module should drive the length and height of a brick wall as well as the placement of openings within the wall. Designing a brick wall that is "on module" will look better and save time and construction cost due to the lack of cut bricks in the wall. **Thin brick** is approximately 1/2 inch thick and installed much like a tile over a plywood or cementitious backer board substrate.

The design of a brick wall is highly dependent upon the arrangement of the bricks and mortar. A **brick course** consists of one row of brick and the accompanying mortar joint where the bricks can be placed in a variety of positions. **Brick positions** are available in a variety of types, and the most common include stretcher, header, and soldier. Brick courses can be arranged into patterns, which is referred to as a brick bond type (Fig. 9.23). **Brick bond types** include running, stacked, Flemish, and English bond, among others (Fig. 9.24). Brick joints are also very important to any brick wall for visual and performance reasons. **Mortar joint types** vary widely, with the most common types including concave, flush, raked, struck, and weathered joints. The joint type can result in a wall that appears more monolithic, such as with a concave or flush joint, or deep shadow lines can be expressed with the use of raked, struck, or weathered joints. Mortar joint type is critical to the durability and longevity for exterior walls, but, when evaluating mortar joint types for the interior face of exterior brick walls or for interior walls, more flexibility is afforded for the designer to achieve the aesthetic goals without having to consider the impacts of nature.

Concrete

Concrete walls rely on temporary forms, typically made from plywood and studs with steel ties holding the plywood in place, to hold the wet concrete in place until it can harden and support itself. The material and texture of those forms will transfer to the concrete as it hardens, such as a wood grain pattern in the case of plywood. The texture of the forms and the placement of the ties can be dictated by the designer to achieve a particular finished appearance for the wall. Other concrete finishes are achieved by an additional installation step after the concrete has hardened and includes bush hammering to expose the aggregate, acid etching to remove the outermost concrete surface

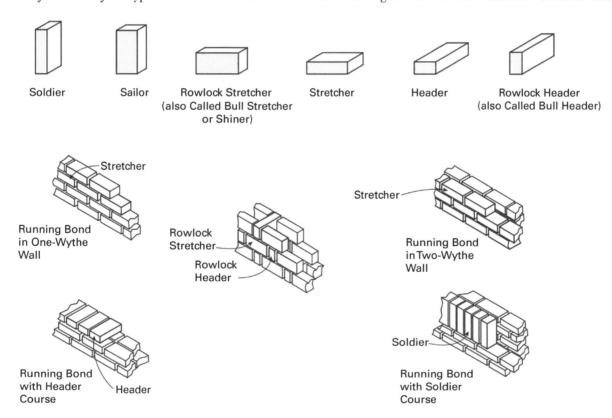

Figure 9.23 Brick masonry can be arranged in a variety of positions to achieve a desired appearance, or to achieve a certain structural goal, such as the rowlock in tying two wythes together.

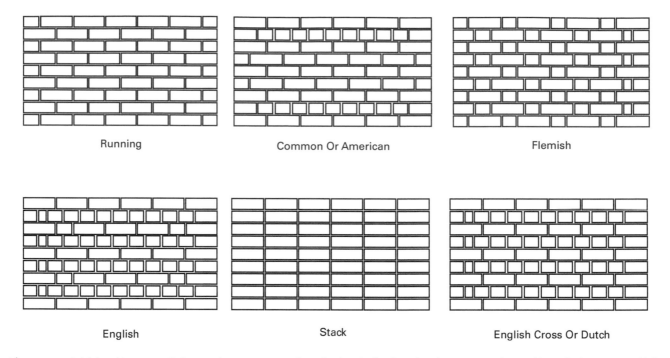

Running   Common Or American   Flemish

English   Stack   English Cross Or Dutch

Figure 9.24 Brick bond types greatly impact the appearance of a wall. Historically, these bond types were also used in walls that were multiple wythes thick in order to tie the wythes together.

and provide a slightly dimpled texture, and sandblasting that will result in a textured surface corresponding to the coarseness of the sand (fine, medium, heavy).

Concrete Masonry Units

As discussed earlier, concrete masonry units are most often used for the interior construction of walls that will receive some other type of finish over them, but occasionally CMU remains exposed. Modular concrete masonry units are 7 5/8 inches W × 15 5/8 inches L × 7 5/8 inches H and utilize a 3/8-inch thick mortar joint resulting in an 8-inch high and 16-inch long design module. Notice that this aligns with modular brick and the goal is consistent to design on module, avoiding any cut units. CMU utilizes an open cell structure that can be filled with concrete and steel reinforcing to create walls that are very tall and can bear heavy loads.

Standard CMU is fabricated with a lightly textured face that can remain natural, receive a polished finish, or be painted. CMU is also available in a variety of other textured finishes including split-face (Fig. 9.25), slump, and sculptured patterns, such as fluted, angular, and other geometric patterns. Concrete masonry units are also available with open faces in geometric patterns called screen blocks.

Figure 9.25 This load-bearing split-face CMU wall is receiving steel rebar in the open cells, which will later be filled with concrete.

Glass

The earliest known uses of glass date back to 4000 BC when glass beads were as highly valued as precious gemstones. Up until the development of clear glass in AD 100 at Alexandria, all glass possessed some coloration due to mineral and chemical impurities. Once clear glass was developed, the Romans refined techniques to use glass in architectural applications which spread across much of Europe over the next 1,000 years. As glass artisans developed their craft, the glass became associated with the location of the artisans, the best example being Murano glass from Murano, Italy (Fig. 9.26). Murano glass is known for its vibrant colors, bold form, and exceptional artistry.

Architectural glass has grown to an entire industry today and is used extensively in architecture and interior design. Glass walls are very useful in providing acoustical privacy and defining the edges between spaces while allowing daylight to penetrate deeply into the interior of buildings. Architectural glass today is primarily made using the float method. **Float glass** is made by pouring molten glass onto molten tin and allowing the glass to reach its flat equilibrium as it cools, resulting in a glass sheet of consistent thickness. When additional safety is needed, **tempered glass** is used, which will shatter into many small fragments rather than large angular pieces, lessening the likelihood of serious injury. In cases where high security is a concern, **laminated glass** should be used (Fig. 9.27). It creates a sandwich of two or more layers of glass with an interlayer that will hold the overall unit together in the event the glass breaks. The interlayer can be clear, or include a pattern to enhance the aesthetics of the design or provide additional visual privacy while still allowing some light to pass through. Another added benefit of laminated glass is improved acoustical performance, increasing privacy between spaces.

Plaster

Plaster has been in use for centuries, including in ancient Egypt and Greece where murals were painted over the plaster for decoration. Romans developed the use of frescoes where the plaster would be painted while still slightly wet so that the paint could penetrate the surface of the plaster, resulting in a very durable decorative effect. Plaster was also used to create very intricate moldings on columns, pilasters, walls, and ceilings.

Plaster is a fine craft requiring several steps for a successful and high quality installation. Prior to the plaster application, **lath**, made of wood strips (Fig. 9.28), metal mesh, or gypsum board strips, is attached to the wall framing. Plaster is installed in three coats:

- **Scratch coat**: bonds to the lath.
- **Brown coat**: levels the surface.
- **Finish coat**: very smooth and receives the final finish, such as paint.

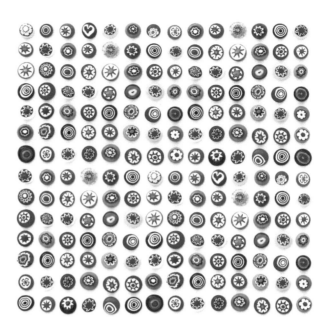

Figure 9.26 Murano glass, from Murano Italy, is prized for its highly crafted artisanal beauty.

Figure 9.27 Clear interior glass partitions are used to divide space while preserving acoustic privacy and allowing daylight to penetrate as far as possible to interior spaces.

Figure 9.28 Plaster is installed in layers over lath which is fastened to wall studs.

Plaster will readily absorb moisture, so it should be sealed prior to applying paint or adhesive for wall coverings. The material is formable, allowing it to follow curves beautifully if skillfully installed. In the hands of a skilled installer, plaster provides an exquisite wall surface with a visual softness unmatched by sheet goods such as gypsum board. This skilled installation is in short supply, requires time and a high monetary cost, making gypsum board an often preferred alternative.

Gypsum Board

Gypsum board is a generic term that refers to a panel made of gypsum with a paper facing on each side of the board and around the edges. Several companies manufacture gypsum board and the product names will often be used freely in place of the generic term, such as Sheetrock, manufactured by the US Gypsum Corporation. Gypsum board is an economical replacement for plaster

and lath that saves time and cost in construction due in large part to the labor required for plaster and lath. Typically, gypsum board is available in 4 feet W × 8 feet L sheets and 1/2-inch thickness for residential and ceiling applications and 5/8 inch for nonresidential applications, but other sizes and thicknesses are available. Thinner sheets of gypsum board are often used for curved applications and thicker versions can be used to achieve high fire ratings.

Gypsum board has many positive attributes, including its ability to be fire retardant. Fire retardant gypsum board, referred to as Type X, is used when an interior fire-rated partition is required by building code to protect occupants from fire along a path of egress, such as a corridor leading to an exit stairwell or door. Fire rating requirements increase as the risks to occupants' safety increases, so, to meet these requirements, designers can add more layers of Type X gypsum board to a wall construction. Other valuable functions exist with specialty types of gypsum board including mildew resistance, antimicrobial gypsum board, and water-resistant gypsum board (referred to as WR or "green" board due to the color of the paper facing). These specialty types of gypsum board can be used in areas that may be prone to these conditions such as basements (mildew resistance), hospitals (antimicrobial), or bathrooms (water resistant).

Gypsum board is typically installed horizontally by screwing the board to the wall framing and then filling the screw holes with joint compound and sanding smooth (Fig. 9.29). Seams between boards are taped, mudded, and sanded to a smooth texture prior to applying the final finish. Outside corners are protected with metal corner

Figure 9.29 Gypsum board is installed in large sheets and the joints are taped, mudded, and sanded to achieve a seamless appearance.

guards that are fastened to the gypsum board and receive multiple applications of joint compound and are sanded to achieve a seamless finish. This process is especially important prior to applying any paint or coating to the wall, as imperfections in the gypsum board are clearly visible after applying the final finish.

Paints and Coatings

Paint has been used for millennia as a means to alter the interior environment. The oldest known example of paint is in the Pettakere cave on Sulawesi Island, Indonesia, dating back to 33000 BC. Even in the earliest examples, paint can be classified as "a group of emulsions generally consisting of pigments suspended in a liquid medium for use as decorative or protective coatings" (National Paint and Coatings Association).

Today, paints and coatings are the simplest, fastest, and most cost-effective method to alter the appearance of a space. In addition to the countless variations of hues in value and intensity, paints and coatings are available in several different **levels of sheen**, or shininess:

- Flat/matte
- Eggshell
- Satin
- Semi-gloss
- Gloss

A higher sheen offers ease in cleaning but will show imperfections in the surface below, while a flat finish will hide many imperfections but will be very difficult to clean. Functionally, paints and coatings provide protection for the surface beneath against rust, fading, and even fire.

The components of paint include pigments, binders, solvents, and additives. **Pigments** are powdered solids that provide the color and brightness qualities of coatings while hiding the surface underneath. High quality paints tend to have a higher quantity of pigment that can hide the surface underneath with fewer coats. **Binders** adhere the pigment to a surface and directly impact the useful life of the coating, as lower quality binders will cause the pigment to flake off more quickly. Types of binders include latex, alkyd, resin, and urethane. **Solvents** are liquids that provide the suspension of the other materials and aid in the application of the coating. Solvent types include water, which is often paired with a latex binder, or an oil and alcohol solution that is often paired with an alkyd. When the solvent dries, the binder adheres

the pigment to the surface. Without the solvent, the pigment and adhesive would not spread over the surface. **Additives** provide specialized functions for the coating, including additional UV protection, mildew-cide, or thickening agents for use on particular types of surfaces.

Many types of paints are specifically formulated for use in certain circumstances on certain substrates. It is the responsibility of the interior designer to understand what the strengths and weaknesses are of the various types of paints and coatings (Fig. 9.30). Latex paint is one very common type of paint used in building interiors. Latex is a binder paired with water as a solvent making clean-up simple during application, and it dries quickly allowing the characteristic odor of latex to vanish quickly. Latex leaves little to no overlapping roller marks, but will show brush marks. This paint of type is recommended to cover plaster, gypsum board, masonry, wood, and even acoustic tile when necessary. Other coating types such as enamel, epoxy, stain, and clear coatings possess their own positive and negative attributes, which the interior designer should become familiar with.

Wall Coverings

The earliest paper wall coverings can be traced back to 200 BC in China where simple rice papers were adhered to walls. The practice developed in China and the Middle East in the following centuries and eventually made its way to Europe sometime between the twelfth and fifteenth centuries. The earliest European wall covering fragment dates from 1509 at Christ's College in Cambridge, England. The English made significant advancements in the printing methods used to create wall coverings, including hand-painting, woodblock printing, and stenciling techniques. Across the English Channel, the French were creating their own wall coverings with great success, including the establishment of the first paperhangers' guild in 1599 and the invention of flocked wall papers in 1620, which resemble velvet in texture and often embrace floral patterns (Fig. 9.31). The Frenchman Jean-Michel Papillon created the first matching and continuous pattern in 1675 using a block method of printing, which led to the modern-day versions of pattern designs in wall coverings.

Modern wall coverings can be made from a variety of materials with the express goal of achieving certain aesthetic and durability characteristics. Typical wall coverings consist of three layers, the decorative layer,

Figure 9.30 Paints and coatings provide protection for the surface beneath and also carry much of the aesthetic goals of a space, such as this warm color scheme in an office interior.

Figure 9.31 Flocked wall coverings require special care due to their delicate texture and can be original to a historic interior or they can be recreated utilizing a historical pattern.

intermediate layer, and the backing layer. This three-layer construction results in wall coverings that can be washable, scrubable, stain resistant, abrasion resistant, and colorfast, which few paints and coatings can match. Whether a wall covering is made from paper, vinyl, a textile, or a hybrid, will influence these durability characteristics. Contract spaces require higher levels of durability resulting in most wall coverings utilizing a vinyl-coated paper, paper-backed solid sheet vinyl, or fabric-backed vinyl; for residential spaces where durability requirements are lower, wall coverings can be made from the more robust varieties used in contract spaces, or they can be manufactured with paper or paper-backed textiles.

The aesthetic possibilities of wall coverings are virtually endless as color and pattern options abound. The designer must take the dye-lot of a wall covering and the pattern matching technique into account when specifying wall coverings. A **dye lot**, also known as a run number, is a group of wall covering rolls manufactured from the same print run. Subtle differences in color brightness and saturation are noticeable between two separate dye lots, meaning a transition in dye lots should be avoided within a space. Pattern matching is challenging the more precise the technique, and mistakes are obvious when poorly executed. Pattern matching options include:

- **Random match**: monolithic in appearance; will match no matter how adjacent strips are hung in relation to one another.
- **Straight-across match**: adjacent strips of wall covering perfectly align with one another horizontally across the wall.
- **Drop match**: half-drop match—every other strip aligns horizontally; multiple-drop match—every third, or more, strip aligns.

Straight-across and drop match patterns will have a **pattern repeat**, the vertical distance between two identical points in a pattern, and the characteristics of the repeat will greatly impact the visual experience in a space.

Innovations in wall coverings include relief textures and even embedding organic LED lighting into the material as designers seek to offer new and enticing design options. Conversely, the additional time and cost of stripping and replacing wall covering along with their tendency to go in and out of style deters many clients from wanting to use the material. A designer should clearly describe the positives and negatives of utilizing a wall covering to the client in a residential or contract design scenario.

Wood

Wood is versatile in regards to the aesthetic impact the material can have upon a space. The orientation of wood planks or panels in a horizontal configuration will appear to elongate, or widen, spatial proportions (Fig. 9.32), a vertical orientation will make the space feel taller, and an angled orientation will activate the space through additional eye movement and visual intensity. Wood wall finishes can add a rustic or refined sense to a space depending upon the color, expressiveness of the grain, texture, and level of refinement of the detailing. Wall installations offer more configuration options, including board-and-batten, reverse board-and-batten, board-on-board, shiplap, tongue-and-groove, and expressive reveals.

Figure 9.32 Horizontal wood strips with wide reveals tend to elongate spatial proportions.

In a residential context, where fire code requirements are not as stringent, wood can be used as either solid strips, planks, or as plywood. In a contract design context, the use of non-fire-treated solid wood (such as trim and casements) must be limited to less than 10 percent of the overall wall surface. In all contexts, however, the designer should be aware that wood can be a sustainable alternative compared to many other material types based upon **embodied energy**, or the amount of energy it takes for a material to be harvested, manufactured, and transported to a construction site. Wood requires 1,510 kW-hours of electricity per ton to manufacture, whereas rolled steel requires 12,000 kW-hours per ton and aluminum 67,200 kW-hours per ton. Other factors, including transportation distance from the point of harvest and manufacture to the construction site will add to this energy consumption, which is why locally harvested and manufactured wood products are more ecologically sustainable.

Plywood panels are a common substrate for many wood wall applications. Plywood consists of an odd quantity of layers—usually three, five, seven, or eleven—of thin sheets of veneer arranged in alternating perpendicular grain orientations to create the overall panel thickness, 1/4 inch, 3/8 inch, 1/2 inch, 5/8 inch, and 3/4 inch, typically. The face veneer can be of finish quality, ready to receive paint, stain, or a clear coat finish, while the back veneer serves to balance the plywood construction and prevent warping. Per the American Woodworkers Institute (AWI), plywood is available in three grades, including **premium grade**, which is reserved for the highest quality of workmanship and is the highest in cost; **custom grade**, which is used for the majority of architectural woodwork and wall applications; and **economy grade**, where a basic level of quality, craft, and materials is expected in construction substrates, such as subfloors, exterior wall sheathing, and roof sheathing.

Wood veneers are thin sheets of wood that have been sliced from a log. **Veneer** can be sliced to produce different grain patterns, much like the sawing methods for solid wood. Veneer slice types include the **plain slice**, which produces cathedral and straight grain patterns; **quarter slice**, resulting in a tight linear grain with diagonal flecks; **rift slice**, creating a clean linear pattern; and **rotary slice**, which will create a random grain veneer typically used for the inner layers of plywood, economy grade substrates, or plywood that will receive a layer of primer and paint. Individual pieces of veneer are referred to as **leaves**, and leaves that are sliced from the same log are grouped into a **flitch**. When laying out wood veneer, it is important to strategically place the division between flitches, as the grain pattern and color can vary even when the designer is using the same species of wood with the same type of slice. Once a species and slicing method are chosen, a millworker, with input from a designer, will match leaves of veneer into an appropriate pattern. The three primary matching types include **random matching**, producing a boarded rustic, or informal, appearance; **slip matching**, organizing the veneer in an identical orientation and size resulting in rhythmic repeat of the grain pattern; and **book matching**, mirroring alternating leaves so that pairs of leaves look like facing pages of a book which results in a balanced symmetrical patterns of veneer leaves. When more than one row of leaves is needed to fill a panel or wall, an **end-matching** technique is used, which involves book matching leaves in both the horizontal and the vertical direction, resulting in a continuous symmetrical grain pattern over a large expanse of wall surface.

Decorative Laminates

Particleboard is a less expensive substrate compared to plywood. It consists of saw dust and adhesive that is pressed under heat to create a smooth and very dimensionally consistent sheet good. Particleboard is available in various densities, referred to as low-density, medium-density, and high-density fiberboard. **Medium-density fiberboard** (MDF) is the most common type of particleboard that utilizes very fine particles resulting in a smooth surface useful for a thin application of paints or coatings, a wood veneer, or decorative laminate overlay. With any type of particleboard, exposure to moisture should be avoided, as the material will expand, disintegrate, and lose its strength.

Decorative laminates are commonly used to cover countertops, cabinetry substrates, and wall panel substrates (Fig. 9.33), such as plywood or particleboard, and can be grouped into two categories—low-pressure and high-pressure—referring to the force applied to the thin materials during manufacturing. These materials are very thin, with general purpose laminate measuring .05 inch thick while laminate intended exclusively for vertical surfaces is only .03 inch thick. Laminates possess a moisture-resistant, abrasion-resistant, and easily

Figure 9.33 Decorative laminate wall panels offer additional protection to wall surfaces.

Figure 9.34 Wall tile provides a surface that is highly durable and cleanable in some of the most high-traffic spaces, such as the London Underground.

cleanable surface that can be very useful in offering protection to the surface behind the laminate while providing visual interest. Specialty functions available with laminates include antifungal and antibacterial treatments, and fire-retardant or flame-resistant laminate cores that can enhance the fire-rating of a partition. Laminates are available in a variety of colors, patterns, and textures and many are designed to mimic natural materials such as wood and stone.

Tile

The attributes of stone, clay, ceramic, porcelain, and glass tile in flooring have many of the same attributes when used on walls (Fig. 9.34). One very important difference, however, is in reference to tile thickness, which influences impact resistance. Wall tile is considerably thinner than floor tile and will also use a thin set mortar installation more frequently than flooring tile. Wall tile is often installed over cementitious backer board, which is specially formulated to support tile and prevent moisture from migrating through to the interior of the wall cavity. Tile is often used when a durable, cleanable, and waterproof surface is needed, such as in and around showers and bathtubs or food preparation areas. In these cases, a grout sealer is highly recommended to prevent the grout from absorbing stains often associated with cooking. Tile's heat resistance also makes the material suitable for fireplace surrounds. When used in partial wall applications, tile trim pieces such as a bullnose are recommended. When transitioning wall tile to the floor, a tile cove base piece is typically used.

Acoustic Panels

Acoustic panels are generally installed over another wall surface, such as painted gypsum board or CMU to reduce noise and generally improve the acoustical performance of space (Fig. 9.35). Generally, acoustic panels are made from a fiberglass or mineral fiberboard core and then wrapped in a textile to provide both the desired acoustic performance and positive aesthetics for the wall surface. These types of panels can be hard or resilient, which can provide the added benefit of a tackable surface. Acoustic panels can be designed to be fire resistant, making it relatively simple for designers to meet code requirements in contract design scenarios that require additional acoustical performance. Walls are not the only surface that can provide acoustical benefits for an interior environment. In fact, the majority of acoustical benefits are often provided by the ceiling surface.

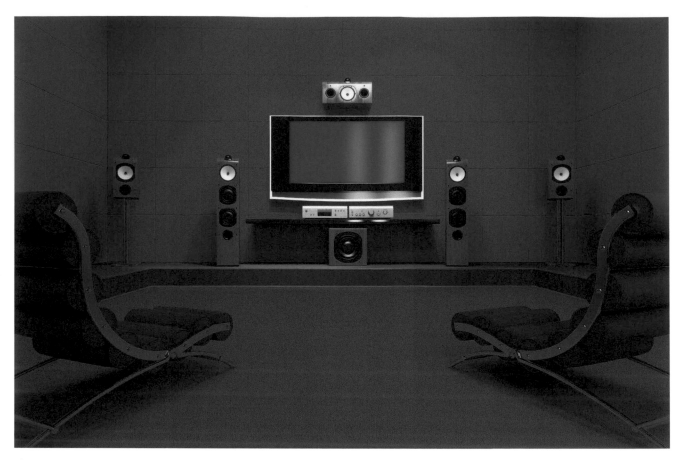

Figure 9.35 Acoustical wall panels can provide both an aesthetic appeal and acoustic performance to this lively lounge space.

Ceilings

Ceilings have historically been the ideal place for creative expression because they do not receive the wear and tear that floors and walls must endure. Consider the ceiling of the Sistine Chapel, the vehicle by which thousands of annual visitors to Vatican City get to experience Michelangelo's frescoes, including the Creation of Adam (Fig. 9.36). These timeless pieces of art would have never survived this long if they had been part of a floor or wall close enough for individuals to touch. Ceilings also provide the opportunity for the architect or designer to take part in great exercises in formal expression.

Ceiling forms include two broad categories described simply as flat and non-flat forms. **Flat ceilings** include standard, tray and double-tray, and coffered forms. **Standard flat ceilings** can be uneventful, lacking in design interest and screaming for more attention, or they can be quiet, yet powerful expressions of minimalism. **Tray ceilings** incorporate a level change near the perimeter of

space and double-tray forms utilize a second step up to a higher plane. Often, these level changes can incorporate soft, indirect cove lighting or subtle changes in material finish that can serve to enhance the mood of any space. **Coffered ceilings** utilize a grid to divide the plane into smaller portions, and often incorporate subtle height changes, wood details, finish changes, and strategically placed lighting (Fig. 9.37).

Non-flat ceilings include shed (mono-pitch), cathedral, vault, and dome forms. **Shed ceiling** forms will often follow a mono-pitch roof form that can serve to introduce additional natural light to the interior through tall walls of glass or strips of clerestory windows (Fig. 9.38). **Cathedral ceiling** forms pitch in two directions reaching an apex, or ridge, resulting in a space grandiose in scale. A cathedral ceiling typically pairs with a gable or hip roof form. **Vault ceilings** result from curved ceiling forms and in cases where the curve is perfectly round, like half a cylinder, that form is referred to as a Roman or barrel vault (Fig. 9.39). **Domes** communicate importance

Figure 9.36 The Sistine Chapel ceiling is populated by extensive frescoes painted by the great artist and architect Michelangelo.

Figure 9.37 Coffered ceilings can find a place in contemporary or traditional settings and offer an enhanced level of visual detail to a flat ceiling design.

Figure 9.39 Vaulted ceilings provide interesting opportunities for expressive lighting and to emphasize the length of a space or a well-defined path of travel.

Figure 9.38 Cathedral ceiling forms provide the opportunity to exploit vertical proportions and rely on a pitched roof form for execution.

for the activities that occur within the spaces they define. Examples include places of worship, legislative buildings, and higher education buildings. When a round dome is placed over a square space in plan, an unusual shape results high on the wall at that intersection called a **pendentive**, resulting in an additional opportunity for artistic expression near the ceiling.

Ceilings carry and conceal many of the interior components related to environmental systems, lighting, and fire suppression in an interior environment. Environmental systems, fire suppression systems, and lighting all benefit from concealing the majority of their components above the ceiling plane in an area called the **plenum** where they

Function Drives Materiality

Project: Gunster

Location: Thirty-fifth floor of 600 Brickell Ave., Miami, Florida

Client: Gunster, Yoakley, & Stewart, P.A.

Design Firm: ASD|SKY

Occupants/Users: Attorneys, staff, and clientele

Site Characteristics: Dense urban downtown

Year Complete: 2014

Cost Estimate: Undisclosed

Facility Size: 20,000 square feet; one level

Project Overview

The project site is a full-floor tenant buildout on the thirty-fifth floor of Brickell World Plaza, a forty-floor, LEED platinum precertified high-rise building in Miami, Florida. Moving to a new space offered the opportunity to reevaluate space allocations and look for planning efficiencies. To better utilize the square footage and allow for more flexibility, ASD|SKY moved the client from their existing model of office size based upon corporate hierarchy to uniform-sized attorney offices along the perimeter glass. Administrative support staff were located adjacent to the attorney offices with a centralized high-density filing system area and communal lounge area easily accessible for all employees.

Public space area requirements included a secure reception area with conference rooms to support various meeting sizes, and serving pantry to service conference area and guests. Given the mandate by the client to employ best practices in law firm design, the reception space was conceived as a multifunctional client zone that accommodates typical confidential meetings that can be converted into an expansive event space to host after-hour gatherings. To accommodate the event functions, an operable glass wall can be concealed into a blind pocket, effectively doubling the open space directly to the exterior glass line. Furnishings were impacted by these considerations, and in lieu of a fixed conference table, multiple mobile tables customized to suit a boardroom were developed.

Aesthetically, the client wanted a departure from their existing environment, which emphasized dark, enclosed offices, heavy wood, and traditional stone flooring. By contrast, the new design developed a visual vocabulary to maximize transparency and access to daylight throughout while maintaining acoustical privacy. The design presents a fresh finish palette with visual richness while clearly speaking to the Miami locale of the office by embracing exterior views of the water and city vista. The challenge that the plan presented for the initial visitor experience proved to be the catalyst for the main feature of the reception sequence. The design of this sculptural piece figuratively captures the firm's dynamism in the aftermath of the 2008 economic downturn.

Material Selection Process

In early design visioning sessions, ASD|SKY displayed a wide range of finishes to the client electronically and in the context of completed spaces for a reaction to the overall look, feel, and mood of a space. This allowed for not only a presentation of various finish materials but also aided in initiating a broader design dialog on topics such as use of color, acoustical impact of material selections, and transparency versus privacy.

ASD|SKY was able to cultivate a strong working relationship with the client such that the design team earned their trust by working closely with them on key design decisions. The client took particular interest in discussing the flooring material options—tone, natural versus manufactured material options, format and size, and installation pattern. Material presentations utilized a loose format, curated to specific palette ranges. This

The monumental brand wall draws the visitor from the elevator to the reception area.

allowed for the presentation to be more interactive, inviting the client to be an integral part of the process with a sense of meaningful contribution to a design that they will live with for the next ten to fifteen years.

The base building construction presented some challenges in relation to the installation of floor materials and other interior components. The existing concrete slab was several inches higher at the perimeter compared to the internal core of the building. The client's desire to have large format stone flooring, which does not react well to sloping floors, and an operable glass partition system with tight tolerances compounded the challenge of creating a level floor. Because the low point occurred at the building core, simply building up this area would create conflict in transitioning to the existing base building doors and floors in the restrooms, stairways, and at the elevator lobby.

Entry Feature Wall

The client's desire for their reception and conference areas to take advantage of the water views over Biscayne Bay initiated the design challenge of the entry wall. This desire required these client interaction

The waiting area is flanked by a sliding glass wall that can unite the waiting area and conference room for large gatherings.

The kitchen is one such area that allows an accent material to draw the attention of the user, creating a very strong visual hierarchy while maintaining balance.

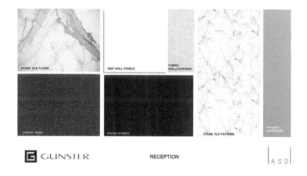

The overall material palette is achromatic while each space incorporates an accent material, such as wood or glass tile.

areas to be located in a corner of the building that was remote from the elevator lobby and the initial approach into the suite. The sequence from the elevator lobby to reception area became a path down a 40-foot corridor, which included passing base building restrooms and service rooms. Instead of the corridor being a design void between the entry experience of the elevator lobby design and the final arrival experience of the reception, ASD|SKY created a space that gave visitors a unique and engaging experience. Without the design and planning challenge, the design team would not have been pushed to create a solution for what has become an iconic design and feature element in this project. The design masterfully intrigues the visitor as one revelation leads to the next along the interior path toward the bay view.

Several very diverse designs were proposed for the feature wall, ranging from conventional to dynamic, but all drew inspiration from the local atmosphere. One concept featured a blue back-painted glass wall with an installation of undulating white metal elements meant to evoke distant sails on the bay. With each option, visitors would experience this gradual transition space as viewing an art installation rather than just traversing a corridor.

The design selected was an option inspired by a cresting wave emerging from a curved wall that opens up to the water view. Still in keeping with the concept of the feature wall being an art installation, each curving piece is unique in its angle and curvature. The fins curve and direct visitors toward the reception space. Its presence and contrast of materials from its surrounding finishes directs attention away from the mundane and invites the user to contemplate something larger than the space itself. The dynamic form sweeps overhead, focusing views to the water even as the wall itself sweeps wider, creating a changing experience on approach to the reception area.

A number of options were explored for the materials of this wall, including hollow extrusions, custom solid castings, and welded metal pieces. Many prototypes were mocked up and budgeted, but the team found that the solid stock aluminum castings provided the best results. Various material properties were analyzed, including limitations on material lengths, weight, fabrication, and reliability of the process required to achieve the desired level of finish. The dark, fumed, figured eucalyptus wood wall served as a backdrop to contrast against the adjacent white finishes to further create an assembly that stands apart from the other

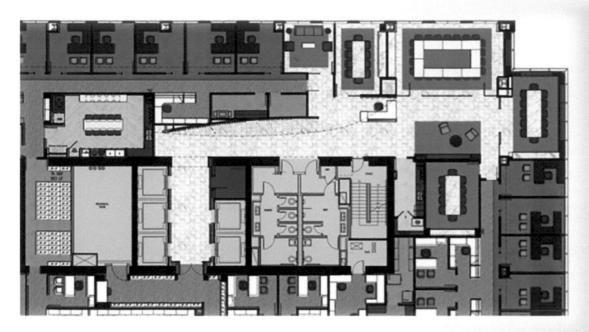

A rendered finish plan can be a useful way to analyze flooring materials and the overarching impact they have on the interior.

light finishes in the space. Extensive 3D modeling and detailed planning was required to ensure that the feature wall could be achieved, including

- ADA projection and headroom clearances were maintained.
- Conflict with floor and ceiling lighting was coordinated.
- Connections were concealed.
- Logistics of hand-carrying the longest pieces into place could be achieved via the elevator and around tight corners.
- The unique form, size, and curvature of the individual metal pieces were considered.

Although creating beautiful spaces is the goal, this project always made the functional program requirements and client's needs a priority. ASD|SKY imposed a challenge on themselves with the floor plan layout and ended up with a more interesting design because of it. A client will never be happy with a space no matter how beautiful the finishes are if it does not also meet their functional needs.

ASD|SKY is a full-service architecture and interior design firm with many offices across the United States. For more information on Gunster, completed in the ASD|SKY Tampa office, or ASD|SKY in general, visit http://www.asdsky.com/.

will not be visible from below (Fig. 9.40). **Environmental systems** involve the delivery of fresh air and removal of contaminated air, more specifically referred to as heating, ventilation, and air conditioning (HVAC), and many of the different methods to address HVAC are described in Chapter 12, the chapter on environmental systems. The ceiling often conceals the ducting that delivers new air to the air diffusers and takes contaminated air away via the returns. **Lighting systems**, which are discussed in more detail in the lighting chapter (Chapter 11), provide electric light to the interior and the ceiling is the primary means by which light fixtures supply light while also concealing the wiring connecting light fixtures to switch controls and the electrical supply panel. **Fire suppression** is an overall strategy within an interior that seeks to limit the spread of fire through a building through the use of sprinklers that are typically located in the ceiling. While the sprinkler heads are visible, the piping that holds the water in the event a fire is detected are concealed above the ceiling plane in the plenum.

Figure 9.40 While many ceilings conceal the plenum, this space embraces the visual impact of the HVAC, lighting, and fire suppression systems.

Designing with acoustics in mind can be very complicated and is described further in Chapter 12, Built Environment Support Systems. Acoustic performance is impacted by the selection of interior finishes and several competing needs must be balanced. For instance, the need for flooring to be durable and cleanable requires them to be hard and, therefore, contribute to noise. Due to cost, lower durability requirements, and ease of renovation, most walls are constructed of gypsum board, also an acoustically reflective material that contributes to higher noise levels. These performance demands placed upon floors and walls requires ceilings to carry the majority of the acoustic performance requirements in an effort to achieve a functional balance within the built environment.

Acoustical Ceiling Tiles

Acoustical ceiling tiles (ACT) are supported by a grid of metal splines suspended by wires from the building structure above the ceiling plane. As discussed, the ceiling plane is dense with lighting, HVAC, and fire suppression components while also needing to provide acoustical performance. Acoustical ceiling tile systems provide for all of these requirements while also being modular. The modular nature of ACT makes design layouts relatively straightforward, as the tiles are commonly available in 2 foot × 2 foot and 2 foot × 4 foot sizes, among others. The tiles are also movable, allowing access to the plenum when repairs are required or when damaged tiles need to be replaced. In spaces such as office environments, ACT can be a great asset when it is time to reconfigure the open office furniture systems, as the ACT, HVAC diffusers, and light fixtures can also be moved if needed. It is much more difficult to reconfigure fire suppression sprinkler systems, however.

Acoustical ceiling tiles are often white, lightly textured, and made of either gypsum or fiberglass, but other colors, textures, and materials are available. The metal spline is available in two sizes of T-shaped grid, in a 15/16 inch or 9/16 inch width, or in a "fine line" grid that incorporates

Figure 9.41 Intricate plaster work in the ceiling is often reserved for historical period designs or for restoration work.

a 1/4-inch reveal. These design options can accentuate the tiled nature of the ceiling system or create a more monolithic appearance. The color of standard ACT can vary per manufacturer offerings, or the material can be painted, but ACT will lose much of its acoustical benefits if painted. Ceiling tile systems can also utilize perforated metal or wood ceiling tiles as well that possess the same benefits of standard ACT described earlier.

Plaster

Historically, ceilings were finished in plaster and painted. The primary benefits of plaster ceilings today include the aesthetic beauty, very smooth surfaces, the possibility of incorporating curves into the ceiling, and the replication of historic patterns in historic preservation and restoration projects (Fig. 9.41). Historic plaster moldings can be restored utilizing the same historic techniques when an authentic reproduction is needed, or new methods including precast plaster pieces and tiles, or a molded polyurethane foam can be used. The designer needs to be careful, however, in matching foam moldings to an existing historic environmental context as many of the foam molding manufacturers follow a different set of proportional ideals and will be clearly out of place to the discerning eye. Authenticity is key in this regard.

While the installation of plaster in the ceiling plane involves the same layering process, it is much more time-consuming and labor-intensive compared to walls. The elevated nature of the ceiling also requires additional scaffolding to support the installer. It should be noted that old plaster ceilings will have a tendency to sag, and, in some cases, may be visible under the right (or wrong) lighting conditions. In general, a smooth ceiling surface will reflect more light than a textured ceiling of the same color, but the textured ceiling will also hide imperfections.

Gypsum Board

Gypsum board is far more common in the ceiling compared to plaster for the same reasons as discussed in context with walls. Gypsum board panels, which are typically 1/2-inch thick to resist sagging, are installed in the ceiling first, and walls second. Similar to walls, gypsum board is taped, mudded, and sanded at the seams and the screw holes are mudded and sanded for a smooth appearance. In cases where textured ceilings are desired, the texture will easily hide the seams and screw holes, but the finished surface will not reflect as much light. Textured gypsum board ceilings can be less expensive than smooth due to the lower amount of skill and time required in installation—it can be much more difficult to achieve a smooth surface than a textured surface in the ceiling plane. Textures can be applied by hand with skip troweled being very common, or they can be applied with a sprayer to achieve an orange peel or popcorn textured finish.

Wood

Wood coffers are one of the most common expressions of wood in a ceiling. Coffers are made up of recessed panels divided by a projecting grid where any portion of the design can be made of wood. Occasionally, the coffer design could mix finishes resulting in strong visual contrast or utilize the same material but vary the texture producing a subtle level of contrast. In very modern spaces, wood is commonly used to wrap from a wall onto the ceiling creating a high level of emphasis on the wood finish and the contrasting finishes around it. The successful execution of this wrapping motion can also result in a very articulate expression of the interior volume as the negative space becomes more apparent. The designer should exercise caution when using dark wood species or stained finishes in the ceiling, as this will cause the overall proportion of the space to feel compressed. In general,

Figure 9.42 The undulating wood ceiling at the Welsh National Assembly in Cardiff Bay leverages the capabilities of the material and draws the eye upward.

Metals

The first metal ceilings were made of tin in the late 1800s as an inexpensive alternative to intricate plaster ceilings. The tin panels were stamped in 1- and 2-foot squares with a variety of geometric and naturalistic patterns. These early metal ceilings offered the added benefits of durability, ease of maintenance, fire resistance, and cost savings over plaster ceilings. Today, metal ceilings can be made of stainless steel, galvanized steel, or aluminum, as a custom design or into a suspended ceiling grid similar to ACT. Metal ceilings are very durable, fire resistant, can be designed to reduce noise, and may discreetly integrate HVAC diffusers, returns, and light fixtures as well (Fig. 9.43). The design possibilities with metal ceilings are very broad.

wood ceilings are very durable, simple to maintain once installed, and can be designed to accommodate many types of lighting, HVAC diffusers and returns, fire suppression sprinkler systems, and even acoustical concerns (Fig. 9.42).

Summary

Selecting finishes is one of the most prized, yet complicated, aspects of a designer's role. The designer must regard finishes as more than a surface, however, and

Figure 9.43 The modern metal slat and panelized ceiling at Don Mills Station, Toronto, provides excellent performance and a visual focus for visitors in this grand space.

consider the entire floor, wall, and ceiling as a system that has tremendous influence on the quality of the entire space. Materials and finishes contribute to a larger design intent that includes function, aesthetics, as well as the physiological and psychological influence upon the users. The coverage of topics in this chapter is not exhaustive, as it only *scratches the surface*.

Key Terms

Additives	Float glass	Quarried
Ashlar	Frieze pile	Quarter sawn
Berber	Grout	Quarter slice
Binders	Gypsum board	Random match
Book matching	Hardwood	Random matching
Brick bond types	Laminate flooring	Rebar
Brick course	Laminated glass	Resilient flooring
Brick positions	Lath	Rift sawn
Broadloom carpet	Leaves	Rift slice
Brown coat	Levels of sheen	Rotary slice
Carpet pile	Lighting systems	Rubble
Carpet tiles	Live sawn	Scratch coat
Cast in place	Load-bearing wall	Semi-shag pile
Cathedral ceiling	Loop pile	Shag pile
Clay tiles	Marquetry	Shed ceiling
Coefficient of friction	Masonry	Slip matching
Coffered ceiling	Medium-density fiberboard	Softwood
Concrete	Modular brick	Solid wood flooring
Custom grade	Mortar	Solution dyeing
Cut pile	Mortar joint types	Solvents
Decorative laminate	Mosaic tile	Standard flat ceiling
Dome	Non-flat ceiling	Stock dyeing
Drop match	Non-load-bearing wall	Straight-across match
Dye lot	Nylon	Strip
Economy grade	Parquetry	Substrates
Embodied energy	Pattern repeat	Tempered glass
End matching	Pendentive	Thin brick
Engineered wood flooring	Pigments	Tip-sheered pile
Environmental systems	Plain sawn	Tongue-and-groove
Fabricated	Plain slice	Tray ceiling
Finish coat	Plank	Vault ceiling
Fire suppression	Plenum	Veneer
Flat ceiling	Precast	Wool
Flitch	Premium grade	

Resources

American Coatings Association. (n.d.). American Coatings Association. Retrieved December 17, 2017, from http://www.paint.org/.

American Concrete Institute. (n.d.). American Concrete Institute. Retrieved December 17, 2017, from https://www.concrete.org/.

Carpet and Rug Institute. (n.d.). The Carpet and Rug Institute, Inc. | Dalton, GA 30722. Retrieved December 17, 2017, from http://www.carpet-rug.org/.

Ching, F. D. (2014). *Building Construction Illustrated*. Hoboken, NJ: John Wiley & Sons, Inc.

International Masonry Institute. (n.d.). The International Masonry Institute | Home. Retrieved December 17, 2017, from http://imiweb.org/.

Masonry Institute of America. (n.d.). MasonryInstitute.org. Retrieved December 17, 2017, from https://www.masonryinstitute.org.

National Floor Covering Association. (n.d.). F03A2 History of Cork. Retrieved December 17, 2017, from http://www.floorcoveringreferencemanual.com/f03a2-history-of-cork.html.

National Wood Flooring Association. (n.d.). NWFA. Retrieved December 17, 2017, from https://www.nwfa.org/.

Natural Stone Institute. (n.d.). MIA BSI—Stone Industry Resources from the Leading Association MIA BSI. Retrieved December 17, 2017, from https://www.marble-institute.com/.

Resilient Floor Covering Institute. (n.d.). Our SUSTAINABILITY Story. Retrieved December 17, 2017, from http://rfci.com/.

Tile Council of North America. (n.d.). Home—The Tile Council of North America. Retrieved December 17, 2017, from http://www.tcnatile.com/.

Wallcoverings Association. (n.d.). Welcome to Wallcoverings Association. Retrieved December 17, 2017, from http://www.wallcoverings.org/.

Review Questions

1. What demands are placed upon flooring that walls and ceilings do not have to endure? How do these demands affect the material characteristics of flooring? Why is it so important to properly prepare the flooring substrate?

2. List the three broad categories of flooring, including general positives and negatives for each.

3. Select one material example from each of the three flooring categories and describe its sustainable characteristics.

4. List the differences between softwood and hardwood. List the types of wood sawing methods, calling attention to the situations where each type is used.

5. List the different types of wood flooring and describe the differences between them.

6. What is the most important aspect of selecting carpet? Which fiber dyeing method is most durable? Describe the conflicting desires/needs of plushness, or softness, and durability in terms of pile type when selecting carpet.

7. When using travertine, which surface, the floor or wall, requires that the voids in the stone be filled?

8. List the typical brick positions, bond types, and joint types.

9. Describe the evolution from plaster to gypsum board wall materials and the reasons why this transition occurred.

10. List the levels of sheen and the contents of paint.

11. What is the primary difference between wall tile and floor tile?

12. List the two broad categories of ceiling forms and the subcategories of each.

13. Why are ceilings typically the primary interior surface used for decoration and dissipating noise?

14. List and describe the environmental systems at the ceiling level.

Exercises

Master Bedroom and Bath Suite

1. Create a client profile (single professional, empty nest retired couple, etc.), select a location (Tokyo, Japan; Bozeman, Montana; etc.) and provide a photograph of the view looking out the primary bedroom window(s). Include the profile, location description, and view image in the final presentation.

2. Select floor, wall, and ceiling finishes for the master bedroom and bathroom based on your client profile, location, and view.

3. Physical finish samples or printed versions of the selections should be presented on a physical or digital "board." Include headings to categorize the spaces (Bedroom, Bathroom) and label each individual finish selection by type (e.g., "wool carpet," "ceramic wall tile," etc.).

10

Furnishings: Millwork, Furniture, Fixtures, and Equipment

Learning Objectives

As a result of reading this chapter, students will possess an awareness of the

1. Various types of architectural millwork.

2. Types of furniture and their respective qualities.

3. Types of doors and windows, their components, and the planning needs of each.

4. Types of window coverings and their hardware.

5. Categories of accessories.

6. Types of fixtures and equipment.

As a result of taking part in the learning exercises at the end of this chapter, students will

1. Demonstrate the ability to identify and select a variety of furnishings for a simple interior space.

2. Demonstrate the ability to compose and/or craft a furnishing selection board.

Introduction

Furnishings are one of the most important aspects of any design to the end users, as these objects within the interior are regularly touched and used within the space. Furnishing types include millwork, furniture, fixtures, and equipment. **Furniture, Fixtures, and Equipment** (FF&E) is a common accounting term used to value the assets of a company. It describes movable items of a building interior that are not permanently attached to the building structure or utilities (water, fuel, electricity). An interior design that maximizes the use of FF&E can be very influential upon the tax strategy of certain clients. Some furnishings, such as custom millwork and cabinetry, countertops, and built-in displays, are designed directly by the designer, whereas others, including modular cabinetry and manufactured furniture, fixtures, and equipment, are specified by the interior designer. In some projects, the client will have a specific piece of furniture, a retail display, or a piece of medical equipment that they purchase themselves, or may have an existing piece that they want to be planned for in the new space. Whether the furnishing is designed or specified by the designer or supplied by the client (referred to as "by owner"), the designer must plan for the piece by thoroughly understanding the size with exact dimensions, if it has specific clearance requirements around the piece, and any special requirements it may have, such as plumbing or electricity supply. Furnishings have a tremendous impact on both the aesthetic and functional qualities of all interior environments and the designer is responsible for integrating them into the space plan.

Millwork

Millwork is divided into two broad categories: custom and manufactured. Within these two categories are cabinetry and countertops, freestanding millwork, and paneling and moldings. The most common material used in millwork is wood, or a wood-derived material such as particleboard, and, therefore, millwork is held to quality standards outlined by the Architectural Woodwork Institute (AWI). Designers need to be aware of the AWI standards for specification, fabrication, and installation as outlined in the *Architectural Woodwork Standards*, second edition. This resource provides clear descriptions of millwork quality grades—economy, custom, and premium—and includes standard terminology that should be used to help ensure that millworkers are on equal footing when competing to work on projects. If a designer does not use millwork terminology correctly, the design outcome could be of a lower quality or higher cost than anticipated.

In addition to important terms related to quality, the designer should have a thorough understanding of joinery types, or how pieces of wood are connected to form larger surfaces and volumes in millwork pieces. **Joinery types** include butt, miter, rabbet, dado, dovetail, mortise and tenon, scarf, splice, lap, and tongue-and-groove (Fig. 10.1). This list is not exhaustive; applies to other woodworking applications, including furniture and wood structural connections; and each of these basic joint types can have several varieties. Joinery also has many cultural influences, and they will vary based on location and training of the maker. An excellent example of this can be found in the highly crafted beauty of traditional Japanese joinery. At the opposite end of the spectrum is the impact of computer numerical control (CNC) milling on the process of millwork and woodworking in general as digital fabrication speeds up the fabrication process and allows designers to play a more integral role in millwork detailing and fabrication. One can see that millwork overlaps with several topics that have already been addressed, such as doors, wall finishes, and ceiling finishes, and those topics should be recalled in context to what is discussed here.

Millwork: Cabinetry and Countertops

The majority of cabinetry is classified as base or wall cabinetry and can be used in a variety of spaces, including kitchens, baths and restrooms, conference rooms, offices, hospital exam rooms, and many others. Manufactured standard base cabinets are typically 34 1/2 inches high and 24 inches deep, except bathrooms where they are typically 28 1/2 inches high and 21 inches deep, and manufactured wall cabinets are available in a variety of heights (12 inches, 18 inches, 24 inches, 30 inches, 36 inches, and 42 inches) and typically are 12 inches deep when installed over base cabinets in kitchens. Widths of manufactured kitchen base and wall cabinetry follow a specific module (typically 3 inches or 6 inches, but differs based upon the manufacturer) starting at approximately 12 inches on the low end and topping out around 48 inches on the high end. Manufactured vanity base cabinets hold a lavatory sink,

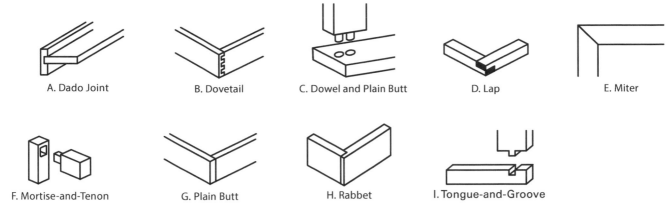

A. Dado Joint   B. Dovetail   C. Dowel and Plain Butt   D. Lap   E. Miter

F. Mortise-and-Tenon   G. Plain Butt   H. Rabbet   I. Tongue-and-Groove

Figure 10.1 Wood joinery can be celebrated, and made visible, or be quiet and concealed. Either way, the designer can specify the type of joinery based on strength, aesthetics, and cost needs for the furniture or millwork piece.

and will therefore range between 30 inches and 72 inches in width, following an incremental module of 6 inches or 12 inches. Custom cabinetry is designed and detailed by the interior designer or millwork fabricator and, as a result, can be built to any practical size and can fit any built condition with precision (Fig. 10.2).

Countertops made of wood, or using a wood substrate, are typically $1^{1}/_{2}$ inches thick, which brings the surface up to approximately 36 inches in the kitchen or 30 inches in the bath or restroom. Countertop materials include wood butcher block, plastic laminate, solid surface, granite, quartz, tile, and concrete, and each of these materials can, and will, vary from the norm of $1^{1}/_{2}$ inches in thickness. Countertops will also overhang the leading edge of base cabinetry by approximately 1 inch, increasing its usable surface area while also decreasing

circulation clearances between cabinetry and design elements across a space from the cabinets. Base cabinets with a countertop that are designed to comply with the Americans with Disabilities Act (ADA) must be equal to, or less than, 34 inches in height to the top of the work surface. The designer should take any specific needs of the users and necessary clearances into account when planning any millwork for the interior.

Built-in displays and storage units, such as those found in residential media and living rooms and corporate conference rooms, can be a great asset to any interior (Fig. 10.3). These millwork pieces may cover an entire wall and can provide for storage and display needs in an efficient manner without having to construct framed walls. Built-in storage and display units are usually fabricated by a custom millworker, but manufactured solutions are also possible, depending on the conditions in the space. Often, custom displays or built-in storage units will require lighting and access to power for electronics through grommets and a built-in chase for electrical wiring, which the designer should include in the design.

Freestanding Millwork

Freestanding millwork includes reception desks for a corporate law firm, point-of-sale stations in a retail setting, and host and hostess stands at restaurants, along with many other applications (Fig. 10.4). These pieces are nearly always unique, requiring the designer to consider the particular needs of both the employee and the visitor. The finish materials, substrates, hardware, storage, electrical needs, fabrication requirements, and installation process must be carefully thought through for

Figure 10.2 Intentionally designed custom cabinetry can bring ample storage to an otherwise compact space.

Figure 10.3 Custom millwork along a wall face, such as this residential media wall, will need to integrate appropriate means to conceal electrical and audio/visual wiring in order to maintain a clean appearance and accessibility to electronic components.

the freestanding millwork piece to be successful. Seated-height work surfaces are approximately 29 inches high, standing transaction height surfaces are 42 inches high, and ADA compliant transaction surfaces for wheelchair users can be between 28 and 34 inches high.

Paneling and Moldings

Millwork wall panels can be solid wood, but are more often constructed of wood veneer over a plywood or particleboard substrate. Wood paneling can have a vertical or horizontal orientation in the form of planks, which will greatly impact the proportion of a space. Vertical planks will enhance the apparent height of a space while horizontal planks, or slats, will emphasize the length or breadth of a space. Vertical wood paneling is available in several configurations, including v-groove, board-and-batten, and board-on-board, while the most common type of horizontal planking is shiplap. Flat millwork panels rely heavily on artful and detailed attention to grain matching as discussed in Chapter 9 in context with wood wall finishes.

Moldings are milled from solid wood, utilize a routed particleboard substrate and veneer covering, or an injection molded foam with the intention of being painted (Fig. 10.5). Moldings can be used to create coffered wall or ceiling panel designs and cover the joints between boards or panels. One common type of molding is a chair rail that is used to run the perimeter of a space along the walls at approximately 36 inches above the floor. A chair rail divides the vertical proportion of a space while functionally protecting walls from wear and tear due to chairs scraping along them, particularly in dining spaces.

Furniture

Of all the discreet objects of an interior space, furniture is arguably the portion that receives the most interaction and use from clients. For this reason, furniture receives a tremendous amount of thought, deliberation, and care during the design process by the designer and client (Fig. 10.6). Specific pieces of furniture are often coveted

Figure 10.4 Freestanding millwork can also be designed with curvilinear forms, such as this reception desk.

Figure 10.5 The wood moldings around this built-in bookcase demonstrates wall base, chair rail, and crown molding in addition to the trim around the windows.

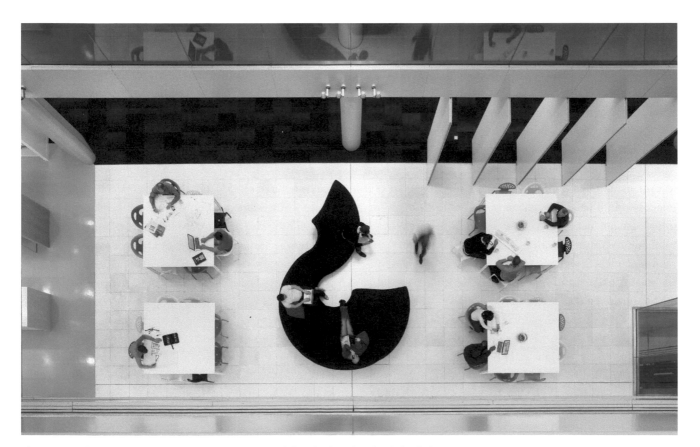

Figure 10.6 The seating and table clusters in this space define the functional and circulation areas.

by clients and designers alike, passed from generation to generation, and great lengths are employed to preserve and restore well-crafted iconic pieces of furniture. Furniture has evolved from a purely functional means to enable daily life functions, such as eating, sleeping, and sitting, to become a way to express the status and personality of the owner.

Whether stated or not, every interior will subscribe to some idea of style, and the furniture should be selected and specified to support the overall design intent of the space. Style can be tied to a specific historical period, which is described in more detail in the chapter on history of architectural and design styles (Chapter 2), and if a piece is more than 100 years old, the style is broadly considered **antique**. Period furniture typically follows many of the conventions of a broad design period in relation to form, proportion, and craft. Some clients prefer to hold to a purist approach to selecting period furniture that matches the period of the interior, whereas others see furniture as an opportunity to deviate from a period or style, selectively mixing styles based on taste, resulting in an eclectic interior.

Broad classifications of style can sometimes be confusing, as terminology may be used incorrectly, so it can be useful to describe styles in contrasting terms for purposes of clarification. One common confusion exists around the terms antique and vintage. As mentioned, in order for a furniture piece to be considered antique, it must be at least 100 years old, while **vintage** describes a piece that is considered to be a prime example of a type of furniture from a specific period or style, for example, a 1948 Womb Chair by Eero Saarinen for Florence Knoll is an example of vintage Mid-Century Modern (Fig. 10.7). Designers and clients need to be aware that reproductions of vintage furniture are very common and the visual differences can be very subtle while the quality could be substandard.

Another set of stylistic terms that is easily confused is traditional and rustic. **Traditional** furniture pieces are characterized by a formal posture and forms and decorations from the Victorian period while **rustic** furniture is characterized by its natural materials, simplistic forms, and relaxed posture, which can include furniture that exudes an industrial aesthetic. Modern and contemporary are notoriously misused terms that the designer should be able to use with accuracy. **Modern** furniture pieces are attached to the Modernist movement of the early 1900s, an architectural period that embraced modular design principles and

Figure 10.7 The Womb Chair (Knoll, 1946), by Eero Saarinen, an example of mid-twentieth century modern furniture, wraps the human form.

new construction technologies, including the use of concrete and steel. **Contemporary** furniture describes those pieces that are in popular use now, and, by definition, all prior periods of style were, in their own time, contemporary.

Furniture Types

Furniture varies widely by type, and includes chairs, sofas, tables, beds, storage, case goods, and systems furniture. All furniture types rely on accurate and thoughtful designs in context with anthropometrics and ergonomics and are arranged to create spaces with particular goals based on proxemics as discussed in Chapter 4. Chairs are the most ubiquitous of the furniture types as they are present in almost every type of space, and, as such, are available in a variety of sizes and functions. Chairs vary in scale, proportion, durability, firmness, and material, based on their functional use in offices, conference rooms, waiting rooms, lobby spaces, living rooms, and dining rooms. Some chairs, such as office task chairs and some lounge chairs, are adjustable to fit the specific body types and preferred posture of the user (Fig. 10.8).

Figure 10.9 A traditional settee is intended for two occupants and establishes a presence in a well-appointed traditional interior.

Figure 10.8 Task chairs allow the users to make multiple adjustments to meet their individualized ergonomic needs.

Closely related to chairs, sofas are upholstered and provide another means to sit for multiple people at once, or for individuals in relaxed postures. Sofas are termed for their size, posture of the user, and type of upholstery:

- Chaise lounge: provides for one person in a reclined position.
- Settee: intended for two people, small in scale, combination of upholstery and wood or metal (Fig. 10.9).
- Tuxedo: the arms are the same height as the back.
- Lawson: the arms are lower than the back.
- Chesterfield: tufted back and/or seat cushions with fully upholstered sides; no exposed wood legs, base, or trim.
- Sectional: upholstered modular units placed next to one another to create a large sofa.

Tables are diverse, as they are specifically designed to accompany particular types of chairs and sofas. Dining tables are approximately 30 inches in height and should be specifically selected to coordinate with dining chairs stylistically and functionally, based on whether or not the chairs have arms (Fig. 10.10). Conference tables are similar in regard to the type of chair selected in conjunction with the table and they have the added requirement of electricity supplied at the work surface to power electronics. In both a dining space, whether residential or

Figure 10.10 These simple and quiet dining tables complement the expressive forms of the interior.

in a restaurant, and a conferencing scenario, the designer must pay particular attention to the clearances around the table and chairs when the occupants have withdrawn slightly from the table in order to allow adequate space for circulation. Side tables in a living room or lounge setting are specifically selected with the height of the chair or sofa arm taken into account so that the two come very close to matching one another. A similar idea is true for end tables, or nightstands, next to a bed, as the surface of the end table should be close to the height of the mattress.

Beds are available in a variety of configurations, freestanding or built-in, and sizes, twin, queen, king, and California king, to suit the needs of many sleeping scenarios and room sizes. Beds can also efficiently serve multiple purposes, such as convertible sofas, futons, and daybeds, or tuck away when not in use, such as a Murphy bed that hinges or folds from a wall or a trundle bed that slides out from under another bed. Bunk beds are used to accommodate multiple people in a small space by stacking the beds. Beds are also subject to stylistic trends, as illustrated by water beds, four-poster beds (Fig. 10.11), and sunken beds (level or nearly level with the floor).

Furniture pieces expressly used for storage are available in a range of sizes and materials, and they may incorporate doors, drawers, or shelves into the design, and, as such, will have some similarities with cabinetry. Shelving units can be used to organize books and manuals or display personal effects. File cabinets can be made of wood or steel to efficiently store and secure documents. Wardrobes and dressers, or bureaus, offer concealed means to store hung or folded clothing and apparel accessories. Media units (Figure 10.3) find a place in both the home and the contract interior setting as large format televisions and projection screens require significant electronic support for entertainment and business or classroom communication purposes.

Case goods include freestanding desks and credenzas in office settings. These items incorporate a variety of materials, including wood, steel, glass, and decorative laminates, to achieve efficient and ergonomic design solutions for office workers in both the home and contract interior environments. Desks are typically 24 inches or 30 inches deep, 60 to 72 inches long, and 28 to 30 inches high and incorporate file and basic office equipment storage. Some desks will also have a return on either the left or right side and these surfaces will be the same height as the desk, but the depth will typically be shallower, either 20 or 24 inches, and the length shorter, approximately 42 inches. Credenzas can provide additional storage, often rest behind the desk, are shallower than the desk, and typically match the length of the desk. Due to the amount of time one spends working at a desk, ergonomics is especially important and additional components can be added to the desk to improve an individual's posture and health. Articulated monitor support arms, keyboard trays, and elevated footrests are all useful items when seeking to improve health and well-being in context with a desk. In addition, some desks can be raised and lowered with a simple pneumatic lever to allow an individual to stand while working at a computer.

Systems furniture solutions, referred to as cubicles by prior work generations, are most common in open office environments where many people are working individually, or collaboratively, at desks (Fig. 10.12). Freestanding partitions that carry electricity can be used to support work surfaces and storage components efficiently and ergonomically. In many cases, systems furniture partitions are not necessary and the work stations can be configured as a series of work surfaces with low storage solutions eliminating the visual barriers between individuals, but these types of arrangements can also lead to acoustical problems as the open work area can become noisy. Systems furniture also includes movable wall systems that are used to create closed offices and meeting spaces that can be disassembled, moved, and rebuilt in the event of a remodel with relative speed compared to conventional construction. Rounding out the modular nature of systems furniture and movable wall systems, raised floor systems allow for the efficient and flexible delivery of electricity and conditioned air that can be reconfigured relatively simply as an interior work environment changes over time.

Figure 10.11 This four poster bed challenges the traditional assumptions of style.

Figure 10.12 Open office systems furniture solutions provide opportunities for improved collaboration and communication among coworkers.

Furniture Quality and Materials

The quality of a furniture piece relies on attention to ergonomics and anthropometrics, level of craft in the connections and joinery, and the durability of the materials (Fig. 10.13). Furniture should provide comfort and support for the user based on the intended use of the item, and because each type of furniture piece is designed and constructed differently, the designer should provide an opportunity for the client to test and experience the furniture prior to specification and purchasing. Surfaces receiving frequent touch, such as tabletops and desk work surfaces, should receive special consideration in relation to the sharpness of edges and resiliency of the surface against scratches, dents, cracks, and chips. Longevity of movable portions of furniture, including doors and drawers and the hardware that enables that mobility (handles, pulls, hinges, glides, and casters), requires attention in the design phase to ensure sustained use over the life of the piece. Materials are often near the top of the list when designers and clients seek to describe the quality of a piece of furniture they desire for a space, and the most common furniture materials, wood, metal, grasses, and synthetics, are described in turn.

Figure 10.13 This well-crafted nineteenth-century wood writing desk is finished in Japanese lacquer.

Wood is the standard by which all furniture materials are judged, due to its durability, versatility, workability, and natural beauty. Solid wood furniture can be made from either softwood or hardwood, and some pieces will mix types of wood, depending on the use, visibility, and exposure to wear and tear of the various components of the piece. For example, the serving top of a buffet may be crafted of solid walnut (hardwood), while a back panel of the piece, concealed against a wall or by drawers and doors, may be constructed of a select pine (softwood) plywood. The craftsperson will select the wood species based on the unique qualities of that wood type in order to resist warping, shrinking, and splitting. The type of finish will also play an influential role in these functional and durability qualities and will also greatly impact the appearance of the wood surfaces. The designer should also examine wood species and finish options under differing qualities of light and at varying angles, as lighting, temperature, and vantage point can alter the appearance of wood. Many furniture pieces utilize plywood, particleboard, or other wood composite material as a substrate and then apply a veneer or laminate over the substrate. This method improves upon the tendency of solid wood to warp twist, but some of these substrates (especially particleboard and open-cell substrates) may not be able to resist moisture, or may have weak pull strength, leading to failure in the joinery and connections. When using real wood veneers, the same principles apply in regard to finishing that apply to solid wood.

Metal alloys, including iron, steel, copper, brass, and aluminum, with a variety of finish options, including chrome and anodizing, are often used in furniture fabrication. Iron is very heavy and strong, useful in table base applications to support a top of another material, applied as decorative filigree, but also can easily rust, necessitating consideration in finish protection and treatment. Steel, an alloy of iron and carbon, can be corrosion resistant as stainless steel with the addition of chromium to the alloy. Stainless steel is available in a variety of finish levels numbered one through eight, with levels four (brushed) through eight (mirror reflective) typically being used in interior finish and furniture applications. Copper is rich in appearance and relatively easy to work with due to its softness, which lends the material to be manufactured in thin sheets and then formed around a substrate such as wood, plastic, or another metal. Brass is a zinc and copper gold-colored alloy often used for bed frames, table bases, and hardware such as pulls, hinges, and even plumbing fixtures. Aluminum is far lighter than the other metals and it is corrosion resistant when treated properly (see anodizing below) lending to wide use in outdoor furniture applications, appliances, and plumbing fixtures and fittings. Chrome results from a plating process that uses an electrical charge to plate a metal or plastic substrate with a thin layer of chromium, resulting in a reflective surface that is simpler to clean and maintain in addition to the aesthetic benefits the finish provides. Anodizing is a process typically applied to aluminum to make the metal corrosion resistant and to add color to the aluminum finish by submerging the metal in an acid wash to remove the natural oxidized layer then submerging in an electrolytic solution to add a corrosion-resistant coating and coloration if desired.

Furniture made from rattan, bamboo, cane, and rush offer a handmade quality to any space embracing a casual aesthetic. Rattan stems and poles from the rattan palm plant are bent into gently curving forms in beds, tables, and chairs. Bamboo can be used for its sturdy poles as furniture legs in tables, chairs, and beds. Cane and rush are used to craft seats and backs for chairs and sofas by separating the plants into strips, in the case of cane, or weaving the grass blades into cords, in the case of rush, and then weaving them into meshes for use in the furniture pieces. One point of confusion in this area is with wicker. Wicker is actually a technique of weaving grasses, twigs, and other plant materials rather than a material.

Synthetic materials in furniture construction include molded plastics and acrylic and fiberglass, which can be crafted into a variety of shapes (Fig. 10.14). Molded plastics are used in small furniture parts, including protective edges on tables to prevent chipping of the top material and for comfort of the user; the levers, buttons, and other controls on task chairs; and bumpers and light-duty casters for tables and chairs to prevent the floor surface from scratching. Entire furniture pieces can be made from acrylic or fiberglass when light weight and formally expressive colorful furniture pieces are desired. These furniture pieces are intended to be easily moved, cleaned, and sometimes stacked for a flexible and adaptable interior. With all the positives of advancements in synthetic furniture materials, there are some drawbacks. Many plastics scratch easily, some do not fare well under exposure to UV light, they are not easily repaired should they crack, and some varieties of synthetics are not environmentally sensitive. Significant advancements are underway in relation to sustainability,

Figure 10.14 These Louis Ghost Armchairs, designed by Philippe Starck for Kartell, complete the contemporary dining space.

however, as the quantity of recycled content in synthetic furniture products is rapidly increasing.

Upholstered Furniture

Upholstery is a process of covering furniture with a textile or animal hide. Early upholstered furniture consisted of stretching animal hides or textiles over wooden frames to add softness and warmth, increasing overall comfort. Cushions were later developed and placed on top of the textiles or hides, again to increase comfort. As cushions became recognized for their benefits, animal hairs, feathers, and down were added to increase the comfort level and additional hides or textiles were used to cover the cushions resulting in a cohesive appearance and increased durability for the furniture piece. With the addition of machined metal springs in the 1800s modernized upholstered furniture had arrived, and with the addition of synthetic foam cushions and textiles in the early 1900s the industry had reached a level of technological advancement that is expected today. These technological advancements have created two basic types of upholstered furniture: overstuffed and partially exposed. Overstuffed upholstered furniture attaches padding to the frame, and partially exposed upholstered furniture allows portions of the frame (wood, metal, grasses, or synthetic), such as the arms, to be visible, often requiring finishing techniques. The frame padding and the cushions are covered with a textile or hide, known as upholstery.

High-quality upholstered furniture frames are often made of metal, plastic, or hardwood. Hardwood frames are used because they do not split as easily as softwood, and the connections are glued and doweled with extra blocking at the corners rather than simply nailed or stapled. The base, or decking, of the frame supports the metal springs, which should be eight-way hand-tied construction, upon which padding and the upholstered cushions will rest. Under the cushion, polyester batting and burlap basket-weave webbing cover the springs, providing additional support and protection for the back side of the cushions (Fig. 10.15).

Cushions, seat, or back can be attached to the frame, referred to as tight back, which is more common in contract

Figure 10.15 This cut-away shows the layers of upholstered furniture construction.

spaces, or free from the frame typically used in residential interiors. Cushion filling composition is an important aspect of any upholstered furniture piece that the designer is responsible to educate their client on, select, and specify. Cushion filling depends upon the type of project (contract or residential), durability requirements, maintenance, allergies, preference regarding firmness, and budget. Standard cushion fill consists of down, the soft inner feathers of geese, feathers, or foam. Down is high in cost and quality, but tends to lose its shape, so high-end cushions in residential settings where the budget will allow it and the client does not have down allergies will often be composed of equal amounts of down and feathers to help the cushion keep its shape. In cases where cost and allergies are an issue, foam will be used. In contract settings, where firmness, durability, maintenance, and probably a cleaner and contemporary appearance are desired, then a combination of foam and down will be used.

Doors

Doors provide many functional and aesthetic benefits to a building exterior and interior. Functional benefits of exterior doors include providing security against intruders and protection against the natural elements. Interior doors enable and control circulation based on the location and the operation of the hardware. Arrangement of furniture, millwork, light switches, and other interior architectural elements respond to and accommodate the location and operation of doors. Temperature, air quality via ventilation, and also sound transmission can be partially controlled through doors.

Aesthetically, doors and their immediate surroundings make a strong statement. The form of a door, with a rectangular or arched top, has the opportunity to reflect the surrounding architectural style of the building or interior while the size of the door can communicate importance through scale and proportion. A door can also communicate strength and security or openness based on the material of the door, such as wood and steel or glass. The moldings and trim around the jambs and head of doors can be very traditional or contemporary based on the design intent for the space.

Door Types

Door types are determined by their operation type and are classified as swing, sliding, or folding (Fig. 10.16). **Swinging doors** can be single or double acting, meaning they swing in one or both directions, depending on the type of hinge, and can be installed as individuals or in pairs. The most common type is the individual single-acting swing door described as either left- or right-handed based upon the location of the hinge when entering a room from a corridor. **Double-acting doors** swing in two directions and are used to divide two spaces that receive high traffic, such as a kitchen and dining area in a restaurant. A **Dutch door** is divided into two halves such that the top and bottom portions swing independently of one another, allowing a visual and audible connection between spaces. Double doors, such as **French doors**, typically swing in the same direction and provide for a wider opening for circulation or ventilation purposes. Most swinging doors swing from the edge with a hinge attached to the door jamb, but some swinging doors, called **pivot doors**, pivot in the middle of the door with a hinge anchored to the head and the threshold of the opening.

Sliding doors are available in a variety of configurations and rely upon a track with rollers to allow the door to slide across the opening. Sliding doors are simple to operate and do not require as much clearance around them compared to swinging doors and, therefore, are useful to ease circulation and allow for more flexibility in placing

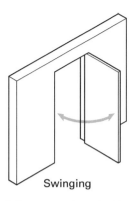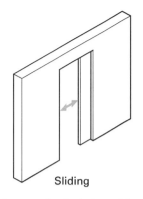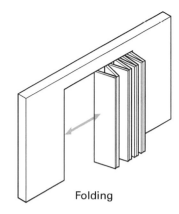

Swinging   Sliding   Folding

Figure 10.16 Doors are categorized into three basic types by operation (swinging, sliding, folding).

furniture in tight spaces. **Automatic sliding doors**, typically made of glass, are common in retail and transportation buildings where carts, luggage, or simply high amounts of foot traffic are present. A sliding door that can be concealed inside of a wall is referred to as a **pocket door**. Doors that are mounted on the face of a wall with exposed track and hardware above the opening are called **surface-mounted sliding doors**.

Folding doors offer the opportunity for multi-use and flexibility between spaces by utilizing a track in the door head and can also require a track in the floor depending upon the weight and sturdiness of the door. The simplest of folding doors, called a **bi-fold door**, is commonly used with closets, allowing the user to fully open the closet to view the contents in an efficient and accessible manner. **Accordion doors** consist of multiple narrow vertical panels and can be used to temporarily divide a large space into smaller spaces. When a space is divided, a secondary means of access to these smaller divided spaces through a swinging door(s) must be planned by the designer. Large folding doors can be used to divide spaces, including indoor and outdoor areas. With large folding doors, it is wise to plan a wall pocket so the folding door panels can be ganged together and concealed allowing for maximum circulation while minimizing visual obstruction.

Doors have a variety of components and the terminology used to describe these parts is embedded within the common vocabulary of design professionals and door and hardware specialists (Fig. 10.17). In the case of raised panel or glass doors, doors are divided into **stiles**, the vertical solid portion of a door; **rails**, the horizontal portion of a door; and

any solid raised panels or **lights**, the glass portions. Flush doors, characterized by their simplicity, can be made of any material, including wood, steel, or glass, and lack the traditional horizontal and vertical divisions. Door edges are divided into three categories: the **head** (top), **jamb** (sides), and **threshold** (bottom, common only for exterior doors). Interior doors often do not have a threshold beneath them, as flooring materials may not transition at door openings, and when flooring does transition at door openings, a simple, low-profile flooring transition strip will suffice. With standard swing doors, one jamb will hold the **hinges** while the other will hold the handle and **latch assembly** that will fit into the strike plate held by the jamb frame.

Door Materials

Door materials are selected based on aesthetics and performance. Aesthetic considerations take into account the overall material palette of the space. Performance characteristics include acoustics, impact resistance, cleanability, fire resistance, and visibility. Wood, both solid and veneer, plastic laminate, painted steel, anodized aluminum, and glass, both clear and translucent, are common surface material choices. The door core affects performance, and common materials include solid wood and wood product substrates such as plywood, OSB, and particleboard; mineral fiber, which is good for acoustics and fire resistance; and metal waffle, which is light weight and relatively strong. Door cores can also be hollow with only enough structural support at the edges of the door to hold the hardware and provide shape. Hollow core wood doors

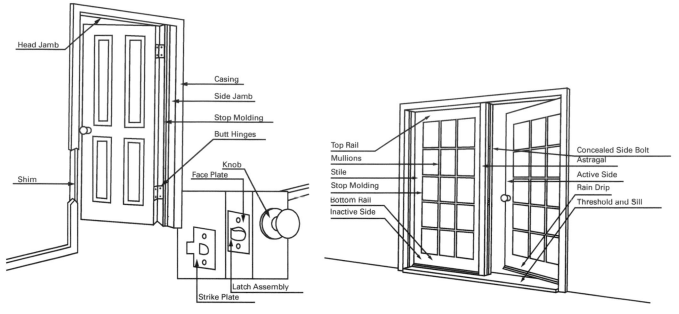

Figure 10.17 Doors possess many detailed parts, each of which impact a door's function, level of security, and aesthetic value.

are inexpensive, but do not offer much beyond visual privacy and low-level security, which makes them suitable for interior residential use. In nonresidential applications, doors require higher levels of performance, resulting in more uses of steel, aluminum, and glass. Wood doors are still used in nonresidential applications, but are often a wood veneer over a solid mineral fiber or fire-retardant treated wood core rather than being made of solid wood.

Door Frames

Door and frame materials must be considered together for functional and aesthetic reasons. Functional goals for doors include security, privacy, and meeting code requirements, and the frame must match the functional performance requirements of the door. For example, if a door is to be installed in a fire-rated partition, the door and the frame must both be fire rated. In residential applications, doors and their accompanying frames are typically made of painted or stained wood. In nonresidential applications, a wider variety of materials are often used, with most frames made of painted steel or anodized aluminum for durability purposes and doors made of wood, steel, aluminum, glass, or some combination of these materials.

Doors and frames are available in standard sizes and are often specified, or purchased, as a unit when installed in a standard gypsum board or CMU partition. Doors must be plumb and square to function properly, but rough construction is rarely perfectly plum and square. To resolve this conflict, a **shim space**, or air gap, is accounted for between the wall framing and the door framing to allow the door to be adjusted accounting for construction imperfections. Molding, or trim, is then used to cover the shim space resulting in a clean and professional installation. Every door frame also has a **stop trim** around all three sides of the opening, which provides a stopping surface for the door when closing.

Door Hardware

Door hardware plays an integral role in the security function of doors, as it will impact the door's operation, opening, and closing (Fig. 10.18). The most obvious hardware component is the lockset which includes the handle used to open the door latch and the lock itself, if one is present. Lever handles are required in nonresidential interiors rather than knobs as levers are simpler to open for those with disabilities. Bar handles and push plates are used on entry doors where the lock is separate from the handle itself. Panic bars are used on egress doors leading into emergency stairwells or on doors leading out of building that used as means of egress. Hinges, pivot axles, tracks, and wheels allow a door to swing, pivot, slide, or fold based on the operation type. Automatic closers are used on fire-rated doors that must return to a closed position when not in operation due to code requirements.

Hardware specification and planning can be a very complex step in the design process, especially for large projects with multiple types of doors and hardware sets.

Door Planning Strategies

Doors are a great tool in helping the designer to achieve planning goals based upon the client's needs for security and privacy and for meeting code requirements. Keep these door planning considerations in mind:

- Too many doors can be a hindrance in situations where ease of circulation between spaces is a high priority. For example, it is better to design airport terminal restrooms without doors so that users can easily wheel their luggage with them.
- In cases where spaces do not have doors but visual privacy is still important (see preceding example), place partitions properly to obstruct views.

- In small spaces that require a door, such as a private office or bedroom, place the door near the corner of the room to ease circulation within the space and simplify furniture placement.
- When considering universal design strategies around doors, the designer should maintain 12 inches (30 centimeters) of clear approach space next to the handle on the push side of a door and 18 inches (45 centimeters) of clear approach space next to the handle on the pull side of a door (Fig. 10.19).
- In order for a wheelchair user to travel through a door opening, a minimum clearance of 32 inches (approximately 82 centimeters) is required when the door is open. Taking into account the door thickness, stop trim thickness, and hinge clearance, a 36-inch (90-centimeter) wide door and frame opening is needed to meet universal design goals.

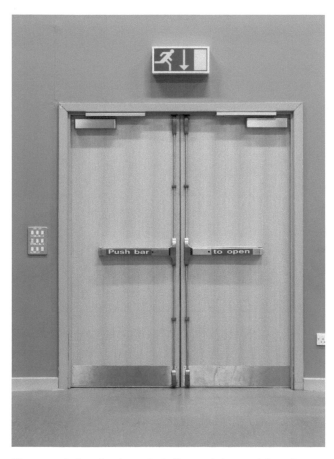

Figure 10.18 Door hardware, including panic bars and door closers shown in this photo, contribute to a door system that meets code requirements providing occupants the opportunity to safely exit a building in the event of an emergency.

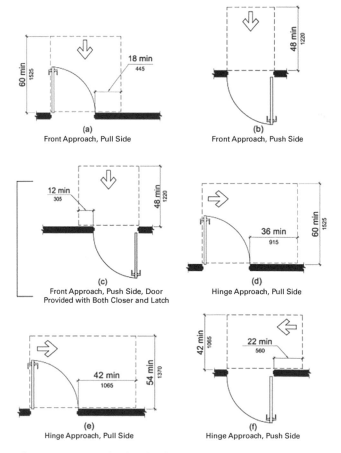

Figure 10.19 Properly planning for clearance requirements around a door is an important aspect of the designer's responsibility when meeting ADA requirements, or seeking to meet universal design ideals.

Windows

Windows, sometimes referred to as glazing, provide a means to allow daylight and outdoor air to enter the interior of a building while contributing to the aesthetics of a building exterior and interior. Chapter 7 on contextual design factors discusses the importance of building location and orientation, which play a critical role in relation to windows. The way windows, along with window treatments, filter daylight significantly impact the users' experience of an interior space. The designer should also be aware if windows are operable, as this will impact the users' ability to control interior temperature, access fresh air at will, and also pose a possible security concern if the windows are located at, or near, ground level. Windows also impact the aesthetics of a building by reinforcing the architectural style of the building. On the interior, windows allow vision to cross multiple spaces while providing acoustical privacy. This can be very useful in projects such as a corporate office where private spaces may ring the exterior of the building and a glass wall and door dividing the private spaces from the shared spaces in the middle of the plan will allow daylight to penetrate further into the space.

Window Types

Exterior windows are classified by their operation, which can be categorized as fixed, hinged, or sliding. Fixed windows do not move in any way, and, therefore, are the most secure of any of the window types, but also do not allow for fresh air intake or for the possibility to be used as a means of egress (Fig. 10.20). Hinged windows include

- **Casement windows**, which are hinged on the side and swing out.

- **Awning windows**, which are hinged along the top and swing out.
- **Hopper windows**, which are hinged along the top and swing in.

Each of these window types allow 100 percent ventilation for the area of the window, but only the awning window also provides some protection against rain while in the open position (Fig. 10.20).

Sliding windows include

- **Single-hung windows**, where only one sash can be raised and lowered.
- **Double-hung windows**, where both sashes can be raised and lowered.
- **Horizontal sliding windows**, where one or both sashes can slide open.

In each sliding window example, only 50 percent of the window area will allow air ventilation when fully open. With some models of double-hung windows, each sash can tilt inwards for ease of cleaning, which is especially helpful on upper stories of buildings.

Window types can also be described by their position in a wall, and include

- **Standard windows**, which have a portion of solid wall above and below them with a sill and head.
- **Floor-to-ceiling windows**, which have their base at, or very near, the floor and the head at, or very near, the ceiling.
- **Transom windows**, which are located above doors, can be operable, and are used to increase ventilation to interior spaces that do not have access to operable windows along exterior walls.
- **Clerestory windows**, have a head height near the ceiling and sill height above normal eye height that

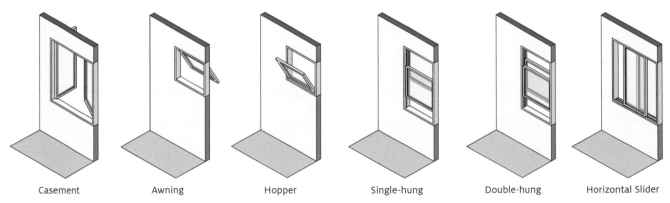

Casement   Awning   Hopper   Single-hung   Double-hung   Horizontal Slider

Figure 10.20 Windows are generally classified by operation: casement, awning, hopper, single-hung, double-hung, and horizontal sliding.

allows light to penetrate the interior while preserving privacy within the interior spaces. This can be very useful within interior walls as well, allowing daylight to reach deep into the center of a large floor plate while allowing tight spaces, such as corridors, to feel larger.

In some cases, windows can be arranged in direct sequence with one another to create entire window-wall systems. These include

- **Storefront window-wall systems**, which can be steel- or aluminum-framed fenestration that spans no more than two levels in height and that can also integrate aluminum and glass doors into the overall system.
- **Curtain wall window-wall systems**, which can span many levels of a building exterior, or an interior atrium, and are typically constructed of aluminum.

Both storefront and curtain wall systems provide the opportunity to create interior spaces that have audible privacy while sharing daylight and opening up a space visually.

Similar to doors, windows possess a detailed set of components with a unique set of terminology that designers and installers understand well (Fig. 10.21). A **sash** describes the two large modules of single- and double-hung windows where one is the inner sash and the other the outer sash. In a traditional window, the glass is often divided into smaller

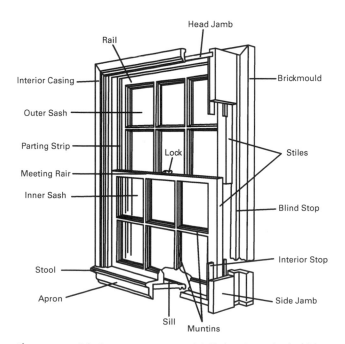

Figure 10.21 Windows possess many detailed parts, each of which impact its function, level of security, and aesthetic value.

lights with a series of **muntins**, while one entire window module is divided from a neighboring window module by a **mullion**. Two commonly confused components are the sill and the stool—a **sill** is the horizontal framing piece at the base of a window that is concealed when the window is closed, while the **stool** is the trim piece on top of the sill and visible whether the window is open or closed. The **casing** refers to the finish trim around a window that conceals the shim space between the wall framing and the window framing. As mentioned earlier, windows are sometimes called glazing, but the **glazing** is specifically the sealant, or adhesive, that holds the glass and the window framing pieces, mullions or muntins, together.

Window Frames

Interior window frames share many characteristics with doors, which have already been described. In cases where a window is installed into a fire-rated partition, both the frame and the window must be fire rated. With windows, the weakness in relation to fire rating is the glass itself, which can break when exposed to flame, so special fire-retardant glass or a layer of fire-retardant material between two layers of glass will provide fire protection. Interior windows in residential applications are often constructed of wood, while nonresidential interior windows are typically steel or aluminum. Steel frames are rolled and, therefore, have a slight radius at the corners, while aluminum is extruded, creating a square corner. Steel is most often painted, which can match the neighboring wall, while aluminum is anodized, an industrial process that protects the aluminum, but is available in a limited number of colors.

Interior glazing walls can also be "frameless," maximizing the visual connection between spaces. In these cases, the glass panes often span from floor to ceiling, which is where a discrete aluminum or steel channel is embedded or mounted to the surface. These channels at the top and bottom hold the glass securely in place. Vertical seems between the glass panels can be left open with a slight gap between them, or be sealed with clear silicone (glazing) to provide some acoustical privacy.

Window Planning Strategies

Planning around and for windows, whether exterior or interior, requires care on the part of the designer. Keep these window planning considerations in mind:

- Orientation of exterior windows in relation to primary sun exposure influences the use of
  - Window treatments.
  - Specification of interior finishes if they are sensitive to UV light.
  - The orientation of digital screens such as televisions and computers.
  - The placement and selection of lighting fixtures.
- Window treatments, particularly flowing draperies, require clearance around the window edges, which can impact the placement of adjacent walls and furniture.
- The type of window, its operation, and height placement within the wall also influence the design of the window treatments.
- Sill heights and the use of full-height walls of glazing impact the placement and selection of tall furniture near these windows.

Window Coverings

Window coverings, also referred to as window treatments, can be conceptualized as a system that provides many customizable benefits for users of an interior space near windows and can be categorized as either hard or soft treatments. Window coverings, in general, provide visual privacy for the interior of buildings as well as between spaces, passively increasing security against theft and providing users with an increased psychological sense of safety as well. Window coverings also mitigate sunlight infiltration, reducing heat gain on sunny days during warm months and helping to control glare on digital devices with screens. Frit patterns, applied vinyl or etched textural applications on glass surfaces, also control transmission of daylight, but these are not expressly window coverings, and are discussed in Chapter 9 in relation to glass. Some window coverings, particularly heavy textile draperies, also provide some insulation benefits by slowing heat loss in cold months. One of the primary benefits of window coverings is the ability of users to adjust and control them at will depending upon needs related to privacy, glare control, heating and cooling, and views between spaces or to the exterior.

Hard Window Coverings

Hard window coverings include blinds, shutters, screens, and grills. Blinds can be horizontal or vertical; made from wood, aluminum, steel, or vinyl; and can be installed within the opening of the window, on the casement, or above the casement surrounding the window. **Venetian blinds** have been in use since the Roman Empire with renewed use during British colonialization of America and other countries, the Art Deco period, and even today. Venetian blinds are a type of wide, more than 1 inch, wood or vinyl horizontal blind, while **mini blinds** are made of aluminum, steel, or vinyl and are less than 1 inch in width. **Split blinds**, such as those made from bamboo or grass reeds, have small gaps between the strips of material that filters daylight, and they often roll up and down to control privacy. **Vertical blinds** often cover windows that reach to the floor or sliding glass doors, are approximately 3 inches in width, twist at the top to control daylight infiltration, and are typically made from plastic or a textile (Fig. 10.22).

Interior shutters are hinged panels that swing over a window to provide privacy, additional security, thermal protection, and control daylight infiltration. Shutters are typically made of wood and can include adjustable louvers, an inner fabric panel, or a raised wood panel similar to a cabinet door. Shutters are typically an expensive window covering system and require particular attention to clearances around the window when the shutters are fully open. Some shutters include pockets in adjacent walls to receive the shutters when fully opened, providing uninterrupted views to the exterior.

Interior decorative **window screens** slide across a window and provide many of the same functional benefits as shutters. Some screens have particular cultural implications, such as Japanese shoji screens, which utilize rice paper to filter daylight and provide interior privacy during the day. Other varieties of screens can use glass or plastic resin panels to achieve the same functional benefits while achieving a variety of artistic goals. Screens require a track at the top and bottom and particular consideration should be given to the clearances at the window edges, understanding that, when open, the screens may prevent 100 percent open views to the exterior if adequate space is not provided at the window edges to receive the screens.

Window grills are decorative carved panels, often fixed, that filter daylight and offer some small level of privacy depending on the openness of the carved pattern (Fig. 10.23). These panels are typically wood, but can also be made of certain types of stone. The intricacies of window grills can cast impactful shadows upon the interior that can drive the character of rest of the interior design.

Figure 10.22 Blinds provide ease of daylighting control at a variety levels.

Figure 10.23 Highly crafted ornate window grills add strong visual texture to the space via the filtered daylight.

Soft Window Coverings

Soft window coverings are made from textiles and can be divided into several categories, including draperies, sheers and semi-sheers, casements, linings, curtains, and shades. **Draperies** are made of light- or medium-weight textiles, such as silk, satin, chintz, and damask; contribute significantly to the visual style of a space; and, therefore, should be designed, and textiles selected, with as much intention as other finishes and surfaces within a design (Fig. 10.24). Draperies are designed to three primary lengths: from near the ceiling down to the floor, from within the window opening down to the stool, and from above the window opening down to the apron. Operable draperies can be either two-way traverse, drawn closed from both sides, or one-way traverse, drawn closed from only one side. Stationary draperies, also called side draperies, are designed to add visual texture and style to a space and rely on other window treatments to provide daylight control and privacy. Textile window coverings possess fullness, or the quality that creates pleats and folds in the textile as it hangs, which is described in terms of multiples of the width of the textile necessary to cover the effective width of the window. For example, in the case of a window that has six feet of effective width, a **fullness factor** of 2x, 2.5x, or 3x would result in a textile 12 feet, 15 feet, or 18 feet wide, respectively. In the case of draperies, light-weight textiles typically will use a 3x fullness factor, medium weight 2.5x, and heavyweight 2x.

Sheers and semi-sheers transmit daylight while softening the harsh effects of direct sunlight on the interior. This common use of sheers necessitates a textile that resists the negative effects of ultraviolet light, such as

Figure 10.24 These full-height medium-weight draperies bring visual focus to this interior while providing privacy.

color fading. Due to the light weight of the textile, sheers will use a 3x fullness factor, and, for night privacy, sheers should be combined with draperies.

Casements utilize a coarser, loose-woven textile, compared to sheer textiles that resist UV light, are easily cleaned, and drape well, such as a leno weave. Utilized primarily in contract applications, and of a moderate weight, casements will often have a fullness of 2.5x the width of the window opening.

Linings are added to draperies to protect them from UV light, which acrylic textiles are well suited for, and provide a consistent appearance when viewed from the exterior. This view from the outside is easily overlooked, but the interior designer should be thoroughly aware of the view from exterior to interior at all times of the day under varying light conditions. In the case of textile window treatments, varying textile types and patterns can be obtrusive when viewed in context along an exterior façade. In many cases, such as high-rise buildings where multiple floors of windows are viewable from the exterior, building owners may require a consistent type and finish of window treatments to maintain a consistent appearance along the exterior.

Curtains are highly decorative window treatments that are known for their use of light textiles, particularly sheers, without a liner. Curtains are generally less expensive than draperies due to the lighter textile and lack of liner. The lack of liner can lead the curtain to have a shorter lifespan due to the impact of UV light and general wear with use. In the case of specifying curtains for a kitchen or dining area, the curtain should be made from an easily washable textile. Many curtains also integrate a heading, where the textile is gathered and pleated resulting in a tightly bound texture at the top of the curtain. The heading can take on a variety of styles and can even be designed with a pocket that receives a hanging rod.

Shades tend to cover less of the wall around a window compared to the other categories of soft window coverings and are composed of textiles or paper that can be raised and lowered to control privacy and daylight. **Roman shades** are available in many varieties, including flat, shirred, soft-pleated, accordion pleated, and balloon, have a bunched appearance at the top of the window when raised, and appear flat, or nearly flat, when lowered. **Austrian shades** are sewn in columns that produce a scalloped lower edge. **Cellular shades** have a honeycomb, or hexagonal, cross section, are often made of paper or a very lightweight textile, are mounted within the window opening leaving the casement exposed, and add insulation to the window opening when lowered. Roller shades are the simplest of the shade varieties. They offer daylight control and privacy at a low cost. Each of these shade types can be designed with opaque textiles to provide a room darkening function as well.

Window Top Coverings

Window top treatments may be constructed of hard or soft materials and serve to accentuate the aesthetics of the overall window covering. Window top treatments serve to conceal hardware, including tracks, rods, and hoops, and can accentuate the proportion of the overall window form, or bring interior consistency to windows that vary in shape and size within a single room. In general, the material used in the window covering does not necessarily dictate the type of material used in the window top treatment. In other words, soft window top treatments could be used with hard window coverings, and vice versa, or the materials can coordinate, which may be advisable in cases of heavily patterned textiles. Soft window top treatments are referred to as **valances**, and can be created using shirred, pleated, or draped textiles (Fig. 10.25). The valance style will typically complement, or match, that of the window covering. Hard window top treatments include cornices and lambrequins.

A **cornice** is positioned along the top of the window to conceal window covering hardware, and is often made from wood or metal and stained, painted, or covered with a textile to coordinate with the rest of the interior. A **lambrequin** is similar to a cornice, but it extends down the side of a window to conceal draperies when in the open position and results in a widening effect of the window proportions.

Window Coverings Hardware

Window treatment hardware can be of a functional or decorative variety and should be coordinated with the window covering and window top treatment, if used. Hardware that is strictly functional, such as a simple curtain rod, or a single- or double-traverse rod, is often intended to be concealed by a valance, cornice, or lambrequin. In other cases, functional hardware, such as sash rods or spring-tension rods, can be concealed by a drapery or curtain heading. Recessed ceiling tracks are especially useful in contemporary spaces using floor-to-ceiling draperies. Drawstrings and cords that accompany draperies, curtains, and blinds should be addressed carefully in spaces where they can be a safety hazard, such as infant nurseries or child care spaces. Decorative hardware provides a functional benefit, but do not necessarily need the concealment of a valance, cornice, or lambrequin (Fig. 10.26). Decorative window

Figure 10.25 This window valance conceals a set of functional drapery hardware.

Figure 10.26 This decorative rod is intended to be exposed, not requiring a valance or other concealment.

treatment hardware can be made from painted or stained wood or a variety of metals, including stainless steel, aluminum, nickel-plated steel, brass, or copper. Decorative rods often include finials and knobs to accentuate the style of the space.

Textiles

The successful application of textiles relies on the designer's understanding of the elements and principles of design. Textiles are prized for their aesthetic impact within a larger design scheme due to their color, pattern, and textural attributes. Textiles can also carry significant cultural importance for the users of a space, which the designer should intentionally and carefully utilize in the built environment. To achieve the aesthetic goals of a design through the application of textiles, the designer must also understand the more technical aspects of this material. This discussion of textiles is abbreviated in its coverage and connects to certain topics in the finishes chapter (Chapter 9), including carpet and wallcoverings as well as upholstered furniture and draperies in this chapter.

Textile Fibers

An understanding of textiles begins with a fundamental knowledge of the most basic component of any textile, the fiber, which can be natural or manufactured (Fig. 10.27). **Natural fibers** originate from nature, are valued for their

Figure 10.27 The great variety of colors and patterns available with textiles result from the fiber, yarn, and weave types as well as the dyeing method.

inherent aesthetic and functional qualities, and fall into three categories:

- **Protein fibers** originate from animals; examples include cashmere from the Cashmere goat, mohair from the Angora goat, wool from a sheep, or silk from a silkworm (Fig. 10.28).
- **Cellulosic fibers** originate from plants; examples include sisal, cotton, and jute, a common fiber used in the backing of many interior materials including carpet, linoleum, wall coverings, upholstery, and draperies.
- **Mineral fibers** originate from rock/earth; the primary example is asbestos, recognized as a carcinogen if it becomes airborne and is no longer used in textiles or other building products, but the designer should be aware of its existence in older interior materials, which may require abatement as step prior to construction of a renovation project.

Natural fibers are not significantly altered from their original state in order to be used in the textile making process, but manufactured fibers by definition are significantly altered. **Manufactured fibers** are made by humans to meet certain aesthetic and functional performance needs that natural fibers cannot, and fall into two categories:

- **Regenerated fibers** are manufactured from plants and require a chemical and/or mechanical process to breakdown the plant material to expose the fiber; examples include acetate and rayon made of wood fiber, and rubber made from the secretions of rubber trees.
- **Synthetic fibers** are manufactured from hydrocarbons (natural gas, oil, and coal) and water, but also recycled from plastic sources, including soda and water bottles; examples include acrylic, nylon, polyester, spandex, and vinyl (Fig. 10.28).

Yarns

Fibers are used to manufacture yarn, which falls into the following categories:

- **Spun yarns** consist of **staple fibers** (noncontinuous length fibers) twisted together to form the yarn; are softer and more plush than filament yarn; and have greater tendency for pilling than filament yarns.
- **Monofilament yarns** consist of a single, relatively thick **filament** (continuous length fiber); are typically transparent, or nearly transparent; and are used for

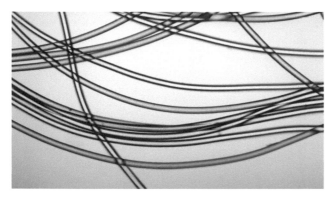

Figures 10.28 a and b Natural textile fibers are harvested from animals (such as wool from sheep), plants, or the earth, and synthetic fibers, such as nylon, shown here, are made by humans.

stitching fabric seams or to create translucent textiles for draperies.

- **Filament/multifilament yarns** consist of many long filament fibers; they are used to create lustrous, smooth textiles.

- **Textured filament yarns** consist of many long filament fibers that have been texturized; they are softer, more fuller bodied than filament yarns in an effort to increase elasticity and create a more natural feel and appearance.

Textile Construction

Most textiles used for upholstery and draperies are woven, made from two sets of yarns interlaced perpendicular to one another. Yarns running the length of the textile are called **warp yarns** and those running the width are the **weft yarns**. High quality textiles are characterized by perfect 90 degree intersections of warp and weft yarns, referred to as **grain-straight**. The primary methods of weaving textiles include

- **Plain weave**: the most basic variation involves one warp yarn and one weft yarn alternating with one another, described as a 1 × 1; a variation includes the basket weave (two warp yarns and one or two weft yarns, 2 × 1 and 2 × 2, respectively) (Fig. 10.29a).
- **Twill weave**: more complicated than a plain weave where a yarn will pass under or over two or more perpendicular yarns in a cascading sequence to create diagonal lines in the weave (Fig. 10.29b).
- **Satin weave**: similar to twill in that a yarn will pass under or over two or more adjacent perpendicular yarns, but without the cascading sequence, which creates a grid pattern rather than a diagonal line emphasis (Fig. 10.29c).

Figures 10.29 a, b, and c The plain weave (a), twill weave (b), and satin weave (c) are common methods used to construct textiles.

Plain weave construction

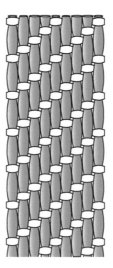

Twill weave construction

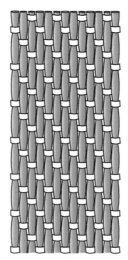

Satin weave construction

Nonwoven textiles are created by bonding fibers with heat or adhesive directly into textiles and omitting the yarn stage of construction. Bonded-web fabric is used as an inner layer in furniture skirting and drapery heading to add thickness. **Felt** is made from wool fiber and is used as an anti-scratch protection layer for furniture, insulation, or to improve acoustic performance in a space. Needle punching is a technique used to manufacture some types of carpet and wall coverings.

Dyeing

Dyeing can occur at any step in the textile manufacturing process—fiber, yarn, or fabric. Dyeing at the fiber stage often results in a higher degree of colorfastness and two options are available for dyeing (see the carpet section in Chapter 9 for additional information):

- **Solution dyeing**: only available for synthetic manufactured fibers, dye is added to the fiber while the fiber is being made, resulting in a through color (similar to a carrot), improving resistance to fading (Fig. 10.30a).
- **Stock dyeing**: available for natural or manufactured fibers the dye is applied to the fiber after it has been

a

b

Figures 10.30 a and b Solution dyeing results in a fiber with through color, similar to a carrot, whereas stock dyeing produces a fiber with superficial color, similar to a radish.

harvested or made resulting in a surface application of the dye to the fiber (similar to a radish) (Fig. 10.30b).

At the yarn step of construction, a yarn can be dyed a single color or multiple colors. Package, beam, and skein dyeing methods are used for differing reasons while creating a single color yarn. Space dyeing is used to create multicolored yarn. Due to the twisting of fibers, it is possible for yarn dyeing methods to be inconsistent when compared to dyeing at the fiber step of textile construction.

Dyeing **greige goods**, or fully constructed textiles that possess only their natural color, is not often used, but does have some advantages. These advantages include flexibility for manufacturers to add the dye at the end of construction based on design specification. This is useful when a manufacturer may not want to inventory large quantities and color variations of a product that is not specified very often. This option can also be employed for custom colors or color patterns.

Printing Textiles

Textile patterns are emphasized by weaving fiber-dyed or yarn-dyed textiles, but pattern can also be created by printing greige goods. Textile printing techniques include

- **Direct printing**: by hand or machine, dye is applied directly to the surface of the textile; techniques include block printing and roller printing.
- **Resist printing**: in conjunction with an inhibiting agent or blocking mechanism, dye is selectively applied to the textile surface to create a pattern; screen printing is a common technique.
- **Digital printing**: digital pattern files are loaded to advanced printing equipment to create intricate textile patterns; jet printing is one technique used by manufacturers.

Textile Performance Enhancements

Depending on the application of a textile as upholstery, drapery, wallcovering, or even carpet, a variety of performance-enhancing additives can be added to the textile. Performance enhancements include

- **Static resistance**: a chemical can be integrated into a manufactured fiber or be applied to yarn in order to reduce static electricity resulting from movement across the textile.

- **Flame resistance**: through a chemical process applied at the fiber stage of textile construction, or through application to griege goods, fire can be prevented from proceeding beyond the ignition phase of the flame-spread process.
- **Soil and stain resistance**: preventing matter from mechanically attaching, referred to as **soiling**, or from chemically bonding, referred to as **staining**, to textiles often requires the application of petroleum-based products to the textile.
- **Water resistance**: dense textiles, that are high in yarn count, are inherently better at resisting water penetration compared to those that are less dense; silicone treatments can also be applied to textiles to slow the absorption of water.

Testing Performance of Textiles

The Association for Contract Textiles developed a method to standardize the description of certain textile performance criteria to aid designers in the specification process. The following performance criteria apply to textiles based on application: furniture upholstery, direct glue wallcoverings, wrapped wall panels and upholstered walls, and drapery (Fig. 10.31).

- **Flammability**: the ability of the textile to resist flame ignition.
- **Wet and dry crocking**: the ability of the textile to resist color transference to another material through rubbing.
- **Colorfastness to light**: the ability of the textile to resist color fading from light.
- **Physical properties**:the ability of the textile to resist **pilling** (creation of fiber balls on the textile surface), the measure of **breaking strength** (the force needed to pull the textile apart), and the ability

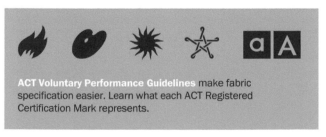

ACT Voluntary Performance Guidelines make fabric specification easier. Learn what each ACT Registered Certification Mark represents.

Figure 10.31 The Association for Contract Textiles provides clear and consistent labeling describing the characteristics of a textile in relation to flammability, wet and dry crocking, colorfastness to light, physical properties, and abrasion.

to resist **seam slippage** (the slipping of yarn at the seam of two textiles when pulling force is applied).
- **Abrasion**: the amount of wear on the textile surface through rubbing and other contact with another textile.

Testing procedures for these performance criteria are provided by the American Society of Testing and Materials (ASTM), the American Association of Textile Chemists and Colorists (AATCC), the National Fire Protection Association (NFPA), and the California Technical Bulletin, which have jurisdiction in the United States. Other countries will have their own requirements governing the use of textiles.

Accessories

Interior accessories can be divided into functional and decorative categories based upon the item's role in the interior. Whether functional or decorative, the designer has the opportunity to purposely compose the placement of a client's existing or proposed collection of accessories to enhance views and focal points within a space and towards the exterior. While accessories can easily be overlooked during the design process, it is in the best interest of the designer and client to identify key elements that will need to be incorporated into the proposed interior that could even provide inspiration for the space that will soon embrace them.

Functional Accessories

Functional accessories include mirrors, clocks, screens, and public restroom accessories (Fig. 10.32). For example, within certain design philosophies such as feng shui, mirrors can play a profound role that transcends the need to examine one's attire and appearance. Mirrors can also be used to magnify lighting, make a space appear larger than it is, and enhance views with security and safety in mind. Clocks provide the functional benefit of recording the passage of time, but they also can provide a subtle background sound in a space, are highly visually stylized, can communicate a client's personality, and can even be heirlooms. Freestanding screens can be beautiful handcrafted room dividers that communicate cultural roots while providing visual privacy between spaces, or bring the scale of a grand space down to the human level.

Public restroom accessories differ from the other accessories described in this section because they require a very high level of attention by the interior designer in order

Figure 10.32 Accessories such as clocks, candlesticks, and mirrors serve functional as well as aesthetic purposes in a space.

to abide by the strict regulations and guidelines governing their placement. The Americans with Disabilities Act (ADA) is the governing regulation in the United States that dictates guidelines, as expressed in the Americans with Disabilities Act Accessibility Guidelines (ADAAG) and American National Standards Institute (ANSI) 117.1, Standard for Accessible and Usable Buildings and Facilities, for the installation of the variety of restroom accessories. Public restroom accessories include soap, toilet paper, sanitary napkin, toilet seat cover, and hand towel dispensers, as well as towel and sanitary napkin waste receptacles, and hand dryers and mirrors. The documents that aid designers in meeting the accessibility requirements of public restrooms are invaluable as they provide many helpful descriptions, commentaries, and diagrams to illustrate the application of the ADA requirements.

Decorative Accessories

Decorative accessories tend to focus on art, including paintings, drawings, prints, photography, sculpture, ceramics, glass, wood, metals, textiles, and plantings. Paintings,

drawings, prints, and photography range widely in value from one-of-kind original oils on canvas to series of lithographs or engravings to posters and personal photography. Each of these types of art may include frames and mats, or could simply be displayed on stretched canvas. Frames and mats serve to offer some protection to the piece while concealing any ragged edges of the art, and these elements should be considered as integral to the overall composition of the work itself as well as the space in which the art is displayed. Sculpture, including ceramics and glass, can be works depicting human or animal figures or be abstract in shape, and can also possess limited function, such as the case with vases, dishes, and bowls. Crafts involving wood, metals, and textiles could be three-dimensional pieces, framed, or relief sculptures and can range in size from table-top pieces to freestanding works of art. All of these examples of decorative art require specialty lighting and means to display them, whether that means hanging on a wall or from a ceiling, freestanding on a shelf or tabletop, or freestanding on an elevated dais. The last example of a decorative accessory, plantings, are unique in that they change with time, require feeding, and have specific lighting requirements in order to live, maintain their beauty, or enhance cuisine (Fig. 10.33). The client may enjoy maintaining interior plantings on occasion, or permanently, and careful consideration should be given by the designer to cleanliness, accessibility, maintenance, and horticulture requirements.

Fixtures and Equipment

Fixtures and equipment include appliances, utility equipment, plumbing fixtures, display systems that are not millwork or furniture, electronic kiosks, signage, and specialty equipment or large tools. These items present some interesting challenges for designers, as they are often manufactured with very specific size and clearance needs and can require mechanical, electrical, plumbing, and telecommunication connections in order to function properly. While the designer is not expressly designing fixtures and equipment, the time needed for coordination with engineering disciplines and manufacturers should not be underestimated.

Appliances

Appliances are most commonly found in kitchens, baths, and laundry spaces and aid in the functions of food

Figure 10.33 As decorative accessories, interior plantings can serve to visually soften hard edges.

preparation and cleaning. Ranges, traditional and convection ovens, microwave ovens, and refrigerators are the most common food preparation and storage appliances, which are available in both residential and commercial grades. Dishwashers and clothes washers and dryers can be found in dedicated laundry spaces, or even in kitchens and bathrooms where residential space is at a premium. Each of these appliances requires an electrical connection, gas connection, or both in some cases, such as a gas range or oven that needs electricity for the ignition switch and digital displays at the controls. Other appliances also require a cold water supply connection, hot water supply connection, waste connection, or all of these, such as a clothes washer. In the case of clothes washers and dryers and dishwashers, an electrical connection is also required for the controls, motors, and any digital displays. Exhaust hoods are common in kitchens; some require a dedicated duct and vent to the outside, and all require electrical supply in order to operate. Appliance materials can vary widely, but are typically type 304 stainless steel in commercial applications, and anodized aluminum, baked enamel, or coated steel in

residential applications. In terms of planning, commercial kitchens require specialized knowledge of code regulations and equipment needs, which should be handled by a commercial kitchen designer (Fig. 10.34).

Figure 10.34 Commercial kitchens will use stainless steel throughout the space for sanitary and maintenance purposes, and these spaces will also have higher ventilation demands compared to residential kitchens.

Plumbing Fixtures

Plumbing fixtures and equipment are found in kitchens, baths, and restrooms, but will also make their way into other types of spaces, including bars, locker and dressing rooms, and utility rooms. Faucets for kitchen and bar sinks, bath and restroom lavatories, and utility basins should be specified with a lever handle rather than knob where accessibility requirements and universal design principles are a concern. Faucets in context with a kitchen sink or utility washtub should be selected with a gooseneck form to allow large pots and buckets to be easily filled with water. Faucet controls may include separate levers or dials for hot and cold supply, or a single actuator can be used to control the water temperature and flow rate. The same type of controls are available for shower heads and bath faucets, which are available in a variety of configurations, including adjustable height shower heads, multiple heads and controls, and deluge functions, depending upon the context and accessibility needs of the users (Fig. 10.35). Toilets are available in either a round or elongated shape, a closed or open seat front, and can be wall or floor mounted. Wall-mounted toilets require structural reinforcing in the wall but allow for ease of cleaning the floor under and around the toilet and open front seats and elongated bowls allow for ease of use by a wider population range. Controls for plumbing fixtures can be manual or automatic, which can reduce water consumption and improve cleanliness. Materials for faucets and shower heads tend to be stainless steel or steel plated with nickel, chrome, brass, or copper, whereas toilets are made from vitreous china, sinks from stainless steel, solid surface, concrete, or stone, tubs from enameled steel, cast iron, or fiberglass, and showers from fiberglass, or tile or stone over cementitious backer board on wall framing.

Display Systems

Retail fixtures are modular or custom designed displays for merchandise. The designer can specify or design these items for a retail client with the express purpose of displaying, storing, and securing merchandise on a sales floor. **Slat wall** is a common panelized flexible display system that can be anchored to walls, or can be used as part of a freestanding display to divide space creating aisles between merchandise displays. **Cable-rail modular display systems** can be wall mounted, ceiling and floor mounted, or freestanding systems that utilize glass shelving and stainless steel cables or rods to display products while preserving open views through a retail environment. Freestanding pedestal displays are utilized in open retail settings to allow patrons to circulate around them and view products from multiple angles. Lockable glass displays are often reserved for valuable items in an effort to decrease theft. A common retail strategy involves bringing the products up close to eye-level rather than near the floor, which allows the lower portion of retail displays to be used as lockable storage that can hold additional merchandise ready to replenish the items that have been purchased. Lighting is also critical to any retail space, and many modular retail fixtures integrate lighting, which requires access to electricity, an important point to coordinate with the electrical engineering consultant.

Large Equipment

In health care settings, the designer is responsible to coordinate the installation of all medical equipment, whether the project has a specialty medical equipment consultant or the owner will be supplying the medical equipment. In context with family dentistry and medical practice, the equipment can range from small countertop infant scales to large dental x-ray machines and examination chairs or tables. Medical specialists, such as ear, nose, and throat (ENT) physicians, may have specialty spaces such as an audiology testing booth to test for hearing loss. Hospitals can have very large pieces of equipment, such as a magnetic resonance imaging (MRI) machine that scans the entire human body (Fig. 10.36). Each of these types of equipment, large or small, requires the designer to

Figure 10.35 A wall-mounted toilet allows the floor to be more easily cleaned, but also requires additional support inside the wall.

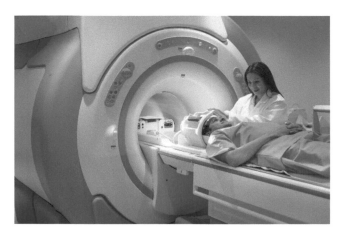

Figure 10.36 Designers need to understand the clearance requirements for large pieces of equipment, such as an MRI machine.

Figure 10.37 Interior designers will often consult with a graphic designer in order to produce large environmental graphics, maps, and signs. The graphic designer is responsible for the graphic composition of these pieces, while the interior designer is responsible for locating them in the plan and the method of attachment to the interior architectural elements.

consider the placement and required clearances around the equipment for proper use and servicing and access to electricity, water, clean and temperature-controlled air, and exhaust.

Signage

Signage is one part of a larger wayfinding strategy that will often use changes in finishes, lighting, and open views to help occupants find their way through a space or across multiple floors of a building, which is described in more detail in Chapter 8 (Fig. 10.37). Complex buildings that utilize signage for wayfinding include hospitals, office buildings, department stores, schools, and multi-family residential buildings. Signage serves to identify whole buildings as is the case with address numbers, entrances through directional identifiers such as "East Entry," retail tenants through brand-specific graphics on windows, corporate tenants on a building's tenant marque in the ground floor lobby space, or the location of a student's physics class by the room number next to the door. Accessibility guidelines dictate the legibility of standard building signage, such as those used for restrooms, by requiring the use of high contrast letters and background colors and the inclusion of Braille for the blind. Many signs are illuminated internally, or on the face, and proper electrical coordination is required. For large projects, a signage contractor or consultant may be used, or a client representative may be identified to ensure that brand consistency is preserved on all interior signage, and the designer will want to coordinate all signage design, placement, and materials so that the overall interior design is cohesive.

Summary

Millwork, furniture, doors, windows and window coverings, textiles, accessories, and fixtures and equipment play a crucial role in the design and fit out of an interior. Some of these items, including certain doors and windows, may be part of the existing space or base building and will not be able to be changed, while others will be specified or custom designed by the designer. Some items will be supplied by the owner and the designer will be required to accommodate those pieces in any proposed design scheme. Other items will require specific and careful coordination with structural, mechanical, plumbing, and electrical consultants or subcontractors. In all, the furnishings of an interior can be the most important aspects of an interior in the eyes, or hands, of the end user.

Two Parts Love, One Part Detail, Equals All Awesome

Project:	The Thompson Nashville Hotel
Location:	Nashville, Tennessee
Client:	The Thompson Hotel Group
Design Firm:	Parts and Labor Design
Occupants/Users:	Hotel patrons and staff
Site Characteristics:	Dense urban downtown
Year Complete:	2016
Cost Estimate:	Undisclosed
Facility Size:	100-seat ground floor restaurant, 200-seat rooftop bar and restaurant, 6,185 square feet of event space, 225 guest rooms

Project Overview

Once synonymous with abandoned warehouses, the Gulch—a LEED-certified community near downtown Nashville, Tennessee—is now one of the city's most vibrant neighborhoods. Parts and Labor Design, a New York City-based design firm, was tapped to create a design concept for the Thompson as Nashville's first true lifestyle hotel. The concept celebrates the city's creative spirit while also embracing a modern experience that is both timeless and fashion forward. Understated elegance, distinct vintage and handcrafted details, locally sourced Nashville artwork, and a residential "home away from home" feel, are all themes found throughout the hotel's lobby.

The experience begins at the canopied entrance, where a clean, modern facade with a wood and brass revolving door ushers guests inside to an expansive lobby. Upon entering, guests are greeted by a locally crafted wooden floor inlay. Here, brass details artistically highlight the global coordinates of the Thompson. Straight ahead, a monolithic mint green stone check-in desk acts as a beacon for entering guests, drawing travelers further into an active lobby space that offers glimpses into the adjacent restaurant and lobby lounge.

The lobby lounge is filled with custom-designed light fixtures and furniture. The public space embodies a vintage charm with a uniquely modern and creative slant. Velvet sofas and reading nooks offer an intimate and warm setting for guests to unwind and relax. The organization of the furniture allows for a multipurpose use of space, giving guests a place to engage in intimate and social interaction, communal conversation, or individual work. Floor-to-ceiling bookcases were carefully curated and filled with items one would find at home—books, plants, photographs, knickknacks, and records—each adding to the hotel's overarching residential vibe. Warm tones and soft finishes round out the lobby's relaxed aesthetic.

Custom millwork, furniture, and lighting beckon the visitor to stay, unwind, and enjoy the space of the ground-floor lobby.

The multi-finish floor inlay at the entrance foretells the level of craft in all of the furnishings.

The design of the restaurant incorporates finely crafted details in the furniture legs and the lighting fixtures above.

To the left of the lobby lounge, on the opposite side of the check-in desk, a custom wood and glass partition serves as grand entry to the hotel's restaurant, Marsh House, with its oversized sliding doors reminiscent of an estate library and sitting room. The 100-seat signature seafood restaurant takes design cues from an American southern estate green room, combining old south elegance with new south creativity. The design team sourced inspiration from a place near and dear to the head chef's heart—a family estate located in New Orleans. Nostalgic, timeless, and fashion forward, its gulf to gulch southern style is embodied in the cocktails, cuisine, and creative interiors.

Custom geometric concrete flooring of gray, cream, and charcoal and a high-gloss green ceiling with mirrored inlays draw the experience deeper into a dining room that is flooded with light from its floor-to-ceiling windows. Guests are first greeted by a lounge area that features plush and comfortable seating. The upscale dining scene mixes marsh-inspired wall coverings with impressive drapery, custom furniture, and impactful light fixtures, all highlighting a well-appointed and luxurious, residential eclecticism celebrated in the South. A partial-height decorative partition thoughtfully divides the main dining and bar area, where a tile and tambour oyster bar serves as the restaurant's main focal point. As guests are led further back through the restaurant they will find an intimate private dining room, which offers seating for fourteen. Green, cream, and gray tones mix with blue hues and warm woods in this space. The bespoke, residential feeling is seamless from lobby lounge to restaurant lounge, and from formal dining to private.

For event needs, the hotel features 6,185 square feet of meeting and event space on the second floor, composed of three dedicated meeting rooms, a 1,219-square-foot outdoor terrace, and a ballroom and boardroom with space for locals and visitors alike to gather for happenings. Custom, deco-inspired chandeliers, luxurious carpets, and wood paneling add a warmth and style of its own to these spaces.

The journey to the breathtaking panoramic city views unveiled from the hotel's L.A. Jackson Rooftop Bar & Restaurant begins with the ground-floor elevator. The high-end rooftop experience begins as the visitor steps off the elevator on the twelfth floor. After strolling down a narrow, white, wood-paneled corridor lined with photographs of music icons, one steps through blue glass entry doors to find flamingo-colored floor tiles that give way to a central, impressive race track bar made of stamped concrete with a contoured wooden top. Dining areas feature stainless steel topped tables and blue velvet banquettes that mix sawtooth detailing with patterned fabric. Custom upholstered ceiling panels overhead feature circular glass chandeliers end to end. Anchoring the back of the main space is a communal table set in front of an eye-catching tropical, modern-themed wallcovering and below a custom chandelier. But before settling into the lounge, bar, or dining room, guests are immediately drawn through the oversized, glass retractable garage doors leading to an expansive patio with breathtaking panoramic city views and an illuminated twenty-foot olive tree. Furnished with a combination of built-in wood banquettes and metal chairs and tables, the patio allows guests to create spaces for intimate conversations or areas to accommodate large groups. With a bold design and

style as strong as its clientele, the 200-seat bar and restaurant embodies a young and culturally driven aesthetic that is upscale and effortless.

A mid-century-modern-meets-'70s sensibility carries from the hotel's lobby, through the corridors, and into the guestrooms, where wood floors are layered with custom rugs and bathrooms boast black and white graphic floors brightened by white tiles and pentagon-shaped mirrors. Wanting each room to have a distinctly residential feel, the design team created an inviting entry foyer within all guestrooms and suites. Further inside, guests will find a living area that leads to the sleeping quarters. To take advantage of the floor-to-ceiling windows, the design team incorporated an open floor plan with a living area that features plush seating, where guests can socialize and entertain while taking in views of the surrounding city. These details, combined with various seating configurations, allow guests to mingle and converse in a laid-back, personal setting. Separating the living and sleeping areas in the king suites is a tiled hearth with cushions, creating a casual setting for conversation.

The residential eclecticism continues throughout the presidential suite, which features a formal dining area where custom leather chairs framed in brass surround a large wood table. Around the corner, a pantry and powder room lead to the bedroom, serving as a transition space between the public and private areas. Once inside the bedroom, one's eye is immediately drawn to a navy blue mohair upholstered headboard and a period-inspired chandelier that hangs above. Detailed with elegant oak-paneled molding, the headboard serves

The rooftop bar and restaurant contrasts the broad views over the city with the intricate details and textures of the textiles and wall coverings.

as a dynamic sculptural art piece. A door leads to an all marble bathroom with a glass transom welcoming additional natural light into the bedroom. An open glass shower is complemented by a polished nickel soaking tub positioned in front of a floor-to-ceiling picture window offering guests a private view of the city. Local artwork is also found throughout the hotel's corridors, guestrooms, and suites, with walls lined in hand-knit tapestries, credenzas, and gold foil pieces. These subtle, handcrafted elements add to the residential feel and further inspire guests during their stay.

Design Process

The design team deftly incorporated the complexities of the location, Nashville culture, and functional goals of the project typology into a cohesive work that entices travelers and locals alike to enjoy the offerings found within the Thompson. The specific storied history of the site as a former rail hub contributes to the tactile nature of the interior while the curve of the adjacent 11th Avenue is reflected in the geometry of the building. Nashville is well known for its music heritage, which is reflected in the design of this project in a rich and meaningful way without treading into kitsch. Building upon these inherent and created characteristics, patrons make the space into a place of common ground for the traveler as well as the native.

To achieve a completed work of this magnitude, the Parts and Labor Design team worked closely with the client to uncover their functional and aesthetic needs and carefully leveraged the design of the custom furnishings to establish the character of each space. The Thompson hotels are indeed part of a chain, with certain brand requirements, however the design team was allowed to explore and create a place that stitches itself into the vibrant culture of Nashville, accentuating the offerings of the Gulch. Throughout the hotel, the team sought to create something that was not only residential in nature but that people would be able to form a relationship with and feel a sense of ownership like one does with their home. Parts and Labor Design typically custom designs about 90 percent of all furniture and lighting so the product is truly unique to the property. The team designed the lighting, furniture, case goods, and interior architecture to intuitively work together and flow from one space to another without

The high-touch details, including upholstery and hardware, contribute to the high-end design of the guest rooms.

losing a sense of the whole. Levels of experience were pursued and aesthetic departures were made in various spaces to add variety while maintaining a cohesive overall design. The team engaged the client through sketches, renderings, models, and mock-ups of key aspects of the design in order to help the client envision how the built space would function and feel.

The interiors of the Thompson Nashville can only be described as specifically purposeful. This extraordinary attention to detail in the furnishings results in a place that is unique to the client and allows the design team to have full control over the design outcome. When the design team takes this approach, no two designs will ever be the same. The team makes it a priority to not reuse furniture or lighting designs from project to project unless there is some client-specific reason to do so. The team has found that this approach ensures that each project is unique, but they also have the privilege to collaborate with a variety of talented designers, fabricators, artists, and craftspeople. For example, each guestroom in the Thompson Nashville has a unique custom rug that resulted from a collaboration between PLD, Tailor-Made Textiles (handmade rugs), and Eskayel (textiles). The level of detail and customization allows the team to express a far greater level of creative freedom that delivers the best product while permitting them to control budget and schedule.

The furniture, millwork, and fixtures for the Thompson Nashville are seamlessly crafted as part of a holistically designed interior by Parts and Labor Design. Parts and Labor Design is a full-service interior architecture and design firm in New York City specializing in finely crafted spaces. For more information on the Thompson Nashville Hotel and Parts and Labor Design visit https://partsandlabordesign.com/. The Thompson Nashville Hotel core and shell architecture was designed by Hastings Architecture Associates (http://www.haa.us/). The creative team at Upspring PR (http://www.upspringpr.com/) contributed much of the written information in support of this case study, for which the author of this text is very grateful.

Key Terms

Abrasion	Filament	Monofilament yarns	Standard windows
Accordion door	Filament/Multifilament	Mullion	Staple fibers
Antique	yarns	Muntins	Static resistance
Austrian shades	Flame resistance	Natural fibers	Stiles
Automatic sliding doors	Flammability	Physical properties	Stock dyeing
Awning windows	Floor-to-ceiling windows	Pilling	Stool
Bi-fold door	Folding door	Pivot door	Stop trim
Breaking strength	French door	Plain weave	Storefront window-wall
Cable-rail modular display	Fullness factor	Pocket door	systems
systems	Functional accessories	Protein fibers	Surface-mounted sliding
Case goods	Furniture, fixtures, and	Rails	door
Casement windows	equipment	Regenerated fibers	Swinging door
Casing	Glazing	Resist printing	Synthetic fibers
Cellular shades	Grain-straight	Roman shades	Textured filament yarns
Cellulosic fibers	Greige goods	Rustic	Threshold
Clerestory windows	Head	Sash	Traditional
Colorfastness to light	Hinges	Satin weave	Transom windows
Contemporary	Hopper windows	Seam slippage	Twill weave
Cornice	Horizontal sliding windows	Shim space	Upholstery
Curtain wall window-wall	Jamb	Sill	Valance
systems	Joinery types	Single-hung windows	Venetian blinds
Decorative accessories	Lambrequin	Slat wall	Vertical blinds
Digital printing	Latch assembly	Sliding door	Vintage
Direct printing	Lights	Soil and stain resistance	Warp yarns
Double-acting door	Manufactured fibers	Soiling	Water resistance
Double-hung windows	Millwork	Solution dyeing	Weft yarns
Draperies	Mineral fibers	Split blinds	Wet and dry crocking
Dutch door	Mini blinds	Spun yarns	Window grills
Felt	Modern	Staining	Window screens

Resources

Alliston, J. (n.d.). *Home*. Retrieved December 17, 2017, from http://www.woodworkersinstitute.com/.

American Window and Door Institute. (n.d.). American Window and Door Institute homepage for certified installers of vinyl windows. Retrieved December 17, 2017, from http://www.awdi.com/.

Architectural Woodwork Institute. (n.d.). Architectural Woodwork Institute homepage. Retrieved December 17, 2017, from http://www.awinet.org/.

Ching, F. D. (2014). *Building Construction Illustrated*. Hoboken, NJ: John Wiley & Sons, Inc.

Haworth. (n.d.). Haworth homepage. Retrieved December 17, 2017, from http://www.haworth.com/.

Herman Miller. (n.d.). *Modern Furniture for the Office and Home*. Retrieved December 17, 2017, from https://www.hermanmiller.com/.

Hinchman, M. (2016). *History of Furniture: A Global View*. New York: Fairchild Books.

Knoll. (n.d.). *Home*. Retrieved December 17, 2017, from https://www.knoll.com/.

Natale, C. (2009). *Furniture Design and Construction for the Interior Designer*. London: Fairchild Books.

Steelcase. (2014, June 16). *Office Furniture Solutions, Education & Healthcare Furniture*. Retrieved December 17, 2017, from https://www.steelcase.com/.

Steel Door Institute. (n.d.). Steel Door Institute homepage. Retrieved December 17, 2017, from https://www.steeldoor.org/.

Steel Window Institute. (n.d.). Steel Window Institute homepage. Retrieved December 17, 2017, from http://www.steelwindows.com/.

Textile Institute. (n.d.). Home. Retrieved December 17, 2017, from https://www.textileinstitute.org/.

Willbanks, A., Oxford, N., & Miller, D. (2014). *Textiles for Residential and Commercial Interiors*. Bloomsbury Publishing.

Review Questions

1. What are the two broad categories of millwork? List the joinery types.
2. What are the typical heights for the following surfaces: seated-height work surfaces, standing-height transaction surfaces, ADA-compliant transaction surfaces.
3. What are the material options for trim and moldings? What is the typical height of a chair rail?
4. List the terms of style associated with furniture. Why can these terms be challenging for designers and clients?
5. List and describe the types of sofas.
6. What are the benefits of systems furniture compared to case goods?
7. In relation to quality and materials in furniture, what situations dictate the use of solid wood rather than wood veneer? What settings are conducive to utilizing metal furniture rather than wood? What advantages do synthetic furniture materials, such as plastics and resins, offer?
8. What materials are typically used to construct the frames of high-quality upholstered furniture?
9. List the three broad types of doors. List the performance characteristics that should be considered when determining door materials. Why are lever handles preferred over knobs? What planning strategies for doors must be addressed in relation to ADA requirements?
10. List the types of windows based on their functionality and describe how they operate, or open. List and describe the types of windows based on their position in a wall. How might the sill height of windows impact planning strategies around a window?
11. How does the window operation impact the selection of window treatment types? List the functional benefits of window treatments. What conditions would contribute to selecting hard or soft window coverings? What type of window covering hardware would likely be paired with a window top covering, such as a valance?
12. Provide examples of both functional and decorative accessories.
13. What types of spaces require special planning expertise in relation to appliances and large equipment? What types of spaces will use specialty display systems? What types of spaces benefit from extensive signage design programs?

Exercises

Master Bedroom and Bath Suite, Continued

1. Reference the client profile, location, and view from the Chapter 9 exercise.
2. Select furniture, millwork, doors and windows, window treatments, fixtures, and accessories to completely outfit the bedroom and bath suite.
3. Images of the selections should be presented on a physical or digital "board." Include headings to categorize the spaces (Bedroom, Bathroom) and label each individual furniture selection by type (e.g., "bed," "vanity storage," etc.).

11

Lighting

Learning Objectives

As a result of reading this chapter, students will possess an awareness of

1. The role of natural and artificial light in the built environment.

2. Interior lighting strategies: ambient, task, and accent lighting.

3. The two broad luminaire categories—architectural and nonarchitectural—and specific types of each.

4. The three categories of lamps—incandescent, discharge, and solid state—and specific types of each.

5. Energy use implications of interior lighting.

6. The safety and health effects associated with interior lighting.

7. Lighting controls, both conventional and digital.

8. The communication tools—the reflected ceiling plan and lighting schedules—that designers use to describe lighting design and layout.

As a result of taking part in the learning exercises at the end of this chapter, students will

1. Demonstrate the ability to identify luminaires, observe existing spatial conditions, and draw a basic reflected ceiling plan.

2. Demonstrate the ability to identify wattage and lumen information on lighting product packaging, calculate efficacy, and analyze lamps based on energy efficiency.

Introduction

Interior designers possess many tools, referred to as the elements and principles of design, as discussed in Chapter 1, which they use to create space. In that discussion light was identified as the element by which the other elements of design can be experienced. The ability of a user to enjoy a design element, such as texture, is directly influenced by light. In fact, the quantity and the quality of light can enhance a wall's desirable textures purposefully employed by the designer in the case of a rough stone wall, or light can hide undesirable textures (to a degree), such as that resulting from a poorly constructed gypsum board wall. Lighting, both natural and electric, has a tremendous impact on how a user experiences a space psychologically, as discussed in Chapter 4, the spatial well-being chapter. In relation to the design process, lighting plays an integral role early in the life of a project as a designer conceptualizes the impact of lighting within a space during schematic design and then creates a design solution that achieves the goals of the concept during design development and construction documentation. In order to create a successful design, a designer must understand the qualities of light in the built environment.

Light Quality

In order for a designer to skillfully wield light, it helps to understand some of the basic science behind lighting technology and the quality of light. In the design context, light is implied to mean the visible spectrum of light, which can be characterized by wavelength. **Light wavelength** is measured in nanometers (nm) ranging from 400 nanometers (violet) to 700 nanometers (red). Notice that to the left of violet (shorter, under 400 nanometers) the spectrum is called ultraviolet, and to the right of red (longer, over 700 nanometers) the spectrum is called infrared, and what lies between, the visible spectrum of light, is very small (Fig. 11.1). It is within this short visible light spectrum that the discussion of light occurs.

Daylight evenly covers the visible spectrum and is the standard by which all artificial light is measured in terms of color accuracy. Some types of light sources, such as incandescent, come relatively close to matching the color properties of daylight. The measurement used to compare artificial light sources to daylight is called the **color rendering index** (CRI), which functions on a 100-point scale, with 100 perfectly matching daylight (Fig. 11.2). For accurate color rendition, a rating of 80 or higher is necessary. Also, recall that the experience of color relies heavily on light as described in Chapter 5, the color theory chapter, particularly that materials and objects possess color in relation to the wavelength of light that they reflect back to the eye.

Light temperature, measured in kelvin (K), and sometimes referred to as color correlated temperature (CCT), is another way to measure light quality. Cooler light colors produce higher temperatures near 8,500 K, whereas warmer light colors produce lower temperatures, between 2,000 K (candle) and 600 K (sunny day). A rating between 3,000 K and 6,000 K tends to produce accurate color rendition.

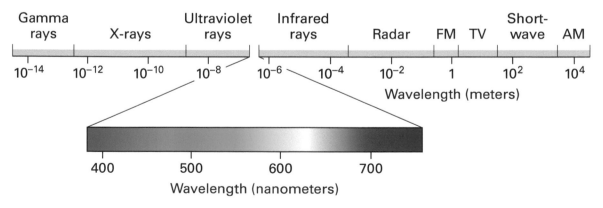

Figure 11.1 The visible portion of the light spectrum is very small compared to the entirety of the light spectrum.

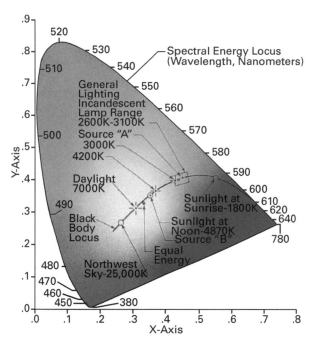

Figure 11.2 This CRI diagram shows the relative location of white light in relation to red, yellow, and blue cast lighting, and an overlay of kelvin temperatures common to electric lighting.

Light Quantity

The quantity of light can be described using multiple terms, all of which contribute in their own way to a broad lighting experience within a space (Fig. 11.3). The first term, **lumen**, describes the amount of light produced by one light source, or lamp (often referred to as a bulb). When purchasing replacement lamps for a light fixture the light output is typically shown on the packaging in lumens.

Closely related to lumens is the lighting measurement of efficiency, called efficacy. **Efficacy** measures the amount of light output in lumens divided by the amount of electricity in watts required to produce that amount of light. Different types of artificial light have varying efficacy ratings due to their ability to efficiently create light. A **foot-candle** is the measurement that describes the amount of light falling on a surface, such as a desk or floor. Specifically, 1 foot-candle is equal to the amount of light shining from a candle to 1 square foot of surface area 1 foot from the light source. The foot-candle measurement is important when designing for certain tasks that require a particular level of light in order to be performed successfully. For example, an operating room requires a much higher level of light on the operating table as opposed to a desk surface in the typical office space. A **footlambert** is the amount of light reflected from a surface. In reality, this is the measurement of light that an individual experiences as it takes into account the qualities of the surface reflecting the light. This measurement is important when the designer is seeking to increase ambient light in a space, or soften glare, through the use of direct or indirect lighting. In general, smooth surfaces that are light in color will reflect more light and, therefore, will have a higher footlambert measurement. A **candela** is the measurement of the intensity of light in a given direction. Many light fixtures are adjustable, or able to be aimed, resulting in a light output that can be carefully directed at a source, such as toward merchandise in a retail environment, or art in a gallery. The intensity of this light needs to be strong enough that it contrasts the lighting levels around the object in order to produce the desired effect.

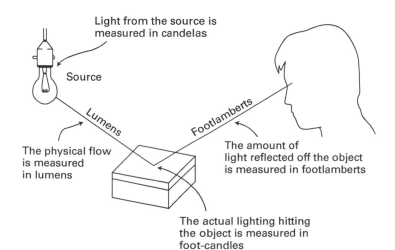

Figure 11.3 This diagram provides a graphic explanation of the common lighting terms used to describe lighting quantity.

Natural Light

Light is generally categorized as either natural or artificial. Natural light has three types:

- **Natural combustion light**: originating from the sun in the form of daylight (Fig. 11.4).
- **Natural atmospheric light**: another type of daylight, created as the atmosphere refracts sunlight through moisture droplets and other particles in the atmosphere.
- **Natural reflected light**: as the moon reflects the sun's light.

Notice the two types of daylight—sunlight and atmospheric light—are not the same. In fact, direct sunlight can be undesirable in a building interior, because it produces glare and will add heat in warm months of the year, further burdening a building's air conditioning systems. Direct sunlight can be anticipated and the negative effects minimized through proper design of overhangs or sunshades on the building exterior, and through window treatments on the interior, as discussed in Chapter 10. Atmospheric light, on the other hand, produces a very even white light, which can add many benefits to an interior during the daytime. Among these benefits are very high visual acuity and decreased energy usage within a space that embraces atmospheric daylight while keeping out direct sunlight. Atmospheric natural light produces the color of light by which all electric light is judged, which is discussed in a later section.

It is important for the designer to also know that daylight can be warm or cool in terms of rendering color based on the location of the building (northern or southern hemisphere) and the position of the sun in the sky (morning or afternoon). In the morning, warm daylight results in spaces with windows on the east side of a building and cool light in spaces with windows facing west. In the afternoon, warm daylight results in spaces with windows on the west side of a building and cool light in spaces with windows facing east. In the northern hemisphere, warm daylight results in spaces with windows on the south side of a building, and cool daylight in spaces with windows facing north. In the southern hemisphere, warm daylight results in spaces with windows on the north side of a building, and cool light results in spaces with windows facing south.

Figure 11.4 This bright day-lit residential interior is benefiting from natural combustion light.

Artificial Light

Artificial light, meaning that it is made by human skill, can be divided into two broad categories—combustion and electric. **Artificial combustion light** originates from fire which can be provided via fireplaces, candles, and oil or gas lamps. Fireplaces require significant infrastructure support depending on whether they are wood-burning, electric, or fueled by natural gas, and could be very heavy if they are masonry. Candles and certain types of oil and gas lamps are portable sources of light. Some gas lanterns are architectural and some are fixed in place; they were the standard for indoor and outdoor illumination up until the invention of the light bulb. Artificial combustion light reasonably mimics the color of light from the sun depending upon the chemistry of the fire.

Electric light first began with the invention of the incandescent lamp in 1879. Today, electric lighting technology is more sophisticated and includes discharge and solid state lighting in addition to incandescent lamps (Fig. 11.5). **Incandescent lamps** produce light by passing an electric current through a tungsten filament sealed in a glass bulb. **Discharge lamps** produce light by passing an electric current through a gas or vapor contained within a glass enclosure. **Solid state lighting** (SSL) relies on very small electrically charged semiconductors to produce light and includes both standard light-emitting diode (LED) technology and organic light-emitting diode (OLED) technology. The types of lamp technologies are discussed in more detail later in this chapter.

Figure 11.5 Evolution of the light bulb: early incandescent, contemporary standard incandescent, compact fluorescent lamp (CFL), and LED.

Interior Lighting Strategies

Lighting strategies can be analyzed based on aesthetic and functional goals of a design. Aesthetically, lighting is important both for the effect that the light produces as well as the fixture itself. The lighting effect can be crafted to produce a certain mood within a space whether that be calm intimacy, energetic productivity, or lively entertainment and sociability. Lighting should enhance the space planning, materials, and furnishings within a space. Lighting can reinforce the space planning by highlighting areas of circulation with a different type of functional lighting than other areas of the plan. Wall materials can be accented with grazing light to emphasize texture while furnishings can be highlighted with a properly placed or aimed directional light fixture. Fixtures are available in a variety of styles and materials and can communicate a very traditional or sleek high-tech aesthetic. All of these opportunities are rooted in the designer's unifying concept for the design as well as his skill in utilizing the elements and principles of design.

Functional lighting strategies rely on the skillful layering of ambient, task, and accent lighting to create a unified lighting design that provides just the right amount of light in the correct place (Fig. 11.6). **Ambient light** is the general illumination in a space that seeks to provide a consistent level of illumination and limit strong contrasts between one zone of light and another. Examples include

Figure 11.6 This space illustrates ambient, task, and accent lighting with a variety of luminaire types, including ceiling-recessed direct down lighting, ceiling-recessed adjustable down lighting, ceiling pendant down lighting, ceiling-concealed slot lighting, and wall-concealed slot lighting.

recessed or pendant light fixtures in the overhead zone. **Task light** is the illumination that focuses on a specified task, such as reading, drawing, cooking, or dental cleaning. Task light fixtures are often adjustable to provide the user with the ability to fine tune the focus of the light, turn it on or off at will, and limit glare. Examples include under-cabinet lighting, desk lamps, and adjustable pendant fixtures in the overhead zone. **Accent light** utilizes a focused beam spread to highlight a specific object or a wash of light to highlight a surface. Fixtures used to create accent light can be located in the overhead zone, or can be associated with a wall, and spatial examples include retail display lighting or lighting used to focus on art work in a museum gallery. As designers utilize ambient, task, and accent light within their spaces, it is important to remember the physical capabilities of the user, as the elderly and disabled will need higher levels of light to see color and textures accurately. A successful lighting design utilizes all three of these functional lighting strategies in combination with one another to varying degrees based on the aesthetic and functional needs of the space.

Luminaire Types

A **luminaire**, or light fixture, is the container for the source of the light, or the **lamp**, often called a bulb, and can be very important, as it will exert influence on the aesthetic and functional lighting qualities of a space. Luminaires can be visible or hidden and will have a strong impact on the quality and quantity of light that contributes to the ambient, task, or accent lighting within a space. Light fixtures can be attached to ceilings or walls and, in rare cases, can be attached to floors, or they can rest on furniture or floors. Light fixtures can occupy the overhead zone, or be located lower in the user-occupied zone of a space. This range of location attributes in combination with the direction the luminaire aims the light tends to drive how fixtures are described. **Direct lighting** involves luminaires where the lamp is visible and often shines the light down, which is why fixtures of this type are also referred to as **down lighting**. **Indirect lighting** shields the lamp by directing the light upward, sometimes called **up lighting**, with a luminaire that hangs from the ceiling, is mounted to a wall below the ceiling, or through the use of a cove light that conceals the luminaire entirely. Light originating from direct lighting

fixtures tends to be more intense whereas that from indirect lighting is typically soft. Fixtures are also described in terms of their installation. **Architectural luminaires** are built-in to the interior architectural surfaces (ceilings, walls, floors) of the interior space whereas **nonarchitectural luminaires** are portable and often are plugged in to an electrical socket or operate on battery power.

Architectural Luminaires

Architectural luminaires are integral with the ceiling, wall, and floor surfaces and, therefore, rely on detailed coordination between engineering consultants, particularly the electrical engineer, and the interior designer to be successful in a constructed space. The drawings, schedules, and specifications should clearly describe the placement, type, manufacturer, and quantity of luminaires for the proposed design.

Ceiling Luminaires

Most architectural lighting is provided via the ceiling and can be recessed, surface-mounted, concealed, or suspended. **Recessed luminaires** serve to create a "clean" appearance to the ceiling and can be small round fixtures, often referred to as cans, large square or rectangle fixtures called troffers, or linear strips available in a variety of lengths (Fig. 11.7). **Surface-mounted luminaires** are available in the same shapes as recessed, that is, round or cylindrical, square or rectangular, and linear, but the visual result tends to be a bit cluttered. Surface-mounted fixtures are very useful in a retrofit scenario where space to run electrical wiring is unavailable or very difficult to access. **Concealed luminaires** in ceilings can often take the form of slot lighting where the fixture, often a linear fluorescent or LED, is not visible from below, but the wash of the light is visible. The result is often a very pleasing and soft illumination that offers both ambient light to the space and accent lighting at the ceiling plane. **Suspended luminaires**, also called pendant luminaires, can be virtually any standard shape (round, square/rectangular, or linear) or they can be very sculptural (Fig. 11.8). Some suspended fixtures have the ability to provide a combination of direct and indirect light, as the fixtures can provide both up lighting and down lighting, which tends to result in a very even degree of ambient lighting. Suspended fixtures are also very useful in tall spaces when the light needs to

Figure 11.7 A variety of ceiling-based luminaires add layers of light to this space.

Figure 11.8 The linear pendant fixtures in this space accentuates the vertical proportion of the volume.

be directed down to a surface, such as a dining table in a voluminous restaurant. In retail spaces, pendant ceiling fixtures are often adjustable so the light can be aimed at a particular display of merchandise. Some fixtures, such as **track lighting**, can be recessed, surface mounted, or suspended. Track lighting is a very versatile type of luminaire, as the individual fixtures can be moved along a track and aimed at a particular object or surface to place the light exactly where it is needed. This can be especially useful in art galleries where the exhibitions are regularly changed.

Wall Luminaires

Architectural lighting provided via the wall can certainly add to the ambient light of a space, but wall lighting tends to be more task or accent oriented. Similar to ceilings, architectural wall lighting can be recessed, surface mounted, concealed, or significantly project off the wall surface (akin to suspended ceiling fixtures). Recessed wall light fixtures can be installed low on a wall to wash light across a floor or stair tread, or installed higher up to provide a small amount of ambient light or accent lighting to act as a wayfinding aid. A surface-mounted wall fixture, often referred to as a **sconce**, is typically very visible in a space and is selected as much for the fixture's appearance as for the quality of light that it produces (Fig. 11.9). Sconces tend to be most useful in an accent lighting strategy, as they generally direct some portion of light back toward the wall and the remaining light out into the space. Concealed wall lighting can take on the form of a light cove that is most often attached high up on a wall approaching the ceiling plane and directs light up the wall and toward the ceiling. Another type of concealed wall light fixture can be a slot light that runs near the bottom of the wall and directs a wash of light toward the floor. In both cases, the fixture is typically a linear fluorescent, or LED, and is not visible, but the lighting effect is. Projecting wall fixtures can be monopoint or linear fixtures that cantilever off the wall and shine their light downward back toward the wall or floor, offering a degree of ambient, task, or accent light. In the case of task lighting and accent lighting, it is critical for the designer to coordinate the placement of the fixture with the task surface or piece of furniture or artwork that the fixture seeks to highlight. In the case of both surface-mounted and projecting wall light fixtures, the designer must take into account their mounting height and the dimension of their projection. If the fixture projects more than 4 inches out from the wall, the fixture must not be below 6 feet 8 inches above the finished floor to meet accessibility requirements.

Floor Luminaires

Architectural floor luminaires have some very specific requirements that differ from ceiling and wall architectural lighting. The primary difference has to do with durability, safety, and cleanability, as the floor surface receives a

Figure 11.9 The surface-mounted wall luminaires (sconces) provide up and down lighting acting as ambient and accent lighting in this space.

much greater degree of wear and tear compared to ceilings and walls. Floor light fixtures function best if they are recessed and covered with a protective lens or glass plate. The challenge can come with replacing the lamps, so the protective plate or lens must be removable, or the fixture will need to be accessible from underneath.

Nonarchitectural Luminaires

Nonarchitectural luminaires can be divided into two groups: portable luminaires and systems furniture fixtures. **Portable luminaires** include table and floor fixtures and will typically be located by the designer on a furniture plan as they are most often found at, or slightly above, the floor plane (Fig. 11.10). The designer selects and specifies portable fixtures with the same level of attention as the architectural luminaires by considering the aesthetic qualities of the fixture in relation to style and quality of light and the functional aspects in relation to quantity of light and lighting strategy (ambient, task, or accent lighting). These luminaires can up light a space adding to the ambient lighting levels, or focus lighting downward in the case of an adjustable floor or table lamp used for reading tasks. The practical consideration for any portable luminaire is access to electricity and the ability to conceal the power cord for aesthetic and safety purposes.

Systems furniture lighting is integrated into the partitions and storage components of workstations commonly found in open office environments. These fixtures add a certain degree of ambient light in the case of torchier-type fixtures that up light the space in and around a

Figure 11.10 Nonarchitectural floor and table luminaires provide task lighting precisely where it is needed.

cluster of workstations. The primary focus, however, is on task lighting at the work surface often delivered through fixtures with an articulating arm or through under-storage strip lighting that can be turned on and off as the user needs.

Lamp Types

Lamp types vary dramatically and include incandescent, discharge, and solid-state lighting categories. Each of the lamp types within these categories possesses light qualities with particular advantages and disadvantages that the designer needs to be aware of. Some lamps produce light with a very high CRI rating but are inefficient, produce a large amount of heat, or can be difficult to maintain, whereas other lamps may be very efficient but also very expensive in terms initial cost. The designer needs to know these attributes so that an informed decision can be made in the best interest of the client.

Incandescent Lamps

Incandescent lamps include the first light bulb invented in 1879 by Thomas Edison. Incandescent lamps function by passing an electric current through a metal filament and heating it to produce a light that ranges between 2,500 K and 3,000 K. The warm light produced by these lamps tends to accentuate warm hues and lessen the impact of cool ones. These lamps are inexpensive initially, but they also have lower efficacy, leading to higher operating costs. Incandescent lamps produce heat that can increase ambient air temperatures and can produce glare if they are not shielded in a shade or with a lens, but they are also easily dimmed allowing the user to carefully control the light output, reduce electricity usage and heat output, and increase the useful life of the lamp in some cases. Typical incandescent lamps are often limited to 1,000 hours of active use, or 125 days at 8 hours of use per day. In the case of fixtures that are difficult to access, such as in very high ceilings, that can translate into frequent trips up a ladder.

Incandescent lamps vary in shape and size, relying on a letter and number designation to differentiate the variety of shapes and sizes. An A19, for example, is a standard shape bulb that is 2 3/8 inches in diameter, where the number indicates the size in eighths of an inch. Some incandescent lamps include integral reflectors within the glass housing (R, PAR, ER/BR lamp shapes) that serve to focus the light output in a focused direction. Other incandescent lamps are low voltage, such as the MR, which integrates a reflector as well, requiring a remote transformer that converts the incoming electrical current from 120v down to 12v or 24v (Fig. 11.11). Low-voltage lamps are relatively small and useful in track lighting. Incandescent lamps, as well as other types, also vary in the way they connect to the fixture; some are screwed in, utilize a bi-pin connection, or a tab connection.

Tungsten-halogen lamps, sometimes simply called halogen, utilizes quartz in place of the metal filament to produce light (Fig. 11.12). These lamps produce a warmer light at 3,000 K, are very bright, and operate at very high temperatures and, therefore, require a shield or lens to limit glare and provide fire protection. The higher initial cost is often justified by the very high quality of light they produce and the longer life (2,250 to 3,500 hours) of the lamp compared to other incandescent lamps. A xenon lamp produces light similar in quality to halogen, but in a low-voltage application.

Discharge Lamps

Fluorescent lamps have been in use since the mid-20th century and utilize a sealed mercury vapor- and argon-filled glass tube with internal phosphorous coating. An electrical current is passed through the tube, which activates the gas and energizes the coating creating light. Fluorescent lamps are available in a variety of shapes and sizes and utilize a letter abbreviation and number to differentiate these qualities. The most common is the fluorescent tube with the T12 (1½-inch diameter), T8 (1 inch), and T5 (5/8 inch), which are manufactured in multiple lengths ranging from 2 feet to 8 feet (Fig. 11.13). A relatively new development in tube fluorescents is the high output version, abbreviated HO, but these types of lamps are often limited to the T5. Other shapes include a compact version, abbreviated CFL, often used in recessed down light applications.

As many types of incandescent lamps are being phased out of production due to government legislation, fluorescent lamps have become more widespread. The main reason for their increased use is due to their higher efficacy compared to incandescent lamps. Fluorescent lamps also produce less heat, last much longer (10,000 to 45,000 hours), and fit into the same fixtures, in the case of **compact fluorescent lamps** (CFL) with a screw-in connection, as many

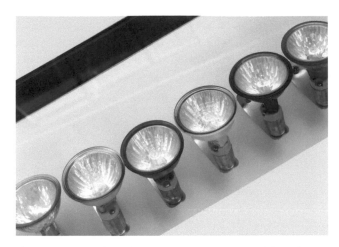

Figure 11.11 MR16 incandescent lamps provide warm light and are often used in track light fixtures.

Figure 11.12 Halogen lamps produce warm light as shown in this multistory lobby.

incandescent lamps. With these benefits, fluorescent lamps do have some drawbacks. They have a higher initial cost, require a ballast to boost voltage for powering on and regulating current during operation which can produce a humming sound in low-quality fixtures, and are more difficult to dim. Older fluorescent lamps had a low CRI, which has been improved in recent years. The designer should keep this in mind when specifying fluorescent fixtures and lamps. The designer should also keep in mind that warm and cool versions of the same lamp type are available. In the event that the wrong temperature (measured in kelvin) lamp is purchased and installed by the client, the lighting effect will be greatly compromised.

High-intensity discharge (HID) lamps seek to blend the benefits of incandescent and fluorescent lamps in terms of color rendition and efficacy, but to varying degrees based on the type of HID lamp. Mercury lamps

Figure 11.13 Fluorescent pendant lighting is commonly used in open office settings.

(blue light, tends to cancel out warm colors), low-pressure sodium (warm, tends to cancel out cool colors), and metal halide (white light with accurate color rendition) are the three types, with low-pressure sodium exhibiting the highest efficacy and metal halide the best color rendition. These lamps are often used in nonresidential applications where energy codes demand very high efficacy, are very long lasting (over 16,000 hours), require a ballast, produce some noise, have a long startup time as they reach their full light output, and are often installed in high ceilings due to their intense light output.

Cold cathode lamps resemble fluorescent in that they are manufactured in tubes filled with gases to produce light and rely on ballasts to regulate electrical input (Fig. 11.14). Cold cathodes, however, are typically reserved for specialty applications where a certain color of light is desired, and they can be used in curvilinear configurations such as retail signage. Many colors are possible with cold cathode lamps, but it is the red variety that often steals the show. **Neon** lamps, which uses

neon gas to create the red color, is what people typically call this larger category of lighting that has many colors. Another type utilizes argon gas to create blue light. The low quantity of light produced from cold cathode limits the lamp to accent uses.

Solid-State Lighting

Solid-state lighting (SSL) utilizes light emitting diodes rather than a filament or gas to produce light. The most common type of SSL is the **LED lamp**, which uses a semiconductor light-emitting diode to produce light. LED lamps possess a very long life (as much as 50,000 hours), have a very high efficacy, and produce a low to moderate amount of heat from the front of the lamp. Sizes and shapes of LED lamps mimic those of incandescent (A19, PAR30, etc.) and also have similar screw-in, bi-pin, or tab connections making adoption of LED lamps into existing fixtures relatively simple. LED lamps are also available

Figure 11.14 The cold cathode tube lighting in this corridor emphasizes the one-point perspective.

Energy Use

in strips and ropes, and, with their low profile dimension, can be tucked into tight areas such as slots in the ceiling or coves on the wall (Fig. 11.15). LED technology also affords the added aesthetic benefit of color changes that can be programmed at gradual intervals.

LED technology has improved dramatically, resulting in lower initial cost, but still much higher than incandescent or fluorescent, and improved CRI, but it is still characteristically cool, or sterile, by some accounts. As the technology continues to improve, the use of LED will only grow, and it appears likely to supplant fluorescent and incandescent if it hasn't already. Two variations of LED are also available, organic light-emitting diode (OLED) lamps, and polymer light-emitting diode lamps (PLED). Both of these lamp types are recent developments to the SSL technology family and show promise in producing a new type of ultra-thin lighting application utilizing films in ribbonlike lighting applications.

As mentioned, one important quality of any lamp is its' efficacy, or efficiency, which is determined by dividing the quantity of light in lumens by the power required to create those lumens in watts. A standard incandescent lamp has an efficacy of 16 lumens per watt (lm/W), a compact fluorescent 60 lumens per watt, and a white LED 150 lumens per watt. Each type of lamp varies in its efficacy depending upon how much of the power coming into the lamp is wasted as heat output rather than being used as light output. In the case of incandescent lamps, as much as 95 percent of the power becomes heat rather than light. This additional heat generation places an added burden on air conditioning systems in warm months and, therefore, compounds the energy impact of the lamp's low efficacy. As a result, many countries, including Australia, have banned the use of incandescent lamps, and many

Figure 11.15 The LED slot lighting in this living space offers the potential for a color changing effect that can be programmed to coordinate with the time of day.

others, including the US, European Union, and Canada, are in the process of phasing them out.

National governing bodies, such as the Environmental Protection Agency (EPA) in the US, play a strong role in setting requirements for energy consumption as it relates to lighting. In the US, the Energy Independence and Security Act of 2007 (EISA 2007) required that lamps cut energy consumption by 25 percent. While the act did not target a specific lamp type by name, it did effectively eliminate the use of standard incandescent lamps due to the limitations of the technology.

Safety and Health Implications

The lighting strategies employed by the designer can positively, or negatively, impact the health and safety of building occupants. Building codes, such as the

National Electric Code (NEC) in the US, seek to protect the basic safety of building occupants in the event of an emergency, such as a fire or power outage. In public buildings, a certain percentage of light fixtures must be wired to a centralized independent power generator or battery system, or specialty fixtures must be provided with their own independent power supply that will turn on in the event of a power failure. Internally illuminated egress signage must be provided at exit doors and along paths of egress leading to exit doors to aid occupants in evacuating a building in the event that the interior begins to fill with smoke and vision is obstructed.

Lamps and luminaires themselves can also become a hazard to safety if they are poorly designed or manufactured. Many nations require that light fixtures be tested and approved by a testing agency, such as the Underwriters' Laboratory (UL) in the US, in order to be installed. The designer must be aware and abide

Utilizing Lighting to Create a Mood or Evoke an Emotional Response

Project:	The Keeper
Location:	Shops at Legacy; Plano, Texas
Client:	Front Burner Restaurants
Architect/Designer:	Plan B Group / Designer: Austin Gauley
Occupants/Users:	Restaurant
Site Characteristics:	Outdoor mall, first-floor tenant space
Year Complete:	2017
Cost Estimate:	$1.5 M
Facility Size:	Tenant space: 7,484 square feet; one level

The Keeper, a seafood restaurant located in the land-locked area of Dallas-Fort Worth, Texas, demonstrates how lighting can play a role in furthering a brand by evoking an emotional response from customers and passersby. The design of the space as a whole is not your stereotypical seafood restaurant. Instead of over compensating with contrived weathered wood, dock posts, and common motifs like rope and life preservers, Plan B Group created a more conceptual atmosphere by only nodding to the idea of seafood or nautical elements.

The dominant lighting feature in the dining space was derived from a major focus of the brand story. The client realized that to create a seafood restaurant in a city without a coast would be a challenge if they wanted the freshest product. They made it their priority to source from local fishermen located in Hawaii, Alaska, and New England and fly it in as quickly as possible ensuring the freshest seafood in the metro area. Taking inspiration from this important distinction in the brand, the design team at Plan B Group visualized the idea in a unique lighting feature for the entire restaurant. The design team abstracted the idea of many shipping routes transporting the freshest seafood through an arrangement of exposed brass conduit that traces around the ceiling and walls of the entire restaurant and connects to each light fixture. The glass globe pendants over every table were integrated into the brass conduit, while other fixtures, such as the brass caged flush-mount fixtures had the conduit appear to run through it. The only time the conduit terminates is at a light

The custom fixtures seamlessly integrate with the overall interior design.

The luminaires' simple and repeated form offers a pleasing background visual rhythm that enhances the dining experience.

Patrons enjoy the custom lighting and signage as a creative means to preserve a memory.

fixture over each dining table in the main dining room, referencing the freshness of each seafood dish that the patrons are enjoying. Selectively utilizing a brass finish throughout the space as an understated reference for a nautical atmosphere, the brass conduit stitches itself into the overall design of the interior.

Not only does the lighting design make for beautiful curvilinear lines running through the space and illuminating the dining experience in a warm glow above each table, it is also an extension of the brand itself. This design feature is conceptual in nature but can also be a great conversation point for service members to talk about and add value to the brand. Patrons can comment about the unique lighting and their waitstaff can inform them of the quick routes spanning the country utilized to deliver their fresh seafood. Also, the waitstaff can educate their tables about the priority of fresh seafood and then can point out the design feature that it aligns with, furthering the discussion and enriching the dining experience.

An additional brand-reinforcing lighting element creates an emotional response for visitors and is part of an outdoor mural and light installation. A mural on the exterior of the restaurant where hundreds of people walk by daily in the outdoor mall consists of nautical elements and the call to action to choose your loved one at a light switch. The light switch runs to a cold cathode light where someone can flip between "She's" or "He's a Keeper." The spot was designed to be an "instagrammable moment" that creates an opportunity for guests and anyone walking by to take a photo and share an experience. The mural has been photographed thousands of times and has been another extension of the brand shared across social media.

Plan B Group is a boutique architecture and design firm in Dallas, Texas, specializing in restaurant design. For more information on the Keeper visit www. thekeeperplano.com, and for more information on Plan B Group, please visit www.planbgroup.net.

by the national laws in authority where the space will be constructed and be sure to specify products that are approved for use in that country.

Occupants' physical, psychological, and economic health can also be impacted by interior lighting. Physical health can be impacted by poor lighting levels, glare, or poorly functioning lamps or luminaires, often manifesting in headaches. Psychologically, occupants can experience elevated levels of stress, anxiety, or tiredness in the presence of low-quality lighting. Finally, the economics of a lighting design can negatively impact the building owner if it is too expensive or difficult to maintain, possibly due to obsolete technology, inaccessible fixtures, or lamps that are very expensive to replace, burnout too quickly, or use too much energy to operate. The design can have a very positive impact on each of these issues at they contribute to the health of the occupants and owners of the built environment.

Lighting Controls

The designer is responsible for collaborating with the electrical engineer to select the type and location of lighting controls that meets the functional, aesthetic, and economic needs of the client. Lighting controls can be manual or digital in their operation and interface. The most common types of controls are the standard toggle switches used for turning light fixtures on and off (Fig. 11.16). Dimmers are used with certain types of lamps and luminaires in order to gradually increase or decrease

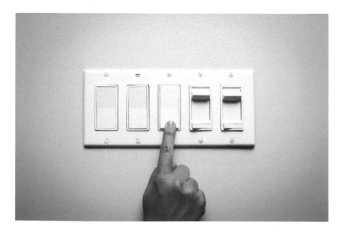

Figure 11.16 This bank of toggle switches and dimmers provides a centralized location to control a variety of lighting levels depending on the function and mood desired within the space.

lighting levels with more precision. Toggle switches can control one or multiple luminaires and more than one toggle switch can control one or multiple luminaires such as when a toggle switch is installed at the top and at the bottom of a stairway to control the lighting over the stair. In this case, the control is referred to as a three-way switch due to its wiring configuration. Switches and dimmers for ambient light fixtures are often placed next to the latch side of doorways at 44 inches AFF (above finished floor) so that they are easy to access upon entry into a space. For task lighting, the toggle switch should be within arm's reach of the task luminaire for convenience. It is common to place multiple toggle switches and dimmers in a row, or bank, to make it quick and simple to turn on multiple zones of luminaires at once. Switch banks are also used when a space has multiple levels of light achieved by varying fixture types, such as a conference room where varying types of presentations are given, each requiring a different lighting scenario. In this scenario, one toggle switch may control the ambient down lighting, another the concealed slot lighting over the conference table, another the wall wash accent lighting, and still another the pinhole recessed task lighting for note taking during dark presentations.

Digital controls have brought the ability of the user to control lighting levels to new heights, especially in spaces with highly complicated lighting designs. In the case of the conference room scenario just described, the bank of toggle switches and dimmers would be replaced with a digital panel or screen with lighting scenario presets that can be executed via a touch screen interface. Digital controls have also enabled the user to control light fixtures from a remote location with the aid of a lighting control app through a computer, tablet, or smartphone. The increase in digital controls is also enabling measurement of energy use and the integration of occupancy sensors that will automatically turn fixtures off when no occupancy is detected in a space.

Reflected Ceiling Plan and Lighting Schedule

The designer uses the **reflected ceiling plan** (RCP) to communicate ceiling finishes, ceiling heights, and the placement of luminaires and lighting controls. Other

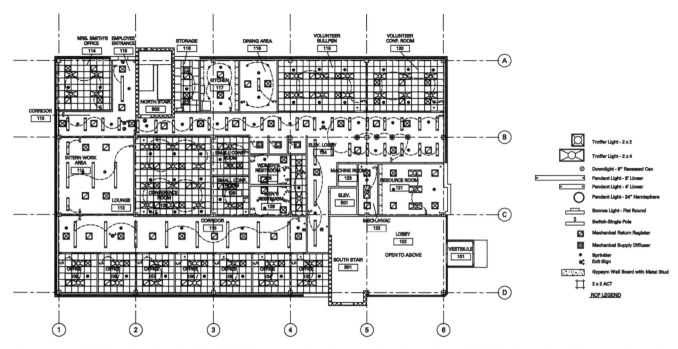

Figure 11.17 The designer's reflected ceiling plan in the construction documentation phase shows the lighting layout in relation to a variety of other components that the ceiling plane carries, including HVAC and fire suppression systems, which are discussed more fully in Chapter 12. The accompanying legend articulates the meaning of each symbol shown on the RCP.

elements, including HVAC (heating, ventilation, and air conditioning) supplies and returns, fire suppression sprinklers, fire strobes and horns, and smoke detectors are also commonly shown on the RCP (Fig. 11.17). The **lighting schedule** consists of graphic symbols that represent the various types of luminaires and controls utilized in the proposed design along with a brief written description of each. Additional items, such as the HVAC and fire suppression items just listed, should also be represented on the schedule. The lighting symbols utilized on an RCP are best understood if they abide by commonly accepted convention in practice. The example RCP and symbol list in Figure 11.17 demonstrate some of these conventions for recessed cans, pendant fixtures, wall washers, and concealed slot lighting.

Summary

The designer has tremendous influence on users of the built environment through lighting. In relation to all other aspects of the design, lighting is the portion that links everything together, as color, visual texture, safety and security, and all other aesthetic and functional properties would be irrelevant without the skillful mastery of lighting. During the design process, designers often seek to express the effect of light through sketches prior to selecting a luminaire or lamp type, but it is this depth and breadth of knowledge that enables the desired outcome to be realized.

Key Terms

Accent light

Ambient light

Architectural luminaires

Artificial combustion light

Artificial light

Candela

Cold cathode

Color rendering index

Compact fluorescent lamps

Concealed luminaires

Direct lighting

Discharge lamps

Down lighting

Efficacy

Electric light

Fluorescent lamps

Foot-candle

Footlambert

High-intensity discharge

Incandescent lamps

Incandescent lamps

Indirect lighting

Lamp

LED lamp

Light temperature

Light wavelength

Lighting schedule

Lumen

Luminaire

Natural atmospheric light

Natural combustion light

Natural reflected light

Neon

Nonarchitectural luminaires

Portable luminaires

Recessed luminaires

Reflected ceiling plan

Sconce

Solid-state lighting

Surface-mounted luminaires

Suspended luminaires

Systems furniture lighting

Task light

Track lighting

Tungsten-halogen lamps

Up lighting

Resources

Ballast, D. K., FAIA, C., & No, N. C. (2013). *Interior Design Reference Manual: Everything You Need to Know to Pass the NCIDQ Exam.* www.ppi2pass.com.

Illuminating Engineering Society. (n.d.). IES|The Lighting Authority. Retrieved December 17, 2017, from https://www.ies.org/.

Winchip, S. M. (2017). *Fundamentals of Lighting.* New York: Bloomsbury.

Review Questions

1. Describe the two methods of determining light quality.
2. Using proper lighting terminology describes how lighting efficiency is measured.
3. Describe how the three different types of natural light impact the built environment.
4. Describe the three categories of lighting technology.
5. Describe the three categories of interior lighting strategies.
6. Describe the two broad types of luminaires. What is another way to describe "down lighting" and "up lighting"?
7. List the different types of ceiling, wall, and floor luminaires ("recessed," etc.).
8. What are the advantages and disadvantages of incandescent, fluorescent, and LED lamps? What types of lamps can be paired with a standard 5-inch recessed direct luminaire, a linear pendant direct/indirect luminaire, a track light system, or a surface-mounted wall luminaire?
9. What are the three types of discharge lamps and what types of scenarios are they best suited for?
10. What can be the effects of legislation that increases efficiency requirements on lighting technology?
11. What negative physical and psychological effects can result from poor lighting design?
12. Describe the importance of properly locating lighting controls in a space. When should a three-way switch be used? What are some advantages of digital lighting controls?

Exercises

Reflected Ceiling Plan

1. Sketch a reflected ceiling plan of your classroom, or other space, on a sheet of graph or sketch paper approximately 81/2 x 11 inches in size. The selected space should include lighting and switching.
2. Draw the walls, door heads, window heads if any exist, ceiling materials, light fixtures, and lighting controls. Create a symbol legend, or key, to accompany the drawing that describes each of the symbols used to depict the required ceiling components.

Sustainability and Lighting Efficacy

1. Visit a home improvement retail center and select three different types of lamps. Photograph their packaging and labels that describe lumens and wattage. Calculate the efficacy of each lamp.
2. Compile your findings, including photos and calculations, into a digital or print presentation.

Master Bedroom and Bath Suite Continued

1. Reference the client profile, location, and view from the Chapter 9 exercise.
2. Select ambient, task, and accent lighting for the bedroom and bath suite.
3. Images of the selections should be presented on a physical or digital "board." Include headings to categorize the spaces (Bedroom, Bathroom) and label each individual lighting selection by type (e.g., "CFL recessed can luminaire," "LED linear cove luminaire," "LED pendant luminaire," "halogen wall-mounted adjustable luminaire," etc.).

12

Built Environment Support Systems

Learning Objectives

As a result of reading this chapter, students will possess an awareness of

1. The role of mechanical systems in the built environment, including

    a. The contributing factors of the human comfort zone.

    b. The importance of indoor air quality.

    c. The role of HVAC systems and their types.

    d. The importance of proper ventilation.

2. The role of electrical systems in the built environment, including

    a. Power.

    b. Telecommunications and data.

    c. Security systems.

3. The role of plumbing systems in the built environment, including

    a. Plumbing supply systems.

    b. Plumbing piping.

    c. Waste system types.

4. The importance of fire monitoring, notification, and suppression systems.

5. The role of acoustical systems in the built environment.

As a result of taking part in the learning exercises at the end of this chapter, students will

1. Demonstrate the ability to identify the many components of HVAC, electrical, plumbing, and fire safety systems visible in the built environment.

2. Demonstrate the ability to draw these components in plan and reflected ceiling plan.

Introduction

Support systems of the built environment include electrical, plumbing, fire suppression, and HVAC (Heating, Ventilation, and Air Conditioning). These systems function to support the daily and ongoing use of the modern-day interior and must be taken into account when conducting code studies, space planning, selecting and specifying furniture, fixtures, and equipment (FF&E), designing and detailing primary interior architectural features, coordinating with consultants, and working through the construction administration process. Mechanical (HVAC), electrical, and plumbing (**MEP** for short) engineering consultants can be brought into the process early, during design development, to offer their expertise and provide suggestions for improvement to allow the support systems to function more efficiently, resulting in overall design efficiency. As discussed in Chapter 6, the professional practice chapter, it is the responsibility of the firm principal and project manager to hire engineering consultants and establish a written contract with each of the consultants. As the project progresses, the project manager and designer will work together to integrate the engineering systems into the overall design.

Mechanical, electrical, plumbing, fire safety (monitoring, notification, and suppression), and acoustical systems are the focus of this chapter. Structural engineering is related in the sense that it, too, is a field of engineering, but it differs in that the interior designer does not typically have input into how structure is integrated into the built environment. Typically, structural engineers work closely with architects to design the structural support of the building that holds up the floors, exterior walls, and roofs. Most of the time, these elements are already determined when an interior designer begins work on a project. For this reason, a brief discussion on structural systems is provided in the chapter on contextual factors of the built environment (Chapter 7). In the event a designer determines that structural intervention is necessary on a project, the designer must hire a structural engineer as a consultant to address that portion of the work, and then integrate their expertise into the design.

Many designers tend to leave support systems to the latter portions of design thinking, the phases of prototyping and testing. For most projects this makes sense, as support systems are detail-oriented portions of the design and outside the primary expertise of the designer. On occasion, however, planning support systems will find its way into the earlier phases, such as empathy, problem definition, and ideation, as clients may express concern with the quality of their current support systems and charge the designer with integrating systems solutions into the new design. The designer may also develop concepts that expose the support systems, such as an exposed ceiling plenum where the HVAC ductwork is visible, in the ideation phase as a part of the aesthetic and functional goals of the design. The design scenario varies from project to project, requiring the designer to integrate systems knowledge into the process at the right time.

Mechanical Systems

HVAC systems address the human comfort zone, and health to a degree, through the heating, ventilation, and air conditioning of the built environment. The **human comfort zone** consists of four factors—temperature, relative humidity, air movement, and radiation of heat (Fig. 12.1). In addition to these four comfort zone factors, HVAC systems can improve **indoor air quality** (IAQ) by helping to control airborne contaminants, such as volatile organic compounds (VOCs), mineral and earth particulates (dust, ash, etc.), and biological contaminants (fungi, bacteria, etc.).

HVAC systems utilize **radiation** (heat transferred through air from warm to cool surface), **conduction** (heat transferred through a solid material), or **convection** (heat transferred through air movement), or some combination of these three, to maintain human comfort (Fig. 12.2). Radiant systems include any system that utilizes a panel or fin tube system to deliver heat to a space. Examples include electric baseboard, radiant panels, hydronic boiler, or steam boiler systems (Fig. 12.3). Each of these systems produces a very even quality of heat, often afford a room-by-room level of user control, and tend to be durable systems. Radiant panels and baseboard systems are generally inexpensive to install but can be expensive to operate depending upon the cost of electricity. Hydronic and steam boiler systems rely on costly boilers for operation and an involved piping system to circulate water and steam to the fin tube radiators through the building. The fin tubes themselves are hot to the touch, capable of causing burns, and can be temperamental but easy to maintain, leading

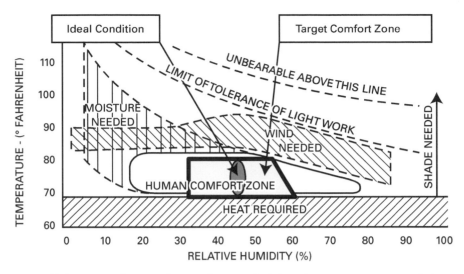

Figure 12.1 This human comfort zone diagram illustrates the balance between temperature, relative humidity, air movement, and heat radiation.

to useful lifespans of seventy-five years or more. Today, hydronic and steam boiler systems are not installed in new construction and baseboard or radiant panels are reserved only for challenging renovations where budgets are tight. The primary drawbacks of all the radiant systems include the inability to filter the air (IAQ), control humidity, provide air conditioning, or produce air movement without the aid of fans. One radiation-based system that is still prized is the fire place, and it is unique as the only HVAC system that also functions as a center for socialization.

Conductive HVAC systems suffer from the same drawbacks as radiation-based systems. The primary example of a conductive system is actually referred to as a radiant system, known as radiant floor heating. Radiant floor heating consists of a system of wiring or fluid-filled piping installed over the subfloor that warms the flooring finish above (Fig. 12.4). The heat from the floor radiates out, resulting in a slight increase in ambient air temperature, but the main benefit comes through physical contact between feet and floor. In cold months, the physical contact between a warm flooring surface and bare, or stockinged, feet can make a significant psychological difference helping the occupant feel warm. Designers should consider the inclusion of a radiant floor

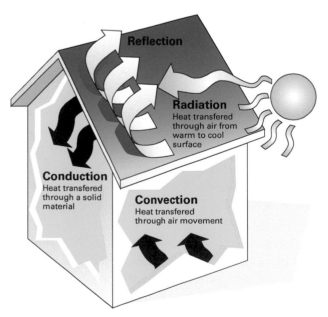

Figure 12.2 This diagram illustrates the how heat can be transferred either through radiation, conduction, or convection.

Figure 12.3 The steam radiant fin tube is one example of a radiant heating system.

Figure 12.4 An underfloor radiant heat system relies on conduction to warm the flooring surface.

Figure 12.5 Standard ductwork installation occurs after framing is complete and prior to finishes.

system in spaces that utilize flooring that can tend to feel cold, such as tile in bathrooms and kitchens.

Forced-air HVAC systems, which rely on convection, are the most commonly used in modern-day buildings, because they have the ability to address all four of the human comfort zone factors and the IAQ components. Warm-air furnaces in combination with a centralized air conditioning system are very common in areas that experience both cold and dry as well as warm and humid climatic conditions, which is the case in the Midwest region of the US. In areas that are more temperate, where cold temperatures rarely reach below 4 8C/40 8F, a heat pump system is more common. Both of these systems can also control humidity, filter the air of contaminants, and utilize metal ducts to deliver the conditioned air throughout the building. In most cases, the ducts run through the ceiling plenum and the air is delivered in the overhead zone through supply air diffusers, or grilles, which can be adjusted to control air flow direction and quantity to a degree (Fig. 12.5). This method of delivery is inherently inefficient, as people do not occupy the overhead zone and additional energy is required to propel the air down to the occupants, especially during the heating months of the year due to the natural tendency of warm air to rise (Fig. 12.6). This problem is less pronounced in cooling months. The introduction of a raised flooring system is a viable answer to this problem, as the conditioned air is delivered through a pressurized open plenum under the floor. These systems are seeing increased use in office settings because they result in lower energy use, a greater degree of individual control, as occupants can adjust individual diffusers at the floor

level to their personal preferences, and flexibility of space reconfiguration particularly when using movable office partitions. These systems add a minimum of 12 inches to the floor height and this increase in height must be accounted for in the space plan while meeting accessibility requirements (typically through ramps).

The heating and air conditioning portion of HVAC tends to attract the most attention, but it is the *ventilation* portion that contributes a great deal to IAQ. **Ventilation** is the air exchange within a room, which is expressed in volume per minute, specifically cubic feet per minute, or cfm, in the US. Natural ventilation is achieved by opening windows, skylights, or doors, while forced ventilation occurs with fans and forced-air HVAC systems. If an interior is not properly ventilated, **sick building syndrome** (SBS) can develop, where indoor pollutants resulting from finishes, millwork, furniture, tobacco smoke, and cleaning products among other sources build up and negatively affect the health of the occupants. If SBS goes unchecked, occupants could develop a building-related illness (BRI) involving an infectious disease such as Legionnaire's disease. Three strategies can be employed to address indoor air pollutants before SBS develops:

1. Eliminate the source of the pollutant. Examples: no smoking policy, non-toxic cleaning supplies policy.
2. Remove the pollutant near the source. Example: a hood over a cooking surface to remove smoke resulting from cooking.
3. Dilute pollutants with ventilation air. Example: open a window or utilize a forced-air HVAC system.

Figure 12.6 Ventilation, adding clean air to the interior, is critical for any interior space. This mechanical diffuser directs air down from the ceiling toward the occupants while return air grilles draw contaminated air out of the space.

Many countries or municipalities may dictate minimum ventilation requirements in order to improve IAQ. In the US, the American Society of Heating, Refrigeration, and Air Conditioning Engineers (ASHRAE) sets this standard through the ASHRAE 62.1 guideline. While mechanical engineers are largely responsible for ensuring that this standard is met in interior environments, the designer must also be aware, especially in context to meeting any prescribed sustainability requirements such as those by LEED (Leadership in Energy and Environmental Design).

The designer can employ several design strategies to integrate HVAC systems into a successful design of the built environment. First, the designer needs to understand the spatial needs of the system being used so that adequate space can be provided for the equipment, including necessary clearance requirements for maintaining and servicing the equipment. Mechanical or utility rooms are required to provide dedicated space for large HVAC equipment, such as furnaces and boilers. Second, the designer needs to understand the positives and negatives of the system so that other aspects of the design can maximize the positives and account for the negatives. For example, if a modular raised floor system is being used, it makes sense to select and specify carpet tile to install over the system to embrace the flexibility qualities of the raised floor system. If a baseboard system is utilized in a space, then other means of introducing air ventilation are needed, such as fans and operable windows.

Electrical Systems

Electrical systems primarily address electrical wiring, switching and other lighting controls, and power supply (Fig. 12.7). On some small projects the designer may be responsible for locating power outlets, lighting controls, and circuit panels, but on most contract projects, the engineer is responsible for these portions while the designer is responsible for coordination between the electrical systems and other portions of the design, such as other systems or FF&E. One aspect of FF&E that requires particular coordination with electrical is systems furniture (Fig. 12.8). Systems furniture workstations are electrified, meaning they have their own internal wiring for task lighting and computer systems, but they require a source for the power, typically a wall outlet or floor outlet that the workstations will plug in to. The location of the power panel containing the circuit breakers is the most important aspect of electrical systems that the designer must coordinate (Fig. 12.9).

Figure 12.7 Electrical and data are both "roughed in" shortly after framing is complete. Notice the plumbing rough-in in the background as well, and reference the prior discussion on HVAC installation to get a broad sense of when these three primary systems are installed in relation to framing and finishes.

Figure 12.8 The designer must coordinate the placement of electrical systems and furniture for convenient and safe use by the occupant.

Figure 12.9 Circuit panels are typically located in an electrical room or utility room near other systems equipment, and the location must be coordinated between the designer and consultant or contractor.

Often, the designer provides an electrical and data closet, or room depending on the project size and complexity, which means the designer must accommodate this space in the space plan. It is up to the designer to coordinate the location of certain critical outlets and the location of and clearances around the power panel with the electrical engineer through the power plan drawings.

Telecommunication and data systems are closely related to electrical power and are commonly addressed by the same electrical engineer on contract design projects. Telecom and data includes hard-line telephone wiring and switching, hard-line data wiring and servers, wireless routing, and cable TV. Telecom and data needs have been changing quickly in recent decades, as technology has moved from exclusively hard-wired applications to a blend of hard-wired and wireless. While wireless applications provide mobility convenience and decrease the need for extensive construction, they are also associated with data security problems, and, as a result, hard-wired telecom and data needs have not been phased out to date, but they could be in the future if the technology improves. Similar to power, telecommunication and data systems require control panels, often located in an electrical closet, or their own telecom and data space, which the designer must provide for in the space plan. Cable TV requires cable outlets and electrical power that the designer must coordinate with FF&E plans. In certain project types, such as offices, call centers, hospitals, education buildings, and any project type that has intensive technology needs, a large server room will be devoted to the centralized computer servers that securely store the organization's data. Not only do these spaces have specific electrical, telecom, and data needs, but they also have very particular air conditioning (HVAC) requirements as the equipment generates high amounts of heat (Fig. 12.10).

Security systems often require low-voltage power and a cable, data, or telecommunications connection to operate properly. Security systems can include perimeter security alerting the system to opening doors and windows, movement within spaces via occupancy sensors, limited access to certain spaces through identity confirmation (card swipe, finger print, retinal or voice scan, etc.) or possession and body scanning, and observation through cameras. The most effective, and most expensive, form of security is through officer patrol and observation. The designer is responsible for some level of design and coordination in projects with any of these methods

Figure 12.10 Data wiring for a large organization or business leads back to a server room where data is stored and transferred between computers.

of security. In some cases, the design and coordination requirements are rather simple, as the case with cameras and/or occupancy sensors, where the designer coordinates placement of these items with HVAC and lighting systems mostly in the ceiling plane via the reflected ceiling plan. In other cases, such as a passenger security checkpoint in an airport that utilizes all of these security systems, the designer must carefully craft all aspects of the design and coordinate with consultants and third parties to meet the functional aspects of the design while also making it an aesthetically pleasing space. In many public spaces, a reception and guard station will need to be designed that provides the person working at the station to see in many directions while monitoring video screens of cameras around various portions of the building (Fig. 12.11).

The most fundamental of electrical systems is power, as many of the other built environment support systems, such as security and HVAC, rely on it to operate. Depending on the size and complexity of the project, the designer may be working with multiple consultants just

within the electrical category, as has been discussed here. The designer's role is not to design each of these systems, but to coordinate between them, creating a cohesive and functional space when the project is complete. During construction, the wiring for power, data, and security systems is installed immediately after rough framing is complete, prior to finishes being installed. Electrical systems are inspected by a building inspector prior to installation of finishes to ensure that the contractor is abiding by electrical codes.

Plumbing Systems

Plumbing systems have two primary functions: (1) supply of water for drinking, bathing, cooking, washing, cleaning and flushing toilets primarily found in kitchens, baths, restrooms, and laundry areas, and (2) removal of waste from those same places. **Potable water**, or drinkable water, is supplied to a building either from a well or municipal

Figure 12.11 Security check points in airports are very intricate, requiring a designer to work closely with specialty consultants and security personnel to properly design these types of spaces.

source at a certain pressure, approximately 50 psi in the US, for the typical functions described earlier. The supply can also come from a cistern/tank that contains **grey water**, which is not fit for drinking, bathing, or washing, but can be used for irrigation or flushing toilets. Grey water reduces the consumption of fresh water because it is often collected from rain water runoff from the roof or some other source on the building site and then stored until needed. The interior use of a grey water system for flushing toilets can become expensive because a separate set of supply pipes must be installed to keep the grey water and potable water separate from one another, but a common waste system is used.

Water arrives to a building cold, passes through a meter to measure water consumption, and then branches into two separate supply lines, one remains cold, and the other runs to a water heater. Water heaters require natural gas or electricity to operate. They can involve tanks that heat water and store it until needed, which is inherently inefficient, or they can be tank-less, rapidly heating the water on-demand, resulting in energy and cost savings (Fig. 12.12). The two supply lines, hot and cold, then proceed to faucets, shower heads, and some appliances, such as clothes washing machines, while only cold proceeds to toilets, hose bibs, and appliances that have a built-in water heater, such as dishwashers. In concept, large buildings, such as high-rises, and small buildings, such as single-family houses, operate as described here, but the scale and gravity impact of tall buildings requires additional attention by the plumbing engineer and designer. Tall buildings will use what is called a **gravity down-feed system** in which the cold water is pumped to the roof, stored, and then gravity draws the cold water down to each level as needed. At each level below, or at each tenant as applicable, the water lines will branch to the water heating system before running out to usage sources as described earlier.

Plumbing supply piping delivers hot or cold water to the usage source and can be made from a variety of materials (Fig. 12.13). Older supply piping was made from galvanized

Figure 12.12 Tank-less water heaters require less space than conventional water heaters because they only heat water as it is needed rather than storing hot water.

Figure 12.13 While piping is never installed as this image suggests, piping has been made from a variety of materials (galvanized steel, copper, and PVC) as technology has improved.

steel, but it showed problems with corrosion, so it was replaced with copper piping. Copper piping is very durable, but expensive, so PVC piping has largely replaced copper in single-family residential construction, but it is still used in non-single-family residential construction. Standard PVC is acceptable for cold water supply, but CPVC is used for hot supply due to the added stress of the high water temperature on the pipe. The designer should be aware of the variety of pipe materials for identification purposes on a construction site and for budgetary impacts in the event that an aging or faulty system requires replacement.

As mentioned, the supply side of the plumbing system relies on pressure to operate, but the waste side of the system simply relies on gravity. As a result, waste piping either runs vertically through walls, or with a slight slope inside of a floor/ceiling plenum. Historically, waste piping has been made from fired clay, which was replaced by cast iron due to durability issues, and today PVC is the preferred material for waste lines. Waste systems harbor gasses that will migrate back into an interior space without the inclusion of a trap. A **trap**, easily visible under most sinks, creates a natural water seal to prevent gasses from coming back into the interior from the sewage system (Fig. 12.14). These gasses can build up and break the water seal in traps, so waste lines also require fresh air to be introduced to the system via a pipe **vent through roof** (VTR). VTRs allow waste gasses that build up in the sewage system to escape to the outdoors rather than to the interior.

Waste removal and disposal systems include a septic tank with a drain field (located on site) and municipal sewer. Septic tanks collect solid waste while allowing liquid waste to flow through to a drain field where the harmful bacteria and viruses are filtered out allowing the harmless remaining liquid to proceed into the soil. The solid waste in a septic tank must be removed and disposed of periodically, requiring the owner to attend to this maintenance. Municipal sewage systems utilize an extensive system of large pipes and pumps to transfer both solid and liquid waste to centralized treatment facilities where harmful contents are neutralized.

The designer should take into account several design strategies to maximize the efficiency of plumbing while minimizing its installed and long-term cost. First, in multistory buildings, plumbing supply and waste lines work most efficiently when they run vertically through a building resulting in plumbing chases. A **plumbing chase** is a void within a wall construction that allows

Figure 12.14 The trap and hot and cold shut-off valves are visible beneath this lavatory, providing easy access for maintenance.

plumbing supply and waste pipes to run vertically between levels in a building. This results in spaces with heavy concentrations of plumbing, such as kitchens, baths, and restrooms, finding their location in the same place on each floor of a multilevel building, sometimes referred to as "stacking" the plumbing. Second, plumbing requires maintenance and repair, resulting in the need to access certain key components such as shut-off valves. The designer should take this need into account by providing access to faucet shut-off valves below lavatories and sinks within cabinetry, and for showers through a **service access panel** behind the shower head wall. The designer can provide for this need through a strategically placed closet that conceals the access panel while also providing much-needed storage. If shut-off valves are concealed within walls, the wall finish will need to be demolished to gain access and repair the problem, then the wall

finish will need to be repaired, resulting in a much higher repair cost. Third, access to waste line clean-outs is just as important as access to shut-off valves. If the waste line is somehow obstructed, it can typically be cleaned out at each sink, toilet, bath, or shower drain, but the building waste line can also become obstructed on a rare occasion. It is in everyone's best interest that access to the main clean-out is preserved and planned for by the designer and plumbing engineer or contractor, *otherwise, things could get ugly*. Fourth, designers must provide space for plumbing system utilities, such as water heaters, with the input of a plumbing engineer or contractor that takes into account the size of equipment as well as manufacturer- and code-required access clearances around the equipment for proper operation, maintenance, and safety.

Fire Monitoring, Notification, and Suppression Systems

Fire monitoring, notification, and suppression systems are dictated by national and local building codes based on the location of the building, occupancy type (assembly, business, education, etc.), and the number of occupants that could be utilizing the space as determined by code. **Fire monitoring** devices include smoke and heat detectors and are located on ceilings or high on walls to more easily detect problems, as smoke and heat will rise. **Fire notification** devices include horns, strobes, centralized audible devices, and many smoke detectors also integrate an audible alarm. In non-single-family residential settings, both an audible and visual alarm is often required to alert individuals of varying physical and sensory abilities that an emergency is present and evacuation of the building is necessary. Centralized audible devices produce prerecorded audible directions to instruct occupants of the type of emergency and necessary actions, whether it is fire-related or not, and these devices can also be used to communicate live instructions to occupants from a centralized security station. Common **fire suppression** devices include fire extinguishers and sprinklers, but many other types and systems are available for particular conditions and spatial types. Fire extinguishers are typically attached to walls, and may be inside of a break-away glass-protected cabinet, near exits or in the common path of travel leading to an exit where they can be easily seen and accessed when needed. Sprinklers are typically in the ceiling, or very high on a wall, and can be fully visible or recessed with a protective cover visible from below.

Interior design considerations in relation to the fire monitoring, notification, and suppression systems primarily focus on the coordination of the design and engineering disciplines. In large and complex projects these coordination tasks can consume a significant portion of the designer's time, and this must be accounted for in the overall schedule of the design work. The designer must balance code requirements with aesthetic desires to create a space that is beautiful, functional, and safe.

Acoustical Systems

Acoustical systems differ from the other nonstructural systems described here in that they require a holistic view of the space planning and finishes. To understand the issues surrounding acoustics, the designer should comprehend some basic science principles of sound and terminology. **Acoustics** is the science of sound. **Sound** is vibration that requires a source (voice, speaker, shoes on a floor), a path (air, water, building structure), and a receiver (ear). And **noise** is any unwanted sound. **Sound intensity** is measured in decibels (dB) where 0 dB is the lowest sound that humans can hear, 120 dB is typically the threshold of hearing pain, and 180 dB can damage a building structure (Fig. 12.15a). **Sound frequency**, sometimes called pitch, is measured in cycles per second (also known as hertz, Hz) where the lower pitches can travel long distances through solid materials such as concrete (Fig. 12.15b).

Strategic space planning, form generation, and informed finish selection and specification embraces acoustics by controlling sound and limiting noise. Noise can come from HVAC systems, conversations, outdoor vehicle traffic, interior foot traffic, and many other sources. Space planning that embraces acoustics seeks

TYPICAL SOUND LEVELS

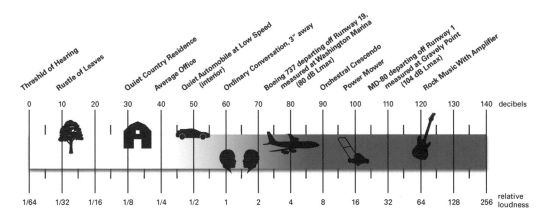

SOUND IS MEASURED 2 WAYS

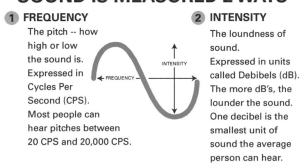

1 FREQUENCY
The pitch -- how high or low the sound is. Expressed in Cycles Per Second (CPS). Most people can hear pitches between 20 CPS and 20,000 CPS.

FREQUENCY
INTENSITY

2 INTENSITY
The loudness of sound. Expressed in units called Debibels (dB). The more dB's, the lounder the sound. One decibel is the smallest unit of sound the average person can hear.

Figure 12.15 Sound is described in terms of frequency (pitch) and loudness. Depending on the function of an interior, or the contextual factors of the immediate vicinity, special acoustical considerations may impact the design of the interior.

Figure 12.16 Convex forms, shown here in the Disney Concert Hall, disperse sound.

to separate spaces that need quiet from sources of noise, and in spaces where this cannot happen, such as open offices, partial-height partitions are used to block some noise from transferring throughout the space. Form also impacts acoustics, as concave surfaces tend to focus sound, creating "hotspots," while convex forms tend to disperse sound (Fig. 12.16), and parallel surfaces with sound reflecting finishes can create echoes (Fig. 12.17 and 18). Finish selection and specification that embraces acoustics seeks to strategically utilize ceiling and wall finishes that absorb some sound and flooring finishes that do not add excessively to the noise level within a space (Fig. 12.19). Again, a good example is the open office that utilizes carpet at the floor and acoustical ceiling tile in the ceilings to limit noise levels.

Several acoustical terms relate specifically to interior finishes and construction types. **Noise reduction coefficient** (NRC) describes the amount of sound absorbed by a material, with 0 indicating 100 percent reflection and 1 indicating 100 percent absorption. A good rating for acoustical ceiling tile falls between .55 and .75, but sometimes higher ratings are required depending on the application. **Sound transmission class** (STC) measures the amount of sound passing through a material or construction, with 0 indicating 100 percent transmittance and 100 indicating 100 percent blockage. A higher STC is a positive attribute of a wall construction, with minimum STC of 40 needed to achieve audible privacy, making normal voice conversation noticeable but not intelligible. **Ceiling attenuation class** (CAC) measures the transmission of sound through a ceiling material and plenum over a wall and into a neighboring space where 0 indicates 100 percent transmittance and 100 indicates 100 percent blockage. A CAC of at least 35 is needed for enclosed offices when designing for

Figure 12.19 Balanced acoustics with adequate surfaces that can absorb sound-limiting noise is important for many environments, including office spaces. If too many surfaces reflect sound, then acoustical problems can develop.

Figure 12.17 Angular forms, demonstrated in the Arctic Cathedral, can limit echoes.

Figure 12.18 A largely rectangular space can utilize textural surfaces to disperse sound and limit echoes.

Environmental Support Systems Enable Creative Solutions in the Workplace

Project: Brasfield & Gorrie

Location: Nashville, Tennessee

Client: Brasfield & Gorrie General Contractors

Architecture Firm: Hastings Architecture Associates; designer: Matt Spaulding

Occupants/Users: Workplace

Site Characteristics: Urban parking garage infill level

Year Complete: 2016

Cost Estimate: Undisclosed

Facility Size: Tenant space: 20,000 total square feet; one level (14,000 square feet) with mezzanine (more than 6,000 square feet)

Project Overview

Driven by the client's mainstay—construction—the design for this collaborative office is a celebration of craft and process while serving as an example for their eleven other offices. A "constructivist" design aesthetic exposes systems and structures to demonstrate and celebrate Brasfield & Gorrie's work as a construction company, seamlessly connecting trades and processes. Raw and refined materials are juxtaposed to further celebrate materials and capabilities. The design plays with the dichotomy between finely detailed finishes and the structures and systems that support them. Everyday building materials, like concrete and plywood, are

The raised flooring platform and one "finished" wall within each pod provides the necessary space to supply each meeting space with electricity and data support.

treated like traditionally high-end finishes (such as marble and walnut), honoring the construction process itself. Environmental support systems, including HVAC, electrical, and fire suppression, are celebrated rather than concealed.

Carved out of the second and third floors of a parking liner of a fifteen-story urban office (also by Hastings Architecture Associates), the raw and open feel of the double-height workspace maximizes natural light, the connection to the street below, and views to downtown Nashville. Transparent, glass-fronted private offices adjacent to the open workspace maintain overall team connections while welcoming natural light into the private offices. A range of small, private, break-out spaces supports the open office, and various meeting spaces allow for flexibility and ample collaboration. Social spaces lend to the casual ambiance, and colorful shipping containers create intimate spaces for meetings and retreat. A living room-inspired gaming area and lounge, and a coffee shop-inspired café promote employee comradery.

Relocating from an enclosed office environment, the design team engaged an employee committee to provide input into the process and keep the office informed with open presentations. The client's prior work space was characterized as a traditional enclosed office space with many private offices, low ceilings, and an overall spatial quality that did not represent their business, nor did it encourage collaboration. This process of client engagement and feedback was a key aspect to collecting employee feedback and preparing them for the major changes to come. The process, and the addition of a "Golden Tee" arcade game to the living room space, immediately created a more engaged and energized staff who enthusiastically took part in the design process, which also translated into their daily work flow after they occupied the new space.

Environmental Systems Impact

The goal of highlighting the construction process within the interior relied heavily on the celebration of environmental systems. In the open work spaces maximizing daylight, enjoying the double-story volume, and preserving views to the exterior even from the mezzanine level were top priorities, so exposing the

The purposeful incorporation of a flexible environmental support system strategy allows the open work environment to maximize the efficiency and collaboration of the users.

HVAC ductwork, electrical conduit, and fire suppression piping in combination with the use of pendant lighting was critical. Exposing these systems, however, creates a need to carefully plan each layout for all of the systems and specifically select the method of attachment for items such as ductwork, conduit, and piping to the structure above. In typical scenarios, with a concealed plenum, arranging the runs of ductwork, conduit, and piping and selecting the anchoring mechanisms would be left to the contractor and subcontractor to decide because they are hidden from view. This highly detailed approach to designing the environmental systems required clear and frequent communication between the design team and the installers. A design-build approach for the systems allowed the team to streamline the design, cost estimation, and installation process due to the client's unique relationships as a general contractor. The designer began the communication process with the systems installers during the design development phase, far earlier than is typical for most projects.

The height of the double-story work space is 19 feet above the finished floor at the perimeter. In an effort to prevent stagnant air from collecting at the top of the space, and making the mezzanine uncomfortable, the design team used air supply diffusers at high elevations and air returns at low elevations in the space. The uninterrupted glass faces east and north, limiting the amount of solar heat gain in warm months. Even so, the glazing is equipped with shear roller shades to

The low profile ceiling feature carries the linear direct down luminaires without interrupting the view to the exterior or the soft daylight entering through the window wall system.

filter early morning light on the east facade while also providing some visual privacy from street-side onlookers if needed. This 19 foot height also led to widespread integration of pendant light fixtures and a suspended wood ceiling element containing linear LED luminaires. The lower height of the luminaires in this tall volume led to a reduced level of electricity consumption through the use of lower wattage lamps. If the fixtures had been mounted higher up in the space, a higher wattage lamp would be required to deliver adequate lumen levels to the work surfaces below and would have distracted from the coveted views of the downtown.

Typically, a space this large with few surfaces to dissipate sound is a concern, but several factors make this space perform well acoustically. The most influential factor, and one that is out of the control of the design team, is that the work performed in this open environment is naturally quiet with loud activities occurring elsewhere. The design-related influencers come through in the floor, ceiling, and HVAC system. A carpet tile was selected to limit noise from footsteps

and rolling chairs, while dissipating ambient sounds. The building structure in the exposed plenum was sprayed with K13 insulation that offers fire protection, a thermal barrier, and also acoustical benefits. The HVAC system provides a low hum, a background sound referred to as passive white noise, to help counteract sounds that could otherwise become disruptive.

The freestanding shipping container privacy rooms presented a unique set of challenges, including how to supply them with power and fresh air. The walls, floor, and ceiling of shipping containers are made from a single layer of heavy gauge steel and lack a void, or a chase, to run electricity. To solve this issue, the design team raised the containers on platforms, built out one wall to include an accent wood panel, and added a low-profile finished ceiling so that electricity could be supplied from a floor core, run under the container, up through the accent wall and overhead to lighting. The accent wall also contains all necessary access to power and data supply for electronic equipment. The ceiling of each container includes a discreet exhaust fan to remove stagnant air while fresh air is supplied by simply opening the door to the space.

The environmental support systems for Brasfield & Gorrie designed by Hastings Architecture Associates are intricately woven together in order to service the needs of the client while making their business come to life for the office workers. Hastings Architecture Associates is a full-service architecture and design firm in Nashville, Tennessee, specializing in a variety of project types. For more information on Brasfield & Gorrie and Hastings Architecture Associates, visit http://www.haa.us/.

privacy. Designing with all three of these concepts in mind is needed to create a space that performs well acoustically, because neglecting any one of them can comprise the quality of the design.

Failing to adequately address acoustics can cause significant problems within any interior environment. In cases where the space is not properly planned, finishes are not correctly selected or specified, or construction quality may be poor, secondary solutions can be sought. **Sound-masking systems** produce low-intensity sound at key frequencies in an effort to cancel, or mitigate, certain types of noise. These systems involve speakers in the ceiling, up inside the plenum, or down in the space distributed on surfaces, such as desks, to produce these low-intensity frequencies. In cases where the speakers are concealed, users may not even be aware that they exist. The designer should be aware of these systems as possible solutions to preexisting acoustical problems, but they are no substitute to great interior design that embraces acoustical principles.

Designing with acoustics in mind is very important for the proper function and enjoyment of everyday spaces. Good acoustics can heighten the enjoyment of a space, whereas poor acoustics can destroy it no matter how beautiful the finishes or forms appear. Integrating acoustical concerns into the design process early, sometimes in the initial empathy stages of design thinking, and following through into construction detailing, or the prototyping and testing phases of design thinking, will increase the likelihood of success in the design.

Monitoring Built Environment Support Systems

Monitoring the systems described in this chapter focuses primarily on mechanical, electrical, and plumbing systems. Monitoring these systems is a significant part of the LEED (Leadership in Energy and Environmental Design) certification system established by the USGBC (United States Green Building Council). Monitoring allows engineers to determine if the various systems are operating as designed while also allowing facilities managers and homeowners to adjust their systems to operate more efficiently and conserve resources. Facilities managers are responsible for the day-to-day efficient operation of large buildings and campuses and will spend a significant portion of their effort monitoring building systems usage, making adjustments to the systems, and scheduling repairs when necessary.

Homeowners essentially do the same thing, but on a much smaller scale. Through smart devices and the **internet of things** (IoT), often collectively referred to as SMART home technology, consumers can monitor their electricity usage, interior temperature and humidity levels, water consumption, and even the contents of their refrigerators. **SMART home technology**, which stands for Self-Monitoring Analysis and Reporting Technology, can automatically make adjustments to built environment systems based on parameters that the homeowner customizes. Through wearable technology, SMART home systems can locate a user and automatically adjust air temperature and humidity, music volume, and lighting, or lock/unlock doors. While the homeowner is away, the user can monitor and change certain controls, such as those related to safety and security should a need arise. While these systems provide many benefits, they can be vulnerable to digital security breaches necessitating the manufacturer and the consumer to be ever vigilant, promptly responding to attacks from the outside.

Summary

Built environment support systems are crucial to the function and enjoyment of any modern-day interior space. Mechanical systems provide occupants with healthy indoor air quality and comfort. Electrical systems provide

Figure 12.20 The often concealed built environment systems work together to support beautiful and functional spaces.

access to lighting, power, data, and security while also supporting many of the other built environment systems, such as mechanical, some plumbing, fire safety, and acoustics (in the case of sound-masking systems). Plumbing provides potable water for consumption, bathing, and washing while removing waste, increasing the health of building occupants and the populace at large. Fire monitoring, notification, and suppression systems serve to protect life in the event of fire or other emergency and limit loss of property in many cases. Acoustics increase the function and enjoyment of interior spaces while also preserving privacy. The interior designer, in relation to these systems, does not rely on reaching an expert-level of understanding, but a professional designer is aware of all these issues and knows how to leverage the expertise of professional consultants to produce great spaces.

Resources

ASA. (n.d.). ASA. Retrieved December 17, 2017, from http://acousticalsociety.org/.

ASHRAE. (n.d.). Home. Retrieved December 17, 2017, from https://www.ashrae.org/.

ASPE. (n.d.). Welcome to ASPE. Retrieved December 17, 2017, from https://www.aspe.org/.

Ching, F. D. (2014). *Building Construction Illustrated.* Hoboken, NJ: John Wiley & Sons, Inc.

Grondzik, W. T., & Kwok, A. G. (2014). *Mechanical and Electrical Equipment for Buildings.* John Wiley & Sons.

IEEE. (n.d.). IEEE. Retrieved December 17, 2017, from https://www.ieee.org/.

Mehta, M., Johnson, J., & Rocafort, J. (1999). *Architectural Acoustics: Principles and Design.* Prentice Hall.

SFPE. (n.d.). SFPE. Retrieved December 17, 2017, from http://www.sfpe.org/.

Tucker, L. M. (2015). *Sustainable Building Systems and Construction for Designers.* New York: Fairchild Books, an Imprint of Bloomsbury Publishing Inc.

Review Questions

1. What phases of design thinking typically incorporate planning of built environment support systems? What circumstances would advance the discussion of support systems to earlier phases of design thinking?

2. What does HVAC standard for? Describe the three types of heat transfer utilized by HVAC systems. What is the most common type of HVAC used today?

3. How can HVAC impact indoor air quality? What is the most important part of HVAC as it relates to IAQ? What is SBS? What are three strategies for reducing indoor air pollutants?

4. What are the primary components addressed by electrical systems? What are some portions of an interior design that the designer must coordinate with electrical planning?

5. Describe telecommunication and data systems and security systems. Why are these two systems linked closely with electrical? What are some coordination concerns that the designer should address in relation to these two systems?

6. What is potable water and how is it supplied to a building? What is potable water used for? What is grey water and what are some possible sources of grey water? What can grey water be used for?

7. What are common materials used for plumbing piping, and what are their advantages and disadvantages? What is a trap and vent through roof, and how do they work together to prevent sewer gases from migrating to the building interior?

8. Describe three planning concerns related to plumbing.

9. Describe how fire monitoring, notification, and suppression work together to provide safety to building occupants.

10. What is the difference between sound and noise? Describe how parallel surfaces and concave, convex, and angular forms influence acoustics of the built environment.

11. How can proper space planning and finish selection lead to an interior with a pleasing acoustical design? What can be added to a space after construction in the event acoustics are poor within a space?

Exercises

Support Systems Observation

1. Sketch a floor plan and reflected ceiling plan of several adjacent rooms and a corridor in your building on a sheet of graph or sketch paper approximately 8 1/2 × 11 inches, or larger, in size. The selected spaces should include electrical power, lighting, HVAC, security monitoring, occupancy monitoring, and fire suppression. Create tracing paper overlays for each type of support system.

2. Floor plan: draw walls, doors, windows, and furniture.
   a. Create an electrical overlay: locate power and data/telecommunication outlets.
   b. Create a fire safety overlay: locate fire extinguishers and pull stations.
   c. Create a symbol legend, or key, to accompany the drawing that describes each of the symbols used to depict the required components.

3. Reflected ceiling plan: draw walls, door heads, window heads, ceiling materials.
   a. Create an electrical overlay: locate light fixtures, electrical components (such as projectors and speakers), security cameras, and any monitoring devices, such as occupancy sensors.
   b. Create an HVAC overlay: locate HVAC supplies and returns.
   c. Create a fire safety overlay: fire suppression sprinklers, smoke detectors, emergency notification speakers and strobes, and any monitoring devices such as occupancy monitors.
   d. Create a symbol legend, or key, to accompany the drawing that describes each of the symbols used to depict the required components.

GLOSSARY

Introduction

Contract design: Encompasses the design of non-residential spaces, including healthcare, education, retail, hospitality, and other spatial typologies; depending upon the jurisdiction, this area of interior design may require certification and/or licensure in order to practice.

Interior decoration: Primarily addresses the finishes furnishings of an interior space.

Interior design: "Interior design encompasses the analysis, planning, design, documentation, and management of interior non-structural/non-seismic construction and alteration projects in compliance with applicable building design and construction, fire, life-safety, and energy codes, standards, regulations, and guidelines for the purpose of obtaining a building permit, as allowed by law. Qualified by means of education, experience, and examination, interior designers have a moral and ethical responsibility to protect consumers and occupants through the design of code-compliant, accessible, and inclusive interior environments that address well-being, while considering the complex physical, mental, and emotional needs of people." (CIDQ, 2019)

Residential design: Encompasses the design of homes, single- or multi-family, by an experienced professional; this area of interior design can often have a more decorative focus and is the least regulated area of the profession.

Space planning: The functional arrangement of built elements, such as partitions, interior windows and doors, in addition to the movable components, or furniture, fixtures, and equipment, in a manner that complies with building codes while meeting the needs of the end user.

Chapter 1

Alternation: A type of patterning that uses two or more contrasting elements in sequence with one another.

Asymmetry: Utilization of a loosely defined visual axis and the visual weight of objects and surfaces on either side of the axis to achieve balance.

Balance: The quality that expresses a natural resting posture, or equilibrium, in a space; categorically expressed through symmetrical, asymmetrical, and radial arrangements.

Chroma: The saturation of a color.

Color: The substantive quality of a surface as it reflects light to the eye in terms of hue, value, and chroma. The quality of light that impacts the perception of an object or surface.

Contrast: Achieved through varying certain elements, such as form, scale, color, light, pattern, or texture, within a design.

Design thinking: "A formal method for practical, creative resolution of problems or issues, with the intent of an improved future result" Faste, R. A. (1987). Perceiving Needs (No. 871534). SAE Technical Paper..

Dominant: The primary element of a design in relation to contrast—the design component that garners the greatest amount of attention at first glance.

Elements of design: The sensory qualities of a design, concise and clearly defined. Categorically, the elements of design are form, pattern, texture, scale, color, and light.

Empathize: Step 1 of 5 in design thinking. In an effort to provide the best possible solution to the design problem the designer needs to immerse themselves in the situation of the users to fully understand the plight of the client.

Failure: Designing and building a space that does not meet the needs of the users, or creates more problems than it solves. Iteration is not failure.

Form: The shape, or geometry, of a space or object. Includes point, line, plane, and volume.

Gradation: Achieved through slight variations in design components that create an overall progression.

Hierarchy: A visual area of focus, or emphasis, within a space that draws the attention of the eye.

Hue: The category of a color and includes red, blue, yellow, violet, green, and orange.

Ideate: Step 3 of 5 in design thinking. The process of identifying possible solutions to the design problem(s) at hand by temporarily suspending disbelief and asking "what if" types of questions.

Iteration: The idea of developing multiple design options for a client to respond to. In design thinking, iteration is the process by which a designer returns to prototyping and testing multiple times in order to arrive at the best possible design solution.

Light: Makes physical qualities visible, whether the source is natural or artificial. The element of design that makes all others perceivable.

Line: A point in motion. Categorized as straight (horizontal, vertical, angular) or curvilinear.

Mass: A solid volume, such as the sphere of an orange fruit.

Negative space: The space that surrounds an object, such as the circulation space around a furniture cluster.

Node: A point can translate into designed space through an intersection of two paths, corridors, or lines on a surface.

Organizing lines: Lines used to guide the design in plan, or to create a sense of proportion in vertical planes of a space.

Pattern: Results from utilizing a certain geometry, or combinations of geometries, repeatedly, even formulaically.

Plane: A line moving in a single direction. Can be described through Euclidian geometries as circle, triangle, rectangle, etc.

Point: A theoretical geometry; an infinitesimally small location in space represented through a dot on a two-dimensional plane or in a three-dimensional space.

Position: The skillful placement of certain design components in a space in an effort to achieve hierarchy.

Positive space: The space occupied within a void, such as a furniture cluster surrounded by circulation.

Principles of design: Design objectives that are achieved by varying combinations of certain elements of design; proportion, balance, rhythm, hierarchy, and unity.

Problem definition: Step 2 of 5 in design thinking. Based on immersing oneself in the users' situation, the designer accurately identifies what a new design must accomplish in order to be successful.

Proportion: The size of an object, or space, in relation to itself rather than in relation to an outside standard.

Prototyping: Step 4 of 5 in design thinking. Through sketching, model building, and other methods, the designer develops a limited number of the best ideas that emerge from the ideation phase.

Radial: Achieved by arranging objects around a center point.

Repetition: The same element repeated over and over.

Rhythm: Evokes a sense of movement as the eye traces various elements of a design through a space.

Scale: The size of a space or object in comparison to what someone would expect it to be based on an accepted standard, such as the human body.

Space: An open volume, such as the sphere of the Pantheon in Rome.

Subdominant: Secondary element(s) of a design in relation to contrast—visual elements that exercise influence on the perception of a space but are perceived after the dominant component is noticed first.

Subordinate: Tertiary element(s) of a design in relation to contrast—the spatial elements that come into focus after detailed inspection of the space.

Symmetry: Utilization of an axial line to arrange identical elements on each side of the line in a mirror-image arrangement.

Testing: Step 5 of 5 in design thinking. Through client interaction, the designer seeks to identify the best prototype, or preferred attributes of many prototypes, that can be developed further in the design process.

Texture: The tactile or visual quality of surface, that is, rough or smooth.

Unity: Encompasses all of the design elements and principles and speaks to base-level structure of the design from which all other elements and principles are derived.

Value: Describes the tint or shade of a color.

Volume: An extruded plane, such as a circle to create a cylinder, or extruded and tapered such as a triangle or square to create a pyramid. Categorically described as space or mass.

Chapter 2

Ambulatory: The circulation area around the apse in a church.

Apse: The semicircular area at the top of the cross plan in a church that contains the altar.

Arcade: Repeated archways supported on columns creating a covered walkway.

Art Deco: The first nontraditional style to gain wide acceptance in America focused largely on aesthetics rather than philosophy and permeated through architecture, interiors, furniture, jewelry, clothing, glass art, graphic art, and film; characterized by stepped forms inspired by the stepped pyramids of ancient civilizations, chevrons and zigzag lines, sunburst reliefs, sharp angles with rounded corners, high sheen materials including stainless steel and aluminum, and the free use of a variety of colors; 1920–1939.

Art Nouveau: The first truly new style since the Gothic, this style drew influence from the English Arts and Crafts, French Gothic, and advancements in wrought iron. It was a reaction against the Ecole de Beaux Arts, a school of art and design in France that sought to revive the use of the classical orders. Art Nouveau style rejected right angles in favor of compound curvilinear lines, asymmetrical balance rather than strict symmetry, parabolic arches rather than pointed or semicircular, glass expanses, and exposed ironwork; 1892–1910.

Arts and Crafts movement: Led by William Morris, John Ruskin, and A.W.N. Pugin, this movement was a reaction against mechanized production coming out of the Industrial Revolution and emphasized interiors and furnishings characterized by authenticity and honesty of materials; exposed joinery; unique textile and wall covering patterns; and highly crafted furniture, millwork, and interior details; 1880–1920.

Attic base: Ionic order column base with an upper and lower ring design separated by a concave molding.

Balloon framing: Wood framing technique where the wall studs would span multiple stories and relied on smaller wood sizes compared to post and beam framing.

Baroque: Beginning in Italy, spreading to France as the primary influence, and then to the rest of Europe and America; characterized by highly ornate details and opulence; 1600–1730.

Bauhaus: A school of Modernist design and craft located in Dessau, Germany, brought each student under the direction of an artist and craftsperson that sought to unify art and technology while neglecting the traditional subjects of mathematics and art history; resulting design styles used expansive glass and unadorned exteriors; 1919–1933.

Byzantine: Evolving from ancient Roman architecture, this style incorporates multiple domes; 330–1453.

Chevet: The ambulatory and small chapels that followed the outer edge of the apse in French Romanesque church architecture.

Colonial revival: Dominated by residential buildings, houses of this style were a conglomeration of various styles, including Georgian and Cape Cod houses that were common during the colonial period of America's history but were modified in favor of simplified construction and architectural detailing; 1880–1955.

Column: A vertical structural support that carries load from the roof or floor above.

Composite order: The fifth Roman architectural order, combined the scroll forms of the Ionic with the acanthus leaf forms of the Corinthian and employed the slenderest column shaft proportions of any of the orders.

Corinthian order: The third of three primary Greek architectural orders, characterized by a narrow fluted shaft and an ornate capital decorated with acanthus leaves and reserved for interior applications.

Craftsman style: inspired by the Arts and Crafts movement in England, this American style sought to simplify the design of the middle-class American home while valuing highly crafted interiors and architecture. Resulted in the bungalow, a house type that utilized one or one-and-a-half stories, high first-floor ceilings, clerestory windows for ventilation, shallow pitch roofs, and deep overhangs to provide shade for windows; therefore, the interior exposed construction details in wood and also incorporated clean-line Asian influences; 1897–1930s.

Crossing: The place where the nave and transepts meet, usually topped with a dome or a groin vault as two barrel vaults intersect.

Curtain wall: Non-load-bearing exterior walls able to be constructed of any material, including stone and glass.

De Stijl: This movement, led in part by Otto Wagner, developed in the Netherlands, while the Bauhaus was active in Germany, and advocated the role of the artist and designer to influence the desires of the public; characterized by abstract forms, non-intersecting planes, and the use of gray scale and primary color schemes; 1917–1931.

Deconstructivism: This design movement evolved as a reaction against Postmodernism and is known for its disjointed and free expression of architectural form divorced from the building interior; 1980s–present.

Doric order: The first of three primary Greek architectural orders, characterized by a smooth or fluted column shaft, a circular capital, and no base.

Egyptian: Ancient Egyptian architecture; characterized by massive stone structures requiring tremendous investment of human labor and technological advancements including the use of post and lintel construction; 3500–1100 BC.

Empire style: The application of Neoclassicism in France.

Entablature: Horizontal band of a building façade located above the columns and below the pediment and made up of the architrave, frieze, and cornice commonly used in classical architecture.

Entasis: A column shaft with a very slight convex form to counter the concave illusion that results from a straight column shaft.

Exotic revivals: This style utilized new materials, forms, or details blended with characteristics from Egyptian, Moorish, and Byzantine buildings of earlier times; 1835–1890.

Federal style: The application of Neoclassicism in the United States.

Flying buttress: Common in Gothic architecture, a structural reinforcement arranged perpendicular to a wall on the exterior of a building that forms an archway with the wall it reinforces.

Free façade: The third of Le Corbusier's Five Points of a New Architecture that recognized that the exterior walls are free from structural constraints and can be more expressive.

Free plan: The second of Le Corbusier's Five Points of a New Architecture that allowed interior walls to be arranged with greater freedom because the structure was carried on columns (pilotis).

Georgian style: The application of Neoclassicism in Great Britain and associated colonies.

Gothic revival: The Gothic style was renewed in England (1820–1870) and America (1840–1860) during the Victorian era.

Gothic: A style of architecture and design that evolved from the Romanesque and is characterized by slender columns, large amounts of daylight, pointed arches, curtain walls, and flying buttresses; 1200–1500.

Greek revival style: The final phase of Neoclassicism applied in the United States and Europe and often relied upon balloon framing technology.

Greek: Ancient Greek architecture; prized for significant structural advancements in stone and the aesthetic codification of architecture through the Greek orders—Doric, Ionic, and Corinthian; 776–146 BC.

International Style: Characterized by simple rectangular forms and right angles, this style embraces advanced construction technologies, the use of concrete and steel structure as a means to provide a free design of the interior plan and building façade, and large expanses of glass often with minimal framing members in the continual effort to eliminate ornamentation; 1930–present.

Ionic order: The second of three primary Greek architectural orders, characterized by volutes, or scrolls, at the capital and an attic base.

Italian villa: Overlapping with the Gothic revival, this style was characterized by asymmetrical arrangements, stucco over brick facades, semicircle arches, and ornate details; 1830–1880.

Italianate: Similar to Italian villa style; 1845–1880.

Klismos: A Greek chair with curved back support and concave tapered legs.

Mesopotamia: Greek for "between two rivers," corresponding to the region between the Tigris and Euphrates Rivers in modern-day Iraq and the location of the world's oldest civilization; 4500–539 BC.

Modernism: This movement produced buildings that prioritized the health of the occupants, embraced views to the exterior, and simplified architectural forms to right angles and straight lines by valuing technological advancements of the early twentieth century, including electricity, steel, concrete, and large-pane glass windows.

Nave: The long center form of a church building that holds most of the parishioners, starting at the primary entrance at the back and proceeding to the transept, or chancel for churches without a transept.

Neoclassical: This style returned to the classical Roman and Greek orders of architecture and resulted from a general dissatisfaction with the indulgent nature of the Rococo and archaeological discoveries at Herculaneum and Pompeii; 1760–1830.

Neolithic: Period of human development relating to the late stone age when ground and/or polished stone techniques were developed; 10000–4000 BC.

Oculus: A circular opening in the center of a dome.

Parametricism: Or parametric design, has developed as a reaction to the prescriptive nature of Modern and Postmodern design, by utilizing digital programs, computers, and algorithms as tools for the designer to address and balance complex functional and formal needs of the built environment.

Pediment: Common in classical architecture, a triangular form above the entablature and columns that establishes a pitched roofline.

Pendentive: A somewhat triangular-shaped curved wall surface above a column or vault that results from a circular or elliptical dome intersecting with a square or rectangular plan configuration.

Pilaster: A column partially embedded in a wall acting as a structural or decorative element.

Pilotis: The first of Le Corbusier's Five Points of a New Architecture that dictated structural loads must be carried on columns rather than on load-bearing walls.

Pointed arch: Common in Gothic architecture, an arch that forms a slight point at its apex rather than a smooth semicircle.

Portico: A porch with roof supported on a series of columns attached to a larger building.

Postmodern: This contradictory style emerged as a countermovement to the International Style and embraced sculptural form expressions in steel reinforced concrete and the liberal use of glass while also recognizing historical influences of architecture expressed in simplified historical forms coupled with advanced building materials; 1960s–present.

Queen Anne: This style utilized many of the same forms as Romanesque revival with some adaptations, such as wrapping porches and steep-pitch roofs, as many of the works were domestic in scale and generally favored the use of wood and brick rather than stone; 1880–1910.

Renaissance: Centered in Italy, this period in history turned emphasis away from the divine and toward the human as the inspiration for art and architecture. Utilizing the classical Roman orders and semicircular arches, this style of architecture articulated facades with columns, pilasters, and pediments; embraced arcades of columns to define open air space; utilized rusticated stone as a dominant material; and embraced a more horizontal proportion compared to the Gothic, which preceded this period; 1450–1649.

Ribbon window: The fourth of Le Corbusier's Five Points of a New Architecture that recognized as an application of the free façade, windows should wrap the building horizontally to provide daylight to the interior equitably.

Rococo: Falling within the Baroque period, this style epitomizes the ideals of the Baroque as the period reaches its full height; characterized by more expressive use of consecutive concave and convex forms, reserved use of asymmetry, and intricate detailing and gilding covering even more interior surfaces compared to the Baroque; 1715–1780.

Roman Corinthian order: The fourth Roman architectural order, similar to the Greek Corinthian order but used for both interior and exterior applications.

Roman Doric order: The second Roman architectural order that kept the slender proportion and inclusion of a base established by the Tuscan order, and added fluting to the shaft.

Roman Ionic order: The third Roman architectural order, included a base, fluted shaft, and scroll capital, but was slenderer than the Greek predecessor and also included a decorative application at the neck of the column, just below the capital.

Roman: Ancient Roman architecture; built upon ancient Greek architectural orders by adding the arch and dome; 753 BC–AD 476.

Romanesque revival: This style was led by Henry Hobson Richardson in America, for which many of his buildings are described as "Richardsonian Romanesque," and utilized signature forms such as semicircle arches in stone; 1860s–1870s.

Romanesque: Known for round semicircular arches, arcades of columns, groin vaults created by the intersection of perpendicular vaults, articulated structural bays, and a tripartite level arrangement in building facades (nave, triforium, and clerestory, from low to high respectively); 800–1200.

Roof garden: The fifth of Le Corbusier's Five Points of a New Architecture that recognized the portion of the building that meets the sky, the flat roof plane, should be designed to be usable, extending the occupied space.

Rotunda: A building or room that is circular in plan and can include a dome ceiling.

Stick style: Possibly draws influence from medieval timber-frame houses, this style decoratively articulates panels of wood shingles or siding in wood frames painted or stained a contrasting color and integrates intricate wood trim details at railings, windows, and overhangs; 1855–1875.

Transept: Either of the two shorter forms running perpendicular to the nave that form the cross shape in a church plan.

Trompe l'oeil: An interior painting method in perspective that expands the perceived size of a space.

Tuscan order: The first Roman architectural order with a simplified Greek Doric, incorporated a base, a shaft lacking flutes, and slenderer proportion than the Greek Doric order.

Tympanum: Common in classical architecture, a highly decorative recessed triangular wall panel within the pediment.

Victorian era: Named for Victoria, Queen of England from 1837 to 1901, the period included the Industrial Revolution during which a rapid series of style changes occurred in Great Britain and America, several of which were revivals of prior styles, which can generally be characterized as heavy in proportion and ornate in detailing.

Chapter 3

Adjacency matrix: A table that communicates priority levels of adjacency, such as "primary," "secondary," and "separate," between spaces by listing the spaces in a column on the left and arranging a 45-degree-turned grid to the right with intersecting cells symbolically communicating adjacency levels.

Blocking diagram: This diagram combines information from the bubble diagram and the programming table into a rudimentary scaled plan diagram that shows spatial arrangement in context with any existing conditions.

Bubble diagram: This drawing diagram communicates priorities of adjacency between spaces by using simple geometric shapes, such as circles, and a variety of line types to indicate circulation patterns and also communicates other important considerations, such as views to the exterior or sources of disruptive noise that can impact placement of spaces.

Build: The fourth stage in the design process from the client's POV involves a shift in focus toward the general contractor or construction manager to execute the design vision created by the designer in collaboration with the client.

Client's POV: The client, the individual or group who initiates the design process, views the design process in five stages: originate, focus, design, build, and occupy.

Concept: Near the conclusion of pre-design, the designer will work to coalesce an overall guiding principle, or set of principles, that will guide the project through schematic design in relation to spatial function and aesthetics.

Construction documentation: The fourth stage in the design process from the designer's POV is geared toward creating a set of large-size drawings and detailed specifications by which the design can later be built.

Contract administration: The fifth stage in the design process from the designer's POV is when the designer advocates for the client on the construction site by observing the construction process and meeting with the general contractor or construction manager to ensure that the design intent becomes reality.

Design development: The third stage in the design process from the designer's POV adds layers of detail and nuance to the design, including more detailed selection of finishes, furniture, fixtures, and equipment; the beginning analysis of construction detailing; outline specifications; and a preliminary cost of construction estimate.

Design process: Differing based on point of view, a formalized approach to creating a vision for a building interior that incorporates how a space will interact with an individual's five senses and impact a user psychologically.

Design: The third stage in the design process from the client's POV witnesses the transition of the larger responsibilities toward the designer as the professional creates design options, solicits client feedback, refines the design intent, and prepares drawings and specifications for construction.

Designer's POV: The designer, the individual or group who controls the design process and ushers the client through its various steps, views the design process in five stages: pre-design, schematic design, design development, construction documentation, and contract administration.

Evidence-based design: Throughout the design process a professional designer uses established and new research to inform decisions in the design process.

Focus: The second stage in the design process from the client's POV begins as the client hires a designer, signs a contract, and concludes after the client and designer have identified and articulated the priorities of the design.

Occupy: The fifth stage in the design process from the client's POV fulfills the goal of the entire design process as the client is now able to move into the new space and begin using it. In theory, this phase never ends, as the users are always in some process of occupying the space and possibly making small modifications to the built environment.

Originate: The first stage in the design process from the client's POV begins as the client considers the need for a new, or additional, space and concludes when the client determines it is necessary to hire a designer to address their spatial needs.

Parti: Working in conjunction with a concept to communicate the guiding ideas behind the design, this diagram captures the essence of the design either in plan, section, elevation, or in a three-dimensional view, such as an axonometric.

Post-occupancy evaluation: (POE), often consists of an on-site observation by the designer coupled with a survey or interview of the client and users after they have been using the new space for an appropriate amount of time. The observation and survey should seek to uncover how the design intent matches up with how the client and users actually use the space.

Pre-design: The first stage in the design process from the designer's POV begins with the designer developing new business, meeting with a prospective client, signing a contract, and conducting research on the client and in support of the new project.

Programming: Based on specific research of client and user needs and precedent set by successful built projects, a document listing spatial needs complete with space names, area sizes, and particular furniture, fixture, and equipment requirements is created.

Schematic design: The second stage in the design process from the designer's POV involves the functional and formal studies of the design as the designer analyzes spatial adjacency requirements using adjacency matrices and bubble diagrams and creates iterations of form arrangements through blocking diagrams and two-dimensional and three-dimensional sketches.

Chapter 4

Aesthetics and beauty: The sixth of eight needs in Maslow's hierarchy of needs, this need addresses a person's need to pursue creativity and witness beauty.

Aging in place: Enabling an aging user who is experiencing various physical and mental challenges to utilize a space as fully and independently as possible for as long as possible.

Anthropometrics: Data resulting from the body measurements of a broad population sample, which is used to design many consumer products such as furniture.

Barrier-free, or accessible: In the context of interior design and architecture practice, a space that is in compliance with all aspects of the ADA.

Biomimetic: A synthetic process, often in manufacturing, that seeks to emulate a natural process.

Building-related illness: An acute case of illness results in occupants that have been infected by bacteria, viruses, or certain forms of fungi due to problems in the built environment, such as a breakout of Legionnaire's disease resulting from poorly maintained HVAC systems.

Closed Loop: A manufacturing strategy that embraces planning for obsolescence by utilizing materials that can be reused or recycled one day, reducing the amount of waste in manufacturing, reusing materials whenever possible, and recycling materials for new uses.

Ergonomics: From the International Ergonomics Association, "the scientific discipline concerned with the understanding of interactions among humans and other elements of a system, and the profession that applies theory, principles, data and methods to design in order to optimize human well-being and overall system performance."

Hearing: One of the five physiological senses, this sense contributes to an individual's ability to navigate a space, perceive space beyond the visual, engage in audible communication, and contributes to mental concentration.

Knowledge and understanding: The fifth of eight needs in Maslow's hierarchy of needs, this need addresses a person's desire to excel cognitively and gain knowledge.

Leadership in Energy and Environmental Design: (LEED), the sustainability standard for the built environment dictated by the United States Green Building Council (USGBC) that measures degrees of sustainability through a point system.

Life cycle: The series of stages of development and use of a product in the built environment, such as a piece of furniture, starting with raw material harvesting, steps in the manufacturing process, through the useful life in the space, and including disposal, reuse, or recycle of useful components once the product has reached its end.

Maslow's hierarchy of needs: Includes eight human needs that include physiological, emotional, mental, and spiritual arenas of human existence.

Mobility challenges: A permanent or temporary reduction in physical strength or endurance reduces a person's ability to traverse a building interior.

Personalization: A theory of human behavior in the built environment observing that people have the tendency to adapt a space to reflect their individual desires, traits, and characteristics; to stake claims to certain portions of a space (territoriality); and to increase their comfort levels in a space.

Phototherapy: The use of full-spectrum lighting or light boxes to mimic the type of light produced by the sun in an effort to treat seasonal affective disorder.

Physiological: The first of eight needs in Maslow's hierarchy of needs, this need addresses thirst, hunger, rest, and shelter.

Privacy: Connected with a need for security and Territoriality theory, this theory of human behavior in the built environment states that people have a desire for varying degrees of acoustical and/or visual concealment, or compartmentalization, depending upon the activity.

Prospect-refuge theory: Proposed by Jay Appleton in *The Experience of Landscape* in 1975, a theory of human aesthetics proposing that people have an innate desire for opportunity and safety.

Proxemics: Proposed by Edward T. Hall in *The Hidden Dimension* in 1963, this theory of human behavior in the built environment observes the way people behave, communicate, and socialize in built space as population density changes.

Safety: The second of eight needs in Maslow's hierarchy of needs, this need addresses the desire to be free from threats of violence and fear.

Self-actualization: The seventh of eight needs in Maslow's hierarchy of needs, this need addresses the desire for someone to reach their full potential once their basic and growth needs are met.

Self-esteem: The fourth of eight needs in Maslow's hierarchy of needs, this need addresses an individual's need for self-confidence and respect from others.

Sensory disabilities: An individual's reduced ability to use any of the five physiological senses; results in design guidelines that require the inclusion of design characteristics that allow individuals with sensory disabilities to utilize the built environment as fully as possible.

Sick building syndrome: Illnesses can result where occupants experience an increase in sickness frequency, such as headaches and fatigue, due to problems in the built environment.

Sight: One of the five physiological senses, this sense allows an individual to navigate a space and enjoy visual aesthetics of the built environment.

Smell: One of the five physiological senses, this sense is grouped with taste as an olfactory sense and contributes to an individual's dining experience, can impact wayfinding, and the ability to identify dangers or problems in the interior.

Social belonging: The third of eight needs in Maslow's hierarchy of needs, this need addresses areas of love and acceptance in a person's life.

Sustainable development: From the World Commission on Environment and Development in 1987, "seeks to meet the needs and aspirations of the present without compromising the ability to meet those of the future. Far from requiring the cessation of economic growth, it recognizes that the problems of poverty and underdevelopment cannot be solved unless we have a new era of growth in which developing countries play a large role and reap large benefits."

Taste: One of the five physiological senses, this sense is grouped with smell as an olfactory sense and contributes to an individual's dining experience and can influence memory recall.

Territoriality: A theory of human behavior in the built environment observing that people have the tendency to claim entire or partial ownership, whether permanent or temporary, of a space.

Touch: One of the five physiological senses, this sense contributes to the interpretation of textures and the sensations of comfort and warmth.

Transcendence: The last of eight needs in Maslow's hierarchy of needs, this need addresses the desire for someone to help others meet their needs.

Universal design: An approach to designing spaces, and components within spaces, that allows inhabitants to fully utilize the built environment despite any physical challenge, mental challenge, or age.

Chapter 5

Accent: A color or material that contrasts with the rest of the design scheme and draws the eye adding emphasis to a composition.

Achromatic: A color scheme that does not rely on color, but instead uses white, black, and variations of gray.

Additive method: A process of mixing primary colors by overlapping light colors to create the secondary colors of light.

Analogous: These color schemes utilize colors adjacent to one another on the artists' color wheel.

Artists' color wheel: The middle layer of Munsell's color system at maximum chroma, these colors are often used by artists and designers to begin creating and analyzing basic color schemes.

Chroma: The intensity of a color.

Cool colors: Inclusive of green-yellow through violet on the color wheel, these colors are perceived to retreat away from the viewer.

Cool light: Encompasses light temperatures at 6,000 to 8,500 K, this light category accentuates cool colors, violet, blue, and green, while neutralizing warm colors, red, orange, and yellow.

Direct-complementary: These color schemes utilize two colors positioned directly opposite one another on the artists' color wheel.

Hue: The basic category of the color based on the three primaries and three secondaries: red, yellow, blue, orange, green, and violet.

Law of chromatic distribution: A three-part, color-application strategy that embraces economy and longevity of a design by using neutral colors that coordinate easily with many other colors on the floors, walls, and ceilings; applying moderate intensity of color, pattern, and texture on primary furniture items; and, using high chroma colors on smaller items, such as accessories.

Monochromatic: A color scheme that focuses on a single hue and adds variety by varying the value and chroma of the color.

Munsell color system: An objective numerical system to describe color. Hue is measured in radial degrees, similar to pie pieces, around a central vertical axis; value is measured by the central axis on a scale of 0 (black) to 10 (white) from bottom to top; and chroma is measured in distance away from the central value axis with the more saturated colors at the outer edge and the muted colors at the center close to the vertical axis.

Neutral: A category of colors often involving some variation of brown.

Primary colors of light: Includes red, green, and blue wavelengths of light that when mixed create other colors of light.

Secondary colors of light: These light colors, yellow, cyan, and magenta, are created by mixing two primary colors of light in equal amounts.

Shade: Adding black to any color darkens the value of a color.

Split-complementary: These color schemes utilize a color and the two colors adjacent to its direct complement on the artists' color wheel.

Subtractive method: As white light strikes a surface, all colors of light are absorbed, or subtracted, with only certain colors of light being reflected and then interpreted by the human eye.

Tertiary colors: The combination of a primary and secondary color.

Tetrad: These color schemes use four colors equally spaced around the artists' color wheel.

Tint: Adding white to any color lightens the value of a color.

Tone: Adding gray or the complement of a color will mute the color's chroma.

Triad: These color schemes use three colors equally spaced around the artists' color wheel.

Value: The brightness of a color.

Visible light: A small portion of the electromagnetic spectrum between infrared and ultraviolet light rays that ranges from 700 to 390 nanometers in wavelength, which is visible to the human eye and includes red, orange, yellow, green, blue, indigo, and violet colors.

Warm colors: Inclusive of red-violet through yellow on the artists' color wheel, these colors are perceived to advance toward the viewer.

Warm light: Encompasses light temperatures at 600 to 2,000 K, this light category accentuates warm colors, red, orange, and yellow, while neutralizing cool colors, violet, blue, and green.

White light: Contains all the colors of the visible spectrum in equal amount and is observed in daylight.

Chapter 6

Accounting and finance: The role in a design firm that tracks the financial health of the firm to ensure that monies are on hand to pay salaries and other costs of doing business, and ensure that clients' fees for individual projects are being properly tracked so that the firm does not spend more time on a project than they will be paid for in order for the firm to be profitable.

Accreditation: A thorough evaluation of a university program's content and approach to design education by an unbiased third-party organization, such as the Council for Interior Design Accreditation (CIDA) in the US, helps to ensure high standards of education.

Area fee: This fee structure charges the client for design services based on the quantity of area that will be designed and has similar risks and benefits as the flat fee.

Billing cycle: The regular period for soliciting payment for design services from the client, such as every 30 days.

Code of ethical conduct: Interior design professional organizations formalize a system of ethics that all of their members are expected to follow so that the public, clients, fellow interior design professionals, and the interior design profession all benefit.

Contract: A long-form agreement outlining in extraordinary detail all of the legal arrangements and binding relationships for all the parties involved.

Corporation: A stand-alone legal entity, separate from the shareholders who own it, able to file a lawsuit and be sued by individuals or other corporations, and shields owners from personal risk beyond their initial monetary investment.

Cost-plus: This fee structure places a greater emphasis on purchasing services for the client by applying a markup to furniture costs.

Council for Interior Design Qualification: (CIDQ), one of the primary interior design certification bodies in the world, and the only one in the United States and Canada, which oversees the NCIDQ examination, a measure of basic interior design competency that includes space planning ability; building code compliance understanding; and basic knowledge of finishes, furniture, and lighting specification.

Designer and client relationship: Fundamental to writing contracts and executing business agreements this is based on the designer acting as an advocate for the client, representing their best interests in all matters related to the design.

Designer and consultant relationship: Hierarchical in nature, the consultants, including engineers and specialized designers, answer to the lead interior designer.

Designer and contractor relationship: Relying on the client as the central figure, the contractor (either general contractor or construction manager) organizes and executes the work based on the contract documents generated by the designer.

Direct personnel expense: (DPE), typically between two and a half and three times the hourly salary of the design team member that covers the individual's salary and benefits plus overhead costs and profit.

Flat fee: A guaranteed fee amount that provides the client with peace of mind knowing what they will be paying in design fees, while the designer has the opportunity to increase profit margins or could lose money on the project depending on the accuracy of projecting the number of hours that will be necessary to complete the project.

Hourly fee: With similarities to the hourly billing rate, this means of billing for design services must cover the salary and fringe benefits of the design team member plus overhead costs.

Human resources: That roles that works to manage human capital in a firm beginning with recruiting and hiring new personnel, analyzing options for employees' compensation and fringe benefits, conducting performance evaluations, and evaluating the grounds for employment layoffs and termination.

Interior decoration: A design-related profession where the focus is on the application of finishes and selection of furniture with some consideration to flame spread classification of materials within the built environment.

Interior design: A profession that focuses on space planning, comprehensive building code compliance, and construction detailing in addition to the application of finishes and the selection of furniture.

Intern designer: Functioning in a supporting role on design projects, this position implies that the individual has not yet completed their education and/or their professional certification process.

Junior designer: An individual who has completed his or her education and is logging work experience hours as they complete a variety of tasks in a support role on projects.

Kitchen and bath design: A specialization of interior design, professionals who focus their efforts here will complete the space plans and specify all of the intricate components of kitchens and baths, including finishes, millwork, appliances, hardware, and lighting.

Letter of agreement: A short-form binding agreement written in language that is more user friendly to non-attorneys.

Limited liability company: (LLC), a business structure that blends the benefits of a partnership and a corporation where the laws governing the formation of this structure vary by state with particular restrictions occasionally in force for those offering professional services such as interior design.

Marketing and promotion: The role in a design firm that seeks to expand the business of the design firm by purposely seeking out the next client and developing relationships with them, fostering long-lasting relationships with current clients, and maintaining positive contact with past clients in an effort to secure repeat business.

National Council of Interior Design Qualifications: (NCIDQ), see Council for Interior Design Qualification (CIDQ).

Overhead costs: Resources that do not directly generate revenue for a firm, such as cost of licensure, utility bills, and salaries for human resources and accounting in a design firm.

Partnership: An agreement between two or more individuals to own and operate a business where some portion of the financial assets and liabilities of the company are conjoined with the owners' personal finances.

Practice act: Requires that an individual be licensed to practice interior design, and declares it unlawful to practice without a license.

Professional ethics: An individual's standard of making decisions of right and wrong in a professional arena that impacts all areas of interior design practice, including education, certification, legislation, and practice legal structures.

Professional organizations: These groups serve the interior design community in an effort to unite design practitioners, share best practices, and enhance the role of interior design in society.

Project designer: An individual with limited experience who has completed and passed the certification exam and is likely working on small- and medium-sized projects with some peripheral input from a senior leader in the firm.

Project management: Acts as a bridge between the business administration side and the design side of a firm in an effort to create the highest quality design projects in a timely and profitable manner.

Project manager: A seasoned interior designer who will direct the operation and function of the design team, manage the design process schedule, coordinate consultants and specialists, and coordinate communication with the client.

Reimbursable expenses: Business expenses billed to a client that include travel expenses for long trips or overnight meetings, and printing costs for large-scale drawings or photocopies.

Retainer: An advanced payment to the designer at the time the client signs an agreement.

Risk management: The process that seeks to minimize the firm's exposure to legal risk, which starts before a designer begins work on a project, includes the writing of fair contracts, hiring competent and conscientious employees, purchasing appropriate insurance coverage in the event a suit is brought against the firm, and then appropriately managing disputes if and when they occur through mediation, arbitration, or litigation.

Sales representative: Working for finish, furniture, lighting, and accessories manufacturers, these professionals understand the design process intimately and act as liaison between the product manufacturer and the designer who specifies the products.

Senior designer: Directs the design decisions on large, high-profile projects where several project designers may be responsible for some portion of the work.

Sole proprietorship: A company owned by one person where the financial assets and liabilities are conjoined with the owner's personal finances.

Technology and information management: The role in a design firm that seeks to effectively manage technology and access to digital information.

Title act: Controls the use of a title, such as "Certified Interior Designer," in order to help the public understand which individuals have met the requirements to use the title as outlined by the governing body, but does not regulate the practice of interior design, nor does it prevent someone from performing such services.

Chapter 7

Balloon framing: A structural system that utilizes continuous studs running up more than one story from foundation to roof structure.

Building codes: Regulations based on prevailing architectural practice adopted by locales governing the design and construction of buildings in order to protect the health, safety, and welfare of the public.

Dead load: The unchanging vertical load that the structure places upon itself by its simple mass.

Egress: The means to exit a building, which is particularly important in the event of an emergency.

Grade: The ground plane, which can be relatively flat or significantly sloping.

Lateral load: Horizontal load that places pressure on a building from the side and often originates from wind or shifting soils.

Live load: The changing or movable sources of vertical load, such as mobile equipment, furniture, and people within the building.

Load: The forces exerted by gravity and the natural elements upon a building.

Platform framing: A structural system achieved by supporting the floor structure (the platforms) with wall framing and then building the next level wall framing on top of the floor structure.

Rebar: Steel reinforcing bars used to strengthen the tension capabilities of concrete construction.

Rural: Based on the U.S. Census Bureau definition, any geographical area possessing less than 1,000 people per square mile.

Stage of life: A distinct step of growth, progress, or development in an individual that can include personal categories, such as marital status or the presence of dependents, as well as professional categories, such as entry-level or high-level leadership, that is more descriptive than simple generational characteristics.

Substructure: Those portions of a building that are constructed partially or fully below grade.

Superstructure: All above-grade construction and includes above-grade floor and subfloor structures, walls, columns, and roofs and all the materials associated with these components.

Urban: Based on the U.S. Census Bureau definition, any geographical area possessing 1,000 or more people per square mile.

Urbanized areas: Based on the U.S. Census Bureau definition, any geographical area of 50,000 inhabitants or more.

Vernacular: The unique application of an architectural style in a particular place, which can contribute to the identity of a community and can exert influence on new design projects.

Vertical load: Loads that result from the forces of gravity, categorized as dead load and live load.

Chapter 8

Axonometric: A three-dimensional drawing showing three sides of an object that depicts vertical edges straight up and down and receding sides with parallel angled lines so there are no vanishing points.

Circulation space: Open floor area that allows users to travel within a space in order to navigate around, or through, architectural elements and to use interior components.

Elevation: A scaled drawing that illustrates a two-dimensional projection of a vertical surface, such as walls, and their associated components, such as millwork, lighting, and accessories.

Floor plan: A scaled drawing depicting a top-down view of a building interior showing all elements that are within four vertical feet of the floor plane including walls, doors, windows, furniture, fixtures, and floor finishes.

Guardrail: Prevents a user from falling over the edge of a stairway or opening in a floor.

Handrail: Provides a user something to grip and steady themselves while ascending or descending a stair.

Isometric: A specific type of axonometric drawing that portrays three sides of an object with equal foreshortening to each side of the central vertical edge line where the angled sides are drawn at 30 degrees from horizontal.

Landing: An intermediate platform on a stairway that allows the stair to change direction, allows users to rest as they ascend, and protects users from excessive injury if they happen to trip and fall.

Node: A place where multiple paths intersect, an intermediate destination, or a hub of activity along a path.

Nosing: The portion of a step on a stair where the tread transitions to the riser and projects out beyond the riser.

Occupied space: Floor area that is consumed by architectural elements, including walls, columns, and doors, and interior components such as furniture, millwork, or equipment.

Perspective: A three-dimensional drawing, not to a scale, of a space from a specific point of view looking at a specific point in space.

Reflected ceiling plan: A scaled drawing that illustrates the design of a ceiling as if a mirror was placed on the floor and shows walls, windows, door openings, ceiling finishes, changes in ceiling height, skylights, openings in the ceiling or floor above, light fixtures, and other components.

Rise: The finished floor to finished floor height that used to calculate the exact dimensions of a stair and its various detailed parts.

Riser: The vertical face between the treads of a step on a stair.

Run: The horizontal distance covered by a stair from the top nosing to the bottom nosing, including any landings.

Section: A scaled drawing that illustrates a vertical cut through a building, or series of spaces, showing the height of individual spaces, the multiple levels of spaces that stack upon one another, and the thicknesses of walls, floors, and ceilings, as well as movable components such as furniture.

Space planning: The act of creating a new layout, called a space plan, for an interior space that carefully depicts occupied space and circulation space.

Tread: The portion of each step on a stair that supports the foot.

Vanishing points: The points in a perspective where lines converge off in the distance; serve to categorize the type of perspective drawing as one-, two-, or three-point perspective.

Wayfinding: The process of an occupant navigating a space or a series of spaces, occasionally with great effort.

Chapter 9

Additives: Provides specialized functions for the coating, including additional UV protection, mildew-cide, or thickening agents for use on particular types of surfaces.

Ashlar: Cut rectangular shapes of stone.

Berber: A carpet pile type that generally consists of a coarse loop pile but is also available in a cut pile and shag; named after handwoven wool squares made by North African tribes, but is now machine made.

Binders: Adheres the pigment to a surface and directly impacts the useful life of the coating, as lower quality binders will cause the pigment to flake off more quickly.

Book-matching: A type of veneer matching technique that mirrors alternating leaves so that pairs of leaves look like facing pages of a book, resulting in a balanced symmetrical pattern of veneer leaves.

Brick bond types: Brick courses can be arranged into patterns, and include running, stacked, Flemish, and English types among others.

Brick course: One row of brick and the accompanying mortar joint.

Brick positions: Brick can be oriented in a variety of ways; the most common types include stretcher, header, and soldier.

Broadloom carpet: Crafted on a wide loom, this carpet material is available in large sizes, most commonly 12 feet in width.

Brown coat: The second layer of plaster levels the wall surface.

Carpet pile: The tufted natural or synthetic carpet yarn that tends to characterize the appearance of the carpet.

Carpet tiles: Crafted on a loom, this carpet product varies in size but is most commonly 24 inches x 24 inches.

Cast in place: Poured on the construction site.

Cathedral ceiling: Pitch in two directions reaching an apex, or ridge, resulting in a space grandiose in scale.

Clay tiles: Masonry modules fabricated from clay used predominantly as flooring or a wall finish.

Coefficient of friction (COF): A value that describes the amount of force required to cause two objects to slide past one another while making contact. In context with flooring, a higher COF means it is more difficult for someone to slip.

Coffered ceiling: Flat ceilings that utilize a grid to divide the plane into smaller portions, and often incorporate subtle height changes, wood details, finish changes, and strategically placed lighting.

Concrete: A composite material made of coarse aggregate (stones or pebbles), fine aggregate (sand), cement, water, and possibly other additives for specialty uses that relies on formwork to provide its shape until the material can harden and support itself.

Custom grade: Per the American Woodworkers Institute (AWI), plywood used for the majority of architectural woodwork and wall applications.

Cut pile: A carpet pile type that can be made from firm or frizzy yarns and appears more luxurious than loop pile, but also shows wear sooner than loop pile.

Decorative laminate: Commonly used to cover countertops, cabinetry substrates, and wall panel substrates, such as plywood or particleboard; a very thin finish that protects the substrate while providing visual interest.

Dome: A half-sphere ceiling geometry.

Drop match: This method to match and install wall coverings has two basic varieties: half-drop match (every other strip aligns horizontally) and multiple-drop match (every third, or more, strip aligns).

Dye lot: Also known as a run number, a group of wall covering rolls manufactured from the same print run.

Economy grade: Per the American Woodworkers Institute (AWI), where a basic level of quality, craft, and materials is expected in construction substrates, such as subfloors, exterior wall sheathing, and roof sheathing.

Embodied energy: The amount of energy it takes for a material to be harvested, manufactured, and transported to a construction site.

End matching: A type of veneer matching technique that involves book-matching leaves in both the horizontal and the vertical direction resulting in a continuous symmetrical grain pattern over a large expanse of wall surface.

Engineered wood flooring: Characterized by species that will only consist of the top layer while the bottom layers are made of plywood, thickness can vary between 3/8 inch and 3/4 inch depending on quality. Thicker products can be sanded and refinished, whereas thinner varieties may not provide this option.

Environmental systems: Includes the delivery of fresh air and removal of contaminated air; more specifically referred to as heating, ventilation, and air conditioning (HVAC).

Fabricated: Made by human hands or industrial processes and, in the case of masonry, includes brick, and ceramic, porcelain, and clay tile.

Finish coat: The third layer of plaster is very smooth and receives the final finish, such as paint.

Fire suppression: An overall strategy within the interior that seeks to limit the spread of fire through a building through the use of sprinklers that are typically located in the ceiling.

Flat ceiling: A non-sloping ceiling.

Flitch: Veneer leaves that are sliced from the same log.

Float glass: A method to manufacture glass by pouring the molten glass onto molten tin and allowing the glass to reach its flat equilibrium as it cools, resulting in a glass sheet of consistent thickness.

Frieze pile: A carpet pile type that is a variation of cut pile using highly twisted yarns set in a snarled configuration that will hide footsteps much better than cut pile.

Grout: Fills the gaps between masonry modules.

Gypsum board: A panel made of gypsum with a paper facing on each side of the board and around the edges used in wall and ceiling construction as a replacement for plaster.

Hardwood: Sourced from deciduous trees and reserved for finish surfaces such as flooring, furniture, and millwork.

Laminate flooring: This flooring material contains little to no hardwood, includes a printed paper layer that resembles wood with a protective coating for wear, and has poor moisture resistance due to a particle board under-layer.

Laminated glass: A type of security glass that includes a sandwich of two or more layers of glass with an interlayer that will hold the overall unit together in the event the glass breaks.

Lath: Made of wood strips, metal mesh, or gypsum board strips, lath is attached to wall framing and supports layers of plaster in a plaster wall construction.

Leaves: Individual pieces of veneer.

Levels of sheen (paint): Shininess often described in levels, flat/matte, eggshell, satin, semi-gloss, and gloss.

Lighting systems: Includes interior electric lighting that is mostly provided via the ceiling, and the switching controls used to operate the lighting.

Live sawn: A method to process and saw logs, this process results in a variety of grain patterns incorporating characteristics of plain, quarter, and rift sawn, is least desirable in appearance, is often painted due to the range of the grain pattern, results in the largest size boards, and is low cost.

Load-bearing wall: Walls that support their own weight and additional weight above that could include a higher level of a building or roof.

Loop pile: A carpet pile type where the surface consists of uncut loops of twisted yarn that can vary in height and color.

Marquetry: An simple elaborate curvilinear pattern of wood flooring including some measure of inlay in many cases.

Masonry: Stone, brick, or tile assembled in modules and installed with mortar and/or grout or dry-laid.

Medium density fiberboard: The most common type of particle board that utilizes very fine particles resulting in a smooth surface useful for a thin application of paints or coatings, a wood veneer, or decorative laminate overlay.

Modular brick: The most widely used brick type, 3 5/8 inch W x 7 5/8 inch L x 21/4 inch H.

Mortar joint types: Several techniques exist to form mortar joints, with the most common types including concave, flush, raked, struck, and weathered joints.

Mortar: Used to secure masonry pieces to a substrate.

Mosaic tile: Classified by size at less than 6 square inches in face area, fabricated from a variety of materials, and used predominantly as flooring or a wall finish.

Non-flat ceiling: Ceiling form that includes shed (mono-pitch), cathedral, vault, and dome forms.

Non-load-bearing wall: Walls that support their own weight and serve to divide larger interior volumes for functional or aesthetic purposes.

Nylon: The most common synthetic carpet fiber, which does a better job at resisting static electricity and stains compared to wool.

Parquetry: A simple geometric pattern of wood flooring utilizing shorter strips or planks of wood and can include checkerboard, basket weave, and herringbone variations.

Pattern repeat: The distance between two identical points in a pattern.

Pendentive: The high wall surface near the ceiling that results from a round dome placed over a square space in plan.

Pigments: Powdered solids that provide the color and brightness qualities of coatings while hiding the surface underneath.

Plain sawn: A method to process and saw logs, this process results in a soft, consistent cathedral pattern in the wood grain, is the most common and widely used sawing types, creates medium to large size boards, and is low to moderate in cost.

Plain slice: A type of veneer that produces cathedral and straight grain patterns.

Plank: A configuration for wood flooring consisting of narrow boards, 3 to 8 inches wide.

Plenum: The volume above the ceiling plane and below the floor or roof structure above.

Precast: Created in a factory, then delivered to the construction site.

Premium grade: Per the American Woodworkers Institute (AWI), plywood reserved for the highest quality of workmanship and the highest in cost.

Quarried: Masonry cut directly from the earth, includes stone slabs or tiles.

Quarter sawn: A method to process and saw logs, this process results in a linear grain pattern with periodic diagonal flecks, is occasionally specified as an upgrade to plain sawn, results in medium to narrow size boards, and is relatively high in cost.

Quarter slice: A type of veneer that produces a tight linear grain with diagonal flecks.

Random match: This method to match and install wall coverings is monolithic in appearance and will match no matter how adjacent strips are hung in relation to one another.

Random matching: A type of veneer matching technique producing a boarded rustic, or informal, appearance.

Resilient flooring: A flooring material characterized by its dimensional memory, or the ability to return to its normal size and shape after receiving pressure.

Rift sawn: A method to process and saw logs, this process results in a very tight linear grain pattern often highly prized in modern wood finishing applications, is rarely used, results in narrow size boards, and is very high in cost.

Rift slice: A type of veneer that produces a clean linear pattern.

Rotary slice: A type of veneer that produces a random grain veneer typically used for the inner layers of plywood, economy grade substrates, or plywood that will receive a layer of primer and paint.

Rubble: Uncut irregular sizes and shapes of stone.

Scratch coat: The first layer of plaster that bonds to the lath.

Shag pile: A carpet pile type consisting of soft cut pile with long yarn that tends to lay down, exposing the side of the yarn.

Shed ceiling: Often follow a mono-pitch roof form that can serve to introduce additional natural light to the interior through tall walls of glass or strips of clerestory windows.

Slip matching: A type of veneer matching technique that organizes the veneer in an identical orientation and size, resulting in a rhythmic repeat of the grain pattern.

Softwood: Sourced from conifer trees and typically used for wood framing, including studs, joists, and rafters, and for sheet goods, such as plywood.

Solid wood flooring: Characterized by wood species, typically 3/4-inch thick, finished with several layers of polyurethane or an acrylic, and able to be sanded and refinished several times during its life cycle.

Solution dyeing: A dyeing method used only with synthetic fibers, as the color is added when the fiber is still in its liquid state resulting in a through-color fiber.

Solvents: Liquids that provide the suspension of the other materials and aid in the application of the coating.

Standard flat ceiling: A flat ceiling that lacks level changes.

Stock dyeing: A dyeing method used for either natural or synthetic fibers, where color is applied to fibers that have already been made, or harvested, resulting in a fiber whose color is superficial.

Straight-across match: This method to match and install wall coverings requires adjacent strips of wall covering perfectly align with one another horizontally across the wall.

Strip: A configuration for wood flooring consisting of narrow boards, 21/4 inch wide.

Substrates: The construction materials under the finishes.

Tempered glass: A type of safety glass that will shatter into many small fragments rather than large angular pieces, lessening the likelihood of serious injury.

Thin brick: Similar to modular brick in terms of face size, but approximately 1/2 inch thick and installed much like a tile over a plywood or cementitious backer board substrate.

Tip sheered pile: A carpet pile type that consists of a loop pile with some loops sheered creating a combination loop and cut pile.

Tongue-and-groove: A wood joinery method whereby the protruding profile of one piece of wood fits into the slotted receiving profile of the neighboring piece of wood.

Tray ceiling: Flat ceiling that incorporates a single or double level change near the perimeter of the space.

Vault ceiling: Curved ceiling forms.

Veneer: Thin sheets of wood that have been sliced from a log.

Wool: The most common natural carpet fiber, which has historically set the standard by which all other carpet fibers are judged.

Chapter 10

Abrasion: The amount of wear on a textile surface through rubbing and other contact with another textile.

Accordion door: A type of folding door, consists of multiple narrow vertical panels and can be used to temporarily divide a large space into smaller spaces.

Antique: A furniture piece that is over 100 years old.

Austrian shades: A type of textile window covering that raises and lowers and are sewn into bunching columns creating a scalloped lower edge.

Automatic sliding doors: Typically made of glass, these sliding doors are common in retail and transportation buildings where carts, luggage, or high amounts of foot traffic are present.

Awning windows: Hinged along the top and swing out.

Bi-fold door: Simplest of folding door types, includes two leaves hinged together and top track to guide the door.

Breaking strength: The force needed to pull a textile apart.

Cable-rail modular display systems: A type of display system common in retail and gallery spaces that can be wall mounted, ceiling and floor mounted, or freestanding; it utilizes glass shelving and stainless steel cables or rods to display products while preserving open views through a space.

Case goods: Freestanding furniture used primarily for storage and/or display purposes.

Casement windows: Hinged on the side and swing out.

Casing: The finish trim around a window that conceals the shim space between the wall framing and the window framing.

Cellular shades: A type of textile or paper window covering that raises and lowers that possesses a honeycomb, or hexagonal, cross section.

Cellulosic fibers: Textile fibers that originate from plants, including sisal, cotton, and jute.

Clerestory window: Possess a head height near the ceiling and sill height above normal eye height that allows light to penetrate the interior while preserving privacy within the interior spaces.

Colorfastness to light: The ability of the textile to resist color fading from light.

Contemporary: Furniture pieces that are in popular use now.

Cornice: A hard window top treatment, often made of wood or metal, that covers the hardware.

Curtain wall window-wall systems: Span many levels of a building exterior, or an interior atrium, and are typically constructed of aluminum.

Decorative accessories: Items in an interior that can be movable or fixed that provide an aesthetic benefit to the user and tends to focus on art pieces.

Digital printing: Digital pattern files are loaded to advanced printing equipment to create intricate textile patterns; jet printing is one technique.

Direct printing: Dye is applied by hand or machine directly to the surface of the textile; techniques include block printing and roller printing.

Double-acting door: Doors that swing in two directions and are used to divide two spaces that receive high traffic.

Double-hung windows: A window where only both sashes can be raised and lowered.

Draperies: Made of light or medium weight textiles, such as silk, satin, chintz, and damask, and serve to filter daylight and preserve visual privacy.

Dutch door: A swinging door divided into two halves such that the top and bottom portions swing independently of one another allowing a visual and audible connection between spaces.

Felt: Made from wool fiber and used as an anti-scratch protection layer for furniture, insulation, or to improve acoustic performance in a space.

Filament: continuous length fiber.

Filament/multifilament yarns: Consist of many long filament fibers; used to create lustrous, smooth textiles.

Flame resistance: Through a chemical process applied at the fiber stage of textile construction, or through application to griege goods, fire can be prevented from proceeding beyond the ignition phase of the flame-spread process.

Flammability: The ability of a textile to resist flame ignition.

Floor-to-ceiling windows: Locate their base at, or very near, the floor and the head at, or very near, the ceiling.

Folding door: This door type has at least two leaves that hinge and relies on a track in the door head and can also require a track in the floor depending upon the weight and sturdiness of the door.

French door: A double door that swings in the same direction and provides for a wider opening for circulation or ventilation purposes.

Fullness factor: A multiple of the full window width, expressed as 1.5x, 2x, 3x, etc., that indicates the amount of additional drapery material that is called for in the design of the window covering.

Functional accessories: Items in an interior that can be movable or fixed that provide a purposeful benefit to the user, for example, mirrors, clocks, screens, and public restroom accessories.

Furniture, Fixtures, and Equipment: (FF&E), a common accounting term used to value the assets of a company that describes movable items of a building interior that are not permanently attached to the building structure or utilities.

Glazing: Specifically, the sealant, or adhesive, that holds the glass and the window framing pieces together.

Grain-straight: High quality textiles that are characterized by perfect 90 degree intersections of warp and weft yarns.

Greige goods: Fully constructed textiles that possess only their natural color.

Head: Top of a door opening.

Hinges: Allows a door to swing, typically attached to the jamb.

Hopper windows: Hinged along the top and swing in.

Horizontal sliding windows: Windows where one or both sashes can slide open.

Jamb: Side of a door opening.

Joinery types: Methods used to connect pieces of wood in order to form larger surfaces and volumes in millwork pieces.

Lambrequin: A hard window top treatment, often made of wood or metal, that extends down the sides of the window, and covers the hardware at the top and the bunched drapery when drawn open.

Latch assembly: Attached to the door, fits into the strike plate at the jamb and allows the door to remain closed and locked.

Lights: The glass portions of a door.

Manufactured fibers: Textile fibers originating from human-made methods to achieve a specific functional requirement that natural fibers cannot achieve.

Millwork: Divided into custom and manufactured types, this grouping of wood-based interior components includes cabinetry, countertops, freestanding millwork, paneling, and moldings, all of which are held to quality standards outlined by the Architectural Woodwork Institute (AWI).

Mineral fibers: Textile fibers that originate from rock/earth, including asbestos.

Mini blinds: A hard horizontal blind that is narrow, less than 1 inch in width, and made of aluminum, steel, or vinyl.

Modern: Furniture pieces associated with the Modernist movement of the early 1900s, an architectural period that embraced modular design principles and new construction technologies, including the use of concrete and steel.

Monofilament yarns: Consist of a single, relatively thick, filament that is typically transparent, or nearly transparent, and used for stitching fabric seams or to create translucent textiles for draperies.

Mullion: The wider framing components used to separate one entire window from a neighboring window.

Muntin: The narrow framing components in traditional windows used to divide the glass into smaller lights.

Natural fibers: Textile fibers originating from animals, plants, or the earth.

Physical properties: The ability of a textile to resist pilling, the measure of breaking strength, and the ability to resist seam slippage.

Pilling: The creation of fiber balls on a textile surface.

Pivot door: A swinging door hinged in the middle of the door with an axle anchored to the head and the threshold of the opening.

Plain weave: The most basic weave type uses one warp yarn and one weft yarn alternating with one another, described as a 1 x 1; a variation includes the basket weave, 2 x 2.

Pocket door: A sliding door that can be concealed inside of a wall.

Protein fibers: Textile fibers that originate from animals, including cashmere, mohair, and wool.

Rails: The horizontal solid portion of a door.

Regenerated fibers: Textile fibers manufactured from plants and require a chemical and/or mechanical process to breakdown the plant material to expose the fiber, including acetate, rayon, and rubber.

Resist printing: In conjunction with an inhibiting agent or blocking mechanism, dye is selectively applied to the textile surface to create a pattern; screen printing is a common technique.

Roman shades: A type of textile window covering that raises and lowers with particular varieties, including flat, shirred, soft-pleated, accordion pleated, and balloon.

Rustic: Furniture characterized by natural materials, simplistic forms, and relaxed posture.

Sash: Two large modules of a single- or double-hung window, or horizontal sliding, where one is the inner and the other the outer sash.

Satin weave: Similar to twill in that a yarn will pass under or over two or more adjacent perpendicular yarns, but without the cascading sequence, which creates a grid pattern rather than a diagonal line emphasis.

Seam slippage: The slipping of yarn at the seam of two textiles when pulling force is applied.

Shim space: The air space between the door frame and wall frame allowing the door to be installed plum and square.

Sill: The horizontal framing piece at the base of a window that is concealed when the window is closed.

Single-hung windows: A window where only one sash can be raised and lowered.

Slat wall: A common flexible display system of panels that can be anchored to walls, or can be used as part of a freestanding

display to divide space, creating aisles between merchandise displays.

Sliding door: Relies on a track with rollers to allow the door to slide across the opening, simple to operate and do not require as much clearance around them compared to swinging doors.

Soil and stain resistance: Preventing matter from mechanically attaching, or from chemically bonding, to textiles often requires the application of petroleum-based products to the textile.

Soiling: The process of matter mechanically attaching to a textile.

Solution dyeing: Only available for synthetic manufactured fibers, dye is added to the fiber while the fiber is being made resulting in a through color (similar to a carrot) improving resistance to fading.

Split blinds: Made from bamboo or grass reeds, have small gaps between the strips of material that filter daylight, and often roll up and down to control privacy.

Spun yarns: Consist of staple fibers twisted together to form the yarn that results in a softer and more plush texture than filament yarn, but with a greater tendency to pill than filament yarns.

Staining: The process of matter chemically attaching to a textile.

Standard windows: Include a portion of solid wall above and below them with a sill and head.

Staple fibers: Noncontinuous length fibers.

Static resistance: A chemical can be integrated into a manufactured fiber or applied to yarn in order to reduce static electricity resulting from movement across the textile.

Stiles: The vertical solid portion of a door.

Stock dyeing: Available for natural or manufactured fibers the dye is applied to the fiber after it has been harvested or made resulting in a surface application of the dye to the fiber (similar to a radish).

Stool: The trim piece on top of the sill and visible from the interior whether the window is open or closed.

Stop trim: The piece that runs around all three sides of a door opening, which provides a stopping surface for the door when closing.

Storefront window-wall systems: Steel- or aluminum-framed fenestration that spans no more than two levels in height and can also integrate glass doors into the overall system.

Surface-mounted sliding door: Sliding doors that are mounted on the face of a wall with exposed track and hardware above the opening.

Swinging door: Categorized as single or double acting, depending on the type of hinge, and can be installed as individuals or in pairs.

Synthetic fibers: Textile fibers manufactured from hydrocarbons (natural gas, oil, and coal) and water, but also recycled from plastic sources, including soda and water bottles, acrylic, nylon, polyester, spandex, and vinyl.

Textured filament yarns: Consist of many long filament fibers that have been texturized that results in a softer, fuller body than filament yarns in an effort to increase elasticity and create a more natural feel and appearance.

Threshold: Bottom of a door opening, typically dividing the interior from exterior of a building.

Traditional: Furniture pieces that are characterized by a formal posture and forms and decorations from the Victorian period.

Transom windows: Located above doors, can be operable, and are used to increase ventilation to interior spaces that do not have access to operable windows along exterior walls.

Twill weave: A more complicated weave than a plain weave where a yarn will pass under or over two or more perpendicular yarns in a cascading sequence to create diagonal lines in the weave.

Upholstery: The process of covering furniture with a textile or animal hide.

Valance: A soft window top treatment, often made of a textile, that covers the hardware.

Venetian blinds: A hard horizontal blind that is wide, more than 1 inch, and made of wood or vinyl.

Vertical blinds: Often cover windows that reach to the floor or sliding glass doors, are approximately 3 inches in width, twist at the top to control daylight infiltration, and are typically made from plastic or a textile.

Vintage: A furniture piece that is considered to be a prime example from a specific period or style.

Warp yarns: Yarns running the length of the textile.

Water resistance: Dense textiles that are high in yarn count are inherently better at resisting water penetration compared to those that are less dense; silicone treatments can also be applied to textiles to slow the absorption of water.

Weft yarns: Yarns running the width of the textile.

Wet and dry crocking: The ability of a textile to resist color transference to another material through rubbing.

Window grills: Decorative carved panels, often fixed, that filter daylight and offer some small level of privacy depending on the openness of the carved pattern.

Window screens: Slide across a window and provide many of the same functional benefits as shutters.

Chapter 11

Accent light: Utilizes a focused beam spread to highlight a specific object or a wash of light to highlight a surface.

Ambient light: General illumination in a space that seeks to provide a consistent level of illumination while limiting strong contrasts between one zone of light and another.

Architectural luminaires: Luminaires built-in to the interior architectural surfaces (ceilings, walls, floors) of the interior space.

Artificial combustion light: Originates from fire, which can be provided via fireplaces, candles, and oil or gas lamps.

Artificial light: Light made by human skill, divided into two broad categories: combustion and electric.

Candela: Measures the intensity of light in a given direction.

Cold cathode: Manufactured in tubes filled with gases to produce specific colors of light for specialty applications, such as retail signage.

Color rendering index: The measurement used to compare artificial light sources to daylight; it functions on a 100-point scale with 100 perfectly matching daylight.

Compact fluorescent lamps, CFL: Similar technology to fluorescent lamps, this lamp is more compact and fits into the same socket and housing as incandescent lamps.

Concealed luminaires: Luminaires whose housing and light source is concealed, creating an indirect lighting effect that washes a wall, ceiling, or floor surface.

Direct lighting: Includes luminaires where the lamp is visible to the eye.

Discharge lamps: Produces light by passing an electric current through a gas or vapor contained within a glass enclosure.

Down lighting: A type of direct lighting where the luminaire shines the light down from a higher point, such as a ceiling.

Efficacy: Measures the amount of light output in lumens divided by the amount of electricity in watts required to produce that amount of light resulting in a rating of efficiency.

Electric light: Began with the invention of the incandescent lamp in 1879, and relies upon an electric current.

Fluorescent lamps: Passes an electrical current through a mercury vapor- and argon-filled glass tube that is internally coated with phosphorus in order to create light.

Foot-candle: Describes the amount of light falling on a surface.

Footlambert: The amount of light reflected from a surface.

High-intensity discharge, HID: Combines the benefits of incandescent and fluorescent lamps and includes mercury, low-pressure sodium, and metal halide lamps.

Incandescent lamps: Produces light by passing an electric current through a tungsten filament sealed in a glass bulb.

Indirect lighting: Shields the lamp from direct view.

Lamp: A light source, sometimes called a bulb.

LED lamp: A type of solid-state lighting that uses a semiconductor light emitting diode to produce light.

Light temperature: Measured in kelvin (K), this is another way to measure light quality, with cooler light colors measuring near 8,500 K, warmer light colors measuring 600 K to 2,000 K, and accurate color measured between 3,000 K and 6,000 K.

Light wavelength: Measured in nanometers (nm), the visible light spectrum ranges in wavelength from 400 nm (violet) to 700 nm (red).

Lighting schedule: Consists of graphic symbols that represent the various types of luminaires and controls utilized in the proposed design along with a brief written description of each.

Lumen: The amount of light produced by one light source.

Luminaire: Light fixture.

Natural atmospheric light: A type of daylight created as the atmosphere refracts sunlight through moisture droplets and other particles in the atmosphere.

Natural combustion light: Light originating from the sun in the form of daylight.

Natural reflected light: Sunlight reflected from the moon.

Neon: A type of cold cathode that uses neon gas to create a red color of light.

Nonarchitectural luminaires: Portable luminaires that are plugged in to an electrical socket or operate on battery power.

Portable luminaires: Nonarchitectural luminaires that include table and floor fixtures.

Recessed luminaires: Luminaires whose housing is behind the finish surface of a ceiling, wall, or even floor.

Sconce: Surface-mounted wall luminaire.

Solid-state lighting: Relies on very small electrically charged semiconductors to produce light and includes both standard light-emitting diode (LED) technology and organic light-emitting diode (OLED) technology.

Surface-mounted luminaires: Luminaires whose housing is visible in front of the finish surface of a ceiling or wall.

Suspended luminaires: Also referred to as pendant, these luminaires hang from a ceiling.

Systems furniture lighting: Nonarchitectural luminaires that are integrated into the partitions and storage components of workstations commonly found in open office environments.

Task light: Illumination that focuses on a specified task, such as reading, drawing, cooking, or dental cleaning, and these fixtures are often adjustable to limit glare and to provide the user with the ability to fine tune the focus of the light, turn it on or off at will.

Track lighting: A versatile lighting type that incorporates a track for individual luminaires that may be aimed to slide along

Tungsten-halogen lamps: A type of incandescent lamp, it utilizes quartz in place of the metal filament to produce light.

Up lighting: A type of indirect lighting, commonly used with pendant fixtures that shine light up toward a ceiling surface or wall fixtures that direct light up a wall.

Chapter 12

Acoustics: The science of sound.

Ceiling attenuation class: CAC, measures the transmission of sound through a ceiling material and plenum over a wall and into a neighboring space.

Conduction: Heat transferred through a solid material contact.

Convection: Heat transferred through fluid movement, such as the natural or forced movement of air.

Electrical systems: Addresses electrical wiring, switching and other lighting controls, and power supply.

Fire monitoring: A strategy that involves identifying the presence of fire before it gets out of control through passive monitoring devices, such as smoke and heat detectors.

Fire notification: A strategy that prioritizes human safety with early broadcast of the presence of fire using devices that include horns, strobes, centralized audible devices, and many smoke detectors also integrate an audible alarm.

Fire suppression: A strategy that prioritizes human safety and limits the damage of fire through various devices, including fire extinguishers and automatic sprinklers.

Gravity down-feed system: Water supply system in tall buildings where the cold water is pumped to the roof, stored, and then is drawn down via gravity to each level as needed.

Grey water: Water not fit for drinking, bathing, or washing, but can be used for irrigation or flushing toilets.

Human comfort zone: Consists of four factors: temperature, relative humidity, air movement, and radiation of heat.

HVAC systems: Heating, ventilation, and air conditioning systems address the human comfort zone and indoor air quality issues.

Indoor air quality: (IAQ), a critical characteristic related to the quality of the built environment where the strategy is to control airborne contaminants, such as volatile organic compounds (VOCs), mineral and earth particulates (dust, ash, etc.), and biological contaminants (fungi, bacteria, etc.).

Internet of things: IoT, consumer products possess the ability to connect to the world wide web allowing consumers to remotely monitor important data, such as electricity usage, interior temperature and humidity levels, water consumption, and even the contents of their refrigerators.

MEP: Mechanical, electrical, and plumbing engineering consultants are integral players in a successful design team.

Noise reduction coefficient: NRC, the amount of sound dissipated by a material.

Noise: Any unwanted sound.

Plumbing chase: A void within a wall construction that allows plumbing supply and waste pipes to run vertically between levels in a building.

Potable water: Drinkable water.

Radiation: Heat transferred through electromagnetic waves.

Security systems: Can include active systems, such as security guards and stations, or passive systems, such as perimeter monitoring systems at doors and windows, motion detection devices, identity confirmation devices at entry points, and cameras, all of which rely on low-voltage power, cable, data, or telecommunications connections.

Service access panel: A means to provide access to plumbing fixture shut-off valves that are concealed within walls or above ceilings.

SMART home technology: Self-Monitoring Analysis and Reporting Technology can automatically make adjustments to built environment systems based on parameters that the individual customizes.

Sound frequency: Pitch, measured in cycles per second (also known as hertz, Hz).

Sound intensity: Loudness, measured in decibels.

Sound transmission class: STC, measures the amount of sound passing through a material or construction.

Sound-masking systems: Produce low-intensity sound at key frequencies in an effort to cancel, or mitigate, certain types of noise.

Sound: Vibration that requires a source (voice, speaker, shoes on a floor), a path (air, water, building structure), and a receiver (ear).

Telecommunication and data systems: Closely related to electrical power and commonly addressed by the same electrical engineer, this specialty includes hard-line telephone wiring and switching, hard-line data wiring and servers, wireless routing, and cable television, all of which have been changing quickly in recent decades as technology has evolved to include wireless capabilities.

Trap: Creates a natural water seal to prevent gasses from coming back into the interior from the sewage system.

Vent through roof: VTR, allows waste gasses that build up in the sewage system to escape to the outdoors rather than to the interior.

Ventilation: The removal of contaminated air and replacement with clean air, also described as air exchange and expressed in volume of air per minute, specifically cubic feet per minute (cfm).

CREDITS

Introduction

I.0 Astronaut Images/Caiaimage/Getty Images
I.1 Kurt Hutton/Hulton Archive/Getty Images
I.2 Julian Elliot Photography/Photolibrary/Getty Images
I.3 View Pictures/UIG via Getty Images
I.4 Hero Images/Getty Images

Chapter 1

1.0 Raimund Franken/ullstein bild via Getty Images
1.1 Franke, Garber, Jansen
1.2 JEAN-SEBASTIEN EVRARD/AFP/Getty Images
1.3 Bladt/ullstein bild via Getty Images
1.4 View Pictures/UIG via Getty Images
1.5 O|X Studio, Inc.
1.6 View Pictures/UIG via Getty Images
1.7 Nuno Valadas.iStock.com
1.8 Chung Sung-Jun/Getty Images
1.9 Steven B. Webber
1.10 O|X Studio, Inc.
1.11 & 1.12 Fairchild Books
1.13 & 1.14 Steven B. Webber
1.15 Loop Images/UIG via Getty Images
1.16 View Pictures/UIG via Getty Images
1.17 Pepmiba/E+/Getty Images
1.18 Alexander Hill/View Pictures/UIG via Getty Images
1.19 © West/JWestProductions.com

Chapter 2

2.0 ilbusca/iStock.com
2.1 Ulrich Baumgarten via Getty Images
2.2 Jeremy Red/Shutterstock.com
2.3 DeAgostini/Getty Images
2.4 Mienny/iStock.com
2.5 Athanasios Gioumpasis/Getty Images
2.6 Prisma/UIG/Getty Images
2.7 Frédéric Soltan/Corbis via Getty Images
2.8 DEA / E. GANZERLA/De Agostini/Getty Images
2.9 & 2.10 Steve B. Webber
2.11 Albert Moldvay/National Geographic/Getty Images
2.12 Electa/Mondadori Portfolio via Getty Images
2.13 DeAgostini/Getty Images
2.14 fstockfoto/iStock.com
2.15 Michael Gordone/Shutterstock.com
2.16 Henry Townsend
2.17 Steve B. Webber
2.18 andrés arias / Shutterstock.com
2.19 Emilie1980/iStock.com
2.20 Chicago History Museum/Getty Images
2.21 Izzet Keribar/Lonely Planet Images/Getty Images
2.22 Thierry Falise/LightRocket via Getty Images
2.23 Julian Calverley/Corbis/Getty Images
Chapter 2 Case Study O|X Studio, Inc.

Chapter 3

3.0 artpartner-images/Getty Images
3.1 & 3.2 Franke, Garber, Jansen
3.3 & 3.4 Alexandria Pfiester
3.5–3.8 Kiera Malcolm
3.9 & 3.10 Mary Elizabeth Johnson
3.11 Bombaert/iStock.com
3.12 fanjianhua.iSock.com
3.13 Searsle/iStock.com
3.14 John Ewing/Portland Press Herald via Getty Images
3.15 Franke, Garber, Jansen
Chapter 3 Case Study Workshop Architects

Chapter 4

4.0 Simon Watson/Stone/Getty Images
4.1 Hero Images/Getty Images
4.2 pidjoe/iStock.com

4.3   Mel Yates/DigitalVision/Getty Images

4.4   Fry Design Ltd./Photographer's Choice/Getty Images

4.5   Wavebreakmedia/iStock.com

4.6   FatCamera/iStock.com

4.7–4.9   Fairchild Books

4.10   monkeybusinessimages/iStock.com

4.11   Photo by Jill Pable. Architecture by Clemons Rutherford Architects.

4.12   Design Resources for Homelessness/ designresourcesforhomelessness.org

4.13   laughingmango/iStock.com

4.14   Fairchild Books

4.15   Rixipix/iStock.com

4.16   Steelcase

4.17   bruceman/iStock.com

4.18   pogonici/Shutterstock.com

4.19   Astronaut Images/Caiaimage/Getty Images

4.20   Design Resources for Homelessness/ designresourcesforhomelessness.org

Chapter 4 Case Study   Environmental Works Community Design Center; Architect: Bill Singer, Director of Architecture. www. eworks.org; Photographer: Jill Pable, Design Resources for Homelessness, designresourcesforhomelessness.org

Chapter 5

5.0   John Greim/LightRocket via Getty Images

5.1   Fairchild Books

5.2   ktsimage/iStock.com

5.3   Fairchild Books

5.4b   Gile68/iStock.com

5.4a   nadtytok/iStock.com

5.5–5.7   Fairchild Books

5.8   PeterHermesFurian/iStock.com

5.9   Thoth_Adan/iStock.com

5.10   Plan Shoot/Multi-bits/The Image Bank/Getty Images

5.11   Hoxton/Tom Merton/Getty Images

5.12   dit26978/iStock.com

5.13   SklepSpozywczy/iStock.com

5.14   benedek/iStock.com

5.15   Per Magnus Persson/Getty Images

5.16   Martin Barraud/Caiaimage/Getty Images

5.17 & 5.18   ShutterWorx/iStock.com

5.19   ThomasVogel/iStock.com

5.20   View Pictures/UIG via Getty Images

5.21   Glow Décor/Getty Images

5.22   Design and rendering by Emily Haynes

Chapter 5 Case Study   Photos by Ryan Gamma, Floorplans by Architects Lewis + Whitlock

Chapter 6

6.0   Dimitri Otis/DigitalVision/Getty Images

6.1   DNY59/iStock.com

6.2   Steve Debenport/iStock.com

6.3   Wavebreakmedia/iStock.com

6.4   DNY59/iStock.com

6.5   International Federation of Interior Architects/Designers

6.6   Kelvin Murray/Taxi/Getty Images

6.7   Hill Street Studios/Blend Images/Getty Images

6.8   Dimitri Otis/DigitalVision/Getty Images

6.9   Portra/DigitalVision/Getty Images

6.10   Kelvin Murray/Taxi/Getty Images

6.11   Hero Images/Getty Images

6.12   Rob Daily/iStock.com

6.13   nihatdursun/iStock.com

6.14   PM Images/Stone/Getty Images

Case Study 6.1   studio m/Daniel Newcomb architectphotography. com

Case Study 6.2   studio m/Peter Murdock

Case Study 6.3   studio m/James Ray Spahn

Case Study 6.4   studio m/Uneek Images

Chapter 7

7.0   Peerakit Jirachetthakun/Moment/Getty Images

7.1   Reza/Getty Images

7.2   Geber86/iStock.com

7.3   Michael Zwahlen/EyeEm/Getty Images

7.4   Yongyuan Dai/the Image Bank/Getty Images

7.5   Ulana Switucha/age fotostock/Getty images

7.6   Fairchild Books

7.7   Ingolf Pompe / LOOK-foto/Getty Images

7.8–7.10   Fairchild Books

7.11   MyLoupe/UIG via Getty Images

7.12   David Cooper/Toronto Star via Getty Images

7.13   hdagli/iStock.com

7.14   eugenesergeev/iStock.com

7.15   fullvalue/iStock.com

7.16   Fairchild Books

7.17   Peter Dazeley/Photographer's Choice/Getty Images

7.18   Hero Images/Getty Images

7.19   Manuel Romano/NurPhoto via Getty Images

7.20   Westend61/Getty Images

7.21   pixzzle/iStock.com

Chapter 7 Case Study   Photos by Ryan Gamma, Floorplans by Architects Lewis + Whitlock

Chapter 8

8.0   ShutterWorx/iStock.com

8.1 & 8.2   Franke, Garber, Jansen

8.3   Milkos/iStock.com

8.4–8.9   Sarah E. Kost

8.10   Jim Dawkins

8.11   Steven B. Webber

8.12   Waring Abbott/Getty Images

8.13   Bernard Weil/Toronto Star via Getty Images

8.14   GIUSEPPE CACACE/AFP/Getty Images

8.15   making_ultimate/moment/Getty Images

8.16   Hero Images/Getty Images

8.17   Nikada/iStock.com

INDEX

RCP. *See* reflected ceiling plan (RCP)

rebar, 140, 180

recessed luminaires, 252

Red and Blue Chair, 40, 41

Red House, 38

reflected ceiling plan (RCP), 153, 154, 262–3

regenerated fibers, 232

reimbursable expenses, 129

Renaissance architecture, 34–5

repetition, 19

residential design, 3

resilient flooring, 183–5

resist printing, 234

retainer, 129

reuse, 85

rhythm, 19–20

ribbon window, 39

Rietveld, Gerrit, 40

rift sawn, 181

rift slice, 196

Ringling Museum of Art, 144–7

risk management, 118, 126

Rococo architecture, 36

Roman architecture, 29–31

Roman Corinthian order, 30

Roman furniture, 31

Roman Ionic order, 30

Roman shades, 230

Romanesque architecture, 32

Romanesque revival, 37

roof garden, 40

roof structures, 140–1

rotary slice, 196

rotunda, 30

rubber floors, 184

rubble, 188

rugs, 185–7

run, 166

rural areas, 135

rustic furniture, 216

S

Saarinen, Eero, 47

safety, as need, 79

Sagrada Familia, 39

St. Peter's Basilica, 34–5

sales representatives, 117

sash, 227

satin weave, 233

SBS. *See* sick building syndrome (SBS)

scale, 14–15

schematic design, 58–60

Schröder House, 40

sciences, spatial, 76–8

sconce, 254

scratch coat, 191

screens, window, 228

Seagram Building, 42

seam slippage, 235

seasonal affective disorder (SAD), 75

seating
Aeron Chair, 47
Barcelona Chair, 47
Carbon Chair, 47
chaise lounge, 217
Chesterfield sofa, 217
Cross Check Chair, 47
Eames Lounge Chair, 47
Lawson sofa, 217
LC4 Chaise Lounge Chair, 47
Louis Ghost chairs, 47, 221
Red and Blue Chair, 40, 41
sectional sofa, 217
sofas, 217
Steelcase Think Chair, 84
task chairs, 217
Victoria and Louis Ghost Chairs, 47, 221
Wassily Chair, 47
Womb Chair, 47
Zigzag Chair, 40

secondary colors of light, 95

sectional sofa, 217

sections (drawing), 154–5

security systems, 272–3

self-actualization, 80

self-esteem, 79

semi-shag pile, 187

senior designers, 117

sensory disabilities, 74

sensory interpretation of space, 72–4

service access panel, 276

settee, 217

Seven Principles of Universal Design, 75

shade, 97

shades
Austrian, 230
cellular, 230–1
Roman, 230

shag pile, 187

shed ceiling, 198

shim space, 2244

sick building syndrome (SBS), 86, 270

sight, 72

signage, 159, 239

sill, 227

similarity, 10

Simon, Herbert, 8

simple use, 75

single-hung windows, 226
Sistine Chapel, 199
slat wall, 238
slate floors, 176, 177
sliding doors, 222–3
slip matching, 196
SMART home technology, 283
smell, 73
social space, 83
Society of Decorative Artists, 41
sociology, of color, 101, 106
sofas, 217
softwood, 181
soil resistance, 235
soiling, 235
sole proprietorship, 119
solid state lighting (SSL), 250, 257–8
solid wood flooring, 182
solution dyeing, 186, 234
solvents, 193
sound, 277
sound frequency, 277
sound intensity, 277
sound masking systems, 283
sound systems, 277–9, 283
sound transmission class (STC), 278
space, 11
    circulation, 157, 171
    negative, 11
    occupied, 157, 171
    positive, 11
    sensory interpretation of, 72–4
    volume and, 11
space planning, 3, 160–4
space planning categories, 157–8
spatial behaviors, human, 78–83
spatial sciences, 76–8
spatial well-being
    and human spatial behaviors, 78–83
    and sensory interpretation of space, 72–4
    and spatial sciences, 76–8
    sustainability and, 84–90
    and universal design, 74–6
Spaulding, Matt, 280–3
specializations, 117
split blinds, 228
split-complementary color schemes, 99, 100
spun yarns, 232
SSL. See solid state lighting (SSL)
stacking diagram, 60
stage of life, 134
stain resistance, 235
staining, 235
stairs, 165–8

standard flat ceiling, 198
standard window, 226
Stanford University, 8, 16–18
staple fibers, 232
Starck, Philippe, 47
static resistance, 234
Steelcase Think Chair, 84
stick style, 37
Stickley, Gustave, 38
stiles, 223
stock dyeing, 186, 234
stone flooring, 175
stone walls, 188
stool (window), 227
stop trim, 224
storage furniture, 218
storefront window-wall systems, 227
straight-across match, 195
strip (wood flooring), 182
Studio M, 122–6
Stumpf, William, 47
subdominant component, 20
subordinate elements, 20
substrates, 174
substructure, 138
subtractive color process, 96
sun exposure, 135–6, 137
superstructure, 138
surface-mounted luminaire, 252
surface-mounted sliding doors, 223
suspended luminaires, 252–3
sustainability, 84–90
sustainability guidelines, 86–90
sustainable development, 84
swinging doors, 222
symmetry, 18–19
synthetic fibers, 232
systems furniture lighting, 255
systems furniture solutions, 218

T

tables, 217–18
task chairs, 217
task lighting, 14, 252
Tassel House, 39
taste, 73
technology and information management, 118
telecommunication systems, 272
temperature, light, 248
tempered glass, 191
terrazzo, 180
territoriality, 82
tertiary colors, 97
testing phase, 9–10, 18, 23